Painted Black

Painted Black

FROM DRUG KILLINGS TO HEAVY METAL—
THE ALARMING TRUE STORY OF HOW
SATANISM IS TERRORIZING
OUR COMMUNITIES

Carl A. Raschke

1817

HARPER & ROW, PUBLISHERS, SAN FRANCISCO
New York, Grand Rapids, Philadelphia, St. Louis
London, Singapore, Sydney, Tokyo, Toronto

And I saw a beast rising out of the sea . . .

——Rev. 13:1

FIRST EDITION

Library of Congress Cataloging-in-Publication Data
Raschke, Carl A.
    Painted black
    Carl A. Raschke.—1st ed.
        p.   cm.
    Includes bibliographical references.
    ISBN 0-06-250704-4
    1. Satanism—United States—History—20th century.   2. United
States—Religion—20th century.   I. Title.
BF1548.R37   1990   89-45953
133.4'22'0973—dc20   CIP

90 91 92 93 94 RINAM 10 9 8 7 6 5 4 3 2 1

This edition is printed on acid-free paper that meets the American
National Standards Institute Z39.48 Standard.

Contents

Preface

In May 1967, as a graduate student in Berkeley, I was present at a noon rock concert at the University of California's Sproul Plaza.

It was approximately five weeks before commencement of the hippie "happening" known as the Summer of Love in San Francisco's Haight Ashbury across the bay. The crowd of students and so-called street people was both randy and festive. College women circulated in cut-off jeans and halter tops. The odor of marijuana smoke hung in the air. A woman with Rapunzel-like blonde braids, wearing a white peasant dress with an orange floral print, passed out flyers for some now-forgotten political cause. Dogs of all sizes and colors ambled through the crowd, detached from their owners.

The concert was to be a surprise. Nobody knew what band would be performing, and even as it was announced over the public address system, the name sounded as eerie as it was unfamiliar. The band was called the Second Coming.

The year 1967 seemed "apocalyptic" to many who lived in the Bay Area. The Vietnam conflict, and the street demonstrations against it, were mounting toward an apex of ferocity. Egypt's President Nasser was mobilizing all the Arab armies of the Middle East in preparation for a war, he announced, that would destroy the nation of Israel and drive the Jews "into the sea." For two summers now the black ghettos had been exploding in firestorms of rage and violence. LSD was as popular as the new Beatles album, *Sergeant Pepper's Lonely Hearts Club Band*.

Raised a Presbyterian, I thought "the Second Coming" referred to Christ's return. I did not realize at the time that it may well have meant something else.

The year before, a balding man in his late thirties with a Van Dyke beard had proclaimed the "Second Coming" as well. His name was Anton LaVey. The "coming" was of Satan.

I first heard for sure that there were satanists in the land in 1981 from a twenty-six-year-old refugee from the occult underground, whom I shall call John Jones. John grew up in Pueblo, Colorado—a far cry from the city by the bay. He told of observing, as a teenager and a small-time drug dealer, mysterious rituals in abandoned houses late at night. He told of two young thugs in his high school who occasionally would kidnap hitchhikers and transport them blindfolded to the ceremonial sites, where they would stab their victims with knives and say prayers to the Prince of Darkness. I thought John was sincerely convinced of what he was describing to me. But I was not sure I believed him.

In 1981, nobody believed there were "bad" people such as the satanists John described. Because nobody believed it, I could not even discuss the subject matter with academic colleagues. I tried hiring one of my students as a research assistant to investigate the matter. After several weeks he gave up and said to me, "Dr. Raschke, everybody thinks this is just too weird." Why would Dr. Raschke be interested in such a topic, after all? Or so they must have reasoned. The entire topic of satanism could easily be dismissed as a paranoid fantasy.

In the spring of 1988, I was cited in a newspaper story that went out over the Associated Press wire. I was quoted as saying that within only a few years the "paranoid fantasy" had become a national epidemic. By then it was both reasonable and socially acceptable to talk about the problem of satanism. Books were coming out on the subject. Television documentaries were in production. Even Geraldo Rivera was getting into the act.

Skeptics continued to dismiss the public concern as mere hysteria inflamed by media sensationalism. One scholar with whom I talked went so far as to make the rather silly claim that satanists were a pure fabrication of the journalistic profession.

In the summer of 1988, I was asked to serve as an expert witness in two court trials involving satanism. The first case was the murder in Joplin, Missouri, of a young man named Steven Newberry. Newberry was killed by two of his cronies who had been high on drugs, heavy metal music, and "satan worship." I was called as a witness for the defense of Pete Roland, one of the murderers, to testify about the tenor of the young man's beliefs. My testimony was aimed at persuading a jury the young man should not receive the death penalty, because his beliefs had led to a state of "diminished competence." Today the young man, named Theron "Pete" Roland, is serving a life sentence.

The second case was a libel trial in Victoria, British Columbia. A guest on a radio talk show had claimed that he had once belonged to an occult group that had tried to make a "sacrifice" of him and his wife in keeping with a "satanic" tradition. The leader of the occult group sued for defamation. I was asked to explain satanism to the jury, which would determine if indeed the occult group could properly be called "satanic." The jury decided such a label was fitting.

Still, the conventional wisdom remained that although there might be genuine satanists out there, they did not commit crimes, let alone murder. Pete Roland was an aberration, the argument went. Then came the grisly spectacle of the mutilated bodies buried beneath the mud and chaparral outside Matamoros, Mexico.

The American intelligensia has a tremendous capacity for what psychologists call "denial." The trained academic mind has a difficult time accepting that there are people who could willfully do evil for the sake of doing evil. Evil, we have been told, is a "social" or "structural" disorder to be remedied by political or therapeutic means. It has nothing to do with a corruption of the human heart. And, besides, *good* and *evil* are relative terms anyhow.

The consequences of this denial, however, become ever more dangerous as the months go on. An analogy with the drug problem is worth considering.

Right now we are in the midst of an international drug crisis. About the time that I began my research into a subject area that supposedly did not exist, the common view was that there was not, and could not be, such a thing as a "drug problem." The trend was toward the legalization of narcotics. Hollywood celebrities were snorting cocaine at parties with few compunctions and with unprecedented abandon. Coke was glamorous; it was the "drug of choice" for the new success-minded "yuppies," successors to the sixties generation. Even *Scientific American* ran an oft-quoted article summarizing research that "demonstrated" there was little danger in cocaine use. Coke was deemed a "harmless recreational drug."

Today, an international crisis has been spawned, and billions of dollars are spent to fight the ravages of the "harmless recreational drug." In this case the intelligentsia was deceived disastrously. It has been deceived again about satanism and the "occult revival," which has accelerated along with drug experimentation and cocaine abuse. Aleister Crowley, the arch-satanist of the twentieth century who fashioned himself the "Beast 666," had his own, blinding revelations of satanic truth while high on coke. He commended it as the drug of choice for those who would plunge into the abyss of black, magical mysteries.

This book is both a documentary and a guide to the deep structure of the phenomenon that has captivated the attention of mental health professionals, law enforcement officials, religious counselors, and the media— the general public notwithstanding. It aims to be comprehensive. Satanism is not a "new religion" deserving the sort of latitudinarian tolerance or respect one would be expected to accord under the U. S. Constitution, say, to an emergent sect of South Pacific pantheists.

Satanism *is* a sophisticated and highly effective motivational system for the spread of violence and cultural terrorism, all the while hiding behind the cloak of the First Amendment. It is an ideology that has found a strategic application in the criminal underworld, even if it was not invented there.

This book would not have been possible at all without a horde of helping hands, visible as well as invisible. I would first and foremost thank my wife and colleague, Susan, who labored tirelessly for a year and a half carrying out library research, organizing my papers, doing transcripts, editing the manuscript, and fending off sundry nuisances that would otherwise have delayed completion of the project. I would also like to thank Dr. Kent Richards, the consulting editor who brought the project to the attention of Harper & Row.

Finally, I would express my gratitude to the following individuals: my personal research assistant, Don Allard, for two long months of strenuous legwork and compilation of source materials in preparation of the final manuscript; my university research assistant, Martin Katchen, for his uncanny ability to ferret out obscure sources of information, his encyclopedic range of observation, and his matchless insights into the significance of certain psychological and historical documents; my son, Erik, for assistance in filing and assembly of information; Kathy Goldston and Andrew Scrimgeour at Regis College for aid in acquiring materials that were difficult to obtain; Kevin Selby for his heroic efforts in gaining documentation and interviews with regard to the Pete Roland case; Linda Blood for her marvelous bibliography, her access to sources, and her special knowledge of key segments of satanism in America; Michael Langone and the American Family Foundation for advice and contacts; Steve Marsh for his interpretations of complex puzzles and for providing storage for more files than my own basement would hold; Lucille for providing living quarters during the first phase of research and writing of the book; Dale Griffis for his mentoring and avuncular oversight; "John" for showing me what was afoot in the first place; and John Southwick and the Palmer Divide Fellowship for their unflagging support in the area that ultimately mattered the most.

Denver, Colorado
September 1989

Part I.

THE SIEGE

CHAPTER 1.

The Horror

My soul is dead. I am not a human being.
——*Mexican satanic cultist* ALVARO DE LEON VALDEZ
*during a press interview following the discovery of
the Matamoros murders*

The fry-cake flat, desolate, and sparsely populated coastal plain that follows the crook of the Gulf of Mexico from southern Texas down across the Rio Grande was probably the last place on earth anyone in American law enforcement would have expected to yield the deeper secrets of the growing national menace of what is popularly termed "satanism." And if it had not been for an astonishing series of circumstances, coincidences, and missteps by one of the most notorious cliques of satanic cultists in the region, the secrets would probably have remained under wraps for much longer.

Before discovery of the gruesome remains of fifteen victims of cult kidnappings and "sacrifice" on a remote ranch west of the Mexican border city of Matamoros in April 1989, the multiplying reports of "occult-related" crimes throughout the country, most of which had been encountered by local police from southern California to New England, were frequently met with suspicion and even ridicule by some authorities. After Matamoros, the climate changed considerably.

The horror of satanic crime—often entailing deliberate and brutal torture, mutilation, or dismemberment of victims—could no longer be dismissed as Christian fundamentalist ravings, galloping social hysteria, or the lurid sorts of media-inspired popular imaginings that one recent author and cult apologist had termed "urban legends." Not only were the bodies themselves visible to an international television audience, the cultists' own confessions were trotted out in detail to legions of journalists from both sides of the border, primarily because of the coercive character of the Mexican judicial system and a hard-driving, publicity-seeking Matamoros police commander. In effect, the distasteful episode was dissected with probably more intimacy and interest than the Charles Manson murders in California almost a generation earlier. Press coverage was so thorough that it even upstaged Geraldo Rivera, who before

Matamoros seemed to have cornered the market on satanist sensationalism.

As the newspaper and magazine articles began gushing forth, a new perspective, not merely on the squalid Matamoros affair, but on the intricate and generally overheated satanist controversy, which had been building for years, flashed into view. What in the media had taken on the aura of an ongoing, true-life, "Friday-the-Thirteenth" style of horror script almost immediately seemed quite intelligible without any kind of supernatural props behind it.

In fact, the Matamoros case conformed in almost textbook fashion to what many criminologists and a few anthropologists had been saying about the darker recesses of the occult for decades—it was a "bonding" mechanism that ensured both loyalty and control within tight-knit, conspiratorial groups. In this setting, the mechanism was needed for criminal enterprise of the most elaborate and dangerous type.

The Matamoros cultists were drug runners who operated one notable turnkey enterprise within the vast underground empire of Latin American *narcotraficantes* stretching from Peru and Colombia through the central Mexico mountains to the streets of America's cities. According to the confessions of the accused, their distinct style of "religion"—which the police wrongly at first identified with the Afro-Caribbean traditions of *santeria* and then with its alleged "shadow side" known as *palo mayombe*—had been improvised from a variety of sources compassing Mexican peasant folk magic, the Hollywood horror movie *The Believers*, and the warped fantasies of Adolfo de Jesus Constanzo, the charismatic cult leader who belonged to the Mexican social celebrity network. Constanzo was eventually killed in a shootout with federal police in Mexico City.

Such an ad hoc blend of the ancient and the contemporary, of cultural kitsch and common superstition, of private folly and collective mania, make up what is most appropriately called *satanism*, which is certainly not a religious tradition in the usual sense. In the Matamoros story are contained many of the important clues to satanism and its presentday siege of American culture. But the story would never have been told had not an unbelievable chain of events come into play.

Mark Kilroy, a premedical student at the University of Texas in Austin, was about as much an all-American, fun-loving, career-minded minion of the white middle class as any twentieth-century writer of tragedy could have possibly designed. Indeed, Kilroy's destiny on March 14, 1989, just one day before the ides of March, did not appear to be anything other than the sort of banal beach blow-out that has been the secular ritual of college students let loose for spring break since the invention of beer and bikinis. Kilroy, along with a group of old high school chums, joined the cavalcade of dented Chevys and shiny vans en route from countless campuses in the South and Midwest to what was the central portion of the

United States' answer to Fort Lauderdale—an austere and interminable stretch of sand known as Padre Island. "Let's Padre" was the pun scratched with soap scum on a few of the automobiles careening down U.S. 77 between Corpus Christi and Brownsville at the southernmost swatch of Texas. It betrayed the brash, literally devil-may-care flippancy and abandon of the annual beach crowd.

Kilroy and friends had nothing more in mind than carousing and picking up women. When they decided after a day at Padre Island to make the trek across the Rio Grande from Brownsville to Matamoros on the Mexican side, it was all in keeping with the step-by-step initiation process of spring break celebrants. For years the Matamoros bars and night clubs had brought in top dollar from a lowered drinking age. When Kilroy's party had tired of beach blanket bingo, they headed for the noisy bistros and brightly lit cabarets on Avenida Alvaro Obregon. They ended up at a honky-tonk bar called Los Sombreros. Unbeknownst to them, the previous summer this bar had been the site of a bloody shootout between the son of a Matamoros nightclub owner and a sullen thug nicknamed "El Duby." The thug was employed by the Hernandez family, which allegedly controlled the bulk of the illegal drug market in the area.

The gunplay had been part of an escalating trend of violence that had a subtle but dramatic impact on the drug scene in the Mexican state of Tamaulipas. This both ensured the growing influence of members of Adolfo de Jesus Constanzo's bizarre cult and their ultimate apprehension by the Mexican police, known as the *federales*. First, the violence severely damaged the Hernandez family's presumed drug supply lines from the south. The Hernandez family then recruited Constanzo because of his ties to the Colombian cocaine lords. Second, it contributed to a police shake-up in Matamoros, which brought into the picture Juan Benitez Ayala, the Matamoros police commandante who ultimately busted the satanists.

That night, however, things were fairly quiet at Los Sombreros, and the Kilroy party soon left in search of a livelier atmosphere. They stumbled into the London Pub, retitled for that week the Hard Rock Cafe in order to entice spring breakers with the popular and well-known American franchise name. The party was raucous, and Kilroy faded into the nearly all-gringo bash until about 2 A.M. when the guys reconvened and set off on foot for Brownsville, where they had parked their car. Kilroy had decided to walk home a young coed, who had won a Padre Island beach beauty contest, known as Miss Tanline. Just before the bridge to the United States, Kilroy paused to say good-bye to Miss Tanline, while his buddy Bill Huddleston snuck behind a tree to relieve himself of too much beer.

When Huddleston returned, Kilroy was gone.

For about a week it was a routine missing person case which, because of the violence and corruption south of the border, was bound to cause more than average consternation among Kilroy's parents and friends.

Kilroy's disappearance coincided with a rash of assaults against spring break tourists. An eighteen-year-old University of Texas coed walking from Whammy's Bar to the international bridge had been gang raped by four Mexicans. A Mexican truck driver had been robbed and stabbed to death while pausing to pass through customs. Dean Scott Buchanan, a University of Texas engineering student, was beaten and robbed beside the bridge. And a guard at a Matamoros car wash had been shot and killed by unknown assailants. Mexican authorities said the impoverished neighborhoods near the river were chronic high-crime districts and that inhabitants of the barrio had been known to assault American visitors.

A $15,000 reward was offered by the Brownsville business community for information concerning the whereabouts of Kilroy. The family, which had inside connections to the U.S. Customs Service through an uncle in Los Angeles, was able to trigger within a short span of time a well-publicized search for their son. The task of tracking Kilroy fell to special agent Oran Neck, a tough and highly regarded customs official in the Brownsville area.

Customs investigators took Kilroy's drinking partners Bradley Moore, Brent Martin, and Huddleston on a tour of the Matamoros nightclub district in order to retrace what had occurred. The youths admitted they had all been drunk, and it was not clear whether any recollections were totally accurate. However, Huddleston remembered a man with a facial injury motioning toward Kilroy in front of Garcia's restaurant. Under hypnosis Huddleston described the stranger as a slender Hispanic, about 5 feet 8 inches tall, who was dressed in a blue plaid shirt with bright pants. The man, who spoke English, had a rounded scar, a recent wound of some type, on his left cheek. Kilroy had paused to talk to the stranger before he vanished.

For weeks police remained stumped about the Kilroy case. They postulated foul play but could not come up with any motive or suspects. If Kilroy had been kidnapped, they reasoned, ransom demands would have been presented. Fox Television heard about the disappearance and flew to Brownsville to recreate the events of the night of March 14 for their popular series "America's Most Wanted." Amid the brawling and reveling of spring breakers who still packed the sidewalks of the Avenida, the Fox film crew took footage of Sombrero's and the Hard Rock Cafe, where Kilroy and his friends had spent the larger part of the evening.

A leading Hispanic politician from Texas also lent his public support. San Antonio mayor Henry Cisneros called a news conference. Speaking on behalf of the parents, he grimly but ardently declared, "I have no presumptions about what one more appeal can do. I do know these are very good people who have been dealt a bad hand." A few days before, Cisneros had volunteered to assist in the case because, as the Brownsville area sheriff put it, "he knows a lot of people in Mexico."

At the same time, two inmates in a Galveston jail made an attempt to extort $10,000 from the Kilroy family over prison telephones, threatening to cut off Mark's fingers if the money was not paid. The plot was not uncovered by police until after the corpses were dug up in Matamoros.

On April 9, a crucial break in the case occurred that could scarcely have been predicted. Suddenly an invisible hand seemed to be working to unravel the entire tapestry of weirdness, confusion, lack of reliable witnesses, and, of course, the cloying silence of those who had some true inkling of the situation.

For several days, Mexican and United States law enforcement agencies had been conducting a joint drug interception campaign along the Rio Grande. Roadblocks had been erected on both sides of the border in order to search cars and snare suspects.

Serafin Hernandez García, nephew of reputed crime boss Elio Hernandez Rivera, approached one of these roadblocks—but he refused to stop. Serafin had been indoctrinated with the idea that his immersion in satanic practices would make him completely immune to the police. As far as he was concerned, running a roadblock invited no untoward consequences. After all, he was invisible. Unfortunately, it was not an everyday police roadblock, which did often let known narcotics traffickers pass with impunity. It was the *federales* backed up by the Mexican army. All authorities had to do was follow Serafin to the Rancho Santa Elena owned by his family and used for smuggling activities. Police were looking for drugs, not Mark Kilroy. But during the search, an American customs man, as part of a routine procedure, showed a photograph of Kilroy to the ranch caretaker.

To his surprise, the caretaker recognized the face and acknowledged Kilroy had been held at the ranch, pointing to a nearby storage shed. American investigators found nothing unusual about the shed, which contained melted candles, cigar butts, and empty liquor bottles. It was just a lot of refuse, they concluded. Yet the Mexican cops went into a frenzy. To them the leavings were the unmistakable signs of the most-wicked form of black magic. To both the bemusement and the chagrin of American officials, the *federales* demanded that the shed be exorcised before going any further. After calling in a Mexican *curandero*, a specialist in "positive magic," to expel the demonic presence at the ranch, the police took into custody Elio Hernandez Rivera, Serafin Garcia, and two other persons from the ranch.

The Hernandezes confessed to the murder of Kilroy and began to reveal all about the workings of the cult and its leaders. They fingered Adolfo de Jesus Constanzo, as well as a Brownsville college student named Sara Villarreal Aldrete. She acted as the "high priestess" of the group, or as Texas attorney general Jim Mattox phrased it in his down-home drawl, "the witch." Aldrete was an honors student by day at Texas

Southmost College and a *narcotraficante* by night. At her home in Matamoros, police came across an assortment of "voodoo" paraphernalia and a blood-spattered altar of sacrifice. Aldrete's neighbors, her class-mates, and her teachers naturally expressed astonishment and dismay. As is always the case when the "nice" boy or girl next door is unmasked as a vicious criminal, they cited innumerable examples of her benevolence, industry, and sincerity.

Aldrete, however, had fled the scene of the crime along with Constanzo, and there was much talk about her role as Constanzo's lover and her "multiple personalities." As events unfolded, the press learned that Constanzo, a homosexual, rarely had sex with women and that Aldrete had served principally as "bait" to lure members into the cult or male victims to their doom. Although she insisted from prison that Constanzo had taught her everything about magic, the story sounded thin. Aldrete had probably picked it up within her own family or childhood circle of affiliates—a common tendency within the poorer strata of society along the Rio Grande.

Kilroy had been killed, police said, with the blow of a machete to the back of his head. Later on, his legs had been hacked off to make it easier to dispose of the cadaver. The cult had selected him out of the swarms of college students because, it was first reported, he bore some physical resemblance to Constanzo, who ordered his disciples to pluck a spring breaker for the ultimate sacrifice. Snatching an American Anglo off the street was always risky business, but Constanzo was bold enough and crazy enough to do it. The danger heightened the possibility of gaining incredible "magical power."

Among other things the cult members were convinced that the kidnapping and sacrifice of an American would secure them super-natural protection on the north side of the river, which they currently lacked, as a recent series of drug busts and the breakdown of their supply lines indicated.

Kilroy's body parts were boiled in an iron kettle with animal blood. The cult members then passed around and drank the "witch's" brew as a kind of sickening "communion" among themselves. They believed that the blood and the energies of violence it contained would make them unconquerable soldiers in the war of evil.

Matamoro's police commandante Benitez knew he had an international sensation on his hands. In a manner quite alien to American judicial practice but to the delight of journalists, he paraded the suspects before television cameras and prompted them to make lengthy confessions for the public record. Meanwhile, other bodies were found. Benitez made suspect Sergio Martinez dig up the decapitated corpse of a teenage boy in front of the eyes of the press. A few hours later a local farmer was asked to remove a stack of hay so that more bodies could be sighted. About the same time the *federales* smashed into Constanzo's house in Atizapan, a

Mexico City suburb, and confiscated electronic high-security equipment, weapons, and two marble altars.

According to neighbors, Constanzo and his cohorts had pulled out a few nights before with large, unmarked boxes in tow. The largest combined manhunt in the history of the Mexican and American drug wars was launched. "We have never, ever, ever had the interest in any other crime [that we have] in this," customs agent Oran Neck told reporters.

The extraordinary attention given by police was spurred not only by snowballing media concern but by a strategic decision of American authorities. With the avalanche of tips and reports coming in all over the world, here was a rare opportunity to make some rapid headway in mapping the movements and source of drugs in the Western Hemisphere.

Contrary to the conventional American news reports during the week the corpses were unearthed, the role of cultists in the disappearance of Kilroy did not come as a complete surprise. As *nordamericano* journalists learned the minute they began probing the cultural context of the Matamoros murders, the practice and fear of black magic is pervasive in the Rio Grande Valley. The legacy of witchcraft goes all the way back to the Spanish conquest. As Marc Simmons, a contemporary anthropologist writes, "On the lower Rio Grande, and below San Antonio, an infusion of traits and practices from Old Mexico continues to build innumerable links between witches along the border and their fraternal kinsmen farther south."

It was not just that the current occult revival in the Western world, connected with the "New Age" phenomenon, had brought back into the mainstream of Hispanic societies the old, pre-Colombian beliefs and ceremonies. Nor was it just that the American style of pop satanism fashionable among alienated teenagers—associated with sexual orgies, grave robbings, church desecrations, menacing graffiti, and animal killings—had slunk into Mexico with the tourists and taken on a native, virulent form. Ironically, it was that the relative success of the U.S. government's drug interdiction campaigns in south Florida had diverted on a major scale the Central American drug transport channels to the long border between Mexico and Texas. The increased drug activities along the western Gulf Coast made municipalities like Matamoros "boom towns" of sorts. But this also brought in its wake piranhalike competition among the traffickers, resulting in ever more vicious, frequent, and barbaric incidents of killing.

In the darkening world of kidnapping, murder, torture, and ever-present machine-gun fire, not to mention mounting pressure from the American antinarcotics crusade, the Mexican drug "families" and their operatives north of the Rio Grande began turning to a source of "otherworldly" protection and encouragement that seemed to them superlatively effective. The solution was black magic. The press and its

American academic commentators have consistently tried to treat the Matamoros happenings as a freakish phenomenon that might be clipped from the pages of National Geographic magazine or as an anomalous sort of topic requiring a brief lecture in a university-style Religion 101 course. Yet Constanzo's disciples were not as out of place as the lofty Anglo mentality might surmise. They were the ones who happened to have been caught. The word in the underground, as a writer for a valley newspaper observed, was not how rare and startling Constanzo's venture had been; rather, it was the likelihood that similar horrid spectacles would eventually be brought to light.

, Other victims besides Kilroy included Ruben Vela García, Jose Luis Garza Luna, Esquiel Rodriguez Luana—all agricultural workers; Ernesto Rivas Dias, a twenty-three-year-old welder on vacation in Matamoros; and Jorge Valente del Fierro Gómez, a municipal policeman. Del Fierro had been known in Matamoros as *la madrina* of the federal judicial police. In Hispanic slang, a *madrina* is an employee whose name does not appear on the payroll and who enjoys protection from law enforcement while receiving a salary and collecting bribes for his superiors. He also acts as a police informant while serving as a kind of ombudsman with the underworld.

In the past, the anonymous residents of what Mexicans in the Brownsville vicinity termed *el otro lado*—the "other side" of the river— had simply refused to talk about what they knew was going on. The *narcotraficantes* availed themselves of satanism the way the Salvation Army uses the Bible. In fact, the locals who knew about them had a special name for them—*narcosatanistos*. Those on *el otro lado* would not talk, not only because they were terrified of everyone in authority, from the lowest magistrates to the judicial police, but more importantly because they actually believed in the power of the Devil. A *maquiladora*, or American-owned factory on the border hiring Mexican labor, had to be shut down temporarily because a piece of machinery was thought to be hexed. Police commandante Benitez kept strings of peppers and garlic as well as white candles in his office to parry evil spirits. And when the *federales* first came upon Constanzo's "sacrificial hut," or "devil's cathedral," on the Santa Elena Ranch, where Kilroy and other victims had met their doom, their first instinct was to summon a "white magician." In the end they resorted to burning the place down—not for hygenic reasons but to destroy the wicked "energies" of the spot.

If the natives were convinced that clouds of evil blew in and out of the valley like so many July thunderstorms, they surely knew of powerful sorcerers and occult *bandidos* who resorted, whenever feasible, to doing tangible types of evil on the surrounding populace. The Matamoros scandal arose mainly because it was a white, American *turista* with family connections to his own federal government whom a rather brash Mexican *brujo*, or "black witch," chose for his victim. Otherwise, the mass grave that harbored Kilroy probably would have been gorged with many more nameless skeletons. It was not kosher for a Mexican satanist to abduct a blonde, blue-eyed American off the street. The risks were enormous. But Constanzo wanted to gain the magical "power" that came from pulling off such a high-stakes deal. It was his arrogance, rather than his lack of orthodoxy, that caused the dogs to bark.

At the ranch, Mexican and American law enforcement officials uncovered a bloody altar, "voodoo" paraphernalia, La Palma cigars, cheap rum, human body parts, animal bones, chicken and goat heads, thousands of pennies, gold beads, and an iron kettle filled with the most foul mixture of blood and flesh—a veritable witch's cauldron. The fluid in the cauldron, which contained brains, hearts, lungs, and testicles, had been drunk in regular rituals by the cult members to "sanctify" themselves, or as Lt. George Gavito of the Cameron County Sheriff's Department explained with a quote that made all the wire services, "so the police would not arrest them, so bullets would not kill them, and so they could make more money."

The animal remains belonged perhaps to the religious accoutrements of Afro-Cuban magic, which had been growing in popularity among poor Hispanics in America's urban centers. The act of removing the human victim's vital organs, as they did with Kilroy, could be traced to the remnants of the Aztec sacrificial customs, which the Mexican country people refer to as *santismo*. In earlier times it was known as "nagualism." The cops called it *palo mayombe*, but that was a misnomer. Historic *palo mayombe* focused on the "power" supposedly derived from bones of other criminals stolen from graveyards. The more wicked the corpse had been in life, the more ferocious he would prove in his etheric guise. The spinal column of a clean-cut gringo kid from Santa Fe, Texas, who at one time might have made the Mouseketeers, just would not have semed very impressive to an authentic palomayombist, even though white bones were valued more than brown ones. Contanzo, like his American counterparts who had steeped themselves in the fashionable black arts as dictated over the years by such magical luminaries as Aleister Crowley and Anton LaVey, founder of the Church of Satan, could only be called a satanist. What made him stand out was his extreme cruelty, which went with the drug trafficking.

It is difficult to judge whether it was the drugs that created the Matamoros horror or the satanic belief system. Most likely it was an inseparable combination of the two. Both Oran Neck, the U.S. Customs agent who put the feds in hot pursuit of the kidnappers, and Mark Kilroy's father blamed it almost exclusively on drugs. Various *curanderos* (Mexican herbal healers and magicians, who came out of the woodwork to offer their opinions to newspaper investigators) claimed it was all because of the prevalence of black magic. Constanzo's cult, however, did not sacrifice and cut up human beings for sadistic kicks. They had their own logically consistent, if not commonplace, rationale.

Their rationale was the same as that of primitive headhunters, who have always believed that violence and gore have a supernatural nimbus around them. In order to harness those supernatural forces, one must kill, torture, and maim. The fact that those same gross and primitive ideas could find their way into the thought mechanisms of educated Mexicans in the twentieth century is not as implausible as it might initially appear. The assault on the modern "rational" attitude toward the universe has been in full swing worldwide among intellectuals themselves since at least the late 1960s. Offbeat religiosity has been the staple of cultural radicalism and artistic chic since the Beatles journeyed to India and started meditating. Constanzo lived not in a mud-block hut but among the Mexico City literati. He was a counter-culturalist who developed his own "training program" for the drug cartels. At bottom, it was the beliefs that carried the day.

The Mexican narcotics gangs, and particularly the Hernandez mob that many thought virtually owned Matamoros, were specially known for their apparently gratuitous cruelty. One of the Santa Elena victims, a Mexican policeman, had been murdered in the most inhumane manner conceivable: he had been slowly skinned alive. As it turned out, an earlier and widely publicized incident of savage torture inflicted on a drug-fighting peace officer—the murder of the American drug enforcement agent Enrico Camarena in 1985—was tied to the activities of the Hernandezes. Their cruelty obviously was not merely to intimidate their enemies, for it was often done out of sight. It was more the expression of intense private passions. And those passions were likely to be what we might describe as "religious" in character.

Constanzo used religion to win friends and influence people at all levels of society and for a host of logistical purposes. At first he seemed content to climb into the catbird seat with the Mexican glitterati by playing the familiar role of charmer and soothsayer with extraordinary "psychic" powers. But he quickly ascended, if he had not already been there from the beginning, to the position of drug captain in charge of the large-scale movement of contraband. At the time of the Santa Elena bust, Constanzo was already under investigation for smuggling illegal aliens into the United States. Constanzo built his diverse satrapies of sordid crime by at once scaring the pants off his clients, his flunkies, and his enemies with his knowledge of "magic."

His expertise was hereditary rather than learned. A woman who knew Constanzo's family in Miami, where he had grown up, told the newspapers that his mother, Delia Gonzales Del Valle, "was in *santeria*." Delia's mother had apparently also been a practitioner in Cuba. Norma Brito said that when she moved into the house she had bought from the family, she found altar remains of *santeria* ceremonies. Evidently, in order to keep the neighbors quiet, the family would go out at night and leave headless chickens as well as dead geese and goats in the streets and on doorsteps. Mutilated animals on somebody's property are a common death threat in all forms of blood cultism, including contemporary satanism.

The family may not have been into *santeria* per se; they may have been *paleros*, or practitioners of *palo mayombe*. The issue of where *santeria* shades off into *palo mayombe*, or where *palo mayombe* in turn lapses into satanism, is more than an academic bagatelle. It touches directly on the degree of potential criminal application of all occult practices. Cult followers and their apologists, together with a sizable portion of university social scientists who examine the more unusual side of religious behavior, are wont to draw hard distinctions between "bad" and "good" occultism, as if they somehow existed in entirely different universes without common linkages or crossover. In this context, *palo mayombe* is ipso facto "dark," whereas *santeria* by definition is of the light. It is like saying that Jimmy Swaggart could not have consorted with prostitutes, or Jim and Tammy Bakker could not have skimmed off money, because ipso facto they were "Christians." Verbal distinctions frequently can be wielded either to tar or to exonerate a particular religious group without any attempt to consider the connection between orthodoxy and deviance.

In the scramble to pin a label on Constanzo's obnoxious brand of belief, the press was treated to some rather odd bending of categories by the academic experts they interviewed. For instance, Rafael Martinez, a cultural anthropologist from the University of North Florida in Miami, who was called in by the Cameron County Sheriff's Department as part of the inquiry into Constanzo, claimed the Santa Elena horror was not even *palo mayombe* in the customary sense. "What we've got here is an isolated case, a self-styled *palo mayombe*," he said. Constanzo was a "psychopathic killer who took the practice of *palo mayombe* into his own hands." Nor was Constanzo involved in satanism, for "if you say demonic, you're looking at the Devil."

Whether Constanzo actually believed in the Devil is irrelevant—it was the mutilated corpses that made the difference. Such rhetorical nit-picking tends to brush aside the fact that there is a dynamic of involvement in the occult that under the right conditions erases most of technical distinctions between "black magic" and "white magic" or between *santeria* and *palo mayombe* or its "perverted" forms. The dynamic is, stated simply, the attainment of power for oneself and the warding off, if not the destruction, of adversaries. Satanism should never be considered a religion per se; it is the carrying of magic and intrigue in its violent hues to the utmost extremes. Constanzo *was* a satanist, because he went beyond the basic moral and ceremonial boundaries established by the magical traditions, which he had learned at his mother's knee. The trespass enabled him to become something quite different than scholars of religion would be trained to consider, and therein lay his cunning and strength.

At the age of fourteen Constanzo was considered by his mother, Delia Gonzales Del Valle, a "psychic" prodigy. According to Del Valle, Constanzo "knew things." Supposedly, he had a vision that Marilyn Monroe's death was not a suicide, and he gained something of a reputation in his mother's immediate occult circles for his out-of-body experiences and his predictions of the future. Whether these recollections have any validity is somewhat beside the point. It is clear from Constanzo's sketchy biography that he was not simply a drug dealer and that the Matamoros incident was, as even Kilroy's father began to reiterate within weeks after finding Mark's body, more than drug violence. Constanzo and his gang did not use drugs themselves. They were occult entrepreneurs who moved into the drug-transporting business because of its enormous profits and who enjoyed a competitive advantage other narcotraficantes lacked—they were "invisible" to the police.

Constanzo's mastery of occult mind control was a talent he took with him from Miami to Mexico City, and it accounted for his rapid rise to power in both high society and in the tightly controlled, Colombian-based drug cartels. Constanzo was, in fact, a Hispanic "New Ager," the Latin American equivalent of a California psychic who nonetheless converted his understanding of metaphysical mumbo-jumbo into a particularly successful criminal conspiracy. He combined his knowledge of Afro-Cuban magic with mysterious and secretive Mexican traditions of human sacrifice dating back to the Mayans and Aztecs. It was not the Afro-Cuban, or "santerian," elements that gave Constanzo's cult its ghastly pallor. It was the "Mexican mystique," witnessed by the Spaniards during the conquest, of blood and the infliction of torture on human captives.

In Mexico City, Constanzo reportedly drew clients who would shell out thousands of dollars per session for his psychic "readings" and ritual "cleansings" (which involved pouring blood over a client) and his knowledge of astrology. Those who visited him in the Zona Rosa, Mexico City's tourist and nightclub district, included top government and police officials as well as actors, singers, and other popular entertainers. They would seek advice on such matters as when to release an album, which motion picture to make, or in what real estate to invest. Florentino Ventura, former Mexican chief of the international police agency Interpol who committed suicide in 1988, was also named by two of the cult members as one of Constanzo's clients.

Constanzo apparently gained considerable influence among the civic leadership of Matamoros by the same mystique. If he could not persuade through the power of suggestion, he would often turn to intimidation. Pop singer Oscar Athie told Mexico City journalists that he had been painfully harassed for over a year by Constanzo's people because he would not perform in concert for them and pay for a cleansing. "They said that they were witches and that Constanzo had powers, and for $2000 or $3000 I could be cleansed for good luck," he said. "I told them I wasn't interested. They kept calling me. They became angry and called back to say that I was going to die slowly of a serious illness."

It is quite common for witches and others in the occult subculture to bully and intimidate each other through "psychic warfare." Yet Constanzo was, even at the outset, someone far more important than a parlor-room "sensitive" or a self-employed tea-leaf reader. A homosexual, Constanzo had also set up a male pornography ring, which may have been his first serious link to the professional criminal underworld. When the *federales* raided Constanzo's apartment in the capital, they found numerous nude pictures of gay males. The cult has been linked to a string of gorey homosexual killings in the Zona Rosa.

In May, Mexican police made further arrests of cult members, including Enrique Calzada and Salvador Antonio Gutierrez Juarez, a.k.a. Jorge Montes. At the time, police claimed that Montes had admitted helping Constanzo murder a gay man in a Mexico City suburb. At the same time, a Juan Carlos Fragoso was taken into custody. Fragoso was suspected in the ritualistic murder of a transvestite named Ramon "Edgar" Baez Elias in the Zona Rosa. The transvestite had been flayed and his heart torn out while he was still alive in the fashion of the ancient Aztec priests.

For Constanzo and his lieutenants, it was an easy step from pornography to the drug trade. In fact, it was their entrance into drugs that brought them to Matamoros in the first place. The Hernandez family, which reportedly dominated trafficking along the Rio Grande, had been steadily losing influence to the subsidiaries of the better financed international syndicates through a series of gangland killings of its key members. Up until about 1986 the Hernandezes had purchased drugs from Casmiro Espinoza, called "El Cacho," who was assassinated in Matamoros. On the death of El Cacho, Saul Hernandez became *jefe* of the drug-smuggling organization, but he had only slim ties to the top suppliers down south. A year later he was shot to death in front of the Piedras Negras bar in Matamoros, and the stage was set for Constanzo.

According to Commandante Benitez, Constanzo "accidentally" showed up in Matamoros and met the Hernandezes. He agreed to tie them in with the vendors and intermediaries they needed but only if he could introduce them to his cult of human sacrifice. Constanzo showed the Hernandezes how his black magic not only could make them ever more powerful but how they could brutalize their opponents with a gusto that their traditional cultural scruples might have prohibited. When Victor Saul Sauceda, a schoolmate of cult member David Serna and a former Matamoros policeman, witnessed the murder of small-time cocaine dealer Carlos de la Llata, he was grabbed by the Hernandezes and carried to the ranch, where they flayed him.

It was not necessarily revenge for some significant criminal indiscretion. Sauceda was for the most part an innocent. It was suggested by one informant that Constanzo had told them the direct experience of Sauceda's terrible torture would give them even greater "power." In Mexican *brujeria*, or black magic, abject torture is a strategic ploy to capture the soul of an enemy or victim. The soul of the victim is taught through the ordeal to fear the murderer completely and for eternity. At the same time, the "energy" from the pain and fear of the victim is appropriated sacramentally by the torturer in order to enhance his magical strength and theoretically his soul. The idea is a very primitive one, but satanism has always been a return to archaic psychology in some sense. The notion, spread in the American media by certain "experts" who had little feeling for what had happened in Matamoros, that the cult killings were the work of "sick" people entirely misses the point. Constanzo and his followers were not irrational; they were merely reverting to a magical worldview and logic that were starkly imprinted in the pre-Christian strata of their own society.

Many scholars, furthermore, would like to believe that the Matamoros atrocities were relatively isolated, that Constanzo was some kind of lone wolf and occult weirdo. But within a month after the initial ballyhoo in the press had subsided, federal investigators began making connections that placed the Matamoros situation in a much more sweeping context. Customs agents realized that the slayings at the ranch bore striking resemblance to mass murders committed about the same time at the Mexican border town of Agua Prieta about 120 miles southeast of Tucson, Arizona. On March 27, two Americans and three Mexicans from the state of Sonora had been found shot to death in a shed. Two days later, twelve more bodies were pulled out of a well and septic tank. The corpses had been mutilated and tortured. Police also confiscated 225 pounds of marijuana, one hundred grams of cocaine, twelve high-powered weapons, and eleven vehicles with highly sophisticated communications equipment.

One of the victims in the Agua Prieta case was a Mexican police official whose wife had been killed along with him. Customs authorities said that the torture killings in both Matamoros and Agua Prieta followed similar patterns. The drug lords were not only taking out police informers and their accomplices, they were doing it with a very grisly flourish. One woman had her fingers severed from her hand. On February 1, ten *federales* were arrested in Matamoros for suspicion of robbery and drug trafficking. They later admitted to the crimes and were found to have in their possession about $5 million.

In June 1989, federal drug agents raided a house in San Mateo County south of San Francisco and came across a sacrificial altar, animal organs, human skulls, and a human spinal column used in rituals. The remains and paraphernalia were almost identical to what had been unearthed at

Matamoros. They included a cauldron stuffed with human and animal body pieces as well as blood and sticks. A Drug Enforcement Administration (DEA) group supervisor in Sacramento informed reporters that the suspects, who were Colombian as well as Cuban, belonged to a massive cocaine trafficking network. The suspects were Angel Rivera, 53; Dennis Belez, 35; Lazaro Jalarraga, 45; Harold Castaneda, 32; Guido Trujillo, 29; and Edith Grajales, 26.

Exactly a year earlier, during a drug raid in Houston, law officers found an altar and paraphernalia resembling what had been discovered at Matamoros. The Hernandez ring was thought to be linked to the $20 million in cocaine seized in the raid. The FBI in Houston speculated that many drug dealers in the metropolitan area were under the influence of Constanzo in some way. The FBI indicated it had tracked Constanzo coming in and out of Houston for the past year. Besides lighted candles, police nabbed from the raid a statue of a figure that looked like the Buddha and "paperwork" with the last name "Rivera" written on it. In Mexico City, little statues of the Buddha were Constanzo's trademark. Houston police linked the cult to drug busts in Pasadena and Corpus Christi, Texas, as well.

Finally, the Texas attorney general's office decided to take a second look at earlier statements by convicted mass killer Henry Lee Lucas, waiting on death row, that he had been connected with a satanic cult operating along the border of Texas and Mexico. Lucas had called the cult the "Hand of Death." Lucas's credibility had been in serious doubt because he had first "confessed" to the murder of 600 persons all around the United States, then withdrew his statements and said he was responsible for the death of only three victims, including his mother. Three years earlier Lucas had drawn a map of cult killing sites for a Catholic lay worker from Georgetown named "Sister" Clemmie Schroeder, who had served as his spiritual advisor. Jim Boutwell, the sheriff of Texas' Williamson County who aided in a Texas Rangers task force that gathered the Lucas confessions, told a valley newspaper that investigators had verified Lucas was involved in cult activities. He also noted that he had seen a map similar to the one supplied by Sister Clemmie.

Earlier Lucas had told the *Dallas Times Herald* that he was "going to show them" that something large-scale and bizarre was going on. Lucas had also insisted to another news reporter that he "belonged to a cult" and that "for initiation you would have to go out and kill a person." According to Lucas, the cult killed by contract while performing ritual cremations and crucifixions of both animals and human beings with the aim of bringing "the devil back to life." Lucas contended a man in Shreveport, Louisiana, first approached him about joining the cult, which had members all over the country. "They think I'm stupid, but before all this is over everyone will know who's really stupid," Lucas later said. "And we'll see who the real criminals are."

The "real criminals" may not have been the affluent and well-educated Mexican yuppies who tagged after Constanzo throughout his descent into the hell of drug distributing but an even more recognizable and sinister criminal organization—the notorious Chicago mob whose pedigree runs back to Al Capone. Federal court documents obtained by and described in the *Brownsville Herald* in July 1989 contained allegations that thousands of pounds of cocaine and marijuana had been siphoned across the border by the Matamoros cult to supply high-ranking syndicate crime bosses in suburban Chicago.

The central figure in the network, according to the same documents, was fifty-eight-year-old Manuel "Poncho" Jaramillo, a former resident of Chicago Heights who at the time was based in Mission, Texas. His colleagues included Albert Caesar Tocco, a reputed Chicago mob leader who had been arrested by the FBI and charged in a forty-eight-count federal racketeering indictment. Jaramillo was closely associated with the Hernandez family and has been suspected of commandeering, not only narcotics, but a money-laundering enterprise. The U.S. Customs regional office in Houston confirmed an "ongoing investigation" was under way into relationships between the Chicago mafia and valley drug suspects.

Federal scrutiny of the Hernandez family's connections with Chicago organized crime began in August 1988. Confiscation by customs agents of 597 pounds of Mexican marijuana from a fishing vessel in the Gulf led to the arrest of a thirty-seven-year-old Harlingen, Texas, man named Michael Habiniak, who was discovered to be a business partner of Jaramillo's former wife in a Texas corporation called La Esperanza Mining Company. La Esperanza, the *Herald* reported, said they imported ore precipitate from northern Mexico, but customs agents surmised that the company was a front for drug smuggling and money-laundering operations.

The vice president of La Esperanza, according to Texas secretary of state records, was businessman David McCoy of McAllen, Texas, a federal narcotics suspect. A government motion entered in the case of Habiniak stated that "investigation by the U.S. Customs has revealed a criminal enterprise connection between some of Habiniak's associates in the Rio Grande Valley and in Chicago, Illinois, with Albert Caesar Tocco of the Accardo organized crime family." In January 1989, a federal grand jury in Corpus Christi convicted Habiniak of conspiracy and distribution of marijuana. Further investigation by the customs service coupled Habiniak and Jaramillo to the drug-connected abduction of Ovidio Hernandez Rivera, a Constanzo cult member, and his two-year-old son. During Habiniak's detention hearings, federal officials insinuated that Ovidio Hernandez and his family were locked in closely with Jaramillo and the drug business. Three other members of the Hernandez family have been identified by the Mexican prosecution as ring leaders of the satanic cult.

Who exactly was Jaramillo? *The Star*, a Chicago Heights newspaper, had profiled him as a "model citizen" in the late 1970s when he worked as a superintendent at Ford Motor Company and was a Republican party activist. Jaramillo, however, was named in a 1988 federal grand jury subpoena as part of a continuing probe surrounding his alleged connections with Tocco, the south Texas drug business, and the mayor and the police captain of Chicago Heights. In July 1987, a confidential informant set up a cocaine buy in Texas between Jaramillo and an uncover agent for the DEA. Jaramillo showed the agent a suitcase filled with $350,000 in cash and said he had spent about $6.5 million the previous day on a Mexican marijuana deal. Jaramillo had warned the agent that "anyone who double-crosses me is dead."

The DEA then arrested Jaramillo and confiscated, along with the money, a .45 caliber handgun and an Illinois license plate. Prosecutors later dismissed the drug complaints against Jaramillo but kept him under suspicion. Transcripts from federal courts also correlated Jaramillo closely, not just with the Hernandezes, but with Tocco. One document stated that "investigation by U.S. Customs has revealed a criminal enterprise connection between [Jaramillo] in the Rio Grande Valley and in Chicago, Illinois, with Albert Caesar Tocco of the Accardo organized crime family." Tocco, who comes from Chicago Heights, has been described by the FBI as a major crime boss. He has been indicted on 172 separate violations of the Racketeer Influenced Corrupt Organization (RICO) Act, and a bureau wanted poster has characterized him as "a known member of an organized crime family in Chicago . . . sought in connection with his involvement in controlling 'street tax' concerning extensive 'chop shop' activities, gambling operations, prostitution activities, and the control of land used for the disposal of toxic waste."

It may well have been that the top-secret structure of the criminal organization that ran drugs from Mexico through south Texas to the Chicago mafia was virtually the same as the makeup of the cult. One of the mysteries associated with the supposition of broad-reaching satanic cult networks has to do with the nature of the organization itself. The conventional wisdom has generally held that the cults themselves, particularly those of the simple adolescent variety, are nothing more than loose-knit, entrepreneurial undertakings that are stitched together only by common attitudes, literature, and beliefs—if even those factors can truly be construed as a common denominator.

Certainly, widely separate groups may all read Anton LaVey's *Satanic Bible*, or they may cast spells from the occult classic *The Necromonicon*. Yet they do not consort together, nor do they "conspire" in some clear-cut, regimental fashion. A point regularly missed, however, is that the conspiratorial tie-in between diverse cells in the cultic organization may not have anything to do with religion at all. On the contrary, the linkage may be quite mundane and commercial. In this case the unifying element was overland drug operations.

As the confessions of the Hernandezes underscore, satanism functioned as a sort of motivational corporate training program for the family business. It not only imparted a heady feeling of power and invincibility to the adherents, in the same connection it inspired terror and the will to maintain extremely tight loyalties—absolutely critical assets for the drug trafficking profession. It is not at all surprising that Constanzo and Sara Aldrete were infatuated with the movie *The Believers*. The magical practitioners in the film are portrayed as insuperable and almost all-knowing. In one telling scene, a victim of the fictional cult screams in a jail-cell interview that the "believers" can even "walk through walls."

Interestingly, the cult in the motion picture has a hidden hierarchy that is not noticeable at first but becomes manifest as the plot lurches toward the final, dramatic scene where the central character, a police psychologist, is compelled to sacrifice his own son in the presence of the assembled devotees. *The Believers* theatrically strives to hammer home the sense that the cult, though protected by its own facade of upstanding citizenry, is "everywhere," and therefore its influence cannot be resisted. The surprise conclusion, in which the hero's girlfriend turns out to have secretly converted to the "religion," enhances this kind of psychology.

In a less stagey manner, the real-life saga of Constanzo and his troupe of "believers" revealed similar themes.

First, the DEA speculated out loud that Constanzo actually had not died in the shoot-out. The condition of his corpse initially prevented positive identification, and Mexican newspapers reported that two people had been observed fleeing the apartment building as the *federales* closed in. Later, however, after Mexican police said they had cross-checked fingerprints, U.S. Customs officially went along with the premise that Constanzo was dead.

Second, after the shoot-out, Mexico City police handed over to Commandante Benitez a diary from Constanzo's apartment ranking the different cult members. Constanzo called himself *padrino*, or "godfather." He referred to others as *paleros*, or "priests," and *rayados*, meaning "marked with an arrow." Benitez said that there had "to be someone higher than Constanzo . . . someone he turned to when all his problems started." Benitez implied that the transformation of Cuban *palo mayombe*, which historically has relied upon bones taken from graveyards, was due to cultic training emanating from the United States. A self-described priestess of "white magic" named Charlotte Chambers, a business partner with the Occult Shoppe in Houston, told journalists that Constanzo had combined Aztec warrior sacrifice with the use of satanism. Flaying alive was typical of the ancient Aztec treatment of prisoners. "I am getting a very real picture that someone in the U.S. had a lot to do with this," she commented.

Satanic killing as a "training exercise" was meant, quite simply, to create both a megalomaniacal urge to murder without remorse—just as terrorists and professional assassins are steeled to fear no one and to shrink from nothing. When the police surrounded Constanzo's gang in their Mexico City hideaway, Constanzo ordered Alvaro de Leon Valdez to execute him with machine gun fire. It was the supreme gesture of ruthlessness and obedience for a warrior occultist.

Indeed, to take the very life of the cult's own charismatic general, its primal font of magical puissance, outdid any imaginable 'sacrifice' that might have been attempted. To refuse was to be tortured in hell, as Valdez had tortured his adversaries in real life. Valdez was nauseated at the prospect, yet he obeyed. He was only "following orders." Valdez most likely could never have mustered the courage had he not done a dry run with the murder of Kilroy. Kilroy's death had reportedly earned Valdez his "stripes" within the cult itself. When Constanzo demanded that Valdez cut off Kilroy's legs, he instructed, "Do this so your fear will go away."

This particular snippet of Valdez's confessions raises the disturbing question of whether the mutilation of Kilroy did, in fact, take place when the young man was still alive. Cutting off the limbs of a corpse would seemingly not have been an ordeal nor stirred any significant scruples for a hardened criminal such as Valdez. During that "initiation," Valdez apparently was inculcated in the basic theology of satanism, which involves a profession of undying hatred for Christians. Kilroy, in fact, was about as emblematic of white, Anglo, Christian culture as any victim to be chosen.

According to Valdez, Constanzo "said that all Christians were animals, and when you earned your stripe your soul died." If Sara Aldrete had in truth practiced "Christian *santeria*," as she insisted to the press and to the police, she was probably despised equally by Constanzo. But there is no evidence of that fact.

The key to the entire, sordid affair, however, was probably Aldrete. In public interviews following her arrest, Aldrete gave off airs of the poor, hard-working, little barrio girl who had raised her lot in life through education and who had been seduced, then innocently led down the spiral staircase into unspeakable infamy through the wiles of Constanzo. She claimed she had not gone to Mexico City willingly with Constanzo after the *federale* bust at the ranch but had been virtually a prisoner against her will. Her close associates testified to the quality of her character. "She was a normal girl, and there was never anything unusual about her," reported her next-door neighbor.

Police in Mexico City, on the other hand, asserted that she exhibited the traits of multiple personality. There was the charmer who dramatically performed and protested her purity before the television cameras, the haughty and defiant gang moll who tussled with federal interrogators, and the vulnerable and tortured private soul who had been observed alone in the jail cell. Israel Aldrete Villarreal, Sara's father, had his own perspective. "She loved children, she loved animals, she loved the beggars who need money," he said. "We never saw anything bad in her." A taxi driver recalled how Sara had given money to his niece after she had ruined her car in a fender-bender on the streets of Matamoros.

Israel Aldrete did know that his daughter practiced *santeria*. He had gone into her private room on the second floor and observed an altar, likenesses of saints, and fruit but "nothing else, nothing satanic." Sara stressed to police that her fascination with *santeria* had been the outgrowth of her crush on Constanzo. "He was mysterious, and I wanted to find out what it was about him, why he was like that," she said. At first Constanzo beckoned to Aldrete with playthings of the occult, according to her story. He would do readings of tarot cards, make psychic predictions, and speak of strange and ungodly forces at work in the universe. After a while he would "admit" that his powers stemmed from his mastery of the art of *palo mayombe*, and Sara wanted to learn much more.

It will probably remain a matter of involuted argument and speculation for a long while whether Constanzo really practiced "classical" *palo mayombe* or whether he was a satanist. The dispute is far more academic and irrelevant than most people would care to admit. All forms of occultism by their very nature are entrepreneurial and experimental. Orthodox religions with their standard doctrines and approved ceremonies rely on public observance and scrutiny. The plumb line of piety is the commonality of practice. Just as we know when the Pledge of Allegiance has been recited incorrectly because "everybody" knows it by heart, so we can judge when a religion changes course, even if we do not actually subscribe to its tenets, because there are perceptible external standards for deciding whether it is "traditional" or not.

In the occult, things are quite different. The occult, strictly by definition, is opaque, private, and elusive. (The word itself derives from the Latin meaning "obscure" or "concealed.") For that reason it can be easily changed to suit the needs of the entrepreneur, even though most occultists routinely insist that they are embroiled in a form of devotion that is unchanging and antique in the extreme. The history of the occult is the chronicle of thousands of strange, constantly shifting, and half-intelligible "systems" of very personal belief. When belief is encircled with barbed wire, horrid things can easily take place inside the perimeter.

It would probably not be too wild a guess to say that Constanzo was trained in *palo mayombe* or the black facets of *santeria*. But under the pressure of succeeding in the drug business, he imported the practice of human sacrifice, which he mimicked from well-established but quite proprietary and top-secret strands of Mexican occultism. For instance,

Mexico City police found eight corpses, including that of Edgar Baez Elias at the bottom of a lagoon in the Zumpango River. Each of the victims had been hideously tortured and their hearts excised. Police ascribed the killings to Constanzo.

Constanzo's followers said he had educated them in the correct, magical procedures of the Aztec priests, who would rip the heart from the victim's body cavity and gulp down the blood before it was drained away. The belief, on which the ritual system of the greater Aztec empire had been built, was that the throbbing heart sequestered the energy of the sun, which had to be "fed" with constant sacrifices. The ritual sites at Mexico City were stained red with the blood of hundreds of thousands of victims killed in this manner. After the sacrifice, the body parts—particularly the brain and vital organs, which contained the "soul-life" of the sun—were boiled with blood in an iron kettle for ritual consumption. The Spanish soldier Bernal Diaz, who accompanied Cortez on his conquest of Mexico, reported seeing many pots—the kind used by Constanzo—near the Great Temple of Tlatelolco.

Constanzo also adopted the very old Mexican folk magic of the *nagual*. The *nagual* is a guardian spirit—frequently a bird or some other animal of "power"— with whom the magician identifies in order to both master and participate in the universe of black magic. The popular American author Carlos Castaneda has written extensively about a fictionalized version of nagualism in his stories of the Yaqui Indian sorcerer Don Juan. Nagualism, which has been preserved through secret, magical groups in Mexican and Central American *campesino* culture since the fall of the Aztecs, was frequently revived by peasant revolutionaries. Maria Candelaria, the heroine of the Tzental uprising of 1712 in Guatemala, was a priestess of nagualism. Nagualism was never absorbed by Christianity, as was voodoo by Haitian Catholicism. Its underlying tenet was fervent opposition to the Christian/European conquest of the New World. Nagualism was basically an underground warrior religion. The nagualists thought that through their magical techniques they could render themselves totally invisible to their enemies and impervious to their weapons. In effect, Constanzo trained the Hernandezes, "warriors" in their own right, in nagualism.

Human sacrifice has always been a high "prestige" item among black magicians. Few would dare to do it, probably out of fear they might be caught. But the one who, like the Nietzschean superman, would dare to overstep the moral boundaries would certainly be rewarded magically. Some of the documented elements of "conventional" *palo mayombe* were discernible among the artifacts found at the shed. The use of the big iron cauldron with blood and the remains of living creatures mixed together is one recognizable feature. The cutting of the arm, the burning of candles, the smoking of cigars to "attract" the energy of the spirits—these items could be documented. Even obtaining the brain of a *mundele* ,or "white person," as a special prize can be glimpsed in the selection of Kilroy.

Yet the slaying and torturing of enemies in preparation for sacrifice has never been typical of even the most bizarre cultic form of *palo mayombe* in the past. That practice, as indicated, came from elsewhere. In *palo mayombe* itself, the bones of a person already gone are desired, because in the occult mind-set it is the lingering powers of life, not death, that the magician seeks to capture. Constanzo was obsessed with death. It was his hatred of his victims, especially Anglos, that distinguished his magic.

The use of magic as a camouflage for sadism and cruelty is to be found in satanism per se. Mingled with the Aztec mystique of killing and torturing adversaries in battle, Constanzo's "religion" occupied a distinct niche, one that would only have emerged in the violent subculture of the narcotics suppliers. If Sara was the "witch," as the Texas attorney general vowed, it was something she learned, not in the herbal shops of the *santeros*, but in the dark and decadent back allies of the American underground.

The gang members themselves sought to protect Sara from the most severe accusations and recriminations. To some of them, she was not a witch at all, but a benevolent mother figure ranking somewhere between a school marm and the Virgin of Guadalupe. Alvaro de Leon Valdez, among the most surly of the throng that had been arrested, said Sara had never been present at the ritual murders. Sara herself maintained that she had not even a hint of the cult killings until she had taken flight with Constanzo and she heard about them on television. She inquired of Constanzo, and he allegedly replied, "You want to know?" That story, of course, did not jibe with her well-known obsession with *The Believers*.

It requires some mental gymnastics to think that Aldrete could have promoted the viewing of the film among cult followers but not had death and murder on her mind. *The Believers* tells a story of a bizarre, and unnamed, African religion that has been adapted by Hispanic followers and white cultists in New York City and centers on child sacrifice as a means of achieving divine powers and averting personal harm. It has little to do with "Christian *santeria*" but strongly suggests that beneath the veneer of gentle-minded pagans beheading barn animals lurks a devious, criminal, and incredibly powerful system of social influence and control.

The protagonist of the film, Dr. Cal Jamison, has his first brush with the cult when his son Chris brings home a shell used in black magical rituals in Central Park. By picking up the shell, Chris becomes "chosen" as a sacrifice. The family's Puerto Rican maid sizes up what is happening and endeavors to use the spells and ceremonies of *santeria*, which she practices, to protect the child. The father becomes scared and angry, rebuking the maid. It is never clear from the movie to what degree "black magic" and "white magic" really stand in opposition to each other, and one gradually infers that the two are one in the same.

Meanwhile, a frightening web of intrigue, cult-directed scare tactics against the father and his girl friend, and weird encounters develop until Jamison learns how powerful and pervasive "the believers" truly are. As he is sucked into their clutches, and he recognizes how difficult it will become to rescue his son, he feigns complicity until the finale when instead of thrusting the sacrificial knife into the boy, as demanded by the cult, he stabs its leader, snatches Chris, and runs. In the end he defeats the cult with bullets rather than sorcery.

Ironically, the breaking of the illusion of magical invincibility as portrayed in the movie is exactly what happened to Constanzo's true-life "believers." The Matamoros cult members may have envisaged themselves as the same type of secret, tentacular, cunning cadre of "controllers" depicted in *The Believers*, and there is some suggestion they may have regarded the conclusion of the story as a warning about transgressing the rules of magic.

When the police surrounded his apartment in Mexico City, Constanzo knew that his magic had failed. The same was true with the Hernandezes, which paradoxically may illumine why they gave up and confessed so easily. Just as an old-fashioned Japanese *samurai* would coolly and without remorse disembowel himself with his sword when he had broken the code of honor, so the Matamoros cultists calmly and with no show of conscience threw themselves at the mercy of the police when it became evident the logic of their occult universe was no longer in force. Satanist psychology will probably never be delineated clearly in a court of law. Yet one can advance the following hypothesis. In "sacrificing" Kilroy to gain extraordinary power, Constanzo went out on a limb that would either make him insuperable or totally vulnerable. As the cops closed in, his followers knew that what he had claimed for power was really overweening pride, or as the Greek tragedians called it, *hubris*.

And thus the spell was broken. But the siege of American culture would continue. The canard of a large-scale, satanist conspiracy would finally gain plausibility with an unusual twist that both traditional believers and skeptics could accept at one level. The conspirators were not black-hooded malefactors holding candle-lit rituals in New York office buildings late at night. They were the *narcotraficantes* themselves.

In December 1989 the U.S. Army invaded Panama and found in the apartment of Gen. Manuel Noriega, who had been indicted in Miami on drug trafficking charges, much the same paraphernalia as Constanzo had owned. A detailed investigation by a military cult expert turned up some quite amazing findings.

Chief Warrant Officer James R. Dibble, the army's chief of staff at Fort Campbell, Kentucky, who teaches courses at an area college on the occult, went to Panama right after the American invasion to analyze the magical bric-a-brac in Noriega's possession. In Building 152 at Noriega's headquarters at Fort Amador on the outskirts of Panama City, Dibble came across a freezer that contained about 30 so-called *trabajos*—black magical "weapons" aimed at both present and past American presidents, U.S. Senator Jesse Helms, Henry Kissinger, Panama's archbishop Marcos McGrath, and a Miami judge. The objects were put into the freezer so that the actions of Noriega's "enemies" might be "frozen," Dibble explained. In addition, a picture of Ronald Reagan was covered in red candle wax with the intent of immobilizing him. Noriega considered red an extremely powerful color. When Noriega was apprehended by DEA agents, he was wearing red underwear—to ward off spirits.

Other discoveries included an altar to St. George, a lock of Noriega's own hair, buckets of blood, Buddha statues (which Constanzo also kept), and representations of frogs. Like Constanzo, Noriega had mixed together in the fashion of an electric blender a wide assortment of native Hispanic black magic and European satanism. He had combined *santeria* with *brujeria*, *palo mayombe* with Egyptian esotericism, voodoo with the Catholic cult of *Condomblé*. According to Dibble, most Latin American drug traffickers captured in North America have been found to ply the black arts.

"They use it in a malevolent manner to protect themselves not only from police but also from rival drug dealers. If we discount or do not give credence to their religious convictions, we have underestimated the enemy," he said. Apparently, many law enforcement and religious experts had done precisely that.

Rather gruesome indicators that similar practices had made their way into the United States turned up the previous fall in the Florida Keys. The body of Sherry Perisho, thirty-nine, was found floating in the ocean on the evening of July 19, 1989, the night after a full moon. Her midsection had been sliced open and her heart removed. It was the second incident in a relatively brief period and within a ten mile radius that smacked of ancient Aztec ritual.

Monroe County Sheriff's investigator Ed Miller blamed the Perisho slaying on what he termed "devil worship." "All we can determine is that he killed her for her heart," he told the press.

Another victim was twenty-year-old Lisa Sanders, an invalid who lived on No Name Key. Sanders had been invited to a party one night by some teenage neighbors. She left the party either out of fear or disgust with what was happening. The next morning police found her corpse down the road from the party in a rock grotto. She had been strangled and, once again, her heart torn out.

CHAPTER 2.

Murder on Main Street

I don't know why we killed Steve. It was like any other animal we killed.
——*Confessed Missouri murderer* JIM HARDY,
*explaining the motive for his "sacrifice to
Satan" of high school crony Steve Newberry*

For all the sheer terror the Matamoros slayings may have elicited in the crania of white middle-class America, there was still something foreign about them. The brutality had been dispatched on *el otro lado*. The perpetrators themselves were *latinos*. Many of the "experts" purred that the whole thing could be traced to the remnants of some barbaric rites that predated Columbus. It had happened "down there," but it could not happen here.

Strangely, *it* had happened over a year before Matamoros, squarely in perhaps the most American principality of the American heartland—Joplin, Missouri. Yet the national press, with the exception of a breathless snippet from Geraldo Rivera's fall 1988 extravaganza on satanism, had barely taken notice. The Joplin case was about "boys" on *this side* of the demographic, and cultural, border. The parents of one of the murderers had been pillars of the community. Therefore, drug trafficking and "satanic murders" could only happen in Mexico.

Joplin, Missouri, is an aging commercial city with a population of approximately 40,000 souls. It was built by mining, railroads, retail trade, and later trucking at the approximate midway point on the heavily traveled interstate route between Oklahoma City and St. Louis. In addition, it is not too far from the geographic center of the forty-eight contiguous states. Joplin is "middle America" in the most literal sense of the word.

The city is listed by author Hugh Bayless as among the top fifty in *The Best Towns in America: A Where to Go Guide for a Better Life*. Not long ago the U.S. Commerce Department published a report dryly observing that "Joplin is the nation's least expensive metropolitan area" in which to dwell. Because of its distinctive geography, the city has grown up as a major transportation hub. The municipal airport is the leading facility for the four-state region of Kansas, Missouri, Oklahoma, and Arkansas. Three railroads—the Kansas City Southern, the Missouri Pacific, and the Burlington Northern—service the area, making it an attractive site, at least in the past, for manufacturing and industry.

The city fathers proudly christened their community the "Crossroads of America." On approach to Joplin along the main highway from the southwest, the signs begin appearing: "Joplin—Gateway to the Ozarks." The unemployment rate is lower than is routinely the case around the heartland. According to a Chamber of Commerce brochure, Joplin has the oldest continuous community theater in Missouri. It also boasts a civic concert association, a pops orchestra, a historical museum, a mineral museum, and an art center.

Notwithstanding its position as nerve center of the American Middle West, Joplin is also Anywhere, USA. With its numberless Baptist churches, fraternal associations, and civic booster groups, Joplin might be called a little shop of traditional values looking out on to what at one time was America's celebrated "main street"—U.S. 66. Before construction of the interstate highway system, Joplin's now decaying downtown bore the entirety of traffic— as well as the lion's share of business— from the road that more than a generation ago was known as "the highway of the heartland."

They took down the escutcheon-shaped road signs for Highway 66 almost a decade ago. Motorists on what is now I-44 whiz about the periphery of Joplin and fail to catch a glimpse of its central commercial district. Like establishments on main streets all across the country, which have been bypassed by the times, Joplin's little shop of values has long been struggling along on what is now the sleazy part of town.

The distemper became manifest in early December 1987 when police discovered the corpse of Steven Newberry, a local high school student, at the bottom of an abandoned well deep in the woods just outside town. The killers had deliberately sunk the body. The rumor had already begun to spread that Newberry had been murdered by satanists from the high school at Carl Junction, Joplin's northern suburb. "We're investigating rumors of cultlike activity," Jasper County chief sheriff's deputy Larry Parill told the newspapers.

It was a strange case and an even more unusual style of homicide. Two girls at the high school had been eavesdropping on one of the suspects, who bragged about having rubbed out a nerdy underachiever named "Steve" who was rumored to deal drugs occasionally. The girls contacted police, and within a very brief stretch of time detectives and sheriff's deputies swooped down on Ron Clements, Theron "Pete" Roland, and Jim Hardy—familiar school chums of Newberry. The arrests were complicated, and local scandal-mongers were emboldened by the fact that young Hardy happened to be Carl Junction High School's senior class president.

A handful of kids around school "knew" that Hardy's minimafia was eventually going to get Newberry. Hardy, the reputed capo, already had positioned Newberry at the top of his hit list, according to various tales then circulating. One account tucked inside the Joplin police reports held that Newberry was marked for failing to pay his bill to a local cocaine trafficker. To investigating officers, such a motive seemed straightforward and far more cogent than satanism.

Yet the tale was already coursing in the community—and was regarded as unvarnished truth by a few hangers-on—that Newberry had been the long-planned victim of a sacrificial killing. The scandal was even more pronounced because Hardy's father was a prominent accountant who did business with the Small Business Administration. Hardy's mother had been the secretary to the local state senator, who was a very prominent legislator and who was closely related to the Missouri attorney general.

Before securing a warrant for the arrest of the "Hardy boys," police had already unearthed the murder weapons—a pair of baseball bats with which Newberry had been pummelled with seventy blows on the head and across the torso. An engineer for the Joplin-based Farmer's Chemical Company, who was checking for vandalism on the grounds of the company's abandoned plant at the edge of town, stumbled across one of the bats. Soon thereafter Newberry's corpse was recovered from the well, which was hidden by thickets. A dead kitten was also retrieved along with the youth's body.

The police report on Roland was routine and terse, giving no hint of events still to unfold:

Suspect was arrested at C.J.H.S. Carpentry House without incident, Miranda read 10:31 a.m. Transported to C.J.P.D. Suspect gave oral recorded statement to participation in murder. Third suspect Jim Harding [sic] not at school. After interrogation by county officers, R/O asked Roland about use of drugs the day of homicide—Roland stated they had smoked some pot earlier in the day at Hardy's house but none of them were high during murder.

Within a week some rather curious items began cropping up in local police logs. An offense report dated December 9 mentioned an informant who "came to the station [and] said his little sister has been getting bad phone calls about him—he thinks it is some of the satanic occult group that is not in jail—he said he used to be one of the occult worshipers at one time but he quit and now they are mad at him." On Friday the eighteenth, Carl Junction police officer J. F. Dean noted a case of grave tampering at one of the local cemeteries. The grave turned out to be Newberry's. The bouquets of flowers laid by mourners had been removed and tossed in a northerly direction from the burial site. In the fantastic lore of adolescent satanism, north represents the kingdom of darkness. There were also unexplained shoe prints of a man and a woman pressed into the soft earth beside the gravestone.

Five days prior to the Newberry slaying, the cops in Carl Junction had encountered a baffling case of property destruction at a vacant home in Joplin with equally lurid undertones. Two officials at the Farm and Home Administration (FHA) in nearby Carthage had filed the complaint. Unknown vandals had forced entry into the dwelling by smashing the brackets on a storm window, pilfered a refrigerator, stripped off a segment of wall paneling in the kitchen, and dumped beige paint all over counters and cabinets. Because of the extent of the damage, investigators reasoned that the perpetrators had been present inside the house on several different occasions. Were it not for the graffiti spray-painted in red about the premises, the incident would probably have remained of small consequence in the minds of police. On the oven was scratched the familiar juvenile expletive "fuck you." But nearby on the wall could be discerned a glyph of the Devil with horns and the popular satanic triad of numbers 666 in the shape of a pyramid. The ceiling fixture in the dining room had been drenched in red, and overhead appeared a second demonic drawing along with the inscription "Your soul belongs to satan!!" The vandals turned out to be the same as Newberry's killers.

The week before Christmas, detectives interviewed a kid known as "Mark" whom a clerk in a Joplin convenience store had overheard whispering about the fate of Newberry. The kid claimed he had first-hand knowledge of the murder and that Newberry's "execution" had been ordered by a mysterious body designated the "Council of 18" who had "handed down the death verdict." The youth also maintained that the council had required Newberry to be slowly and severely bludgeoned because it was necessary in satanic ritual to drink the victim's blood and "taste the brain." Although such scuttlebutt may have seemed preposterous to investigating officers at the time, it was completely in keeping with what was later learned at Matamoros.

On December 16, Carl Junction officer Tom Brown interrogated a teenage girl named Tina. According to notes compiled by Brown, Tina had expert acquaintance with active satanic cults in southern Missouri. One cult dubbed itself the Midnight Angels—an obvious mimickry of the Hell's Angels. The second group was headquartered out of town and proved to be more mysterious, authoritative, and sinister than its Joplin counterpart. Referred to simply as "the Crowd" and boasting about thirty members, the cult reportedly was comprised not just of adolescents but of young adults and middle-aged women and men.

The Crowd allegedly met regularly at an empty building known as Old Prosperity School, which they were planning to burn down to efface evidence of their sacrifices and ceremonies. Another officer remarked in his logbook that, while Tina's story was "possibly real" to her, some of the particulars in his opinion may have been "while under the influence." At the same time, he added that "all warranted consideration."

On Sunday the thirteenth, an elderly gentleman by the name of Spike Melugin, who lived in the countryside, walked into the police station and recounted how he and his grandson had stumbled upon a place supposedly used for satanic rituals in a cave near his home. Inside the cave was a large, central fire area surrounded by several smaller ash pits. Melugin became decidedly unnerved at the sight of what looked like a partially filled grave. Punching a stick down into the earth, he discovered the soil was deep and loose. On the previous Wednesday afternoon, right after school had let out for the summer, Melugin had observed five young men prostrate on the ground, as though they were praying. In passing, Melugin also noted that someone had wedged a knife up the vagina of his neighbor's female dog.

In the meantime, information began to dribble in about Hardy. The driver of the school bus on which Hardy rode each day said the youth was constantly bothering the little kids. The mother of a fourth grader groused to school authorities that Hardy was passing out drugs and "teaching satanism." Hardy's mother countered that the driver had been fabricating such accusations and that the driver had a vendetta against Jim.

School records showed that Hardy had been docked many times for disorderly conduct, including breaking through a rear emergency door, using profanity, throwing objects at the bus driver, and spitting tobacco on the floor. A confidential police informant, identified in the files simply as "L.N.," confirmed that Hardy was a drug abuser and that he was particularly fond of LSD, or "acid." The informant portrayed Hardy as both unpredictable and sadistic. He recalled one incident in 1985 or 1986 when Hardy had deliberately run over with his car a fellow on a bicycle because it "was fun."

Hardy had repeatedly said it was "fun to kill" and wished he could actually carry through with his secret, consuming desire. Hardy was also obsessed with torture and fantasized about an agonizing, protracted death for his imagined victims. The informant explained to the cops that Hardy's preoccupation with the Devil made him seem "possessed." Hardy and Clements would chatter on about the different "demons" who had visited them and with which they consistently communed. A student at Carl Junction High, who had been intimately acquainted with Hardy, told about a recent conversation in the school lunchroom in which Jim went into rhapsodies over his planned murder. "What a trip it would be!" Hardy reportedly said. "It'd be neat."

Hardy's visions of mayhem were evidently stoked by a ferocious drug habit, especially a dependence on cocaine. The drugs seemed to have produced a megalomania that scared even his most loyal friends. There was no evidence Hardy had ever acted upon his wishes prior to the savaging of poor Steven Newberry. But his much advertised satanism already could be blamed on various pogroms against small animals—cats, puppies, rabbits, and squirrels. Hardy had a preference for torturing and killing kittens. He would drown them in ponds, drub them with rods, strangle them with clothes line. The most astounding fact in the Newberry case was that none of the murderers had bothered, even for days in advance, to conceal their intentions.

Hardy had confided to a high school buddy named Tony as far back as September that he aimed to "sacrifice" Newberry. Hardy, Clements, and Roland had also chattered about their macabre design on several occasions in the school lunchroom and were easily overheard by other students.

The consensus of classmates after the murder was that Hardy and his hangers-on were nothing more than "weirdos and sickos." But those opinions had been forged in the breach. All along, no one had actually believed the Hardy boys would carry through with their warped sense of drama. After all, their figures of speech were nothing more than "metal talk"—the kind of frightening bravado that so-called stoners who listen to "thrash rock" indulge in. Defenders of the heavy metal bands even today doggedly insist that the lyrics about death and unspeakable modes of sanguinary savagery are not toxic, that they are a perverse yet inconsequential form of acting out.

When the awful deed was done, however, Hardy and Roland still felt compelled to brag about it. On this occasion, one teenager who happened to be listening put in a call to the police. When the arrests came, a sheriff's deputy observed how nonchalant the suspects appeared. The same total lack of remorse had been observed among the disciples of Constanzo. "That bothers me more than anything," the deputy said. "I don't care how brutal a murder you've worked. There's always some remorse. These boys have shown none that I've seen yet. It kind of makes you wonder what this new generation is thinking."

Oddly, Newberry himself must have been alerted to the plot. His mother mentioned to friends how her son had become obsessed with the "idea" that his cronies were conspiring to get rid of him. Newberry suffered recurring nightmares about an impending, horrid death. He began telling close associates as early as 1986 that the three had targeted him, and he went so far as to compose a story, which both Tony and his mother read, describing himself supine at the bottom of a well gazing up into the ghoulish face of his assailant. His assailant was Hardy.

It was altogether possible that the choice of Newberry for the "sacrifice" was neither as random nor as episodic as both the police narrative and later trial testimony suggested. While not implicated in the killing, a close friend of the Hardy boys I shall call "Barry" had employed his exceptional artistic talents to draw an actual storyboard for the murder. Barry was notorious for his grisly collages that detailed all sorts of brutality and sadistic adventures. One sketch he passed around school showed a body stretched out on a table with a slobbering fiend ripping the heart out. Sometimes, according to a police report, Barry tested his own impulses. It was not what psychotherapists would call psychodrama. Apparently it was the real thing. A girl named Rebecca, according to a police report, informed the cops that she had witnessed Barry slashing his tongue several times with a filet knife, then cooly proclaiming how he suffered no pain.

One commonplace bouncing around in conversations among Joplinites was that the Newberry slaying could be explained rather simply as a Mafia hit. Nobody knew, of course, who the Mafia might be or whether the ancient underground empire of the Sicilians had ever opened a branch office in the Ozarks. But in light of the south Texas findings, the hypothesis does not seem all that implausible.

Indeed, it was no secret that the Hardy boys were not only locked into every conceivable form of substance abuse; they were also small-town sales reps within the drug trafficking conglomerate. "Everybody" in Joplin, a number of teenage witnesses said, used and condoned drugs— even the patrons and matrons of the civic establishment. Cocaine allegedly wafted about, like a mid-January Ozark snow squall, at virtually every gathering of socialites. As much nose candy was supposed to be partaken on any given Saturday evening in Jasper County than in all the mansions and villas of Beverly Hills. That was most likely an exaggeration, but even local police would admit the rate of consumption was extraordinarily high for a place with its particular demographic profile. The lawyers and accountants placed orders and scarfed the stuff. The bikers and the backwoods brokers ran it along the interstate from Los Angeles, Texas, and Colorado. A known drug dealer with the moniker of "Robert Adams," convicted a few years earlier for putting out a contract on a Jasper County sheriff's deputy, said Newberry had been killed for double-crossing the syndicate. He remarked that "Pete and Jim were paid well for their part." Adams, who sported a 666 tattoo, claimed Newberry had been singled out because he was believed to have stolen a stash of coke and two pounds of marijuana. Adams said a number of interested parties, who were never identified in the police investigation, had stopped by the well right after the killing to confirm that the deal had been consummated.

The mystique of the Crowd in southwestern Missouri was almost as formidable as the legend of the Illuminati—the alleged, great satanist conspiracy of all ages. The Crowd, which elected the Council of 18, was rumored to be billeted at the local junior college and the adjoining national guard armory in the neighboring town of Neosho. The title "the Crowd" was derived from the name of the army facility in Neosho— Camp Crowder. The Crowd reportedly had ties to several major *covens*, or occult groups, just across the state line in Kansas. Jim Hardy's phone bill indicated that he had called various towns in Kansas on different occasions. He had also put in repeated calls to Neosho.

Neosho itself is a sleepy community snuggled amid rolling, oak-clogged hills and hollows with meandering streets and rambling, ochre-brick storefronts that resembles most Ozark municipalities. The town is grappling for economic survival, and the city fathers have gone out of their way to offer just about any kind of economic incentive to firms that might locate there. A largely undeveloped office park has been mapped out near the junior college. The Chamber of Commerce says it is interested in luring firms doing defense work, and it points with pride to a planned expansion of the armory in the next decade. The armory was used as one of the leading internment camps for German prisoners right after World War II, according to local history records.

In 1941 the U.S. Army approved a contract with the Kansas City engineering firm of Burns and McDonnell to construct a training camp in Newton County. Survey work began in May of that year. The camp would compass 8900 acres. It would be known as Camp Crowder after Maj. Gen. Enoch H. Crowder, a West Point graduate who taught military tactics and received his law degree from the University of Missouri. Gen. Crowder had been in charge of Selective Service during World War I. He had also worked as judge advocate general, the highest position in the legal department of the army.

Camp Crowder was a telecommunications hub during World War II. It was also a cultural and artistic center for the military. Klaus Mann, son of the great German novelist Thomas Mann, visited the installation. Cartoonist Mort Walker spent a sizable portion of time there and drew on daily life at Crowder as a model for his later, world-syndicated comic strip "Beetle Bailey." The first contingent of German prisoners arrived at Crowder on October 6, 1943. They had been captured from Rommel's regiments in North Africa.

At the end of the war there were 2000 POWs at the camp. The German prisoners, many of whom were top-ranking officers, were well treated. They were not allowed to do degrading work and lived at about the same level as their captors. In the 1950s, Camp Crowder became a disciplinary barracks for military prisoners. The camp was abandoned by the army and became the site of an armory during the 1960s. Local residents talk about its planned rehabilitation during the 1990s.

In the course of investigating cult activity in the vicinity of Joplin, a young man with peripheral links to the Hardy group, who is also a former member of the Crowd, agreed to an interview on the condition that his real name not be used. "Eddie," as we shall call him, is in his late teens or early twenties and at the time of the interview was employed as a retail clerk at a shopping mall in Joplin. Contact with Eddie was made through one of the paralegal assistants assigned to the court trial of Pete Roland. The paralegal had met Eddie during his own pretrial inquiries.

Eddie claims he was recruited into the Crowd in 1977 at about age seven. An unidentified "prominent" member of the Joplin social hierarchy made discreet overtures to Eddie and said he was willing to "offer the world" if only the child would give his life over to the Prince of Darkness. At the time Eddie's mother and father were going through a tumultuous divorce, and as with any child of that age suffering the trauma of family upheaval, Eddie was susceptible to whoever might play the role of surrogate parent. The man, according to Eddie, promised him everything of which a child could dream—distant travel, exotic friends, and "loving" companions. The man turned out to be a satanist.

As it happened, the "exotic friends" were drugs—marijuana, mescaline, LSD, cocaine—and the faraway places were hallucinogenic states reinforced through the weird, Xanadu-like world of satanist believers. The believers themselves were the "loving" comrades. They puffed up Eddie's ego to the point he felt like he was crown prince in waiting for the galaxy itself, while at the same time they chipped away at the structure of his personality, sometimes ruthlessly with their thought-transforming rituals and terror tactics. The scenario is familiar to experts on mind control. If Eddie had been a bit less brilliant and more diffident, he might have lost it. But as he approached adulthood, he started to realize what was happening and hatched plans for a departure.

The chief reason for Eddie's exit from the Crowd was his doctor's warning that he would soon be a dead man from drug and alcohol abuse. Although the cult performed sacrifices and conducted ceremonies, the real function of the Crowd became "a purchasing service for the occult." "If you get people addicted to drugs and alcohol," he says, "they won't leave the occult. It's drilled into their minds." Eddie's thought processes and methods of reasoning, even after his formal departure from the satanist cult in which he was raised, disclose so much of what is transpiring in America today.

The linkage between the rise of satanism and the drug culture is so transparent it is often overlooked by most experts. Even the revelations about Matamoros have not solidified the connections in people's minds the way they should. "People think they know so much," Eddie said, laughing.

They really don't know what's going on. [The cult] gave me everything I wanted when I wanted it. We would go out into the countryside and have these rallies. I remember a big rally in 1979 or 1980 with thousands of people there. And the leaders of the group would arrive in a semi-truck, and they would distribute free drugs to whoever showed up. There would be high school kids, bikers, truckers— you name it. And the people who organized the rally would say they would come back and there would be more.

According to Eddie, the Crowd managed most of the day-to-day drug operations in southern Missouri:

They didn't just own the trucks. They owned planes and trains. If you were a druggie, you associated the good things of life with satanism, and that is how they began to recruit. It started many years ago. It's a network just as large as the federal government has for transporting its own goods. The trucks would bring in the drugs if you requested them.

After Matamoros such a statement seems far less speculative than before.

Because of its central location, the biggest industry in Joplin is the warehousing and shipment of the country's manufactured products. Again, the boosters have put up signs. The signs say,"Joplin—the Motor Freight Capitol of America." Joplin has more headquarters for national trucking companies relative to its population than any principality in the United States. In the 1960s it was a power base for the teamsters' union. One incident involving the sabotage by dynamite of a truck outside Joplin during a ferocious strike in the late 1960s spurred congressional probes into racketeering by that infamous union.

Could Joplin have grown up as the commercial hub of the tentacular drug underground because of its advantageous position for truckers in much the same manner as Pittsburgh became the steel capital because it was situated at the confluence of two great rivers? Would it have been possible for satanism in America to grow at the pace it has since the opening of the present decade had not "getting stoned," if only on the sly, become fashionable with America's educated elites? Did Joplin really invent satanism? Or was it the obvious "next step" in the transformation of a society?

Anton LaVey, founder of the Church of Satan in San Francisco in 1966, who would as happily take on donning the vestments of the Antichrist during the 1990s as any mortal, proclaimed the coming of the great "eon of darkness" exactly at that divide in contemporary history when hallucinogenics became as popular as herb tea.

Eddie had virtually no serious religious upbringing of any kind. His values were suburban America's. His cultural heritage was what he saw on the television. So it was not all that unusual for him to find a substitute not only for Mom and Dad but for God. While growing up stoned, Eddie began to steep himself in the darker dimensions of the "faith," which he claimed was erected upon the ideas and traditions of the Church of Satan.

Although the Church of Satan was officially undraped in San Francisco in 1968, Anton Szandor LaVey became titular head of the satanic movement in 1960, according to Eddie. Satanism as a religion, as opposed to the "church" of Satan, goes back a long way. An eccentric and rakish Englishman of the Edwardian era named Aleister Crowley made what has popularly, but too crudely, been called "devil worship" fashionable among the English aristocracy and the American bohemian class. Crowley also extolled cocaine and certain psychedelic substances as crucial to the personal development of satanists, much as peyote is to Southwestern Indian shamans and chanting is to Hare Krishna devotees.

Nearly a century before Crowley, around the middle of the nineteenth century, there rose to fame in France a renegade Catholic rector called Alphonse Constant, who changed his name to Eliphas Levi. Levi was considered the Michelangelo of the suppressed traditions of "black magic" in the Christian West. Levi exerted a powerful influence on a whole generation of avant-garde intellectuals in continental Europe, Britain, and the United States.

Levy's most notable apostle in America was one Albert Pike, a Confederate general from Arkansas and Robert E. Lee's chief of army intelligence. Immediately after the Civil War, Pike became the premier "reformer" within the brotherhood of American Freemasons. He assumed the leadership of the Southern Jursidiction of Scottish Rite Masonry and gained notoriety for his benevolent ministrations on the fraternity's behalf. But Pike also has a less glorious and murkier credit to his name. Pike was one of the original architects of the Ku Klux Klan, which, contrary to common belief, was not at its inception primarily a racist club for semiliterates. The white robes, cross burnings, conical hats, and use of such titles as "grand dragon" and "imperial wizard" derives from the strange lore developed by Levi.

During the period of Reconstruction in the South right after the Civil War, the Klan was fundamentally a terrorist organization motivated by magic and mysticism, whose larger purpose was to drive out the Northern occupation army. Since the Union administrators, known as carpetbaggers used freed slaves to accomplish their political objectives, it was only natural that the Klan would take aim at blacks.

The deep-rooted racism of Southerners, of course, had a lot to do with the attitudes and strategies of the Klan. But the night-riders were more interested in scaring off black political agents than what much later would be invidiously referred to as "nigger baiting." In order to be effective, terrorists need to learn not only the most severe art of secrecy; they also must hold doggedly to some religious point of view. Today's Islamic terrorists are an excellent illustration.

The amalgam of violence, secrecy, and fanaticism that went into the original constitution of the Klan became the basis for the rise of satanism in the South over the past decade. As recently as twenty years ago the heavy metal troopers of Joplin who egged on the Hardy boys probably would have joined the Klan. A large cave outside of town used by adolescent satanists today was the command post for Klan activity during the revival of the order in the 1920s. In fact, southwestern Missouri and northwestern Arkansas have always been one of the Klan's main strong-holds. Right after the Civil War, Pike hung out, and as far as the legends run, received his "religious" inspiration in that section of the Ozarks. The

University of Arkansas in Fayetteville—slightly more than an hour's drive from Joplin—owns the world's sole collection of Pike's papers, correspondence, and privately published books.

Significantly, the same locale was the base of operations for the Aryan Nation gang from 1983 to 1985 when it hijacked and robbed an armored truck in northern California, assassinated a Jewish talk-show host in Denver, and gunned down a Missouri state trooper. The group was also tried by a federal jury in Ft. Smith, Arkansas, for sedition and attempting to "overthrow" the government of the United States—a rare charge usually reserved for powerful, criminal terrorists.

The merger of white racist terrorism and satanism is a somewhat recent, and dangerous, phenomenon that has been closely watched and documented by law enforcement agencies across the country. The so-called skinheads, who regularly beat up minorities, are based in Ray, Oklahoma. Police informers tell of the conflation of conventional, hard-core satanist bodies with what remains of the Aryan Nation's guerilla operation. The new unit reportedly goes by the title of "the Foundation" and has its "home office" in the piney woods just north of Houston. It is not clear at this writing whether such alliances are for convenience or for ideological objectives. The answer may be a little of both.

In rock music, the symbols and paraphernalia of hate movements, particularly nazism, have been the staple diet of so-called metalheads for more than a decade. Pete Roland exhibited a fascination with nazism, much of which he drew from the lyrics and imagery of his favorite "thrash" bands. A picture discovered by police in Roland's room shows a leering skeleton with a Nazi pith helmet emblazoned with a swastika. Roland explained during a jail interview that the drawing was his own fantasy of genocide, a kind of commemoration of Hitler. "I thought all the time about Auschwitz," he said. "That's what I wanted to do."

One teenage girl told a journalist outside the courtroom during the trial that she had been present late at night at a satanist ceremony in the woods organized by Hardy. The highlight of the evening was a Klan-style cross-burning. A friend of Roland said in an interview that when he was seven years old, or about the year 1977, he was taken to watch a crowd of men in white robes burning a cross on the lawn. The boy claims that the Klan is, and always has been, "a factor" in Joplin.

Yet punkers, skinheads, and neo-Nazi riffraff are not the stuff of "real" satanism, so far as Eddie is concerned. Roland himself amounted all along to what is termed, in the slang of metal culture, a wanna-be. A wanna-be puts on all the airs and gives off all the pretension of a celebrity, but in truth he is hiding his ignorance and dearth of skills by merely pretending. "A real satanist would never get caught," Eddie said flatly and with a confidence smacking almost of haughtiness. "They certainly wouldn't find a body." Eddie contended that before he "got out" he had been a real satanist. A real satanist studies and plies the art of magic much in the same fashion a novice monk learns Latin and devotes himself to prayer.

A satanist does not pursue the subject of Latin, but he does endeavor to master an obscure and impenetrable language known as Enochean. Enochean is what witches are supposed to speak. It sounds a little like a cross between Chinese and Arabic. Enoch, according to the Bible, was one of the first men on earth. He did not die but one day merely "was not," whatever that may imply. Magicians in the West have zeroed in on the mystery of Enoch to give themselves some kind of respectable pedigree. The Elizabethan occultist John Dee reportedly compiled and codified the strange idiom to the extent that it became a standard, albeit "secret," argot of Rosicrucians, Masons, and sundry occultists. Eddie insists LaVey wrote down and made a "science" out of the magical language of Enochean with much the same forte as Wilhelm von Humboldt did with German. LaVey is far more powerful within the occult underground than his cultivated reputation as a buffoon and a cynical, P.T. Barnum-style huckster would suggest. "If LaVey says jump, you jump," according to Eddie. "There is nobody in the world more powerful than LaVey."

Eddie's tendency toward sensation and hyperbole might lead to the hasty judgment that he has trotted out the overworked specter of a worldwide satanist conspiracy. Eddie thinks there is no satanist conspiracy per se. There are, nonetheless, drug cartels, which are conspiracies in the legal sense of the word. Satanism is the preferred belief system of those who commandeer the trucks and planes.

The process of discovery south of the border has made that supposition almost emphatic. LaVey started selling satanist "estates and offices," that is titles and honors, in the mid-1970s to whoever possessed hard cash. Satanism is a religion of abject fear, which can prove useful when the aim is to prevent drug couriers from being detected or captured. Constanzo's gang believed they were invisible to police and that bullets could not injure them.

The police report on the Newberry killing was both macabre and revealing:

"CASE #DR87-1717. . . .
REF: Homicide—Steven Newberry
    Brent Dunham advised that Jim Hardy is a Devil worshiper and does give a number of hand signs to this effect. He also said that he has several items of Devil worshiping, things that Jim Hardy has made him aware of. After the first interview with Ron Clements, he had been arrested for Investigation of Murder and transported to the County Jail, where the next morning, Dec. 8, 1987, at approximately 8:30 A.M., Clements was again brought to an interrogation room at the Jail and was talked with about the homicide. At this point he agreed to tell us everything about the homicide and advised that the other two parties were

involved in the killing and also that one of the bats did belong to him, and the other three had belonged to Pete Roland. . . .

He advised that they had killed Steven Newberry because he was both mentally and physically inferior and that they had planned to kill him on Halloween night but had not because things did not work out. . . .

He advised that after the homicide that the three had done as much cleaning up of the area as possible and that they had gone to Jim Hardy's house at approximately 8 P.M. He advised that they had made up their story about dropping Steve off at Barneys and they would tell the story. . . .

Clements did give R/O and Officer Wiseman permission to search his room and to take these items as evidence. Officer Wiseman later did go [to] the Clements' residence, and did obtain a permission to search the home from the mother. Officer Wiseman did take into his custody the items of clothing that Clements had advised that he was wearing when the homicide was committed. . . .

The following morning, R/O, Officer Randolph, Officer Pat Hayes and Tom Brown of the Carl Junction Police Department went to the area where a house was being built, by the Vo-Ag class of the high school for the purpose of contacting Pete Roland. . . .

At 10:39, Roland was read his rights and did sign a waiver of rights form and gave a statement to these officers. In this he gave a number of details and did advise that he, Jim Hardy and Ron Clements had committed the homicide and that they had been planning this for about two months. . . .

Ron advised that the twine used in the tying of Steven had come from his house and that they had used the whole roll. Roland advised that Steve was taken to the area on the promise that the four would sacrifice a cat and that Steve had taken part in the sacrifice. He advised that they had no motive for killing Steve Newberry, other than they had wanted to have a human sacrifice and that they had picked Steve as the victim of the subject of this sacrifice. . . .

Roland advised that he had rolled a large stone, to the area of the well, after they had beaten Steve to death. He advised that the first one to strike Steve was Jim Hardy, and that this was a glancing blow off of his face. He advised that Steve ran at this point and that he had reached the road, and had ran a short ways up the road. He advised at one point, while facing them, Steve had asked—"Why me?"—and that Ron Clements had advised—"Because it's fun." . . .

Roland advised that he has been involved in the killing of two cats and that one of the cats had been cut open and they had smashed the guts under their feet into the ground. . . .

He advised that Jim Hardy had broken his bat during the beating of Steven Newberry and that he thought that he and the others had hit Steve a total of approximately 70 times. . . .

Later in the day Pete Roland was returned to the scene of the crime and did give a video re-enactment of the crime, in which he described the details of the killing, with the approximate location of the different persons during the time of and after the time of the homicide. . . ."

On December 9, Officer Wiseman interrogated fifteen-year-old Jerry Dale Hoffman, who said that he and two other boys had been riding their bicycles about two years earlier with Scott Hardy, Jim's brother. Hoffman recalled that Jim Hardy himself and another kid had stolen away to a spot near Farmers Chemical where a circle was spray-painted in white on a concrete culvert.

At the center of the circle was a five-pointed star, or pentagram—the telltale emblem of the occult. An inverted pentagram is the signature of satanism. Hoffman said that Scott Hardy warned him not to step or ride through the circle. "If you do, you'll be possessed by the Devil," he said lackadaisically. Hardy said the drawing on the ground belonged to his brother Jimmy. Hoffman took the police to the the spot where the circle had been traced, but it was no longer perceptible.

On December 11, detectives had a conversation with Tony Vickers, seventeen, at Carl Junction city hall. Vickers said Newberry had told him that Hardy and Roland were contemplating him as a prospective sacrifice. Vickers handed police three drawings by Barry, the young artist with a flair for "demonic" portraiture. One drawing portrayed a demon hand with long fingernails crushing a cross in his fist. The second depicted a devil floating in the air with an iron bar and a chain with a hanging skull. The third showed Satan on his throne. Vickers said that he had viewed other satanic artwork by Barry, including an etching of a male torso astride an altar with three boys holding a human heart at arms lengths above the head.

On December 11, Robert William Testerman, seventeen, gave his story to police. Testerman asserted that the Hardy boys had taken Newberry into their cabal because "they then had someone to make fun of and that any time they went anywhere it was Steve who always paid for things." Testerman added that "Steve was the one who would buy the drugs, whenever anyone wanted to get drugs." At the same time the three were fond of ridiculing Newberry. Among other indignities, they constantly accused him of having body odor. Testerman pointed out how Hardy, Clements, and Roland may have been enamored by the sixties movie *A Clockwork Orange*. In that British film a band of young toughs went around pummeling people with clubs. The group wore white apparel and black makeup.

One of the terms used repeatedly in the movie was *ultraviolent*. According to the police report, Testerman advised that Ron had borrowed this book from him and that he was very excited about the book and told him how great it was. Clements had inscribed the phrase ultraviolent on his baseball bat that, but for a last minute choice, would have been used to bludgeon Newberry to death.

Newberry's sister Cyndi told law enforcement officials that, on the evening on which her brother was murdered, Hardy boasted to her about the time he had sadistically killed a barking dog. "I don't like dogs," Hardy said coolly, then grabbed the dog, stabbed it with a knife, soaked the wound with gasoline and set the dog afire. Hardy described in livid detail how much "fun" it had been to watch the tormented animal race around in circles.

Cyndi also advised police that her brother had said to her once that he and the Hardy boys had committed the same type of atrocity with another dog. This time Hardy poured gasoline down the dog's throat and watched the wretched hound explode into flames. Each time Barry drew a picture of the group's glorious sacrifice the victim was represented as a tiny, trusting, canine creature on whom a swift, unexpected, and devastating blow was about to fall.

One boy, who was obviously a friend not only of Hardy but of Roland and Clements as well and who hung out with them daily throughout the court proceedings, gave the rundown on Jim's rise to power at Carl Junction High School. The boy, whom we shall call "Tom," had known Hardy for years, ever since they attended parochial school together. The Hardy family is Catholic. But Jim crowed to his friends on numerous occasions that he did not believe in God—only the Devil. Tom met both Hardy and Clements, who played guitar in the school band. Tom would routinely spend the night with Hardy and Clements, imbibing the strident sounds of such heavy metal groups as Motley Crew, Black Sabbath, Metallica, Megadeath, Flotsam and Jetsam, and Slayer.

Hardy seemed to know all about satanism, and Tom took a keen interest in the topic "because the best rock musicians did it." On one occasion Hardy impressed Tom by exhibiting a wooden plaque with a pentagram burned into the grain. Tom remembered another incident where Hardy took him to his grandfather's sheet metal shop and cut a block for a guillotine. Jim's mother caught them and inquired what they were making. Hardy said it was going to be used on cats.

Hardy may not have been all that idiosyncratic, as far as teenage satanism in southern Missouri is concerned. According to Tom, satanism is "pretty big" in southern Missouri. In Joplin, the adolescent satanists supposedly all show up in secret at a games parlor called the Eight-Ball. You can tell who the satanists are by the paraphernalia they wear.

According to Eddie, however, the satanist fad has reached far beyond the so-called stoners—those who live and eat and breathe heavy metal music— into the delicate fabric of polite society. The port of entry was drugs. "I can walk down the hall of school and see more committed satanists than Christians," Eddie said. "It's like the flu. One person catches it, and everybody catches it." One contracts the "flu" when attending what is known as a "satan party," where both children and adults do drugs, fornicate in the bedrooms, and chatter and gossip about the occult in the same fashion as other suburbanites patter on about their sexual conquests or their tennis games.

But there is also a serious side to the satanic movement, Eddie argues. "Satan for satanists is as God is to Christians. [For them] Satan knows all, sees all." As with God, Satan demands souls. "Satanists are taught: 'We are here to collect enough souls so Satan can draw on them to win the battle with God and get back the throne which is rightfully his.'" One of these days Satan will have a sufficiently large army, and the biblical Armageddon will commence. On the other hand, "there is no absolute timetable" for the satanic apocalypse. "It could be the year 2000. It could be the year when the 'leadership' says it is."

Talk of the final battle may sound like so much pomp and puffery to the jaded journalist or law enforcement specialist, but to Eddie it is very real. "I take the occult seriously. To me it's a war. People in general know very little about its army." South of St. Louis, on the other end of the state, atop the limestone cliffs that border the Mississippi River, police in 1987 raided the cave hideout of a paramilitary cell group. In the cave they found sufficient weaponry, including scores of automatic rifles, to wage a sustained guerilla effort. The group was apparently linked up with the network of racist hate groups in the region. When questioned about their intentions, one of the suspects reportedly told police, "We're doing this for Satan."

According to Roland, Hardy would gloat privately about a future, climactic moment in the history of the planet when the lieges and hordes of Satan would rise up in a successful revolt against God, which would also be a revolution that destroyed the United States. It would be one and the same thing, since America was the Christian God's "chosen people." It was a different version than the fantasy of the white supremacists who hoped to bring down the "Zionist occupation government" of America through bombings, terror, and sabotage of industrial facilities. Roland, however, was only marginally political. Although one of his notebooks contains the scrawl "U.S.A. sucks" and "anarchy rules," Roland's "religion" derived from, and was inculcated by, the "hymn singing" of heavy metal.

Roland's entire mind was metal lined. Morning, noon, and evening he would wander around in a metal haze with his Sony Walkman and his earphones attached, to his head, almost like sensitive electrodes. The lyrics of the metal bands were graven with laserlike force and precision on his unconscious.

Roland's school notebooks confirm such a psychology of disintegration that mirrored his "addiction" to metal music. For a few minutes he would take random but intelligible notes on an American history lesson. Then there would be a blank space where his thoughts would wander. Soon satanic scribbles and doodles would appear down the page, then the almost incantational scribbling of a few lines to a metal song. Finally, he would lapse back into some disconnected notes to the history lesson, which would end abruptly with the following in large black letters: S-A-T-A-N.

Roland's world was a totally "metal" world. The following inventory of personal articles found by Roland's mother when she cleaned out his room after the arrests furnishes some richer insight into the prevalence of the metal "message" within his own framework of language:

MEMO

DATE: June 6, 1988

The following is a list of articles brought in by the mother of Pete Roland found in his room including record albums this is a partial list not all of the record albums and tapes are in this box.

First record album in the box is Krokus, The Blitz, songs included Side One: Midnight Maniac, Out of Control, Boys Night Out, Our Love, Out to Lunch. Side Two: Ball Room, Blitz, Rock the Nation, Hot Stuff, Ready to Rock, record producer Arista.

The Second record album is Krokus, Metal RendenVous, songs on the album, Side One: Heat Stroke, Bedside Radio, Come On, Streamer. Side Two: Tokyo Nights, Shy Kid, Lady Double Dealer, Fire, No Way, Back Seat Rock and Roll, record producer, Arista. Copyright 1980.

Album Number Three from the rock group KISS, title of the animal Animalize, songs included, Side One: I've Had Enough (Into the Fire), Heavens on Fire, Burn Bitch Burn, Get All You Can Take, Lonely is the Hunter. Side Two: Under the Gun, Thrills in the Night, While the City Sleeps, Murder in High Hells. Record production company produced by Paul Stanley, Polygram records.

Album Number Four called Masters of Metal by different artists. Side One: Trashed by Black Sabbath; Mean Streak by Y and T; Breaking the Chain by Dok Ken; Whose Behind the Door by Zebra; Rainbow in the Dark by Dio; Screaming in the Night by Krokus; Lick it Up by KISS. Side Two: Street of Dreams by Rainbow; Run to the Hills by Iron Maiden; Tom Sawyer by Rush; A World of Fantasy by Triumph; You Can't Stop Rock and Roll by Twisted Sister; Dancing in the Street by Van Halen. Copyright 1984 by K-Tel Records.

Album Number Five by AC-DC, For Those About to Rock. Side One: For Those About to Rock (We Salute You), Evil Walks, C.O.D., Spellbound, Put the Finger on You, Let's Get it Up, Inject the Venom, Breaking the Rules, Snowball, Night of the Long Knives. Recording Company, Atlantic Recording Corporation, Copyright 1981.

Album Number Six by The J. Geils Band, Freeze Frame. Side One: Freeze Frame, Rage in the Cage, Centerfold, Do You Remember When, Insane Insane Again, Side Two: Flame Thrower, River Blindness, Angel in Blue, Piss on the Wall. Recording Company, EMI America, 1981 Copyright.

Album Number Seven by Judus Priest, Defenders of the Faith. Side One: Free Wheel Burning, Jawbreaker, Rock Hard Ride Free, The Sentinel, Love Bites, Eat Me Alive, Some Heads are Going to Roll, Night Comes Down, Heavy Duty, Defenders of the Faith. CBS Records, Inc., 1984.

Album Number Eight by Judus Priest, Screaming for Vengence. Side One: The Hellion, Electric Eye, Riding on the Wind, Blood Stone, Take These Chains, Pain and Pleasure. Side Two: Screaming for Vengence, You've Got Another Thing Coming, Feaver, Devil's Child, Producing Company, Columbia Records, 1982 Copyright.

Album Number Nine by Quiet Riot, Metal Health. Side One: Metal Health, Come On Feel the Noise, Don't Want to Let You Go, Slick Black Cadillac, Love's a Bitch. Side Two: Breathless, Run for Cover, Battle Ax, Let's Get Grazy, Thunderbird. Record Company, Pasha Records, CBS Inc., 1983.

Album Number Ten by Quiet Riot Again, Condition Critical. Side One: Sign of the Times, Mamma We're All Crazy Now, Party All Night, Stomp Your Hands, Clap Your Feet, Winner's Take All. Side Two: Condition Critical, Scream and Shout, Red Alert, Bad Boy, We Were Born to Rock. CBS Records Again, 1984.

Album Number Eleven by the Scorpions, Black Out. Side One: Black Out, Can't Live Without You, No One Like You, You Give Me All I Need, Now. Side Two: Dynamite, Arizona, China White, When the Smoke is Going Down. Polygram Records, Copyright 1982.

Album Number Twelve by Pink Floyd, Side One: Young Lust, Comfortably Numb, Run Like Hell, The Trial.

Album Number Thirteen by Ozzie Osbourne, Speak of the Devil. Side One: Symptom of the Universe, Snow Blind, Black Sabbath. Side Two: Fairies Wear Boots, War Pigs, The Wizard, CBS Records, Copyright 1982.

Album Number Fourteen by Iron Maiden, The Number of the Beast. Side One: Invaders, Children of the Damned, The Prisoner, Twenty two Acacia Avenue. Side Two: The Number of the Beast, Run to the Hills, Gang Land, Hallowed Be Thy Name. By EMI Records, Ltd. 1982 Copyright.

Album Number Fifteen by Ozzie Osbourne, Bark at the Moon. Side One: Bark at the Moon, You're No Different, Now You See It Now You Don't, Rock and Roll Rebel, Side Two: Center of Eternity, So Tired, Slow Down, Waiting for Darkness. CBS, Inc., 1983.

Album Number Sixteen by Motley Crue, Shout at the Devil. Side One: In the Beginning, Shout at the Devil, Looks that Kill, Bastard, Knock Em Dead, Kid Danger, Too Young To Fall in Love, Helter Skelter, Red Hot, Ten Seconds Till Love, God Bless the Children of the Beast. Elektra/Asylum Records, Copyright 1983.

Video Tape with Return of the Living Dead On It

Video of Pink Floyd and The Wall

Large Wall Poster by Iron Maiden

Poster of Blackie Lawless from the Rock Group Wasp showing him drinking blood out of a human skull.

Art work, psychedelic oil paint that Pete Roland had but the painting was done by Tony Vechio.

Heavy metal T-shirt by Mega Deaf with a skull and what appears to be demons or devils on the front of the black T-shirt.

Extremely large poster approximately $2\frac{1}{2}$ feet by $3\frac{1}{2}$ to 4 feet ugly picture of some kind of creature. It says their evil became an orgy of bloodshed demons. One of the best horror films of the last decade.

Tomihawk type hatchet and broken glass as though it would be sharp objects with oil paint on it in psychodelic colors. This glass could be used for weapons.

Collage of photographs. One particularly of Pete and a girlfriend giving the finger to whoever took the picture.

A piece of glass, a mirror with AC-DC on it and it has been painted on heavy fucking metal.

Audio Cassette of Black Sabbath and the album name on the cassette is Heaven and Hell.

A cassette by Diamond Reed songs include Land of the Damned, All I Need, Cuz I Want Ya, Wish I Was Rich, Don't Start Without Me, Up and Down, Rock Gun, Bats, Kick in Your Face, Life and Death.

The Plasmatics, songs include, Put Your Love in Me, Stop, Rock and Roll, Lighting Breaks, No Class, Mistress of Taboo, Country Fairs, Path of Glory, Just Like on T.V., The Damned.

Audio casette Vinny Vincent, Invasion.

Pink Floyd audio cassette, name of the cassette the Dark Side of the Moon. Songs include Side One: Money, Us and Then, Any Color You Like, Brain Damage, Eclipse, Side Two: Speak to Me, Breath, On the Run, Time, The Great Gig in the Sky by Capital Records.

Album on audio cassette, Best of Black Sabbath, No song names on the cassette.

Cassette Metalica called Ride the Lightening, Songs include: Fight with Fire, Ride the Lightening, For Whom the Bell Tolls, Fade to Black, Trapped Under Ice, Escape, Creeping Death, The Call of Ktulu.

Black Sabbath, Live/Evil, no song titles on the tape.

Mega Death, Album Name, Peace Sells But Whose Dying. Songs include Side One: Good Morning, Black Friday, Bad Omen, I Ain't Superstitious, My Last Words. Side Two: Program One, Wake Up The Dead, The Conjuring, Peace Sells, Devil's Island.

Van Halen, Fair Warning no songs listed on the audio.

Audio Cassette Wasp.

Audio Cassette by Pink Floyd, The Wall

Medley, Metal Manio Cassette, songs include: Loverboy, Take Me To The Top, Tommy Bolin, song Shake the Devil by Blue Oyster Cult, Don't Fear the Reaper by Judus Priest, You've Got Another Thing Coming by Aerosmith, Dream On. Side One: Fast Way, Say What You Will, Mountain, Mississippi Queen, Heaven, In The Beginning, Strange Dreams, Fools Game.

Tape by the Scorpions, no song titles list on the tape.

Pat Pulling

The metal songs, nonetheless, would not have been able to project their message to Roland unless he had been dazed with drugs the whole time. According to many who knew the Hardy boys, the trio was constantly high on everything from hash to coke to "crystal," a highly addictive street drug. One drawing of Roland's is an odd, surrealistic collage that shows a saw-toothed demon with a butcher knife in its throat and blood cascading down from the right ear into a basketball hoop, which becomes a spigot, and flowing into a drinking glass. The caption of the drawing says, "I got stoned and I missed it." At the head of the page is the following ditty, which parodies a song by the Monkeys: "Hey, hey we're the druggies,/ People say we fuck around,/ But we're to [sic] busy trippen,/ To put anybody down."

Another doodle on Roland's math homework says, "Coke is it, get hooked." There are numerous pictures, penned with the care and craft of a scribe, of marijuana leaves. According to a Columbia, Missouri, psychiatrist who did an evaluation, Roland was introduced to mind-altering drugs at the age of thirteen, "which apparently caused further slipping of grades and behavior deterioration." His drug abuse intensified in ninth grade. "What began as an experimentation with marijuana had rather suddenly increased to include amphetamines, 'mushroom' (hallucinogen), cocaine, and alcoholic beverages. Throughout the 10th, 11th, and 12th grades, he abused these drugs rather heavily during the day, during the weekends, vacations, and almost every evening on school days."

Roland confessed to the psychiatrist that on many days he was stoned all day in school. The drugs had been introduced and supplied by Hardy. He and Hardy would do drugs while drinking beer. The combination, he said, helped him "enjoy music more." "Reportedly, the drug abuse substantially escalated in his senior year, particularly during the months preceding the alleged incident. Drugs had been acquired from a close-knit group of friends and was purchased with stolen money." Yet the drugs were employed largely to enhance the intensity, the lucidity, and the *reality* of the music, which for Hardy, Roland, and Clements was a constant choir of fallen angels casting vengeful curses at society.

The psychiatrist report stated the following:

Mr. Roland reported that he was always interested in rock music, particularly the hardest variety. He was introduced to Satan and Satan worship through heavy metal music (a variety of hard rock music). According to him, heavy metal music is a form of Satan worship. The lyrics of the heavy metal music reflect graphic violence, mutilation, torture, death, annihilation, blood, witches, and related themes. He was introduced to Satan worship by the song, "The Number of the Beast" by Iron Maiden. He stated that he believed in Satan, who is "very real . . . very influential . . . and he influences me, and Earth is dominated by Satan. . . ." While listening to the music either alone or in a group, he would "thrash, scream, bang my head" and go into frenzied laughter, becoming part of a satanic ritual "to release to Satan to the world and in this way, children of the metal movement become stronger than they believe." Most of the time he would be on some kind of drug which would increase the intensity of this ritual. Besides listening to the music and engaging in satanic rituals, he used to spend his time drawing pictures depicting satanic symbols, scenes of violence and death, and writing about violence and torture. It appeared that he was totally engrossed in the music and these satanic rituals. . . . He stated that he and Jim Hardy, during their senior year began killing animals in sacrifice to Satan. He, with his friends, had tortured several animals such as cats, puppies, and dogs . . . "sacrificed them to Satan." At one time, he put his neighbor's cat in a clothes dryer, and later set fire to it and stabbed it. Another time, he hung a dog from a tree and tortured it by "poking it with small and big sticks until it died." Yet, on another occasion, he placed a cat under a board, jumped on it, smashing it to the ground, and injected alcohol with a lethal injection kit . . . there were too numerous instances to report. Immediately after the sacrificial ritual, he felt a sense of accomplshment, a "sense of excitement," followed by "a lost feeling," but had not felt sorry for the animals or felt that his actions were cruel. He stated that it was something expected of a Satan worshiper. Mr. Roland denied being a member of a cult or occult group, but stated that Satan worship could be seen everywhere.

According to the psychiatrist, Roland was neither insane nor mentally deranged. While he had experienced paranoia during drugs, there was no indication of mental illness at the time of the psychiatric assessment. Roland told the shrink that he was preoccupied with thoughts about "torturing, death, fucking, getting rich"—in other words, the very litany of the metal movement. Roland, wrote the psychiatrist, "revealed thoughts of violent acting out and torturing people while listening to lyrics of heavy metal music and identifying . . . scenes of torture and killing. He described that these thoughts were often uncontrollable and reinforced by incessant listening to songs which depict such scenes."

During the car ride to the site at which Newberry was killed, the Hardy boys indulged themselves in the words of a song by Metallica titled "Crash Course in Brain Surgery." They also paid particular heed to the number "Damage Incorporated" with the lyrics "dying time is here." Hardy pulled the car to a screeching halt next to the railroad tracks that ran beside the chemical plant. Roland sensed that something awful was about to happen. The pressure had been building for many days from Hardy, from the music, from the drugs, from the "demon" that Hardy had been cavalierly saying all along possessed him. First Hardy ordered the sacrifice of a cat they had hauled along in a canvas bag. They hoisted up the confined animal and beat it to death with the bat.

Roland later said he felt eerie because the cat made scarcely a cry. Then the foul spirit in Hardy tore off its mask. Hardy turned to Roland and commanded, "Sacrifice Steve to Satan." Roland repeated with almost robotlike obedience: "Sacrifice Steve to Satan."

Hardy, however, seized the bat and struck the first blow himself. "Sacrifice to Satan! Sacrifice to Satan!" Newberry had been injured but was not yet unconscious. The horrified boy shouted "Why me?" Then he picked himself off the ground and started running, while Hardy and Roland gave chase. A short distance away Newberry tripped, and his attackers pounced upon him mercilessly. Roland informed the psychiatrist, "We beat him like vultures and my feeling was to get it over with. It was an undescribable feeling."

Roland had been fantasizing about the sacrifice for many days. Whether the actual event had been inspired by the music is unclear. But Roland had his own peculiar liturgy, which had been assiduously recorded in his school binder. The words were virtually a formula for the murder itself:

Throw him in hell/ Burn him in hell/ Beat him in hell/ Rape him in hell/ Torture him in hell/ Sacrifice him in hell/ Smash him in hell/ Reap him in hell/ Throw him in hell/ Thrash him in hell/ That's where he'll dwell/ Burn him in hell/ Beat him in hell/ Oh no, I can't stand the smell/ Rape him in hell/ Reap him in hell/ Oh yes, you're doing well/ Smash him in hell/ Stab him in hell/ Do it till he has fell.

Newberry "fell" into what the Hardy boys mythically named the "well of hell."

After dumping Newberry's dead body down the well, the Hardy boys returned home and reveled in a stereo concert of more metal music. But now Roland was beginning to feel a profound sense of unease, although the sensation could certainly not be described as moral qualms. A deep-searching anxiety and exhaustion spread over him—the kind of nauseating realization that all the "tripping" and posturing would soon be unmasked as having a steep price to pay. "I was empty. Absolutely empty," Roland said. Interestingly, Roland did not immediately discern that he had actually done something wrong, let alone commit a crime punishable under the law.

The sweet mystery of illusion and trance brought about by the "religion" remained strong. When interrogated by police, he said almost plaintively, "It just did not connect and it was not logical." In a very weird sense his alibi was just like the Nazis at Nuremberg who protested they were just following orders. Roland saw himself as a kind of floppy mannequin, as a transparent expression of the diabolical will of Hardy. "If Jim did not come up with the idea, we would not have done it," he said.

Among Roland's sketches was the famous sacrifice drawing. The drawing seems to capture dramatically the symbolic thought processes of the Hardy boys as they plotted the slaying. Barry had drawn it, he said, almost in a whimsy. At the left side of the picture stands a towering, stern, jackbooted figure who is only visible from the waist down. A tiny dog, perhaps a terrier, stares excitedly and obediently up at the "master," who bellows from his anonymous heights—"Sacrifice to Satan." The master is Hardy, or Satan, or both. Just underneath the dog can be glimpsed the leering countenance of a man brandishing a golf club.

The allusion may be to the clubs from *A Clockwork Orange*, even though the choice of weapons at the well was baseball bats. Furthermore, the picture is oddly reminiscent of the famous logo for RCA Victor, where a puzzled little mutt cocks his ear to the speaker of a phonograph recording beside the caption—"His master's voice." It is clear from a more intimate study of the relationship between Hardy and his hangers-on that Roland is really the "dog" in the picture. In a series of letters exchanged from prison, Hardy refers to Roland as "Little Mutt." Perhaps with solemnity and respectfully, Roland addresses Hardy as "Outlaw Dog."

Roland explained that the names "Little Mutt" and "Outlaw Dog" were snagged from the breeze one day when the two boys were reading a children's book featuring those particular characters. But it is plain from their correspondence that the names had a cryptic and magical connotation for them. In a letter postmarked March 10, 1988, Hardy wrote the following:

... man, you know, how much into Satan I was and he constantly fights at me to get me back. Yet, I have been saved, and I plan to stay on the side of holiness. With that holiness in me and in you I think we'll once again be together. You're right, the Devil tricked us. He really fucked our lives up, but we'll show his evil ass what we're about now . . . ow, ow, outlaw dog, one eye, big eye.

An archetypal symbol of Satan in his "disguises" throughout Western history has been a stray curr, an "outlaw dog." Satan is also the eye in the pyramid, the "big eye." But throughout the letters Hardy warns Roland not to turn "state's evidence." And he reminds Roland about his habit of killing dogs. Roland may have relished with a slight masochistic glee the rendering of himself as a dog. After all, Roland was an abused and battered child. All during his growing up it had been a "dog's world."

Roland was born in Joplin on October 1, 1970, as the second of two children. His sister was three and a half years older. Roland's mother was raised in nearby Carthage, where her father worked as a furniture refinisher. Her father was cruel to her and sexually molested her older sister. (Later she would marry a man exactly like him, a man who would beat the children and abuse his daughter sexually.) Roland's mother graduated from high school in 1965 and immediately left home. A short while later she met Roland's father, an army veteran employed as general manager of a men's care store in May City.

Although she did not love him, Roland's mother decided to marry his father out of fear it would be her "last offer." His father allegedly was disgruntled with his job, according to documents, and he vented his frustrations on the little boy. Sexual molesting of the daughter also began about this time, according to a psychologist's report. His mother recalls an incident where his father repeatedly threw a football at the toddler. One day his father did not come home from work and vanished from town, only to resurface several years later. When his father disappeared, Roland's mother went to work at very low pay and extraordinarily long hours to support the family.

Roland has almost no memories of his early childhood. A lonely little boy, he was constantly kept in the care of his older sister. He was a bed wetter and became something of a behavioral problem both in school and for the social workers who constantly attended to him. For about three months in early 1977 both Roland and his sister were placed with foster families. Roland told a psychologist that he believed at the time both his mother and his father had rejected him. His intense anger at his parents, and the corrupt authority they seemed to represent, would finally play itself out in the nihilistic rage that the metal music and the iconography of pop satanism embodied.

When Roland was eight, his mother started dating another man, who would eventually become Roland's stepfather. About the same time Roland found out that his father had remarried and that his new wife would soon deliver a baby, which turned out to be a boy. The psychological repercussions of this twist of fate are well appreciated by today's therapists. The news devastated young Roland, who came to believe that his father had "replaced" him. The enormous hostility Roland experienced, particularly from this moment onward, became the fulcrum of his psychological development, the beliefs and fantasies promoted by the religious cultism and the music now became plausible.

Young Roland became engulfed in a psychological maelstrom arising out of a fury directed against both an absent and an abusive father, against the rootlessness of his life and the normlessness of his family, indeed, against the whole cultural breakdown that characterized the late 1960s and early 1970s. This pathology, which might well be identified as the underlying psycho-social impetus to the growth of pop satanism, can be called the "Darth Vader complex." In the popular "Star Wars" trilogy by filmmaker George Lucas, which has almost ascended to the level of contemporary myth, the diabolical figure of Darth Vader looms large as a strange emblem of the confusions and contradictions of the "Big Chill" generation. At the opening of the trilogy, Darth Vader is the evil and distant starlord, contrasting sharply with the unknown and long-dead "good" father of Luke Skywalker, the young hero.

At the close of the trilogy the terrible truth is disclosed—Darth Vader *is* Luke's father. The old paternal images have been turned upside down. White becomes black, and the father is revealed as the apotheosis of evil, even though in the end Darth Vader does come to the rescue of his own flesh and blood. After the "death of God," particularly God the father, much the same inversion has happened in American culture. If God has died, Satan must live. Satan emerges, especially in the case of Pete Roland, as the "dark father," of which the name Darth Vader is a homonym—the father who has been there but is no longer, who had abandoned his son and replaced him with a favorite; who has beaten, ignored, and molested his progeny, but who still holds an allurement, a power, and a strange sort of "command" over life. He is the personification of the "new order," as the heavy metal bands sing, of a dark and grim authority to stand over the chaos of the recent age.

When Roland was in junior high, his mother remarried, and thereafter his stepfather emerged as a strong presence. Roland, however, was not fond of his stepfather and strongly resented his stepbrothers, one of whom, however, was responsible for introducing the boy to heavy metal music. Roland's admission to the playhouse of adolescent diabolism took place in seventh grade, the period when virtually every pubescent male and female in America changes overnight into a social creature. He would snatch a bottle of wine and listen to his stepbrother's metal albums, which included AC/DC and Alice Cooper.

Toward the end of junior high he had seriously tried marijuana, and by high school he had been tabbed an academic underachiever whose life-style matched the "stoner" idyll of sex, drugs, and rock 'n' roll. His mother would come home in the early afternoon and find her son completely drunk or blotted by drugs. Roland was also given to acts of vandalism against neighbors and started hanging out with social misfits, including an ex-convict and a local drug pusher. When his mother asked Pete why he ran in such company, his answer was, "Because I want to be with people as bad as I am."

In the summer of 1986, Roland's parents sent him off to live with an uncle on his father's side. The uncle, who owned a farm, sought to discipline his nephew and laid down rules against drinking and drug use. For a while Roland's behavior, and his grades, improved. But by Christmas 1986 the uncle's heart condition made it necessary for Pete to return home. At first the mother was gratified by the dramatic improvement in her son's attitude and outlook. Pete would help around the house and act politely to friends and acquaintances. The pattern, however, deteriorated rapidly after Roland's sister, who married and became pregnant just before separating from her husband, came home to deliver a baby. Roland was furious at the baby's crying. His grades started declining, and again he withdrew through his headphones into the clash of metal music. It was about this time that Roland grew close to Hardy, even though he had known him since early adolescence. His mother recalls that his habitual rudeness and hostility gave way to actual threats of violence.

Roland seemed drawn to Hardy because he was the class president and was bent on changing him from a "nobody" into someone significant. Pete told his mother that Hardy "knew everybody and everything." When Roland went to work at a local steakhouse, a neighbor informed the mother that her son had been seen using the meat-cutting devices to kill animals.

Roland's "conversion" to satanism apparently ensued when he heard the following song lyrics: "666 the number of the beast, the one for you and me, possess my body and make it burn." Hardy loaned him a handful of metal tapes and admonished him not to repeat the lyrics because they had "special powers." Roland began listening to "thrash rock" while snorting and sometimes free-basing cocaine. He would beat his head to the music, scream, and bang on things. Hardy would tell him he was feeling the effects of "Satan's power." Hardy also taught Roland to torture cats and dogs. As a child Roland had loved animals, but the new black gospel urged him to transport his soul beyond the bounds of evil.

The taking of life and the spilling of blood was not just the required initiation procedure. It was a sacrament, as one might say in today's New Age lingo, of "personal transformation." While coming down from a high on psychedelic mushrooms, Roland watched Hardy kill a dog. Roland protested but then saw the dog's head flop around and discovered a "feeling" of mastery never experienced before. After each killing, Hardy would intone, "Sacrifice to Satan." The more Roland tagged around with

Hardy, the more he fell completely under his sway. "Jim is higher than me," he told a prison psychiatrist. "I am a coward—stupid and dumb."

Roland began killing animals on his own to "please Jim." Jim was "so proud of me," he confessed. His ritual tortures of animals became more exotic and professional. He would cut off the animal's limbs and gouge out the eyes. Once he put a dog in a clothe's dryer and broke into hysterical laughter as he watched the beast's face on fire from the dryer. He would also stare for lengths of time at the dog's corpse. "I was fascinated to see the guts," he said. It was a "momentous thing for me and Jim to look back on and talk about."

Another ceremony Hardy taught Roland to perform was defecation upon a Bible, a traditional satanic gesture harking back to the black masses of the fifteenth century. He began routinely drawing the satanic symbol of the goat's head. He told himself that his devotion and adoration toward Satan gave him his own personal "charisma." Hardy confided to him that the power would increase tremendously if he could "kill a person." Much the same psychology had operated with the Matamoros cult.

Roland came to believe he had psychic abilities and could manipulate the minds of others. All along, though, he remained disappointed because he yearned to look straightaway at the face of Satan, who never showed himself. "The Devil never came to me," Roland recalled. "He spoke to me through the music." At the same time Roland would linger for hours before the mirror, mugging and making "evil" faces. "The faces stayed there," he swore. On one occasion the mimickry actually frightened him. He became obsessed with horror movies, of which his favorite was *The Texas Chainsaw Massacre*. At the end of the summer of 1987, Roland had assured himself that "killing is a way of life."

Roland explained to the psychiatrist that the animal slayings and mutilations forged a bond between Hardy and himself. Meanwhile, he remained in dread of the possibility that Hardy might abandon him if he did not "perform" the routines of sacrifice. The week before Halloween 1987, Hardy came up to Roland in English class and whispered that he had an "important message." When class was over the two met, with Clements in attendance, beside the school lockers. Jim asked, "Can you now kill someone?" Since Roland did not want to buck Hardy, he said, "Sure." At that point Hardy demanded that he take part in the murder of Newberry.

During the following days Roland started to look upon the intended sacrifice as an act of personal redemption. Increasingly depressed, he complained to friends that he had no control over his life and that he was an instrument of forces beyond his comprehension, which he was obliged to appease. The killing of Newberry would not only satisfy Hardy, it would greatly please Satan.

The murder of Newberry was originally slated for Halloween, "Satan's holy day." But the plan had to be postponed because Hardy's parents would not give him the car. By now Roland was completely terrified of Hardy and thought he was an awesome magician whose spell could not be counteracted. Several months before, Hardy had told Pete that if Pete ever struck him, Hardy would come back from the dead as an avenging demon and rip him to tatters.

On the Friday night before the slaying, Roland downed an entire fifth of Southern Comfort. Sunday, Hardy phoned him and reminded him of their appointment. The murder would have to take place on a Sunday, he insisted, so that it could be a desecration sufficiently pleasing to Satan. Roland reviewed in his mind phrases from a song by Metallica called "Black Sabbath," which dealt with the sacrifice of a "first-born" on the Lord's Day.

Until then the group had not discussed the specifics of how Newberry would be killed. Someone suggested using an axe belonging to the victim. But eventually it was decided that Roland, who happened to be the strongest, would strike Newberry first. Jim instructed him to knock Newberry on the spine and paralyze his legs.

The vandalizing of the FHA house in Carthage, perpetrated by the Hardy boys, was undertaken for precise magical, or ritual, purposes. Strewing food and spray-painting satanic symbols was intended to demonstrate both the seriousness of their plans and their power. The messages were also intended to solicit the direct interest of the Prince of Darkness. Yet once the deed was accomplished, and the sight of the dead Newberry had seeped in, such ceremonial piety dissolved as rapidly as a March spring. A primitive and homicidal madness overcame the trio. Roland's memory of the seventy blows was hazy, as if a strange amnesia had overcome him. But all they did was pound him and pound him, he said. Like the cat they killed first, Newberry made little noise, except for a few agonized moans. It was as though he, too, was ready for the sacrifice.

When Roland had killed animals in the past, he had been "very happy." When it came to homicide, however, he admitted he was quite distressed and remotely sad, all the while recalling the gist of a line from Black Sabbath: "Things faded to black as nothingness." Roland said, "I felt like an empty void, like I wasn't a person. I was a zombie, someone who doesn't exist. I was freaking out. I was there but not listening. It didn't register." As he left the scene of the crime he thought, "Life's a bunch of shit. I'll never be able to love again."

Roland asked Hardy if they should burn the bats to destroy the evidence. Hardy said they should toss them into woods where nobody would find them, which of course they did. At that juncture, Roland had a sudden and terrible urge to commit suicide. As they walked to the car, Pete asked Jim if Satan now had "Steve's soul." Hardy said he did because they had pronounced the magical words *sacrifice to Satan*. The three went back to Hardy's and hung around for about an hour and a half. Jim said they had satisfied Satan and would not have to eliminate anybody else for a while.

Nobody knew Hardy had both his accomplices on his own private hit list. Jim said his next goal was to kill a baby. Hardy may have had in mind his own offspring, since he was rumored to have fathered an illegitimate child by a local high school girl. According to Roland, Hardy imagined how lovely it would be to drink the baby's blood. He said he had been inspired by a metal song that describes such an act at a "black funeral." The song was part of an album by the group Merciful Fate. The song wails, "With the blood you'll be one." Roland wished he could undo what he had just done. He began secretly wishing for a "second chance," and he told Hardy he seriously doubted that what they had accomplished was truly a sacrifice. Hardy stared at him and said dryly, "You have to believe it."

Roland went home and attempted to watch a movie on television, but nothing appealed to him. He tried to snack, but he had no appetite. It was "mass confusion" in his head, he said. He tried to repent of his entire life, which did not satisfy either. At school the next day he was unable to concentrate, and the tension increased in the afternoon when a private investigator talked with the trio. Their story to the investigator was that they had dropped Newberry off at a store, which sounded plausible.

In the evening, however, Hardy called and in a worried tone of voice insisted they needed to hurry out to the chemical plant and check the well, in case anything "floated up." They even brought along bleach to wipe out the blood on the road. At the scene they discovered to their horror that they had not disposed of the victim's pipe, brush, and sunglasses. Newberry's coat had also risen to the top of the well. They tied a rock around the coat to make sure it stayed on the bottom.

Roland's school chums reported that he was extremely nervous the next morning. When he showed up for building trades class he glanced out the window and saw a police car driving away. The police car, however, returned, and Roland was asked by a school official to speak with the cops. When the cops appeared they informed him he had been charged with first-degree murder. When the police read him his rights, Roland broke down and wept. During the police interrogation Roland was frank, even "cold," a detective later indicated. Congenially, he led the officers to the well and showed where the bats had been deposited.

Later Roland recalled that he was "sick" and that he no longer wanted to "get high." Roland added, "The power left me." The cult members at Matamoros gave much the same explanation when the *federale* raid proved they were not invisible to police or impervious to bullets. But Roland devised his own interpretation from the stock logic of Western folk culture. Satan had "tricked" him, he complained. "I gave up my soul, but I didn't get anything back. Satan stole it. Once you kill something, you'll never be human again. I have apologized to Steve, if he can hear me. I can hardly stand it without the music and the drugs."

CHAPTER 3.

Bad Moon Rising:
The Epidemic of Satanic Crime
in America

What you see may not always please you; but you *will see*.
——ANTON SZANDOR LaVEY, *The Satanic Bible*

Pete Roland confessed to his role in the murder of Steve Newberry, while Hardy and Clements pleaded no contest. All are currently serving life sentences. Roland stood trial in June 1988, not in order to determine his guilt or innocence, but as the consequence of his plea that his satanist beliefs had contributed to a psychological state of "diminished competence." The prosecution was demanding the death penalty for Roland, but the defense interposed the satanist question in order to prevent the kid from going to the electric chair. Although the prosecution pulled every conceivable legal maneuver to keep the issue of satanism out of court, in the end they were unsuccessful. Roland himself admitted to the motive of an attempted sacrifice, which had run all through the psychiatric evaluations and police reports anyway. When Roland took the witness stand, the prosecution was absolutely furious and sought to make the jury believe that the young man was lying about the devil, and that the slaying of Newberry had been an arbitrary and unprincipled act of violence. The jury, however, considered young Roland to be telling the truth, and for the first time a satanic murder had been proven in an American court of law.

But the Roland case was unique because the connections between satanism and homicide had been clearly demonstrated by the confession of the accused himself. Elsewhere, a national epidemic of "satanist-related" crime was growing faster than AIDS, even though the "religious" motivation was frequently deleted once the cases were actually brought to trial. *Believing* in the powers of evil, and of one's own dedication to them, was not a crime—or so said the FBI and various top law enforcement officials. It only mattered once the crime itself was committed.

A pathologist read from the witness stand in a San Francisco courtroom the coroner's report on the disfigured corpse of an unnamed transient the police had dubbed "John Doe 60." His nauseating description could have been lifted from the chronicles of the most barbarous medieval torture sessions. The cadaver exhibited two three-inch cuts to the upper lip, burns and cuts on the neck, multiple stab wounds in the chest, each approximately six to nine inches long. The grisly orgy had been neither haphazard nor gratuitous but suggested a prolonged ritual of sadistic mutilation using a live victim. The pattern of lesions themselves formed a familiar emblem of satanic practice—the five-pointed star, or pentagram. In addition, John Doe had been castrated and molten wax poured into the socket of the right eye. Immediately after those ceremonial procedures the perpetrator of the sordid crime had made a surgical slice all the way from the scrotum to the anal region in order to drain the blood from the body. Clusters of bruises on the back, buttocks, and ankles together with abrasions along the wrists revealed that the hapless wretch had been pummeled prior to his execution.

Officials had discovered the remains of John Doe 60 beneath a truck in the warehouse district of the city by the bay, a short distance from where two decades earlier the so-called flower children or hippies of the sixties had streamed from the midwestern heartland toward California's vermillion sunset, beckoned by the Circean strains of the popular song: "If you come to San Francisco . . ." The bloody human remains had been swathed in plastic and a blanket and bundled with guitar strings. The accused in the slaying was a hulking 45-year-old waiter known in the San Francisco homosexual community as Clifford St. Joseph, who was also reputed to be the capo of a vicious satanic cult. Maurice Bork, his alleged accomplice, testified that he had helped St. Joseph stuff the corpse in a station wagon and drop it in the spot where it had been found. St. Joseph later was found guilty of murder and sentenced from thirty-four years to life. Charges against Bork were dismissed.

The sacrifice of John Doe 60 had been conducted by candle-glow with the heavy metal band Black Sabbath supplying the mood music as well as serving to drown out the screams of the victim. The incision on the victim's lips was a gesture familiar to police experts in occult crime; it was ostensibly to "seal" the secret of the act for eternity. The draining of the blood was the signal feature in the group's fastidious performance of this "unholy communion." It was carefully collected in a golden chalice, a kind of sacred grail, then imbibed with all the solemnity of high mass.

Police in San Francisco, where Anton LaVey founded the Church of Satan in 1966, had issued public warnings for years about what they have characterized as an "infestation" of blood cults and satanic criminals. Sandi Gallant of the San Francisco Police Department's intelligence division had already become something of a national celebrity for her "cult-busting" ferocity and her unsurpassed street knowledge of the satanic underworld. In 1988 she made national headlines for her charges against a U.S. Army lieutenant colonel named Michael Aquino, head of a prominent satanic group calling itself the Temple of Set, for alleged child abuse and molestation at the Presidio.

On June 4, 1987—two weeks before the Pete Roland case was to go to trial—another body was uncovered in southwestern Missouri. The victim this time was a thirty-seven-year-old white woman named Paulette June Sherman, who seemed to have a penchant for extreme fundamentalist religion. The coroner's statement in this instance was just as awful as with John Doe 60:

Subject was found by her husband, Daniel Sherman, when he returned home from work at 10:12 PM. . . . Subject was lieing [sic] on her back, feet facing the bedroom, north. Subject had been stabbed numerous (85) times about the body, with several areas of concentration. It appeared that the assailant had tried to remove the vulva by cutting; there was a cross cut into the victim's abdomen; the heart had been repeatedly . . . tried to be removed; several defense wounds about the hands; the throat had been severely cut; all vessels of the neck area had been severed, both carotid arteries, both jugular veins, esophogus, wind pipe, all cut down to the spine; stab wounds to the back of the trunk, 87, approximately, stab wounds in all. A black plastic-handled steak knife was found near the victim's head. The knife had been bent in a curving angle, app. 45 degree angle, and had probably been bent by striking a bone while cutting. . . .

The assailant had sliced up Mrs. Sherman the way a supermarket meat cutter prepares a package of beef fajitas. A bloody crucifix engraved on the abdomen, excision of the vaginal parts, an evident attempt at cutting out the heart—all comprised the signature of another ritual killing.

Here are other snapshots pasted in the album leaves of the spreading epidemic of satanist-related mayhem and violence, the majority of which have been confirmed by police:

ITEM: In Weld County, Colorado, federal drug agents arrested three individuals while busting a drug laboratory and confiscating a cache of weapons along with "Satan-worship material." A warrant stated that the head of the drug and satanism operation had been giving directions from prison. The house in which the suspects were arrested was surrounded by a barbed-wire fence and protected by a gun-equipped tower.

ITEM: Ten-year-old David Tackett of Pico Rivera, California, alleged that six of his neighbors had regularly been engaged in baby sacrifices, orgies, cremations, cannibalism, blood-letting, and the drinking of urine. The tale was corroborated by nine other children, who claim they were sexually abused during a cult-like ritual.

ITEM: Richard Kasso, seventeen, of Riverhead, New York, committed suicide in his jail cell after having been arraigned for the ritual murder of Gary Lauwers of East Northport. Also arrested was an eighteen-year-old friend. The two youths burned Lauwer's socks and shirt sleeves while chanting around a fire then demanded, "Say you love Satan," before plunging a knife into him. Kasso confessed to police that the slaying constituted revenge against Lauwer for his theft of ten bags of "angel dust," a powerful street drug.

ITEM: In Montana, Stanley Dean Baker was accused of stabbing a man twenty-seven times, dismembering his corpse, tearing out the heart, and eating it. According to published accounts, one of the victim's fingers was in Baker's pocket at the time of his arrest.

ITEM: In 1981 Satanic goings-on were unearthed in Westport, Massachusetts, in connection with the ritualistic murder of two cult members. The accused murderer was Carl Drew, twenty-five, a local pimp known by his girls as "son of Satan," who wore on his left arm the tatoo "Satan's Angels." Drew ordered seventeen-year-old Robin Murphy to slit the throat of a third cult member, twenty-year-old Karen A. Marsden. After offering up her soul to the Devil, Drew lopped off Marsden's head.
Murphy related to the court how Drew's band had pummeled Marsden in the head with rocks, severed her fingers, stripped her, slit her throat, decapitated her, and kicked the head around on the ground. Drew then performed sex on the decapitated body and carved an X on Marsden's chest while babbling in a strange tongue. He then put his thumb in Marsden's blood and etched an X on Murphy's forehead. By such a process, Murphy was supposedly "initiated" into the religion. On March 14, 1981 Drew received a life sentence for the slaying of Marsden.

ITEM: In Ontario, California, ten straight-A teenagers were caught having composed a two-page, step-by-step blueprint for eliminating parents from their lives. Step number ten, tagged "the ultimate sacrifice," involved dissection of parents' bodies then feeding them to the dogs. Afterwards the dogs themselves, according to the instructions, were to be sacrificed.

ITEM: A drug suspect apprehended in Fort Worth, Texas, told authorities he had attended a party in northwestern Indiana at which severed limbs of small children were deployed in "sacrificial" ceremonies.

ITEM: An eight-year old girl in San Francisco recounted an experience in a candlelit room where a wooden cross was hung upside down and baby's legs were scorched in a fire. The squalling infant was then laid on a blanket, while the girl's father compelled her to stab the child through the navel and consume the blood.

ITEM: Five men were hauled before a magistrate in Sacramento, California, and charged with 169 counts of sexual molestation and abuse of children, including the making of "snuff" movies in which kids were butchered on camera. The alleged ringleader, Arthur Gary Dill, who worked at the Citrus Heights Restaurant supposedly molded a satanic cult organization around the snuff pornography operation.

ITEM: Eighteen-year-old Scott Waterhouse of Sanford, Maine, was convicted by a jury of luring Gycelle Cote, twelve, into the woods and strangling her after carefully studying Anton LaVey's *Satanic Bible*. Waterhouse explained to interviewers that the principles of satanism centered on doing anything one feels like doing—"whatever floats your boat, turns your crank."

ITEM: Triple murderer Sean Sellers, seventeen, of Oklahoma City, while awaiting execution on death row, confessed he had been inspired to kill his mother, stepfather, and a convenience-store clerk with a .44 magnum after reading satanic literature brought by a babysitter when he was about the age of ten. Sellers claimed he had inaugurated his own satanic group in Greeley, Colorado.

ITEM: Two men in a van were stopped by the highway patrol near Tallahassee, Florida, and found to have six filthy and abused children in tow. The men contended the children had been given to them by a satanic cult and that they were enroute to Mexico to put them in a "school for brilliant children."

ITEM: In Atlanta, Georgia, where a series of ritualistic murders of black children captured headlines earlier in the decade, similar slayings continue. Apparently the killings did not cease after the arrest of reputed mass murderer Wayne Williams, who was convicted in two of the deaths. Over twenty black children have been murdered in much the same fashion since Williams was put behind bars. But the incidents have gone unreported by the general media. A number of chldren have told police about satanic sex abuse in which, they insist, they were compelled to drink both animal and human blood.

ITEM: A Detroit policewoman and a male companion were ordered to stand trial after allegedly kidnapping a woman and forcing her to take part in satanic sex rituals. District Judge Rufus Griffin Jr., ordered officer Linda Greene of the thirteenth precinct and private detective Arzell Jones held under $25,000 bonds on four counts of first-degree sexual assault, kidnapping, and firearms violations. The suspects were convicted by a jury in December 1983.

The victim said the duo took their victim from a nightclub, dragged her to a motel, beat her, and sexually assaulted her. The victim also testified that Jones ordered her to chant "Satan is my follower. I denounce the words of Jesus Christ." Later Jones attempted to recruit another woman for "some type of ritualistic ceremony," involving black robes.

ITEM: "Who's the guy that's kidnapping and murdering all the girls in Battle Creek?" Michigan detective Michael DeBoer asked. The partially clad bodies of Patricia Rosansky and Karry Lynn Evans were found within five weeks of each other in wooded sites twelve miles apart. One of the suspects in the case was a self-proclaimed satanist who had written friends about his strange beliefs and had been seen wearing a red jacket with 666 embossed upon it. He also boasted of having presided over a black mass in Kalamazoo.

ITEM: In Forest Lake, Minnesota, a young boy named Steve shot himself to death. Steve, however, had long professed a belief in satanism. His body was found with a thirteen-pointed star pinned to his chest together with pictures of his family.

ITEM: In Phoenix, Arizona, 140 dogs were found slain. Nationwide thousands of animal mutilations have been thought to have satanic origins. In Palm Springs, California, Humane Society officials have been studying the alleged disappearance of numerous pets, including pure-bred dogs and cats.

ITEM: Authorities on the south shore of Long Island had reason to believe that a satanist gang cruising in a van had been responsible for the kidnapping and ritualized murder of several young women. Indications of satanism have cropped up with the discovery of the corpses of two of the victims. Police also happened upon a cave, located within walking distance of where the remains of one woman was found, that was decorated with satanic grafitti, including pentagrams, the number of the beast (*666*), and drawings of the "devil's head," known in occult circles as Baphomet.

ITEM: A couple from Lakewood, Colorado, drove 145 miles to a remote mountain area and shot each other in a murder-suicide police described as "occultic" and "satanic." The bodies of Bruce and Pamela Covey, both in their twenties, were discovered by a snowplow operator not far from the town of Walden. First the pair enjoyed a few puffs of marijuana, then the husband pulled a .45-caliber cap-and-ball pistol and shot his wife. Both Coveys wore rings and medallions with satanic insignia. A police search of the couple's apartment turned up numerous occult books and other literature.

ITEM: Jeanette Louise Tracy, forty-one, of Firestone, Colorado, and Michael Dean Tracy, twenty-four, were arrested in March of 1989 in connection with the slaying seven years earlier of the woman's previous husband, Jim Lee Stewart. Stewart's body had been discovered in 1982 at the bottom of a mine shaft near the Colorado mountain town of Central City. Five months later Jeanette Tracy was found guilty of plotting first-degree murder and was sentenced to life imprisonment. Her younger accomplice, with whom she had allegedly been involved in a love triangle at the time of her former husband's death and whom she later married, stood trial on charges that he had bludgeoned Stewart to death with a baseball bat on the instructions of Jeanette.

Michael Tracy's defense attorney argued that his client could not have been guilty of first-degree murder, which requires proof of prior deliberation, because the young man had too low an IQ to know what he was doing. The defense also described a scenario—based on police reports, testimony of Jeanette Tracy's daughters, and expert witness evaluation—in which Michael Tracy had supposedly been constrained psychologically to commit the murder because of the woman's use of black magic and "satanic" spells. Jim Stewart himself had allegedly been asked to draw a large pentagram—a feature of satanic cult ritual—on the basement wall immediately in advance of the murder.

Michael Tracy was found guilty by a jury.

These and many other disarming, sometimes seemingly improbable, scenarios are gaining credible adherents around the country, not just among popular journalists or self-styled ghost-busters, but within the law enforcement, criminology, and mental health establishment. Satanic cases or incidents are frequently difficult to assess because of the crosswinds of hysteria, anxiety, and what might be called the "denial syndrome" of certain professionals trained in the social sciences who reject out of hand, even without good cause, all suggestions—even where only weird behavior is the issue—of the occult itself.

In their information retrieval and assessment, the so-called experts, however, have frequently lagged severely behind the lay public. There has been a tendency among some in the field of the study of religion, particularly those who should know better, to dismiss the entire subject as a tabloid-inspired wave of frenzy simulating audience reaction to, say, the late-night television series "Tales from the Dark Side." An analogy has also been drawn with UFO sightings. But the fact of the matter is that the "observers" in the current satanist siege are social workers, therapists, district attorneys, and police chiefs, not teenagers on their way home late at night from a hay ride. And, unlike rumored alien spacecraft, the satanists have left shiploads of physical evidence, including cadavers.

Believability, however, is not the only stumbling block confronting investigators. The other problem is the veracity of the primary sources of information themselves—children aged three to nine, convicted killers, and ex-satanists. By themselves, the terms *cult* and *devil worship* tend to kindle the general public's suspicions, whose attitudes are influenced by a lifelong diet of late-night movies, paperback novels, and more recently, rock video entertainment. Investigators quickly find their own credibility under scrutiny because of the fearful reactions, and therefore the penchant for denial, that afflict their own professional reputations when the subject is brought up.

The most complex, daunting, and maddening of so-called satanist cases has been the affair with the McMartin preschool in Manhattan Beach, California. On January 18, 1990, the only remaining McMartin defendants—Raymond Buckey, thirty-one, and his sixty-three-year-old mother Peggy McMartin Buckey—were acquitted by a jury in Los Angeles on fifty-two child molestation counts in what had turned out to be the country's longest and costliest criminal trial, and what had also come to be a kind of circus arena for various charges and countercharges from experts about the existence, or significance, of satanic cult influences on children as well as so-called ritual abuse. The jury had deadlocked on twelve other sex abuse charges.

Peggy McMartin Buckey told the press flatly, "I've gone through hell and now we've lost everything." Graham Jeambey, an official spokesman for a national organization known as Victims of Child Abuse Laws (VOCAL), which had taken the side of the defendants, vowed to take up the mattter with Congress and proclaimed that "we've got to exercise some control over these rampant, hysterical activities." The day after the verdict Peggy McMartin Buckey informed the media she had filed a federal civil lawsuit that alleged malicious prosecution and defamation of character. Named in the litigation as defendants were Los Angeles County, the city of Manhattan Beach, former district attorney Robert Philibosian, Children's Institute International (CII) and therapist Kee McFarlane, and Capital Cities–ABC Inc., including its former reporter Wayne Satz. The suit contended that all the defendants in the civil case were part of a conspiracy to indict the McMartin preschool operators. It sought general damages of $1 million as well as unspecified punitive damages.

Whereas the outcome of the McMartin case exonerated the preschool operators of wrongdoing, it did not necessarily resolve any of the broader issues surrounding ritual child abuse. And a number of child abuse experts and district attorneys interviewed in the wake of the jury's deliberations said the upshot would not be any effort to back off on the larger issues that emerged during the trial, or any new era of constrained prosecution. They promised instead greater oversight and more caution in the use of interrogation and the application of the rules of evidence in the courtroom.

Juror John Brees, who suffered the personal misfortune of his wife dying during trial, told a *Washington Post* reporter that the defendants "weren't proven innocent," but that "we just found them not guilty, based on the evidence." Other jurors, who were encouraged by the trial judge to discuss with the press their experience and mode of reasoning in reaching their decision, said that they believed the children had in fact been molested, but that they were simply not sure who had done it. The jurors also faulted the prosecution for its presentation, and suggested that evidence from the video tapes of the children's stories to therapists may have been "contaminated."

The parents of the McMartin children, who had organized into an outspoken interest group during the court proceedings and even begun publishing a national newsletter, appeared not to accept the verdict easily. According to wire service reports, the verdict generated "outrage among parents of youngsters in the case." Prosecutor Lael Rubin said to a press conference that although she definitely respected the jury's decision, she disagreed with it. And she added: "I believe that the families involved in this case and the children . . . cannot be forgotten or overlooked in terms of what they had to endure in the kind of system we presently had."

The McMartin affair had been a three-ring circus from the outset.

The McMartin school was shuttered and closed after the investigation first got underway in the early 1980s. In Los Angeles, a bright, husky, freckle-faced boy—identified in the files as John Doe 9—told officials that at the preschool he had participated in a game called "Naked Movie Star" where children were seduced into performing explicit sexual acts with adults before a video camera. Furthermore, the boy said he had viewed the slaughter of animals on a church altar intended to terrorize the children and compel them to silence about what was taking place in the preschool. The child described an extraordinary occurrence in which robed strangers, moaning and chanting, whirled in a circle around him while he was in the preschool. When asked why he did not tell his parents, little "Johnny" replied, "Because I was scared they might get hurt if I told them."

Other children in the McMartin affair complained of having been sodomized and sexually fondled during "Naked Movie Star." They also maintained they were secretly taken during the day to the homes and businesses of adult strangers in the community, where they were sexually molested and forced to take part in a range of macabre rituals. The children said they had undergone the rituals in a grocery store, a church, a cemetery, and a crematorium.

According to one boy, one of the defendants mutilated rabbits before the children's eyes and warned them the same fate awaited both their parents and them if they snitched. Johnny also told the court about repeated assaults upon him and his friends by people who were clothed like "witches" and "devils," as well about having witnessed the slaying of animals in front of a church missal stand. Johnny was put in psycho-therapy, and each session elicited ever more exotic testimony. He told his mother, among other things, that he believed the Devil was trying to control him.

The McMartin affair began in the summer of 1983 when local police were summoned on a single charge of alleged child abuse at the preschool. By the following January, police had cleared the facility, and in March seven people were arraigned on 208 counts of child sexual molestation. Every child questioned by authorities came up with similar statements about continuing abuse. By November the organization known as Children's Institute International (CII) had interviewed 389 former McMartin pupils, the vast majority of whom had the same repertoire of "memories" of occult molestation and terror.

CII argued that eighty percent of the 389 victimized kids had physical or medical symptoms to prove that they had been abused. The alleged tokens included scar tissue on the child's vagina or anus, rectal bleeding, painful bowel movements, and something called the "wick anal reflex," which occurs only when the rear end has been violently penetrated. Behavioral signs such as continuing nightmares, excessive masturbation, exposing of oneself, and precocious sexual posturing were also visible. One mother glanced out the window and, to her horror, beheld her three-year-old having oral sex with a five-year-old neighbor boy, a technique he could only have learned from deliberate and perverted tutorials.

Dr. Roland Summit, a Los Angeles County psychiatrist acting as media representative for the parents of the McMartin children, said the district attorney had evidence to indict thirty individuals who had never been arrested. In addition, twenty-three of the parents filed a civil suit against the McMartin preschool, alleging child prostitution and pornography. The civil suit submitted that the preschool was really a cover for a large-scale "kiddie porn" production studio. The suit laid out further charges of sadistic cruelty, including acts of urinating on, defecating on, and spanking children. Certain adults, it was claimed, had committed sodomy, rape, forced fellatio and cunnilinguis, and penetrating the children's bodies with blunt objects.

The suit alleged that some pupils were given tranquilizers and habit-forming narcotics. It mentioned bomb threats to the children's homes as well. Other preschools in the Los Angeles vicinity were shuttered because of the accusations.

Even if the satanic cult claims were totally disproven, few investigators would have doubted that the children had been molested sexually. Therapists report that from the outset the children had been talking about sexual play. A five-year-old boy who announced to his mother over and over that he was the "son of Satan" said, "I am stupid. I hate myself. I want to kill myself."

The mother of a five-year-old stated that when she tried to teach her daughter a simple prayer, the child answered, "I tried it your way. There is no God. And he doesn't listen anyway. I just know." The same child awakened in the throes of nightmares and began babbling in an unknown language. Several McMartin "alumni" recalled having been shut up with caskets that were "all dark inside with soft pillows." They were forced to spend a significant amount of time in the caskets, "so we would all know what death was like." In some cases they said they had to share the casket with a corpse.

According to the therapists, the preschoolers now displayed the hand sign of the devil with the index and fifth fingers stretched upward. The common themes in the children's spontaneous drawings were devils, devil figures, demons with occult names such as "Bassago," witches, and decapitation scenes. At the South Bay Center for Counseling, some children reportedly began chanting as if on some deep subconscious cue. Several kids said they had observed the beheading of infants, while others had been coerced into jabbing knives into babies themselves. One or two of the victims attempted to stab or strangle younger siblings, not to mention trying to set fire to their own homes.

A number of months after the beginning of the McMartin pretrial, children in other sections of Los Angeles County began confiding to parents about sexual abuse at the hands, not of school directors, but of neighbors. Media converage of rumored satanism in Manhattan Beach had not yet heated up, so the incidents could not be quickly dismissed as a "copycat" kind of confabulation perpetrated by children.

In the racially mixed community of Pico Rivera, Vicki Meyers said she began to notice odd traits in the life-style of a neighbor, with whom she went jogging routinely, according to news accounts. Meyers said the neighbor bragged excessively about her "superior children" and she had an "inverted cross" a satanist symbol, blazoned on her van. One day Meyers' younger son, Jeff, three, said he was too frightened to go to sleep because there were spiders underneath the bed. Meyers tried to assure the boy that there were, in fact, no spiders. But the child persisted. "The man down the street told me there were. It's the man who pulls my clothes off and puts me in the closet."

On investigation, Meyers and her husband, Jerry, discovered that the man came over to visit her oldest son, Scot. When Scot was queried about this, he admitted to ritualistic sex abuse that had gone on with his youngest brother. A fair-haired youngster with above average intelligence, Scot related how he had been called "the Beloved One" by his abusers and how he had been inculcated in the doctrines of the group. Other Meyers children say they witnessed infants tossed into ovens alive. The Meyers are only one of quite a few families, many of whom have left the neighborhood, whose children have made similiar, shocking accusations.

Although eighteen felony counts of child molestation were filed against the accused, the charges were dismissed by a Whittier municipal court judge in July of the same year by reason of "insufficent evidence." Meyers now lives in Fontana, California and has become her own kind of crusader against ritualistic abuse.

The Pico Rivera families found friends and advocates in the team of investigative journalist Dee Brown and the McMartin spokesperson, Dr. Summitt. According to Summitt, four common elements tend to pop up around the country with regard to ritualistic abuse, which is often connected to satanism: (1) use of cameras, (2) sadistic types of games and rituals, (3) sexual contact between children and adults, and (4) intimidation and threats or spectacles of death. Dr. Summitt was never convinced that a belief in the power of Satan is always the crucial factor behind the abuse. But he has noted that so-called satanic rituals have been utilized by adults as a premeditated strategy to terrorize juveniles into viewing what often turns out to be sadomasochistic, or perverted, sexual demonstrations. The rituals also serve to suborn the children into silence in the event police become involved.

Journalist Brown, a former teacher of special education who had logged long hours on the case, was convinced that the nauseating accounts of the McMartin and Pico Rivera children were not at all fabricated. Freelance writer John Jackson, the only representative from the media community to attend the McMartin trial daily, harbored no doubts the McMartin kids were molested. However, the aims of the abuse were not necessarily purely sexual or hedonistic. In an article in the *Daily Breeze*, Jackson wrote that the McMartin syndrome had raised the specter of a concentration camp, rather than a fleshpot or a brothel. "It points not to money or sex or the devil, but to power that ultimately indoctrinates the child into the belief system of the group."

Jackson's primary evidence for this thesis was that six of the seven McMartin defendants had been women, and that women are seldom repeat sexual abusers of children. Jackson observed that driving a stick dipped in dog feces up the rectum of a three-year-old, as one of the allegations went, is not chiefly a sexual act but an expression of cruelty. Strangely enough, the average pedophile tends to display some sort of perverted affection for the victim. The McMartin defendants gave no hint of emotion whatsoever.

ITEM: In American Fork, Utah, just twenty-four hours preceding one of the most "high holy days of the Church of Satan," an unknown culprit slaughtered two sheep, stole a lamb, and removed the animals' esophaguses and other body parts. "It used to be," American Fork police chief Randy Johnson said dryly to the local press, "that whenever we went into a drug dealer's home or apartment we'd find porn and drug paraphernalia. But more and more we are finding things dealing with satanism." He added, "Drug use and satanism are starting to go hand in hand."

At American Fork Junior High School, authorities stumbled upon a compendium of requirements for joining a satanic coven in the area. The list was handwritten and had been authored by an eighth-grader at the school. Among the fifty stipulations were adoration of the rock group Black Sabbath as well as the Ku Klux Klan, performance of oral sex, use of drugs, burning crosses, killing "666 people," taking out your grandmother, and biting off a dog's head. Beside the list was a pen sketch of a figure clutching two blood-drenched daggers poised above a corpse with the chest cut open!

ITEM: In Cedar Falls, Iowa, high school officials became "concerned" about the burgeoning interest of their charges in the black arts. A senior at Cedar Falls High School said she had been immersed in satanic worship for about four years. Through satanism "you get what you want," she said coolly, "but you pay." At age thirteen, the girl was looking for "something to hang on to, something to belong to, something to make me feel more secure." The girl already had a serious drug problem, and Satan was the answer. "Kids who are feeling low will reach for anything."

ITEM: On Boston's South Shore, police considered filing charges against a pack of alleged "devil worshipers" after raiding their "church," an abandoned munitions bunker deep in the woods of Wompatuck State Park. During the raid the cops confiscated an animal skull, a silver chalice, swords, machetes, and knives. During World War II, the bunker housed guns and ammunition. At the site, police found copious occult symbolism, including pentagrams and a five-sided, special altar of sacrifice. Many of the cult members had dressed themselves in long, black cloaks. Also in the bunker was found a life-size, enamaeled crucifix with barbed wire parodying the crown of thorns worn by Christ during his passion.

ITEM: An Indiana murderer on death row linked the practice of satanism to the activities of the Ku Klux Klan. According to Terry L. Lowery, twenty-six, who murdered thirteen-year-old Tricia Woods in 1985, cross-burning in Indiana had become old-fashioned with its conventional clientele. Killing babies was now the fashionable occupation among the newer generation.

ITEM: A teacher and several parents of junior high students in Fort Collins, Colorado, said they were outraged at the way threats associated with incidents of alleged satanism in the Poudre R-1 School District had been scanted by authorities. Audrey Marshall, a Lincoln Junior High special education teacher, remarked, "I've estimated that 30 to 40 percent of my class alone has been either vicitimized, threatened, beaten or in some way bothered or terrorized by [a large group of satanists]." Elizabeth Kleckner, a parent of one of the high schoolers, swore her daughter had been violently threatened on three occasions by certain girls who bragged about animal sacrifices and flaunted satanist insignia.

ITEM: A woman patient of a California psychiatrist and a student at the University of Missouri, Kansas City, recalled a murder she had witnessed on Halloween years ago by a satanic cult in southwest Missouri, according to news accounts. She recalled black-robed adults wearing ghoulish makeup and chanting in a strange language, while allowing themselves to be bitten by snakes. The woman reported she had been brutally assaulted sexually and hung upside down over a fire. As part of the ceremony, an unidentified man was stabbed to death. Those in attendance drained his blood, drank it, and devoured his flesh. The heart was left intact.

The linkage between satanism and criminality has a genealogy that is neither as complicated nor as obscure as prevailing public opinion often holds. Satanism, if we can believe the many different literary accounts and fashionable rumormongers of the eighteenth and nineteenth centuries, had its beginnings among the decadent nobility and Victorian gentlemen who had simply discovered a sadistically engaging form of anti-clericism. The fascination with brutal crime as a statement of contempt not merely against society but against God himself can be easily found among romantics and disaffected intellectuals from the time of the French Revolution onward. The Marquis de Sade, while not a satanist in the technical sense of the term, espoused the view that the infliction of torture and pain could be regarded as a kind of moral obedience to "nature," which revealed itself as utterly inhumane and heartless.

The notion captivated the imagination of such diverse nineteenth-century figures as Charles Baudelaire, Oscar Wilde, and Friedrich Nietzsche. Baudelaire himself was obsessed with the "powers of the dark," symbolized in the archetypal personage of Lucifer, as the source of both poetic inspiration and human redemption. Much the same sentiment lurks within the famous dictum of LaVey that the goal of human evolution is an "awareness of the flesh" and "satanism encourages its followers to indulge in their natural desires."

In his *Satanic Bible*, which since its first publication in the late 1960s has sold hundreds of thousands of copies and has reportedly been gaining extraordinary sales momentum in the last three years, LaVey himself offers justification, if not with specific intention, for homicide. The "blood of the freshly slaughtered victim" in the satanic sacrifice, he says, serves to "throw the energy" into an "atmosphere of the magical working." The power of the magician is thus increased. The same idea, of course, was fundamental to the murderous magic of Constanzo and his adepts.

LaVey waffles, almost to the brink of bald obscurity, in order to leave the impression that the sacrifice is symbolic, not actual. Yet in the end he minces few words. A "fit and proper human sacrifice," he says, is whoever has done an injustice to the satanist—in other words, someone who "is asking to be cursed" because of their behavior.

LaVey and other apologists for contemporary satanic worship and behavior have routinely protested that they bear no responsibility whatsoever for the "bad moon rising" over the American cultural landscape in the guise of an epidemic of satanist-inspired criminal enterprise. The fault lies with the "sickos" and demented malefactors who do not properly appreciate and who misuse the figurative, or purely theatrical, messages of satanic villainy, the apology goes.

The argument is similar to that of the purveyor of sadistic pornography who insists that his mass retailing of videos and photographs showing women under torture or in cruel bondage cannot possibly have any social impact. The blame should fall squarely upon those "perverts" who are deranged enough to walk into his store and furnish him with a livelihood. Not only moral crusaders, but feminist groups appalled at the rise in gratuitous violence against women have been prone to disagree.

Such a position, moreover, has not been favored by Supreme Court decisions. In addition to rejecting the notion that the severe degradation of human beings in the public media is not susceptible to public oversight and legal restriction because of First Amendment guarantees, the Supreme Court for generations has denied that the user of socially objectional materials is the only one accountable. Oliver Wendell Holmes' dictum that the boundaries of free speech do not extend as far as yelling, "Fire!" in a crowded theater has clear application in the case of satanism as a form of "religious" advocacy.

ITEM: Bunny Nicole Dixon, a teenager from Daytona Beach, Florida, was sentenced to fifty years in state prison after entering a plea of no contest to the kidnapping, satanic mutilation, and slaying of Ngoc Van Dang, a Vietnamese immigrant. Circuit Judge S. James Foxman gave the girl, a ninth-grade dropout, a double sentence because of the horror and severity of the crime. Dixon had been labeled a "satan worshiper" in court by three of her coconspirators. Dang had been abducted and brutally slain after picking up Dixon on an Orlando street.

Another defendant in the case testified that Dixon planned the murder after conducting a satanic ritual with the use of a Ouija board. According to the court hearings, Dixon had been inspired to commit the crime through her constant reading and study of *The Satanic Bible*. She wanted to have sex with the Devil and "to bear the Antichrist." The accused had carved a large, upside-down cross on Dang's chest to mark him as a sacrifice, then hauled him into the woods and shot him seven times.

ITEM: Earl Hill, coordinator of the adolescent chemical dependency program at St. Francis Medical Center in Pittsburgh, told a local newspaper that his agency had in just two years logged up to sixty incidents involving teenagers using drugs in the cult practices of satanism. The kids sacrifice pigs, goats, chickens, dogs, and cats, according to Hill, then cut off their heads and drink the blood. "When we talk to them about a higher power, they say, 'Yes, you mean Satan," Hill observed. The adolescents fortify their rituals with LSD and PCP, or angel dust, according to another counselor. "We're seeing a higher percentage of drug cases involving cult practices," one counselor observed.

ITEM: El Paso teenager Jessie Villalobos was interviewed by police about satanic cult activity in West Texas, which he said had accounted for the deaths of at least three innocent people, according to published accounts." Villalobos, moved to Los Angeles, told of watching members of a southern California cult chop off the head of a 10-year-old girl. "They'll kill again, if the rituals keep on," he said. "They'll just keep on killing."

ITEM: Smart and popular Michelle Kimball, fifteen, of Bristol, Vermont, stunned classmates by committing suicide with a gunshot wound to the forehead. Investigators surmised that the death had been due to her belief in satanism. Michelle had made frequent mention of her adoration of Satan in her diaries. "The devil [is] the person to worship," she had reportedly confided to friends. Kimball also cited lyrics from such "satanic metal" groups as Judas Priest and Black Sabbath. The local newspaper observed that "satanism . . . may appear to parents and friends as just one more manifestation of the rebellious teen years."

ITEM: Police in Douglas County, Georgia, exhumed from a shallow grave the corpse of fifteen-year-old Teresa Simmons and arrested three of her friends, who confessed to killing her. During the burial, the youths had allegedly conducted a satanic ritual, derived from a popular occult book, to the accompaniment of heavy metal music. About the same time, in the town of Roswell, the cops found human fingers in a house. Candles were stuck to the fingernails. Police linked the two murders.

ITEM: In Hoffman Estates, Illinois, a northwest Chicago suburb, the Reverend Jack Dewes of the St. Hubert Catholic Church entered the sanctuary to prepare Sunday Mass. At first he spotted ashes on the floor, then a handwritten letter on the marble altar that said: "Satan is the one and only God to worship. The black hand of death shall be laid upon your forehead and you shall die at the mercy of Satan." The message was signed by "Grim Reaper" and "Cobra of Death." "Satanism has such a strong grip on some impressionable teenagers that they must undergo psychiatric counseling," said Hoffman Estates detective Michael Brady.

ITEM: A coven of self-described "black witches" in Houston, Texas, protested to the newspapers that their reputation was in jeopardy because of all the reports of satanist-related crime. "We don't drink blood. Maybe we'll have a rare steak once in awhile," they told a reporter. Satanists do not even consider "Satan" to be the embodiment of the power of evil, one woman said, and they do not cast spells to hurt people. Satan is, on the contrary, the "embodiment of life." Rituals are for fun—pure and simple. "You put on a robe, it puts you in the mood."

ITEM: In Ignacio, Colorado, local law enforcement personnel sought to reassure parents that they did not have a satanic cult problem in their community, "just some kids dabbling in this stuff." About sixty people, who crowded into the Ignacio Fine Arts Auditorium, were told by police that "every time there's a road kill, the so-called satanists are taking credit for it." Father Bill Groves of St. Ignatius Church said he was convinced that "children involved in satanism are reaching out for a positive influence in their lives."

ITEM: About the same time in the same part of the country, the bludgeoned body of Ernest Weil, sixty-five, a retired Denver aerospace engineer, was found in a car trunk near a Gallup, New Mexico, watering hole. "Satanic graffiti, for lack of a better term," noted Gallup assistant district attorney Anthony Porter, "was written on the rocks around the watering hole, and we believe some of the graffiti appears to have been made from the victim's blood." Nearby rocks bore the bloody lettering S.O.D., which according to Porter stood for "Sisters of the Devil," and the word *Metallica*. Porter said he believed the motive for the killing was robbery, not satanism. Two young Navajos were taken into custody as suspects in the killing.

ITEM: In Gilbert, New York, three men and two juveniles were arrested in connection with the kidnapping and ritual molestation of a fifteen-year-old boy. The quintet allegedly bound the victim, forced him to wear a spiked collar, laid him spread-eagle in the center of a pentagram, and performed a black mass. The victim was released after ninety minutes but was warned that "if you tell anyone what we did to you, we'll come back and kill you." Gerald Miller, a guidance counselor at Pleasant Valley High School, where the adult members of the group attended classes, said he was very concerned that the incident might "become a witch hunt, where a kid who listens to rock music becomes ostracized."

ITEM: The cops in San Diego, California, came upon an abandoned pump house swathed in satanic graffiti. One of the inscriptions on the wall read, "Welcome to Hell." Others proclaimed "Satan lives" and "Sabbath, Bloody Sabbath." A seminar on the problem of adolescent satanism held by the San Diego County Sheriff's Department Juvenile Diversion Unit was attended by over 350 law enforcement professionals as well as probation officers, educators, and mental health personnel. At the seminar, police began to talk avidly of hitherto "unexplained" and peculiar findings, such as scribblings on buildings and altar sites, that pointed to satanic activity. Attendees at the conference heard documented accounts of kidnapping, murder, robbery, dope-peddling, extortion, and sexual aggression related to satanic cults in California.

ITEM: In Dothan, Alabama, vandals broke into a little country church, destroyed the organ, overturned the altar, and ruined the carpet and pews. They also scribbled satanic slogans and a death threat to the president. The messages on the church walls were "Those who enter will kneel upon the Lamb's throat with us," "The beast is calling for you," and "Reagan will die." The satanic symbols were lifted from rock albums.

ITEM: In the east Texas woods near the town of Kountze, local police have actually set up a laboratory and simulation center to train rookies and veteran officers in techniques for identifying and analyzing satanic ritual crime. East Texas in the last few years has witnessed an explosion of satanic cult activity that includes the defacement of buildings, animal mutilations, and ongoing trespass against private property. According to area authorties, the vast majority of the incidents can be correlated with drug trafficking. Two satanic murders, as in Matamoros, included as the victims rival drug operators and informants.

ITEM: In March 1989, rumors began to balloon in Cambria County, Indiana, about satanists who held nocturnal rites in the woods and harassed area citizens. Business people, lawyers, and law enforcement officials claimed to have been harassed by threatening telephone calls. A caller informed the wife of a local police chief that her husband was going to be killed. Vigilante groups began to form. "I have a feeling some kids may be dabbling in satanism for kicks, but I don't think there is a problem," said Sgt. Gary Rumgay of the state police. "I feel the rumors have gotten out of hand." He added that there is no law against people worshiping the devil. "However, we will take necessary action if there is any sign of criminal activity."

ITEM: The Illinois general assembly voted overwhelmingly to approve legislation that would curb satanic crime. Measures sent to the governor were intended to instruct judges to entertain stiffer penalties for people convicted of torturing and kidnapping humans or animals, as well as stealing corpses and desecrating property. The laws would also create a new offense of "ritual mutilation," punishable by up to seven years in prison and a $10,000 fine. Attempts to coerce others into suicide would face as many as seven years in prison.

Law enforcement officials, who by profession usually take a hard-bitten and empirical approach to their subjects of inquiry, have been the most straightforward about the intimate connection between satanism as a "religious" phenomenon and the varieties of criminal behavior.

In its February 1987 edition, *Police* magazine offered a rundown of clues by which criminal investigators might espy occult motivations behind apparently senseless or strange misdeeds. The magazine listed the presence of the satanic pentagrams and scrawlings in the satanic or rune alphabet; dismembered animal or human remains including surgical removal of vital organs; suspects wearing certain kinds of tattoos such as black panthers, goat's heads, inverted crosses, black widow spiders, knives dripping blood; the use of ritual items at cult sites like bells, gongs, crucibles, and stone altars; collections of human bones, which supposedly contain the magical potency of the victim; and the careful manipulation of herbs and drugs.

The National Sheriff has urged that "law enforcement managers [must] realize this renewed interest in Satanism and the occult is a serious national problem. Authorities must meet the challenge by assuring these crimes are detected, reported and prosecuted for what they are: satanic related." The National Sheriff's Association recommends a twelve-pronged approach: increased awareness of the "satanic trend" by law enforcement; maintenance of detailed records on satanic crimes; dissemination of information; collaborative intelligence gathering; state task forces for coordination of occult crimes; state and federal computer utilization; standardized report forms recognizing the distinctive character of occult behavior; development of reliable informants; allocation of adequate department resources; general instruction for police recruits; in-depth training for specialized investigators; and the close involvement of community and private sector resources.

By and large the police response nationwide has been heroic, but confused. While local cops and sheriff's deputies have crammed by the thousands into special seminars arranged with the special aim of teaching about "occult crime," certain kinds of political prejudices and social reservations have intruded. Police are constantly reminded by superiors and civil libertarians that they must not prosecute people for their religious "beliefs," when in fact many of the beliefs in question explicitly encourage criminal activity, which is not guaranteed under the Constitution. Police instead must look for specific violations of the law and only then prosecute or intervene.

The FBI keeps centralized statistics on particular types of crime and serves as an authoritative sounding board for discussions among law enforcement officials. It could easily exert leadership, decanting authentic from bogus information, to help deal with the occult crime wave. Strangely, and in a quite uncharacteristic manner, the FBI has muddied the waters instead.

While hundreds of cops almost every day are confronted with mutilated animal caracasses, drug-related slayings with macabre and occult overtones, religious desecrations, and neo-Nazi acts of violence and terrorism, the bureau's "satanist expert," Ken Lanning, has endeavored to discredit virtually anyone inside or outside of law enforcement who thinks ritual crime in America might somehow be a problem. Lanning's method of operation has been bizarre. Imagine some top official in the Drug Enforcement Administration jetting around the country and screeching that the current concern about cocaine abuse and violence is an infringement on the fundamental right to privacy among Colombian traffickers. And imagine this official also claiming that the "war on drugs" is nothing

BAD MOON RISING / 75

more than a paranoid, hysterical psychosis shared by police officers, mental health professionals, the media, and, of course, the entire American public.

That, however, has been very much Lanning's approach. As a result, satanist criminals have had one of their best friends, if only for legitimate philosophical reasons, at the highest level of national law enforcement. In a paper titled "Satanic, Occult, Ritualistic Crime: A Law Enforcement Perspective," prepared for the National Center for Missing and Exploited Children, Lanning rakes the reader with volley after volley of emotional diatribe, innuendo, nonsequitur, glittering and unsupported generality, and bogus appeal to his own authority as the FBI's "supervisory special agent" for the bureau's Behavioral Science Instruction and Research Unit in Quantico, Virginia. Written with the literacy, the research sophistication, and the rhetorical finesse of a high school sophomore, Lanning's piece—which he has waved about to make the case that there really can be no such thing as serious satanic crime—examines no cases, sifts through no evidence, and cites no literature. It merely growls, bullies, and browbeats with all the subtlety of a charging mastodon.

The essay also trivializes the issue in a rather strange fashion. For example:

Since 1972, the author has lectured about sexual ritualism. This is nothing more than repeatedly engaging in an act or series of acts in [sic] certain manner because of a *sexual* need.

Satanism may also have a positive social function, according to Lanning. "Ritualistic crime may fulfill the cultural, spiritual, sexual and psychological needs of an offender." While gross physical abuse or molestation of children—fondling and exposing oneself—"may be criminal if performed for sexual gratification," once the "acts of ritualistic abuse are performed for spiritual indoctrination, potential prosecution can be jeopardized." Moreover, "in some cases the ritualistic activity and the child abuse may be integral parts of some spiritual belief system." Such statements, however, are not only fulsome; they are also fallacious. Criminal sexual abuse has no cover under the law, even a religious one, although Lanning gives the impression that it may—which is highly irregular for someone in law enforcement.

Religious satanists routinely complain that they are hounded for their anomalous beliefs, which is really not true at all. When the Church of Satan started holding black masses in front of television cameras back in the sixties and chanting, "Hail Satan," there were no arrests, let alone police seminars. The problem came to a head during this decade when law enforcement began to couple increasing incidents of murder, destruction, injury, and cruelty with such beliefs.

The strident argument of satanists, and their "defenders" such as Lanning, that they are under suspicion because of their religious convictions alone resembles the old-line Mafia plaint that busts of syndicate activities were nothing more than outbreaks of bigotry toward Italians. Satanic crime has benefited immensely from the spurious preoccupation with First Amendment guarantees. If practitioners of a religion in their own literature openly urge antisocial behavior, it is certainly not "paranoid" of authorities to keep a close eye on them. The government does the same for members of the Shiite sect of Islam, which sponsors terrorism. Why should it not do the same for satanists?

As Bette Naysmith, chair of the Ritual Abuse Advisory Committee for the Chicago-based Cult Awareness Network, phrased it in a letter to city mayor Richard M. Daley, "Please be assured that our concerns relate to *criminal acts* and not a specific religious belief system. . . . Clearly, we are talking about the criminal acts *committed under the guise of the First Amendment,* under the umbrella of a religious, political therapy. . . . These crimes include, but are not limited to, child abuse, child pornography, child prostitution, theft, fraud, arson, vandalism, illegal drugs, illegal weapons, and murder." From March to May of 1989, Naysmith's organization handled 520 calls involving satanism and ritual abuse from around the country and 55 in the city of Chicago alone.

There are individual cops who have made supererogatory and courageous efforts both to put the problem in perspective and to offer moderate and cogent solutions. Chicago's Robert Simandl, for example, has been a pioneer in showing the linkages nationwide between activities of certain satanist groups. Recently, Simandl undertook to examine claims of thirty patients in Illinois mental institutions who had recounted satanic crimes in different states, including murder, drug trafficking, pornography, child prostitution, and kidnapping. San Francisco's Sandi Gallant has also been instrumental in alerting police around the country to the signs and behavioral quirks of criminal satanism. Among other things, Gallant advised a pair of detectives from Michigan on why a fifteen-year-old satanist shot his brother to death on Candlemas eve, a midwinter church holiday. According to Gallant, "It's the consistency in the stories that continue to make me take this whole thing seriously."

Dr. Dale Griffis, a police captain from Tiffin, Ohio, and a pioneer and leading expert in the investigation of occult crime, has developed a typology that has become operative for many in law enforcement.

The first, and most widespread, type of satanic activity he terms *experimental.* Experimental satanists may act by themselves, or with others, in a generally disorganized fashion. Experimental satanism has erupted within adolescent culture. The kids are simply "searching for power," says Griffis. "The youth of today are often adrift in a world without standards and values, and the occult fills a need for secrecy, identity, power, and provides a belief system that seems to make their lives take on a new meaning."

The second kind is the *occult cult*. The occult cult is characterized by a charismatic leader, as in the Matamoros case. Recruitment for these forms of cults involve sex, drugs, music, or fantasy role-playing games. Their "use of mental manipulation tends to lead toward violent or criminal activity." Such cults will set up ceremonial sites in remote areas and exploit the ritual process to bond members into criminal activity. Such groups pose a serious danger to both the citizenry and to police.

The third group, according to Griffis, is the *self-styled satanist*. Self-styled satanists often have biological or psychological disorders and embellish them with the language or trappings of the occult. They may be construed as individuals with deep-seated criminal tendencies, for which satanism provides a vocabulary to symbolize and act out deviant, patterned behavior. Very often they can be serial killers, sexual deviants, or child molesters. They may be skilled in mind control techniques, stage magic, and mood-setting. Charles Manson, who called himself the "Devil" and would frequently use demonic symbols, is a premier example of the self-styled satanist. The personality profile described by Dr. Joel Norris in his book *Serial Killers* can often be a flashpoint for satanic activity. Griffis estimates, however, that the self-styled category applies to only about 5 percent of satanist-related criminals.

Finally, there is the *traditional satanist*, such as Anton LaVey of the Church of Satan and Michael Aquino of the Temple of Set. Griffis warns about jumping to conclusions in connecting traditional satanism with crime. "The worship of Satan is not new and frankly, little is known about the number of true traditional satanists in society today."

The latter observation may become increasingly irrelevant because the word *satanism* has stuck to an expanding spectrum of violent, deviant behavior for which the term *ritual crime* has come to serve. Whether "traditional" satanists, who assert their right to protection under the First Amendment, ever truly carry out the evil that they vaunt and relish in their writings may be immaterial. Like IBM personal computers, their prized beliefs may have been "cloned" and retailed in a cognate form by a host of singular entrepreneurs and criminal cartels.

It is the cultural impact that counts in the long haul.

NOTES

1. Anton Szandor LaVey, *The Satanic Bible* (New York, Avon Books, 1970), p. 87.

Part II.

THE GENEOLOGY OF DARKNESS

CHAPTER 4.

The Occult Underworld

In the house of pain there are ten thousand shrines.
——ALEISTER CROWLEY

Constanzo, the Hardy boys, and nameless cohorts of satanic cult devotees and "dabblers" could not have proliferated in police files around the nation without a context and a backlight.

The problem of why the siege of American culture flared in the first place follows from the question of why the American counterculture's habit of toying with hallucinogens in the 1960s ballooned into the vast and terrifying "drug crisis" of the 1980s. It also comports with the question of why the culture of postwar folk music evolved into the rock industry, which eventually spawned the cacaphonous, and frequently sinister, "metal" bands of recent years.

Satanism is the name we have conferred, perhaps because of the very eminence of the symbol of God's adversary in Judaeo-Christian history, on the unruly subcurrents of deliberate and ritualized destruction in this late nuclear age. Satanism is the ideology of decadence that has been raised to a computation, to an art form. In the backwash of the well-known proclamation of God's death, explicit worship of the figure of Satan has been growing, particularly among the young who would worship violence as a purpose rather than accept the glib, agnostic premise that there is no purpose at all.

Young Pete Roland was compelled to construct in his mind, through the aid of language and imagery supplied by pop music and occultism, the sense of the presence of an all-seeing and encompassing "dark father." His music-wrought Darth Vader was the sole salve to a psychic burden of chaos and abuse that could be redeemed no longer, as it had been for centuries, by the "blood of the Lamb." In an odd but almost stereotypical fashion, the Hardy boys thirsted for a primitive form of blood atonement. The same can be said, although in a much higher pitch of moral outrage, about the sacrifices performed by Constanzo and his troop of thugs. The grim illusion fostered in the psyches of today's satanic occultists is that of open-ended personal power that can be obtained through rapine and lawlessness.

Yet the illusion did not spring full-blown in battle armor from the fractured head of "Christian civilization." It had been rankling, seething, and fermenting in the entrails of Western culture for decades, if not centuries. Just as illegal drugs after about 1967 suddenly surged out of the back alleys and the blues bars of America's urban ghettoes into colleges and universities and eventually into the living rooms of the professional middle class, so the darkest strains of magical mania seeped out of the occult underworld, where they had rankled for centuries, and into the mainstream.

The occult underworld cannot be gauged by any relevant standard apart from an inspection of the moldering archives of secret societies and lodges, which have remained a pervasive, but routinely overlooked, feature of the Western historical landscape. The history and sociology of these secret organizations is an emergent field in its own right. Yet consideration of the very subject matter among the intelligentsia today tends unfortunately to induce discomfort, as does the very topic of satanism. Particularly in the United States, the notion that secret assemblies are at work to achieve grandiose and clandestine aims has regularly rubbed hard against the grain of American democracy and political liberalism. The idea, however, had been almost an item of stock-in-trade for centuries among Europeans, whose memoirs and chronicles are chock full with tales of palace intrigues, heretical murmurings, and carefully orchestrated assassination schemes. Distaste for talk about veiled intrigue has been carried to such an extreme in the past twenty years that any mention of such activity automatically brings the ignorant response and hysterical cry of "conspiratorial thinking," as if conspiracies were not a fact of life, notwithstanding a staple contribution to the making of world history.

The study of the occult underworld, especially since the late eighteenth century, comprises an examination of "conspiratorial" visionaries who, though not necessarily bent on destroying the entire order of things or storming the citadels of influence themselves, were nonetheless committed with militant intent to upending the political and cultural order of the day. Their motives were less pragmatic than "religious." The central strand winding through the literature of the occult underworld is the passionate judgment that Christian civilization, which has persisted over a thousand years, is corrupt and hypocritical and that a new "natural" regime of instinctual spontaneity and untrammeled free will must burst the fetters of time. Strikingly, such an attitude, which may be described as *neobarbarism*, runs all the way down the line from the French radicals of the 1700s, many of whom practiced a discrete and finely cultivated form of satanism, to LaVey himself. It also constitutes the major message of contemporary "punks" and skinheads. Spokespersons for the new barbarism, such as San Francisco's Robert Heick, talk openly and effusively about the recovery of something known as *primordial instinctuality*—or, as LaVey would say, not so much the veneration of the evil "angel" known as Satan but the plenary, pleasurable, and guiltless exploration of the "darkest" proddings of human existence.

Two centuries ago such a philosophy would have been identified with the self-justifying life-style of the "rake." Yet by the late twentieth century the rake's progress had gone from mere "wicked and ungodly" deport-ment, as the mark of innate human depravity, to a rude metaphysics of vengeance and violence. If occultism itself has traditionally been typecast as "rejected knowledge," then by behavioral criteria alone satanism represents a philosophical apology for what Sigmund Freud termed the "return of the repressed."

The origin and growth of the occult underworld along these lines can be traced all the way back to the first glimmerings of the modern era when the scientific critique of the medieval Christian worldview gained stature. The tradition of "secret knowledge" guarded by an equally secret fraternity or sorority, into which a follower had to be initiated, had been preserved from Greek and Roman times, even under the vigilant watch of the Catholic Church, as part of what has conventionally been called the *hermetic* or *Gnostic* heritage. During the Renaissance—approximately the fourteenth through the sixteenth centuries—hermeticism became not only respectable but fashionable among Europe's educated elites. By the seventeenth century it had permeated the Protestant countries, where it was ensconced as the spirit of *Freemasonry*, or what are popularly known as the Masonic orders. Extolling the God of "nature" and "nature's laws" over the God of biblical revelation, Freemasonry served as the popular faith of the Age of Reason, lasting from the late 1600s to about the time of the French Revolution in 1789.

Masonry was a gentleman's club for religious doubters, or even libertines. And despite popular hypotheses of murky, "Masonic conspir-acies" to overthrow the Christian religion and existing forms of govern-ment that swirled around as far back as the early eighteenth century, the historical tablets clearly indicate that the majority of Masons were really armchair intellectuals who maintained tight organizational control by offering quick-and-easy access to the "ancient mysteries." The "myste-ries" themselves turned out to be little more than imaginatively embroi-dered exercises from old Egypt and Babylon, mingled with some Muslim mysticism. Many of the signers of America's Declaration of Indepen-dence were members of the "secret fraternity" of Masons. But there are few data to support the supposition that such a secret society has ever been in control politically in this country.

The myth of the Masonic conspiracy and its satanic underpinnings appears to have arisen about the time of the French Revolution as the outgrowth of a poorly understood, but well-documented, effort of more sinister occultists to infiltrate and manipulate established Masonic lodges.

During the late eighteenth and ninteenth centuries the more conventional and recognized "secret brotherhoods" became prey for occult
entrepreneurs seeking to subvert Masonic rationalism and its high-toned
ethical philosophy. The entrepreneurs introduced sexual magic and the
advocacy of moral license.

Whereas Masonry originally had appealed to "freethinkers" because of
its challenge to the leaden dogmas of orthodox Christianity, the new
"magical" Masonry had much the same allure to those steeped in the
Enlightenment culture of reason and tolerance. What came to be called
Romanticism, obsessed as it was with the terrifying and the irrational, can
be traced overall to the influence of magical Masonry. It was among the
magical Masons that satanism as a secret order within a secret society
initially surfaced.

A colorful forerunner of modernity's black magical adepts was a group
of prominent Londoners who called themselves the Hell Fire Club, which
thrived around the period of the American Revolution. The Hell Fire
Club was founded by the English baronet Sir Francis Dashwood, heir to a
great fortune and the intimate colleague of King George III. Benjamin
Franklin visited the Hell Fire Club while in England, most likely to gain
political influence. Numbered among its members were the British prime
minister, the chancellor of the exchequer, the lord mayor of London, the
first lord of the admiralty, the son of the archbishop of Canterbury, the
Prince of Wales, and sundry well-known poets and artists, including the
painter William Hogarth. The association itself was dedicated to "Black
Magic, sexual orgies, and political conspiracies," though not necessarily
in that order.

At first, Sir Francis named his group the Friars of St. Francis of
Wycombe. Sir Francis adopted the name of the order as a slur against the
established church hierarchy. In 1752 he obtained a "clubhouse" in the
form of a ruined medieval abbey on the bank of the Thames near Marlow.
In the next century the poet Shelley would go to the abbey to compose
poems. Dashwood decorated the walls of the abbey with obscene Roman
frescoes. He purchased lavish furniture, designed for fornicating, to be
used by the "monks" and their sexual conquests. The "rule" of the order,
which would become infamous as the precise, same motto of a later,
notorious British occultist, Aleister Crowley, was simply "Do what thou
wilt." Inside the clubhouse, Sir Francis would inaugurate the Black Mass
by pouring brandy laced with brimstone into glasses shaped like the
Devil's horns. After the recitation of "Do what thou wilt," they would sing
and drink a toast to the "powers of darkness." Virgins were specially
purchased for ceremonies, and wealthy socialites sometimes attended as
masked "nuns" at the festivities.

For a while the habitues of the Hell Fire Club actually made most of the
important political decisions affecting England. Partisans of democracy
and the new theory of the "rights of man," they prevented George III

from taking what had been contemplated as very drastic steps against the American colonies, thus ensuring the fateful outcome of their war of independence. Although the Hell Fire Club was frequently accused of being "Catholic," most likely Dashwood was influenced significantly by the more perverted elements of club Masonry that had been creeping into London throughout the eighteenth century. Mocking Catholicism was quite common among the Masonic orders, and the prevalence of Egyptian statuary and nomenclature during the "services" of the Black Mass point in this direction.

The most notorious sect of magical Masons, often branded the great legendary malefactors behind *all* world historical conspiracies, were the so-called *Illuminati*, or "the illumined ones." Although conventional historians nowadays are apt to ignore the Illuminati in their treatment of modern Europe and sometimes go so far as to deny their existence, there is no doubt the "illumined ones" not only had a significant place in the early modern era, they also had a broad impact that is beginning at last to be appreciated.

The Illuminati were a furtive association founded in 1776 by a renegade German Jesuit professor, and a disillusioned Mason, named Adam Weishaupt. Weishaupt, who taught for a while at the University of Ingolstadt in Bavaria, wanted both to capsize Christianity and to convert Masonry into a revolutionary brigade. Though dogged by police and spurned by the churches and the lodges alike, Weishaupt and his followers were able to carry out on a remarkable scale, as one of his biographers says, the "subversive purpose" of "the revolutionary education of the members of the Order for the transformation of existing society."[1]

Weishaupt's "revolutionary education," however, was as much occultic as it was political. Credible research has linked the symbols and rituals of Weishaupt's "illumined" body to the sixteenth-century Middle Eastern cult of the Roshaniya—a highly effective, political terrorist squad in the mountain kingdom of Afghanistan. The Roshaniya cult may, in turn, have appropriated from India the elements of black, sexual magic termed *tantrism*. In the hands of Aleister Crowley, tantrism became the focus of twentieth-century satanist rituals.

The Illuminati were self-avowedly conspiratorial. In fact, they urged initiates to assassinate princes and to influence men of status by seducing and winning the confidence of their women. In addition, there is firm evidence that many of the Jacobin leaders of the French Revolution were backed by the Illuminati. Weishaupt's disciples, who voraciously read atheistic French philosophers, had in fact targeted France ten years before the fall of the Bastille. The oath of allegiance to the Illuminati centered on their unswerving willingness to kill, or be killed, both to promote the order and to avoid betrayal. "Lightning does not strike so quickly as the dagger which will reach thee wherever thou mayest be" went a passage from the presumed initiation rite.[2]

The satanic character of Illuminism can be discerned in witness reports of its ceremonies. The chateau of the Marquis de Geradin Ermenonville outside Paris was the site for many of the major Illuminist initiations. Black magic indeed seems to have been a secret and perverted pastime of the French nobility, ranging back as far as the fifteenth century. That was when a certain Gilles de Rais was discovered to have kidnapped children and tortured and murdered them in horrid fashion as part of his performance of the Black Mass. The candidate to the Illuminati initiation was conducted through a long, dark tunnel into a great vestibule adorned with black drapings and genuine corpses wrapped in shrouds. In the center of the hall the initiate would behold an altar composed of human skeletons. Two men dressed as ghosts would then appear and would tie a pink ribbon, which had been dipped in blood and bore the image of Our Lady of Loretto, around the forehead. A crucifix would be placed in his hand, and his clothes burned on a funeral pyre. Crosses of blood would be painted on his body.

As the fire mounted, a voice could be heard from the flames demanding that the initiate swear to sever all bonds with parents, brothers and sisters, wives, friends, and lieges. He would be told that he now abided in "another dimension" of existence and that he gave all loyalty to what later occultists would call a great, invisible "secret chief" that watched over all things. The initiate too would become a "spy" for the chief. He would be taught the art of poisoning and be bidden to become an agent of intrigue for the sake of the hierophant who was speaking to him. Finally, a candelabra with seven black tapers would be set down in front of a chalice of human blood. The initiate would wash himself with the blood and drink half a glassful.

The Illuminist hierarchy and initiatory structure was designed to mimick ordinary lodge Masonry, indisputably for the purpose of confusing and snaring ordinary members of that genial brotherhood. The secret society of Illuminati was divided first into classes and into degrees with such Masonic nomenclature as Master Mason, Scotch Novice, Epot, or Areopagite. Entrants into the so-called greater mysteries were called *Magus*, or "magician." Devotees were given knowledge of a secret script, which they used for correspondence across Europe and which bears some similarity to the seemingly unintelligble graffiti used by today's adolescent satanists.

Illuminist secret societies spread all across Europe during the late eighteenth century. Tadeusz Grabianka, a wealthy Polish estate owner and eccentric, subsidized and propogated the views of a leading Illuminist group in southern France known as the Avignon Illuminati. He was said to have ambitions of being elected king of Poland and made considerable efforts to influence the czarist rule in Russia. Grabianka claimed to be in possession of the "great mystery," which would unite Masonry and Christianity in a new social, revolutionary synthesis.

The point to bear in mind is that Illuminism aimed from its outset to accomplish what alchemists and occultists have called the "great work" as a social and political undertaking. The "magical" objective of the Illuminati was abolition of a millenium of feudalism together with the creation of a universal, utopian society that knitted together all humankind.

At the same time, Illuminist politics were fired by a self-conscious worship of the deepest and most impelling instinctual urgings of the human organism. Only the reign of the violent and repressed would be sufficient to "liberate" humanity from the tyranny of religion, law, and class domination. The notion was to become the turnkey of revolutionary doctrine from Marx to Mao, and it also highlights not just the close connection between nazism and satanism but also the ongoing affinity throughout the nineteenth and twentieth centuries between occultism, social anarchism, organized criminality, and what has been called the *aesthetic terrorism* of the cultural avant-garde.

If Weishaupt's specific cabal had petered out on the eve of the Napoleonic era, as most historical observers concur it had, it was not because Illuminism was irrelevant and exhausted but because its outlook had diffused throughout revolutionary Europe. Thus, the historian James Billington's thesis that Illuminist occultism was, in fact, the watershed of the entire nineteenth century "revolutionary faith" is far more cogent than it appears at first glance.[3] Illuminism was Masonic magic with a *this-worldly* program. But it was not in the realm of revolutionary politics, with its amoral passions and fanatical advocacy of world upheaval, that the "blood cultism" characterizing modern satanism held its grip. It was among the artists, poets, novelists, and radical *literati* of the nineteenth century where the cult found its most stalwart enthusiasts.

In form, if not substance, the satanism of the nineteenth century was a revival of certain heresies of the High Middle Ages, particularly what was known as Catharism in Italy and Albigensianism in France. The *Cathari*, or "pure ones," and the Albigensians, who took their name from a town in southern France, engaged in a type of religious cultism deriving from the ancient Persian faith of Zoroastrianism, which in its later variations became Mithraism and Manicheanism.

The old Persian religion was *dualistic*—it held that the universe was a battleground for the perpetual struggle between the principles of darkness and light. Orthodox Zoroastrianism contended that at the close of time the God of light would subjugate the powers of darkness. But Mithraism especially, as well as Manicheanism, stressed an unending tension between the two cosmic powers, which could be overcome only through an influx of "higher knowledge" into the consciousness of the initiate. Manicheanism was transmitted by way of the Middle East to Western Christianity. It seems to have taken root along the trade routes of the Mediterranean in the wake of the Crusades.

Different Manichean "heresies" were widely popular with the merchant classes and the wealthy nobility, who found them a convenient cudgel in their struggles with the pope at Rome. The papacy finally turned the weapon of crusading against the Manichean heretics, but their teachings persisted on the sly for centuries. Masonry itself may have its roots in the medieval forms of Manicheanism.

The most persuasive evidence for this surmise is the tradition of the legendary crusading fraternity known as the Knights Templar. The Templars were persecuted and dissolved by the king of France in the early 1300s. The crown accused the Templars, probably with little justice, of reviling the cross of Christ and engaging in strange ritual practices, about which scholars have debated for centuries but which seem to correspond in many levels to Catharism or its Manichean counterparts. Stories about the martyred Templars became the foundation for the legacy of the Masons.

Neither the Templars nor the Manichean heretics were "devil worshipers" in the strict sense of the word, even though the former had been charged with secretly worshiping a grotesque horned figure dubbed "Baphomet," whom modern satanists revere. The link between Manicheanism and satanism, and ultimately with the modern occult underworld, can be espied in the dualistic doctrine that "good" and "evil," or light and darkness, are equivalent. Since good has no priority over its opposite, the immersion of the devotee in the black abyss of things and what society might consider depraved conduct represents a valid path in the quest for "salvation."

The connection is made in an obscure, semifictional narrative by the nineteenth-century French decadent J. K. Huysmans. In his book *La-Bas*, translated as "Down There," Huysmans captures a conversation with an occultist named Des Hermies. According to Des Hermies, who defends the growth of modern satanism as a vital therapy against soulless "materialism," Manicheanism never went away. "The Principle of Good and the Principle of Evil, the God of Light and the God of Darkness, two rivals, are fighting for our souls. That's at least clear. Right now it is evident that the Evil God has the upper hand and is reigning over the world as master."[4]

The so-called Black Mass, which the Inquisition accused witches and alleged diabolists of performing, was not first aimed as a parody of the church's Holy Communion. Instead it evolved from Cathar ritual, which changed the meaning of the Catholic rite of redemption into a sacramental affirmation of the balance between heaven and hell. The use of a naked woman as an altar, and the substitution of fecal matter for the consecrated host, were not simply blasphemy. There were direct expressions of the dualistic idea that the horrible and the glorious, the shadowy and the resplendent, must be exhibited together as the supreme revelation of "secret knowledge."

In medieval Catharism, this secret knowledge was identified with the figure of Lucifer, meaning "light-bearer" in Latin and associated in heretical thought with the great illumination that stems from the mind fastening on the dual face of good and evil. In the twelfth and thirteenth centuries there thrived offshoots of the Cathari calling themselves "Luciferians." The Luciferians were noted for such disgusting rituals as kissing a toad or the buttocks of a priest, not to mention the veneration of a black cat.

These same practices, resembling the lurid antics for which witches were customarily despised by the ecclesiastical authorities in later centuries, did not spring from the pagan peasantry. Intead they can be traced to the experimental rituals of certain "invisible colleges" within the Catholic church itself. The chief tenet of the Luciferian Catharists, many of whom deliberately infiltrated the monastic societies in order to undermine orthodoxy, was that the "evil" entity known as Satan had been wronged by God. By bringing down the institutions of Christianity and the political regimes of the day, Lucifer would be restored to his rightful office in the cosmic arrangement.

The Catharists, as a whole, anticipated the Illuminati with their belief that all social injustice was due to the influence of Christianity. Social injustice, in turn, resulted from the primeval great wrong done by God to Satan. The Satanic restoration would coincide with a new era of perfect equality and social justice. The "real saints," as Huysmans' Des Hermies terms them, are the Catharists, libelously misnamed satanists, who will conspire against the bourgeois class in the same manner as their medieval forbears worked to bring down the feudal order of society.

The Black Mass is, in actuality, what in the heretical tradition was labeled the "rite of vain observance." The rite exalts the flesh to an equal plane with the spirit; it balances lust with self-denial, death with vitality, murder with charity, the lowly with the haughty, the oppressed with the oppressor. The psychology behind the rite was quite fitting for dispossessed intellectual classes of Europe after the failure of two major revolutions and the rapid growth of industrial civilization. To the triumphant bourgeoisie whose values centered on self-abnegation, thrift, piety, and hard work, the cultured satanists of the period dwelt on sexual abandon or "free love," material indulgence, anti-Christianity, and living off others for the sake of their "aesthetic"pursuits.

Many nineteenth-century satanists, including Huysmans, had been molded in their views by the poet Baudelaire. Baudelaire had provided the inspiration for genteel satanism through the powerful imagery of his poems, which exalted the Luciferian impulse. Many of his poems can be regarded as a kind of initiatory rite in their own way. Baudelaire's work, which launched what would later be called "symbolist" poetry, concentrated on producing hallucinogenic states of consciousness and the evocation of what he called "infernal reality." "O Satan, take pity on my long misery!" was Baudelaire's famous, rhapsodic plaint.

Following the Catharist theology, Baudelaire saw the Devil as in need of "sympathy." For Satan and God are, in the final tally, different but complementary facets of a single creative force out of which the poet, as magician, can conjure his own universe. A very similar conception emboldened the fantasies of a most infamous satanic cult spawned in the late 1960s called the Church of the Process. The Church of the Process has been implicated in the notorious murder rampage of the disciples of Charles Manson.

In 1896, Jules Bois, a French author, published a book with a preface by Huysmans and titled *Satanism*. The work purported to describe the kinds of satanic rituals secretly fashionable in Europe. Bois's volume appeared four years after a sensational French bestseller, of slightly dubious scholarship, by one Dr. Bataille, a pseudonym. The name of the book was *The Devil in the Nineteenth Century*. The popularity of these works, combined with the wealth of detail they displayed, testified to the widespread nature of the phenomenon. Unlike the current flap, which has focused on adolescent crime and low-level incidents of terrorist activity against the public at large, the French controversy of the 1890s revolved around strange debaucheries and anomalies under the cover of organized religion, as well as in the parlors of Paris's affluent classes.

Bois recounted one distinctive "satanic rite" he witnessed in a church. The ceremony began with the screen of the choir opening. Then a hand was thrust out of a huge mantle. Next, after a clock struck twelve, a black-robed priest thrust out his hands in the configuration of a cross and invoked the dark powers of the world. Then, as the flames of large candles began to flicker, the satanic celebrant dressed himself in the sacristy and came out to perform a "mass," reversing the mixing of wine and water and picking up a reliquary filled with human skulls. The priest read from the Gospel of John but reversed the meaning of the opening stanzas so that instead of the "word becoming flesh," the "flesh becomes word." After a short while he recited the following:

Be blessed, breath of death, blessed a thousand times more than the bread of life, for you have not been harvested by any human hands nor did any human creature mill and grind you. It is the evil god alone who took you to the mill of the sepulchre, so that you should thus become the bread of revelation.

Finally, the votary cast down the cross, exclaiming, "Your reign is finished," and, "Life listen, death speak." An invocation would be made to the three magi of the New Testament, whose skulls supposedly were kept in the reliquary, saying, "It is no longer necessary for me to return to darkness and despair . . . [for] they can arise to find the spirit of the Mani[cheans] which is the Holy Ghost."[5] In the breviary of this "Black Mass," Christ is also referred to as "Jesus of the Mani."

The text Bois cites is too disjointed, and the allusions too obscure, to have been devised for popular titillation. The obvious references to Mani, founder of the Manicheans, and to the ancient Persian "magicians" forcefully confirms the linkage between nineteenth-century satanism and the ancient dualistic faith. Significantly, however, it was neither the Manicheans nor the Cathars but their Masonic doubles—the Templars—who fed most directly into the occult imagination of the age. The Masonic mystique of the Templars gave rise to a fascination and celebration in literary salons and in both left-wing and right-wing political circles of the medieval "warrior monks." One of the most persistent and prolific promoters of the Templar tales was an Austrian scholar who took the name of Joseph von Hammer-Purgstall, or "Hammer" for short. In his *Mystery of Baphomet Revealed*, published in 1818, Hammer laid out some rather florid theories about Templarism as Masonry, as revolutionism, as satanism.

Many of Hammer's more liberal critics have denounced him for drawing these connections, chiefly because he was employed by Austrian Count Klemens Metternich, notorious architect of political reaction during the first decades of the nineteenth century. The critics tend to overlook the obvious ideological threads that make such connections plausible. Where Hammer went wrong was his failure to define Templarism straightaway as the age-old Manichean heresy, which was not so much antiauthoritarian as it was its own kind of secret authority.

The curious fact is that whether Hammer was correct or not, the congruence between Templarism and satanism was picked up by occultists themselves, who began to romanticize the worship of darkness. The great French historian Jules Michelet aided in this interpretation by proferring the idea that the Templars, under stress from repeated military defeats in the Holy Land, had switched from a kind of offbeat Catholicism to the actual practice of magic and even outright diabolism.

The French occultist Alphonse-Louis Constant (a.k.a. Eliphas Levi), who influenced twentieth-century satanism considerably, bought almost completely into the thesis that Templars were diabolists. And his engraving of the Templar idol Baphomet has become a classic article of iconography for today's black magicians, a sort of satanist Mona Lisa.

By the close of the nineteenth century, the myth of the Templars as "dark lords" of the supernatural had gained widespread currency among those who sought to perfect the black arts themselves. The effective "satanizing" of the Templars quite separately from their Cathar legacy can be consigned to the modern era's pontiff of all occult showmen and hucksters, Aleister Crowley.

The lore and reputation of Crowley are gargantuan. One prominent writer on esoteric matters has labeled him "the flower . . . of the entire body of Western occultism and its literature."[6] In addition, it is probably fair to say that no true-life personality—even Anton LaVey—has cast more of a shadow of influence over contemporary satanism than Crowley. Although he probably stole many of his stunts of public exhibitionism from Dashwood's Hell Fire Club, his mastery of arcane matters was prodigious.

Crowley annointed himself the "Beast 666" of the Book of Revelation. He also believed he was the embodiment of the mysterious figure of Baphomet, and he presided over his own satanic, pseudo-Masonic fraternity after the legendary ideal of the "secret," non-Christian society founded in Jerusalem by the Templars—the Ordo Templi Orientalis, the "Order of the Oriental Temple" or O.T.O.

The O.T.O. was actually established around the turn of the century by Theodor Reuss, a German newspaperman and reputed secret agent for the Kaiser hired to spy on the British socialists. Reuss was a student of Tantric yoga, a very old and fiercely guarded tradition of sexual magic that originated in India. The so-called left hand path of Tantric yoga had been associated over the centuries with immoral excesses that included random murder, sodomy, and cannibalism. Tantrism probably also had an effect on the Roshaniya, who in turn left an impression on Weishaupt and his Bavarian Illuminati. Thus, it should come as no surprise that Reuss, in cahoots with an Austrian industrialist known as Karl Kellner, launched in the 1880s what they termed a "Masonic Academy" with "the key" to "all the secrets of Freemasonry and all systems of religion," which they later renamed the Order of Oriental Templars and claimed to be in a direct line of descent from Weishaupt's organization. In 1912, Reuss (a.k.a. Frater Merlinus) passed the leadership of the O.T.O. over to Crowley, who had already achieved a portfolio for himself in the occult underground.

He was born Edward Alexander Crowley in 1875, the son of parents belonging to the fundamentalist Christian sect, the Plymouth Brethren. Much of Crowley's satanism was a calculated and self-willed reaction against what he considered the extremities and stupidities of his fundamentalist upbringing, which at times included physical abuse. His mother, a dim-witted but pious woman, one time in a huff branded him "the Beast" of the Apocalypse. Crowley cherished the insult and let the epithet stick to him for the remainder of his seventy-two years.

In college, Crowley studied to become a poet, but he soon succumbed to a romantic interest in the occult, which was quite common for boys during the last decade of the nineteenth century. In 1898 he joined the Hermetic Order of the Golden Dawn, a magical and pseudo-Masonic community founded by the occult scholar Samuel MacGregor Mathers. Membership in the Golden Dawn included such lustrous literary figures as the Irish poet William Butler Yeats. In the Golden Dawn, Crowley learned to elicit—today we would say "channel"—disembodied "angels" or spirits, the majority of which turned out, to Crowley's perverse delight, to be demonic.

Mathers and many other adepts of the Golden Dawn, however, looked upon Crowley as an "unspeakably mad person," and he was eventually expelled from the order. One of Crowley's mistresses in the secret society went so far as to go to the London police and accuse him of having performed acts of "torture and medieval iniquity." Crowley, however, rebutted her with the assertion that he had been framed, assaulted, and subject to constant "psychic attack" by the other magicians in the Golden Dawn. The allegations and countercharges smacked a great deal of the sort of petty fracases among celebrities that one reads about today in the *National Enquirer*.

As a biographer of the order has written, the character of the Golden Dawn could be summarized

"in the significant phrase *fin de siecle*. Having been founded just prior to the nineties, using the latter word to denote a special period in recent social history, it incorporated within itself all the faults and vices of that period. The fact that it admitted numerous theatrical people to the ranks of its membership indicates the presence of superficiality and self-satisfaction."[7]

Crowley's rise to stardom, together with the acquisition of an international "bad boy" reputation, started in 1907 with his marriage to Rose Kelly, daughter of a popular artist. Rose was not the most intelligent of women, and toward the end of their relatively brief marriage she became a raging alcoholic. But she was a *sensitive*, or psychic, of sorts who encouraged Crowley to pursue his talents as an occultist and magician of the supreme grade. It was during the couple's sojourn in Cairo in 1904 that Rose's intimacy with the spirit universe led to a critical juncture in Crowley's career.

Crowley had been swaggering about the city pretending he was a wealthy Persian aristocrat called Prince Chioa Khan. Crowley performed a magical ritual one evening in their apartment, and while Rose was in a trance state, she began to mutter, "They are waiting for you." Crowley then did further magical invocations, and over several days he started to "channel" communiques from the ancient Egyptian gods, including Thoth and Horus. But it was the ensuing revelations from a mysterious entity calling himself "Aiwass" that affected Crowley the most. Crowley said he had been commanded by the spirits to write down what came to be titled *The Book of the Law*, a kind of esoteric scripture that resembled the poetry of Robert Browning.

Through the book, Aiwass spoke of a "new religion" and a "new eon" that would be distinguished by complete self-fulfillment and the unleashing of private volition and desire. The great "commandment" of Crowley's new age, as dictated by Aiwass, has been recited over and over: "Do what thou wilt shall be the whole of the law." Magic, especially the black variety, Crowley regarded as the most efficacious vehicle to attain mastery over all things. The key to magical sovereignty lay in the "will," or what Crowley in bastardizing the Greek termed *thelemic* religion.

Virtually all historians of the occult sidestep the fact that the teachings of Crowley or Aiwass, depending on whether one takes a psychological or a metaphysical slant, were little more than inferior literary imitations of the German philosopher Friedrich Nietzsche, who was a generation younger than the Beast himself. But while Nietzsche appealed to continental cognoscenti and aesthetes, Crowley pulled into his orbit a hodgepodge of bored British aristocrats, American heirs and heiresses, and even spooks in the military and intelligence sectors.

While Nietzschean philosophy vaunted the artistic life as the premier expression of the "will to power," what Crowley termed "magick" with a k on the end promised the unlimited satisfaction of instinctual wishes along with total liberation from both human and divine laws. Crowley, in fact, spent the remainder of his days immersed in every mode of unusual or deviant sexual experiment, not so much to be loose-moraled as to carry out the mandate of *The Book of the Law*.

Crowley held that all forms of sexual activity were good and noble in themselves. He also insisted that sexuality and genius, or "divine consciousness," were integrally joined to each other. Crowley even went so far as to commend death while having orgasm. From 1909 he had a homosexual relationship with the poet Victor Neuburg, and right after the First World War he founded a "monastery" for sexual wisdom at Cefalu in Sicily. The center, which he called the Abbey of *Thelema*— which means "will" in Greek and which consisted of two mistresses and miscellaneous followers—could have easily been modeled on the Hell Fire Club.

The abbey quickly became a worldwide object of attention for its alleged depravities. Crowley adorned the walls of the abbey with shocking and erotic murals, such as that of the Greek god Pan having anal intercourse with a man, who in turn sprinkled his sperm over the body of a female. The female symbolized Crowley's mythical "Scarlet Woman," mentioned in the Book of Revelation, whom Crowley hoped might be embodied in one of his own paramours and would give birth to a satanic messiah of the new eon as prophesied by Aiwass. Crowley also conducted regularly with his disciples the thelemic version of the Black Mass, which he termed instead the "Gnostic Mass," which may have been a carefully embroidered version of the older Cathar rituals. The centerpiece of the mass was the ingesting of a biscuit, mimicking the consecrated wafer, which Crowley dubbed the "Cake of Light," baked with blood. It is interesting that Crowley's own *Book of the Law* prescribed the use of real human blood in this sacramental foodstuff, as the earlier legends about what was employed in the Black Mass implied. Crowley's own black bible described "the best blood" as that of a menstruating woman, then "fresh blood of a child,"and finally of "enemies." This unsettling passage, which has parallels in other writings of Crowley, without doubt confirms that the Crowley cultists, at minimum, granted themselves a license for human sacrifice. The fact that Crowley established "congregations" throughout Britain and North America committed to his teachings should give a reasonable person pause. A question arises in this regard over whether satanists ever kill people, if not through wanton murder, then at least within the privacy of their own liturgies. Crowley certainly would not have discouraged the practice.

When Crowley died in 1947, he had become the first true occult hero with a public persona in the modern epoch. But even though he earned his fame as a virtuoso of the occult arts, Crowley had also left his signature as a strange sort of "Renaissance man" of the twentieth-century counter-culture and the Bohemian left.

One lasting contribution of Crowley to twentieth-century culture was the popularization of cocaine use and other psychoactive drugs among the avant-garde. In his diaries of 1914 through 1920, Crowley revealed a somewhat scientific examination of the effects of coke on his brain and nervous system, much as certain Victorian gentlemen, including Freud, had been accustomed to doing. By 1920, however, Crowley had taken to building castles in the air and to commending cocaine as an aid to the enhancement of sexual pleasure and of his "magickal rituals."

In his *Diary of a Drug Fiend*, a fictionalized look at his own probing and playing with what occultists and addicts would call the "white lady," Crowley sees the drug, though dangerous, as an expedient for "increasing your natural powers." At the end, the chief character of the novel offers a strong suggestion concerning drugs as an instrument for ushering in the new eon itself. "We obtained the ineffable assurances of the existence of a spiritual energy that worked its wondrous will in ways too strange for the heart of man to understand until the time should be right . . . we had attained a higher state of evolution."[8] Drugs, particularly heroine and cocaine, were a sacrament for Crowley. As his coke-intoxicated hero rhapsodizes, "The taking of a drug should be a carefully thought out and purposeful religious act. Experience alone can teach you the right conditions . . . when it assists your will."[9] The taking of drugs, because they enhanced the sense of private mastery of the universe, were recommended as the perfect fulfillment of the thelemic commandment given in *The Book of the Law*. While on cocaine, Crowley evidently had his first great insight that, as the "sublimist mystic in all history," he was the Beast of Revelation, the "self-crowned God whom men shall worship and blaspheme for centuries."[10]

Allen Hollub, one of Crowley's adepts in a commentary to the magical text *Book of the Forgotten Ones*, remarks that "the Mage must invoke his most primal self by the sacramental use of the proper drugs (blood, raw meat, cocaine, etc., and sex)." At the time of his death Crowley had physically wasted away from overindulgence in drugs.

Yet his pernicious "addiction" can hardly be explained simply in terms of chemical dependence. During the First World War he paid a visit to the Parke-Davis pharmaceutical plant in Detroit, Michigan, and discussed with them preparations of mescaline. He had probably learned about mescaline, or peyote, as the hallucinogenic substance in cactus during his ramblings about Mexico in 1900. Evidence also exists that Crowley first introduced Aldous Huxley, who stood as the gray eminence of the psychedelic drug culture in the 1960s, to mescaline. Their collaboration is not inconsequential, for in his autobiography, Timothy Leary, the sixties guru of social transformation through hallucinogenic mind-blowing, tells how Aldous had urged him in October 1960 to "become a cheerleader for evolution" by pouring "brain-drugs, mass-produced in the laboratories" into the streets of the Western democracies.[11]

The notion of "cheerleading" evolution through drugs dropped right out of Crowley, and it raises some troubling, if not insoluble, puzzles about the conscious role of philosophical occultists in the promotion of the late twentieth-century drug culture. Crowley's new eon, which he alternately described as the age of the hawk-God Horus whose talons would rip to shreds the body of Christ, was metamorphosized in the 1960s into LaVey's Age of Satan. In his writings, Crowley had spoken of the inauguration of the "New Age" by the "bloody sacrifice."

It is not clear, even from the context, whether he had in mind an actual, high ritual to be performed by his "Gnostic" inner circle or whether he envisioned the kind of general, apocalyptic bloodshed that accompanies such calamitous historical events as revolutions and wars. At any event, Crowley, like the satanists who would succeed him, repeatedly talked of the coming era of chaos and, to use the phraseology of Nazi occultism itself, the "triumph of the will." As Crowley's hagiographer Israel Regardie wrote quite recently, Crowley's "psychic" mentor, Ra Hoor Khuit, the "solar form of Horus," disclosed himself as "the regent of this new age [representing] force and fire, and his advent can only bathe this planet in a baptism of fire."[12] LaVey himself in his *Satanic Rituals*, published in 1972, proclaimed the arrival of "the new Age of Fire" as the ascendancy of the order of Satan.[13]

The obscure magical rhetoric of Crowley, and even of his occult admirers in successive generations, is a far too complex subject either to unwind or to analyze, so far as the history of the contemporary satanist movement is concerned. But one does not have to venture too far from the main highways of historical research in the twentieth century to identify how the prophecy of the coming of the age of "force and fire" was at least partially realized in a very familiar guise. In a word, Crowleyism became one of the larger ideological streams feeding the swollen torrent of fascism. By extension, the mystique of Nazism and fascism, even almost half a century after their demise as palpable political movements, has persisted beyond the point of sheer coincidence in the subculture of satanism. Anton LaVey's own fascination with Nazi regalia and ritualism is well documented.

Crowley was not by any stretch of the imagination an "esotericist," as had been many of his occult predecessors. He was an "Illuminist" to the extent that he dreamed great political dreams of "liberation" through the expansion of consciousness and the individual, godlike will through drugs and the occult. Remarkably, the dreams were virtually the same as those of Leary and the sixties. Crowley himself wrote in his *Confessions* that he wanted to "form an archetype of a new society" in which "each human being has his own definite object in life . . . [and] has every right to fulfill this purpose, and none to do anything else."[14] The new order would make a "clean sweep" of all past civilizations. *The Book of the Law*, he said, was nought but a "revolutionary" handbook with an implicit "magical model of society"; it was "practical politics."

The literary remains of Crowley also show quite convincingly that his rumored affiliations with the dark gods of nazism were not merely a case of guilt by association. In 1925 a Marthe Kuenzel of Leipzig, chief of the German O.T.O., was informed by Crowley himself that the first nation to adopt *The Book of the Law*, as dictated by the disembodied "secret chiefs of the order," would rule the earth.

Kuenzel was a close friend of Rudolf Hess, Hitler's right-hand man. By 1927, Kuenzel was absolutely convinced that Hitler was the "magical child," or satanic messiah, and she introduced Hitler to the writings of Crowley. There is no indication that Hitler took Kuenzel seriously. But in the thick of World War II, Crowley did annotate a copy of the book *Hitler Speaks* in which he proudly pointed out correspondences with his own *Book of the Law*.

Crowley's "new law for mankind" could easily have been adopted as the credo of the Nazi S.S. Crowley had also confided to cronies that he had no doubts the two world conflicts had been "released" magically into time as a consequence of the giving of *The Book of the Law*. In his commentary on *Hitler Speaks*, Crowley noted approvingly the fuehrer's announcement of a "new world order." He was particularly enamored with nazism's "slogans, its feasts, and his freedoms," which he saw as thelemic to the core. He speculated that Hitler may even have been swayed by reading his own "sacred text."

It would be decidedly difficult, if not altogether impossible, to argue that Crowleyite satanism was a straightforward "cause" of the Nazi holocaust or that Crowley's hucksters ever really succeeded in seriously fashioning and coloring the madness of the Third Reich.

Still, one cannot deny that the mysterious, magical "workings" constantly undertaken by Crowley mirrored the fantasies and metaphysical delusions of disaffected intellectuals and political activists all across the ruined landscape of Europe after the First World War.

Even if Crowley himself had only a negligible impact in Germany, the old Catharism dressed as satanism reached into the remote soul-life of nazism's political mystics. The Cathar concept of a pure, perfected, and illumined secret order, which would raze the entire spectrum of European institutions while giving vent to repressed "evil" as a creative power, was adapted by the Nazis. The only difference between nazism and nineteenth-century satanism was that the Cathari were no longer bohemians who kept primarily to themselves, but political agitators and government functionaries. The corpses at Dachau and Buchenwald turned out to be even more ghastly than anything that could have been beheld at a black mass. Even the romantic image of the Templars had a profound place in the genealogy of Nazi ideas.

There is significant support for the premise that Hitler regarded the Nazi party as a "holy order" patterned after the Templars. At the Nuremberg rallies during the early 1930s, Hitler's propogandists talked in these terms. And the latest historical research has proposed that the paradigm itself came from a cranky German occultist named Lanz von Liebenfels, who in 1907 had founded the Ordo Novi Templi, or Order of the New Templars.

The so-called O.N.T., which had nothing to do with Crowley's O.T.O., was an attempt to supply a mystic, racial interpretation to the military legends of the Templars. It was the German counterpart to Crowley's pseudo-Masonic fraternity, emphasizing the purity of Aryan blood and "ario-Christian" illumination as the sine qua non of membership. Just as the medieval Templars had been chartered to rescue the Holy Land from the infidels, the "new Templars" would secure Christian Germany from the Jews. The O.N.T. represented, as one scholar has put it, a "crusade for absolute values."[15] The more virulent strands of Nazi racism and the quest for world salvation through eugenic breeding seems to have been originally laid out in the plan for the order of new Templars. Catharist elitism, in its translation from ritual rage against the Christian God to venegeance against the human race overall, reached its most horrid extreme.

The Nazi phenomenon, together with a flurry of demonstrable but not widely reported incidents of "satanism" in the Western world immediately following the Second World War, attest how the occult underworld has been detectible for centuries. In 1955, the German magazine *Quick* reported how a thirty-seven-year-old Australian painter named Rosaleen Norton was discovered to be celebrating black masses in her apartment. After performance of the Mass, Norton would sponsor rather flamboyant orgies. In 1950, a German citizen was interviewed by the respected north

German weekly *Man in der Zeit* and told of having been taken to a secret meeting of a satanic coven that called itself "the great brothers of the black spirit." The rituals he detailed were not all that different from what LaVey published fifteen years later with the establishment of his Church of Satan.

NOTES

1. J. M. Roberts, *The Mythology of the Secret Societies* (New York: Charles Scribner's Sons, 1972), p. 121.
2. Charles William Heckethorn, *The Secret Societies of All Ages and Countries* (New Hyde Park, NY: University Books, 1965), vol. 1, p. 314. See also Akron Daraul, *A History of Secret Societies* (New York: Citadel Press, 1961), p. 230.
3. James Billington, *Fire in the Minds of Men: The Origins of the Revolutionary Faith* (New York: Basic Books, Inc., 1980).
4. J. K. Huysmans, *La-Bas* (New York: Dover Publications, 1972), p. 59.
5. Quoted in Henry T. F. Rhodes, *The Satanic Mass* (London: Arrow Books, 1973), p. 173.
6. Kenneth Grant, *Outside the Circles of Time* (London: Frederick Muller, 1980), p. 31.
7. Israel Regardie, *What You Should Know About the Golden Dawn* (Phoenix, AZ: Falcon Press, 1985 3rd ed.), p. 39.
8. Aleister Crowley, *Diary of a Drug Fiend* (York Beach, ME: Samuel Weiser, 1987), p. 368.
9. Ibid., p. 365.
10. Quoted in Colin Wilson, *Aleister Crowley: The Nature of the Beast* (Wellingborough, Northamptonshire, England: Aquarian Press, 1987), p. 121.
11. Timothy Leary, *Flashbacks: An Autobiography* (Los Angeles: J. P. Tarcher, 1983), p. 44.
12. Israel Regardie, *The Eye in the Triangle: An Interpretation of Aleister Crowley* (Las Vegas, NV: Falcon Press, 1989), p. 499.
13. Anton Szandor LaVey, *The Satanic Rituals* (New York: Avon Books, 1972), p. 220.
14. Aleister Crowley, *The Confessions of Aleister Crowley* (New York: Hill and Wang, 1969), p. 848.
15. Nicholas Goodrick-Clarke, *The Occult Roots of Nazism: The Ariosophists of Austria and Germany, 1890–1935* (Wellingborough, Northamptonshire, England: Aquarian Press, 1985), p. 114.

CHAPTER 5.

The Aesthetics of Terror

All that is dark, buried deep, unrevealed in the mind, should be manifested in a sort of physical projection, as real.
—Antonin Artaud

Up through the nineteenth century, satanic ritualism was a "counter-faith," sometimes with a hidden political agenda, to the dominant Christianity. By the Second World War, under the sway of Crowleyism, it had become a form of cultural revolt appealing to the libertine, who wanted to shake off the shackles of bourgeois morality. By the 1960s, the last great age of "revolution" in the West, it had turned into a self-conscious art form with a utopian fever and an eye toward social transformation. It had become an "aesthetic terrorism."

Kenneth Anger, avant-garde American filmmaker of whom the artistic elites first took notice during the Second World War, was obsessed with the French decadents of the nineteenth century. His works have been described, accurately it seems, as "trance films"—surrealistic dream symphonies evincing the inner dynamics of the human mind through sex, hashish, jazz, rock, and death.

Anger was literally a "cult" figure in the motion picture industry. For in 1967 he announced he was going to produce his "first religious film" entitled *Lucifer Rising*. Anger had also been a follower of Aleister Crowley and in the 1960s joined LaVey's Church of Satan. He also had an indirect connection with the murder of Hollywood actress Sharon Tate by the crazed "scorpion" from the abyss—Charlie Manson.

Anger remarked, rather blandly, to interviewers that *Lucifer Rising* was about a counterpoise of the life and death forces. "It's about the angel-demon of light and beauty named Lucifer," he said. "And it's about the solar deity. The Christian ethos has turned Lucifer into Satan. But I show it in the gnostic and pagan sense. Lucifer is the rebel angel behind what's happening in the world today. His message is that the key of joy is disobedience."

The original footage for *Lucifer Rising* included footage of the Rolling Stones, a helicopter touching down in Vietnam, and alchemical tatoos. The movie was concocted not merely as art but as a ritual event in keeping with the principles hammered out by Crowley. Like experimental artists before him, Anger wanted to be metamorphosized into his own myth.

The year 1967 was the optimal occasion for Anger's personal apotheosis. The Vietnam protests in the streets of San Francisco, where Anger resided, were reaching a crescendo. The hippies had descended upon the city's Haight Ashbury district that summer like rats responding to the Pied Piper. Swarming through the alleys and streets, they settled into the district's decaying, Edwardian flats toting their LSD, their Indian sitar music, and their unchained libidos. And by August they proclaimed that the world had been conquered by their "Summer of Love," fraught with sufficiently powerful and mystical energies to halt the war in Southeast Asia and to inaugurate the Age of Aquarius.

Anger wanted *Lucifer Rising* to be performed as a dramaturgical spectacle right at the fall equinox at the Straight Theater in the Haight. In Anger's opinion, the advent of autumn that year was not simply the passing of one more solar milestone. It was truly the Equinox of the Gods, a magical fete corresponding to the unveiling of the new eon.

The film was never shown because 1600 feet of the original celluloid was stolen from a locked trunk. The suspected culprit was Robert K. "Bobby" Beausoleil, Anger's live-in boyfriend at the house they called the "Russian embassy." Beausoleil was the lead guitar and sitar player for the 11-piece rock band named the Magick Powerhouse of Oz, which Anger had assembled to provide the soundtrack for *Lucifer Rising*. On learning of the heist, Anger flew into a nearly psychotic rage and smashed a priceless, caduceus-head cane that had been owned by Crowley. According to author Ed Sanders, he also put together a puissant rite of "sympathetic" magic, designed to turn Beausoleil into a toad.

Beausoleil, however, slipped away and took up with Manson's "family." After the episode with Anger, Beausoleil had his own "conversion" experience. He was now convinced that he was the "second coming"—it was unclear whether of Christ or Satan. Manson had a similiar suspicion about himself, so the two got along fabulously.

In the meantime, Anger had left San Francisco to go to Washington, D.C., for the famous sixties "happening" in which thousands of counter-culturalists—or "freaks," as they styled themselves—locked arms and magically strove to "levitate" the Pentagon. The so-called Diggers group of hippies from the Haight stood on top of a flatbed truck and chanted, "Out demons, out," while the military brass looked on with both fury and curiosity. Anger, who sported his tatoo of Lucifer, before television cameras, burned a picture of Satan within a consecrated pentagram. As reporters closed in, Anger hissed at them and flaunted his "magic ring."

Before arriving at the Pentagon, Anger had stopped off in New York to meet with the Film-Makers Cooperative. He shocked the cooperative's officers by unreeling cans of unreleased film and burning them. At that juncture, Anger also announced that he would make no more films and that he was about to change his name and assume an entirely new identity. The irony was that "Kenneth Anger" had been a stage name from the beginning. Anger had chosen it for "magickal" reasons, and he was in the process of switching names once more in order to bring about a "change of order," a self-initiation into a higher degree. It was a ritual death and rebirth.

Anger carried the rite so far as to insert an obituary for himself in the *Village Voice*, which led many "nonmagickal" critics to grieve for him on the dumb assumption that he was actually dead. Anger, however, was only making believe for political purposes. It was the blending of the arts of magic, theater, and public relations—a mild version of what has been termed in the avant-garde world the "aesthetics of terror."

In Anger's case the strategy of aesthetic terrorism played itself out, perhaps because of the long-term magical "working" of his ferocious curse on Beausoleil in a violent and sensational manner. The horror in Anger's esoteric art, inspired by his self-professed "Luciferianism," was soon upstaged by a popular Hollywood flick entitled *Rosemary's Baby*, for which LaVey served as a consultant.

Rosemary's Baby, starring Mia Farrow, did for the public what *Lucifer Rising* was supposed to have accomplished on the 1967 equinox—manifest by visual and histrionic flourishes the advent of Lucifer's return to earth and the morning skies of the Age of Satan. Unfortunately, the producer of *Rosemary's Baby*, a foreign film-maker named Roman Polanski, wound up with his own personal terror. His pregnant wife, Sharon Tate, was savagely murdered and her blood spattered on the Hollywood hills in August 1969 by Charles Manson, the Antichrist who had recruited his death squad from among the Haight flower children. The inspiration for the butchery may well have derived in part from Manson's friendship with Beausoleil, who had declared himself a living embodiment of the Devil.

Aesthetic terrorism had become all the rage in California.

The concept of the aesthetic terrorist has been enunciated in an article in *Harper's* magazine by Alberto Moravia. Terrorism, Moravia points out, is an idiosyncrasy of the modern era and of modern thought and fashion. It is the scimitar of avant-garde culture. Terrorism can only thrive where there is constant revolutionary agitation and movement, where there is an obsession with history, where there is an actual set of cultural values adulating change.

In classical culture, according to Moravia, values were "eternal"; they never changed. Values were timeless plumb lines of right and wrong, truth and falsity, justice and injustice. In modernity, on the other hand, values are forever in transit—they are constantly writhing and flipping over into their opposite. The modern revolutionary temper has arisen from the rage to overturn old values and supplant them with shining, new ones. Terrorism becomes a "style" of revolutionary political struggle, because it is not only a regime that must be replaced, it is the people's very moral fabric and intellectual marrow as well. Terror is connected, as Moravia emphasizes, "to the idea of power" inasmuch as "a person who gives the impression of knowing how to foresee the movements of values through time will be the one who gets hold of power."[1]

The concept of art as a revolutionary battering ram that flattens the old values of society and drives their opposite into the shafts of experience developed during the Romantic age. It became a favorite theory among the artistic radicals of the nineteenth century, whose fellowship frequently overlapped with the occult underworld. The growth of aesthetic terrorism as a surrogate for political radicalism had its origins in France, especially within the circles close to Baudelaire, and it seems to have flowered at approximately the same time the political momentum of revolution throughout Europe was waning.

Moreover, the Illuminist yearning for world transformation through occult conspiracy played easily into the hands of aesthetic terrorists. The prestige enjoyed by the occult among artists in twentieth-century civilization, and by extension the interests of occultists in the use of artistic media, turned on the common bond of "magic." Since the first known artworks of human beings were inscribed on the walls of the Trois Freres cave in southern France in conjunction with an ancient and forgotten hunting rite, aesthetics and magic have always been intertwined.

Art images were worshiped as sensible tokens of the gods by early peoples because they were believed to incarnate strange and overwhelming "powers." By the modern period these powers were assigned to human spirit, or the "unconscious." Yet the same artistic psychology persisted. With Baudelaire and the "symbolist" movement in art, which he helped engineer, art came to be understood as a revelation of the inner life and the driving will to power of humanity. "Magic," in Crowley's sense of mastery of the world by the will, or what Nietzsche called "the will to power as art," became extraordinarily fashionable, if only at a sophisticated and self-conscious level. Aesthetic terrorism was the notion derived from avant-garde artistic work, and applied to the occult, that power over things ultimately requires social revolution, which in turn demands a subversion of symbols.

For the supreme "knowledge of good and evil" in the occult sense to dominate over what Nietzsche dubbed the "slave consciousness" of the Christian believer, a campaign of terror must be waged. Bourgeois and Christian values must be ambushed, trampled down, eviscerated, and tossed aside by creating a universal sense of the invincibility of evil. Aesthetic terrorism is a blunt instrument in the war of values. It slices to the heart of what we mean by satanism.

The sixties constituted the high-water mark of aesthetic terrorism as an experimental art form. And it can be viewed as the wider matrix out of which the popular habit of dabbling in the black side of the occult began suddenly to gain ground. In the bohemian district of Vienna in the early 1960s, the Austrian playwright Hermann Nitsch pushed the perspective of aesthetic terrorism to its limits. Nitsch underwrote a number of performances, which he wryly spoke of as "OM," standing for "orgy mysteries." In the orgy mysteries, actors carried out an authentic Dionysian revel, in which the performers, after becoming intoxicated with alcohol and drugs amid frenzed music and dancing, ripped to pieces and disemboweled a live animal, then writhed in the blood and gore.

Although the "happening" was often raided by police, Nitsch persisted with his grueseome, aesthetic "statement" about the darkest rumblings of the human spirit. The objective of the artistic orgies, Nitsch explained, matched the primitive religious impulse to incorporate the "god." It signified the ecstatic union of all opposites and made the celebrant "divine." Nitsch regarded his art as cultural "therapy." The Greek word was *catharsis*, a purging of everything primal and repressed within the collective psyche, what Nitsch in his updated interpretation called "the liberated joy of strong existence without barriers."

In a free-wheeling and rather laudatory survey of Nitsch's "art form," critic Thomas McEvilley has noted how "the artist is seen as a kind of extramural initiation priest, a healer or guide who points the alienated soul back toward the depth of the psyche where it resonates to the rhythms of nature."[2] Rumors were even rife at the time that some of Nitsch's more literal and enthusiastic imitators had cultivated the Dionyisian "initiation" to the point where "dismembering the Deity" had been simulated through human sacrifice, the cutting up of a live victim. If killing did actually occur, it would have fulfilled the logic of aesthetic terrorism as well as Nitsch's "art in the dark."

The credo of the avant-garde in the sixties was no longer that art imitates life, as Aristotle had decreed. Nor was it that life must imitate art, as earlier twentieth-century radicals had held. Art and life were now indistinguishable. "Aggression" became "expression," the eruption through theatrical realism, rather than symbolic movement, of the profoundest pressures of horror, rage, bestial craving, and primordial violence. Art was to be converted into terrorism because "reality must be constantly updated."[3] Reality was viewed as pure time, the unlimited outflowing of desire and the ceaseless propulsion of instinct.

Ironically, aesthetic terrorism as a broader *political* issue first surfaced in 1989 with the controversy in Congress concerning the funding of the photography of Andres Serrano and Robert Mapplethorpe by the National Endowment for the Arts. The flap over whether artworks considered obscene should be funded by a tax-supported, public agency obscured the deeper and more interesting problem of what Serrano and Mapplethorpe were really trying to do.

The fur began to fly over protests by Christian groups regarding an image of a crucifix in a pool of Serrano's urine bearing the title *Piss Christ*. The Christian groups complained that their fundamental beliefs were under attack with state subvention. Defenders of the avant-garde countered that *Piss Christ* was nothing more than a vivid pronouncement of disgust with commercialized religion.

Such an interpretation seemed a little bit disingenuous, if one grasps the mentality of the aesthetic terrorist. The intentions of Mapplethorpe also fell under suspicion. His exhibits have entailed homoerotic and sadomasochistic images of a man urinating into another's mouth, the artist himself doubled over without trousers and a bullwhip dangling from his anus, and children in erotic scenes that cannot be distinguished from child pornography.

Yet other pictures, particularly Mapplethorpe's self-portraits, were even more revealing. In its rather prosaic synopsis of the political uproar, the *New York Times* printed Mapplethorpe's 1982 work *Self Portrait (With Gun and Star)*. The picture shows the artist in the pose of a leather-jacketed terrorist cradling a machine gun with the "star" as backdrop. The star is clearly an inverted pentagram, the supreme symbol of religious satanism. In another self-portrait, he is the Devil with horns. A critical review of Mapplethorpe in *ARTnews* called him "the visual poet of our shadow side" as well as "prince of darkness, angel of light"—a most fitting series of sobriquets for the Luciferian imagination.

The primal blueprint for aesthetic terrorism can be found in the manifestoes of the Dadaists immediately following the First World War. The postwar years were marked in artistic and literary quarters by extreme disillusionment and hostility toward Western civilization. Modern art, which already before the war had progressed from representing the external world to an absorption with its own problems and methods— (captured in the slogan "art for art's sake"), now turned to what in a very general fashion came to be called expressionism. In the same vein art turned rebelliously against itself. Dadaism was really a self-aware type of anti-art. Just as the word *dada* meant nothing at all, so art was supposed to be at best nothing and at worst heinously shocking and revolting. Marcel Duchamp, chief theoretician of the Dadaists, put a urinal on display and called it sculpture. Some Dadaists believed, perhaps far less ironically than many thought, that the ultimate act of artistic creativity was to grab a revolver and start firing it into a crowd of bystanders.

The "aestheticism" of aesthetic terrorism did not necessarily mean sheer pretending as opposed to real action. Nitsch's doctrine of art as *Aktion*, or "action," was intended to promote what the word implies. As Adam Parfrey has remarked, "terrorism can be advanced through art only if art threatens *action*." If aesthetic terrorism is to take place, artistic endeavor must become "symbolic not of its own decadently solipsistic pleasures." Rather, it must describe "action taken beyond the pale of art world confines."[4]

Parfrey cites John Hinckley, Jr., who made an assassination attempt on the life of President Ronald Reagan in 1981, as the aesthetic terrorist *par excellence*. "Embodying the Byronic model of poetry and action, John Hinckley, Jr., made the 'mistake' of valuing visual poetry (Martin Scorcese's *Taxi Driver* as a greater reality), and acting accordingly."[5] Hinckley was the "victim" of an age that would regard his *action* as "psychopathic," according to Parfrey. On the contrary, Hinckley should be lionized as a "Nietzschean hero." John Hinckley was the aesthetic terrorist who "meant what he said." Manson was an even more accomplished aesthetic terrorist, but Parfrey neglects to give any significant due.

Aesthetic terrorism was lived theater in which action upon the stage and action in the street are drawn from the visionary mind of dramatist Antonin Artaud. Born in 1896 at Marseilles, France, Artaud wrestled with mental illness most of his life. At his death in 1948, Artaud, however, had won credit as the "shaman," or inspired seer, of a revitalized avant-garde theater.

The impact of Artaud's genius can be detected in the French student uprisings of 1968, when the government almost succumbed to mobs in the street. On the night of May 16, French students occupied en masse the Odeon-Theatre de France. The incident was not merely a political insurrection. It was theater transposed into historical "action." The script was directed by one of Artaud's former collaborators, Jean-Louis Barrault.

Artaud himself had been an admirer of Hitler, and he had dedicated a copy of his *New Revelations About Existence* to the Führer. In Hitler, Artaud beheld a Bacchic fury that had resulted in a change of world reality. For him, Hitler had triumphantly let loose a lightning storm of destruction and creative fervor, which in a key sense were identical with each other. Artaud asked of an interviewer what difference does it make that "seven to eight hundred million human beings . . . should be exterminated" when, in fact, the outcome was the elimination of the dolts and drudges who did nothing to loft consciousness to a more Olympian plane.[6]

Hitler's holocaust could have been rationalized in Artaud's phrasing as what he characterized as "theater of cruelty." The theater of cruelty stood for a dramatic spectacle that served to activate the "magnetism" in the human organism. Cruelty is not merely blood and violence. It is the affirmation of life in its darkest cry from the wellspring of all. It is the celebration of the fact that "evil is permanent." Cruelty, as the inflicting of terrible pain, stills the crosswinds of good and evil. For pain is the leveler of all injustice and hypocrisy. Murder is creation because it abolishes the cleavage between violent deed and hostile wish, between rage and fulfillment. Artaud talked about the theater as "total experience."

The role of theater, for Artaud, is to do far more than to provoke the imagination; it must transfigure the very spectator so that one becomes an actor. Artaud based many of his musings on the mystical Jewish tradition known as the *Kabbalah*, which has been revered by many occultists in the modern centuries, although it has also been a pillar of orthodox belief as well. In the *Kabbalah*, good and evil are transcended in a great and etheric knowledge of the divine Oneness. In that respect the theater is also, for Artaud, a distinctive brand of "alchemy." In the theater of cruelty, the dross of human expectations and emotions are "magically" manifested as the gold of pure, creative will. To do "evil" both on and off the stage is to act as God the Creator, who is at once the Destroyer.

Artaud's most famous play was *The Cenci*, which he subtitled *A Dramatized Myth*. *The Cenci* is based on a five-act tragedy by the English Romantic poet Percy Bysshe Shelley and concerns the Italian family of Count Francesco Cenci, a sixteenth-century Italian nobleman, reviled in his own day as a sordid sexual pervert and sadist. Artaud hoped that in viewing *The Cenci* theatergoers would be "plunged in a bath of fire" while participating "with his soul and his nerves." According to Artaud, the *mise en scene*, or method of staging, is not an accompaniment to the drama. The two are indivisible. The horrors perpetrated by Count Cenci, therefore, are not concocted primarily to be watched; they must be "acted out" in some way by the viewer, who because of their compelling strength is unable to remain a strict voyeur.

The audience of the play must be seduced at the end into declaring with Count Cenci that "the one legacy I am determined to bequeath is a crowning glory of horror."[7] The character of Cenci is crafted to turn the spectator into a simulacrum of Lucifer, the murky and dangerous, yet unrecognized, aspect of human existence. If art has any goal, vows Artaud, it is to banish the enthrallment of the human agent with morality and to allow a person to experience the ecstasy of both saintliness and wickedness. "Salvation" comes when one can say with Cenci that "I obey my law" and "I seek and commit acts of evil through intention and principle."

The theater of cruelty is "sorcery" in a very telling sense. As aesthetic terrorism, it amounts to a sacramental language for materializing the unwanted demons of experience. It must provide "the spectator with the truthful precipitates of dreams, in which his taste for crime, his erotic obsessions, his savagery, his fantasies, his utopian sense of life and of things, even his cannibalism, pour out on a level that is not counterfeit and illusory but internal."[8] Like Crowley, Artaud also saw the social dissemination of psychotropic drugs as both a revolutionary and theatrical strategy—as a statement of glory that overcomes the suffering imposed by society. "Nature herself is fundamentally anti-social, it is only by a usurpation of powers that the organized body of society opposes the *natural* inclinations of humanity."[9]

Satanism as aesthetic terrorism belongs to what in the avant-garde idiom has come to be labeled *apocalypse culture*. The undying fascination of the cultural avant-garde in the West with Adolf Hitler and nazism, which under the influence of the "black fashions" of punk music and heavy metal rock has been accelerating in the past several years, can be attributed to the feeling that the old must be constantly, and ferociously, assailed in order to substitute what is perpetually novel.

Parfrey quotes Hitler: "We are motion itself, we are eternal revolution. We shall never allow ourselves to be held down to one permanent condition."[10] The success of terrorism rests on the manufacture of unceasing, apocalyptic fright and anticipation. Apocalypse culture emanates from the conviction that nothing must be denied or shielded from the light of day. There can be no longer any modesty or privacy. At last, everything is bared. The tangled relationship between apocalypse culture, aesthetic terrorism, the modern avant-garde, and the much older, covert traditions of the occult underworld has only recently begun to unravel. The link was Dada. "Dada was a legend of freedom only after the fact," writes Greil Marcus, a contemporary cultural historian who has sought to sketch the "secret history of the twentieth century." For "in the act it was a gnostic myth of the twentieth century."[11]

The Dadaists, unlike the artistic decadents before them, fancied themselves political magicians. Dada was launched at the Cabaret Voltaire in Zurich, Switzerland, in 1916 at the peak of World War I. The principals of the new Dadaist salon were Hugo Ball, a German theatrical director and former Catholic mystic; the singer Emmy Hennings; the artist Hans Jean Arp; the Romanian poet Tristan Tzara; and Franz Marc, cofounder with Vasili Kandinsky of the "Blue Rider" school of modern art that promoted the magical use of color. From the Dadaist vantage point, the artist was conceived as both a magician and a saint. The Dadaist agenda was to "cure man of the frenzy of the times through art" while building "a new order to restore the balance between heaven and hell."

Such an occult project was the direct outgrowth of the symbolist movement and French decadent fashions of the 1880s. Abstraction in modern painting, which has long been mistaken as a purely technical process in turn-of-the century painting, was promoted largely by its early enthusiasts with the end of making art into a new religion, an occult vision, or in Marc's memorable phrase a "second sight." The predilection for the occult among both American and European intellectuals from the late 1800s into the first quarter of the twentieth century stemmed from an ideal of "spiritualizing" art—which often meant making it geometric, erotic, primitive, or purely psychological. Dadaism pulled its proposals for an art that would speak a "secret language" of all humankind from musings of the earlier figures of the occult underworld.

For example, Ball practiced an urbane form of necrophilia, carrying about wherever he went the skull of a twenty-two-year-old girl who had died in 1811. In public, he compared the skull to Hennings, his mistress who became his wife. Such an eccentricity appears quite shocking and even "sick" on the surface. But to the Dadaists, civilization and the idealized imagery of womanhood that held it together was a fraud perpetrated by the death instinct. Ball also talked in his diaries about sexually violating the Virgin Mary, a gesture of aesthetic terrorism intended to unmask the sordid behind the holy.

The "secret language" to be spoken amid the crypts of dead, ancient religions was violence and desire—in other words, the compulsion to rape. Dadaists were cultural anarchists to the extent that they believed the entire architecture of social values and political idealism constituted a system that radically "oppressed" the truly spiritual nature of human beings, lodged in the freedom of the will. Dadaism was inextricably linked with anarchism as a direct, avant-garde expression of pure "political art." The Dadaists thought that in the midst of a fallen civilization, as the horrors of the First World War were understood, a means had been at last achieved to carry forth the "great liberation" of humanity's corporate cravings.

Dadaism imagined a great liberation and a great terror as virtually one and the same climax. This unity of the most basic dyad of experience, embellished in later themes of apocaylpse culture, was constructed, as Greil Marcus tells us, out of the occult frenzy for "absolute freedom."It was the "prize seized by the Cathars, the Brethren of the Free Spirit, the Lollards, John of Leyden, the Ranters, and Adolf Hitler."[12] It was also the Holy Rood of intellectual satanism.

Apocalyptic violence as a riot of unbounded freedom, signaling the arrival of the Crowleyean "new eon," has been the hallmark of Anger's films. At the opening of Anger's most important motion picture, *The Inauguration of the Pleasure Dome*, Lord Shiva, the Hindu deity of devastating wrath and destruction, wakens from a long, historic sleep in order to reveal himself in his "incarnation" for the twentieth century. He is the Great Beast 666 of the apocalypse.

Inauguration, subtitled *Lord Shiva's Dream*, was crafted to celebrate the spring equinox of the year 1966, when Crowleyite prophecies of the "new age" were supposed to be consummated and LaVey would proclaim the "second coming" of Satan. According to Crowley's own notes, *Inauguration* is supposed to be set in Crowley's Abbey of Thelema. The face of the historical Crowley appears in the movie.

The film is a surrealistic tableau of mythical episodes with gods and figures culled from the texts of Crowleyite satanism. Anger explained that the script was adapted from one of Crowley's high-order rituals where members of his cult were "possessed" by the identity of dark beings. The actual, recognizable religious ritual Anger dramatized was the Dionysian madness involving the "eating of the god," the primitive and instinctual counterpart to the Christian Eucharist. Anger wrote that "a Eucharist of some sort should most assuredly be consumed daily by every magician, and he should regard it as the main sustenance of his magic life . . . The magician becomes filled with God, fed upon God, intoxicated with God.[13]

The "holy communion" of orgiastic violence—Crowley's "bloody sacrifice" lubricating the new eon—is, in Anger's mind, a veritable "twilight of the gods." Pan, the spirit of the "all," is poisoned by Shiva, whereupon the gods themselves in costume and mask descend into an orgy signifying "the powers of the age of Horus."

As the gods dissolve into a tempest of dancing and orgiastic communion, Shiva stays aloof, watching and directing the rites in full knowledge that he enjoys lordship of the new eon. Prior to the orgy, the Great Beast, Shiva discloses his escort for the festivities—Crowley's "Scarlet Woman," mother of everything horrid and sensually corrupt. Just as Shiva is shown to be the Great Beast, the Scarlet Woman is revealed under her sublimely terrible Indian aspect as the black goddess "Kali"—evil enchantress and wellspring of death adorned with a necklace of skulls.

The poisoning of Pan and the Dionysian confusion are ritually inaugurated by the pouring of a white powder, a magical drug, from an amphora into the cups of the Great Beast and the Scarlet Woman. The drug, which well could be cocaine, symbolizes the "power" Shiva and Kali possess over the eon. The Beast and the Scarlet Woman in Cathar fashion have attained perfect freedom, even over the gods themselves. Film analysts have noted that *Inauguration* is designed to ritualize the raging, psychic elements of the sixties as the epoch of what Crowley termed "force and fire." Anger's "Eucharist" was the theatrical murder of the Christian God, in fact, of all civilized values bespoken in the classical divinities themselves. Anger told the press his film was a major "improvised happening." It was the supreme "communion" with the unfathomable, black abyss of time and history.

In 1969, Anger unveiled his *Invocation of My Demon Brother*. The movie was even more striking than *Inauguration*, although less formally brilliant and epic in its impact. The movie was a genuine conjuring, a video version of the Black Mass, in which Lucifer, the occult "power of light" hidden in the chaos and infernal night, was made manifest. The musical background of *Invocation* was supplied by Mick Jagger on a Moog synthesizer. And the film itself included a lineup from the Church of Satan, including Anger as the Magus in Egyptian garb, LaVey as "his satanic majesty," and Beausoleil as Lucifer.

Through the ritual, the Magus himself becomes the great "Secret Chief," the sovereign of force and fire, the "demon brother" to the Prince of Darkness. He lopes around the stage with a Nazi swastika, which in Anger's mythology is the sign of the true power of Lucifer. A document, perhaps signifying the testament of religion and human culture, is committed to the flames. Then a cat is burned. Finally, the cluster of otherworldly images gives place to a camera pan of Hell's Angels in black leather and silver studs, then a rock festival, then a shot of the Vietnam carnage—altogether conveying the mood that current events are somehow under the dominion of the Crowleyite, black magical system.

In reply to a question about *Invocation*, Anger said that he had "always considered movies evil." The images were to "control" lives and occurrences, he stated. "My reason for filming has nothing to do with 'cinema' at all," he added. "It's a transparent excuse for capturing people . . . I consider myself as working Evil in an evil medium."[14] No more gripping confession about the broad-ranging strategy of aesthetic terrorism could have been uttered.

A decade later, Anger's style of the terrorist aesthetic had become *au courant*, especially in rock performances. But the aesthetic itself, harking all the way back to Artaud and the Dadaists, required an effective, Pygmalionlike means for bringing the "work" of black magic to life. The theater of cruelty, as incorporated in Anger's Dionysian spectacle of heaven's dissolution, was destined to become the social drama of the sixties onward. *Invocation* disclosed the unity of Lucifer and Satan. But it would take street actors to manifest the "working" in real time and in real culture. Their names were Robert de Grimston and Charles Manson.

All along, the secret text, or subterfuge, of the terrorist subculture was that aesthetics, in order to be plausible as both art and magic, must veer toward terror itself. de Grimston was the subculture's worldly philosopher, its Karl Marx. Manson was its Lenin. Without the influence of de Grimston, Manson might have wound up a drug-sotted and sexually overindulged cast-off from the Haight Ashbury, a musician who never made it, a go-between and gigolo for the Hollywood celebrity scene, which he both adored and loathed.

Robert de Grimston and his wife Mary Anne launched the Church of the Process of the Final Judgment in England during the year 1964 in a sectarian split from Ron Hubbard's Scientology movement. De Grimston had been transformed, according to Sanders, into a "clear," as Scientology lingo described the highest state of consciousness and existence an earthling could attain through the organization's expensive "auditing" procedures—a weird combination of Freudian psychoanalysis, Buddhism, Chinese thought reform, and Dale Carnegie motivational training. Becoming a clear in Scientology is like ascending to the beatific vision of God in medieval monasticism. Once you are there, you have nowhere else to go—except perhaps, as in de Grimston's case, to plunder the planet with your newfound, godlike powers.

The Church of the Process was chic, sixties-bred Catharism. The difference was that de Grimston firmly believed that the millenia of dualism were now over and that all the hitherto dispersed forces of both light and dark must now be reconciled in a great hip "lovefest" of cosmic sweep and orgiastic intensity. Christ and Satan would now become reunited as brothers. The elect of the Process Church, who attracted public curiosity in a number of American cities for panhandling at crowded intersections in their flowing, black robes, were gearing up by the mid-sixties to take dominion over all things and to "off," or eliminate, those who might oppose this great, barbarous reunion of the human race's unconscious complexes. Ten years later, members of the Process Church would be accused of having orchestrated the notorious Son of Sam murders in New York.

De Grimston wrote, "If a man asks: What is the Process? Say to him: It is the End, the final ending of the world of men. It is the agent of The End, the instrument of The End, and the inexorable Power of the End." The Process Church reversed the commandment of Moses: "Thou shalt kill." One must "release the Fiend that lies dormant in you," de Grimston exhorted his followers, "for the world can be yours, and the blood of men can be yours to spill as you please." De Grimston appears in cult photographs as a glowering, Jesus looking figure with beard, shoulder-length hair, and Teutonic cross on his black chemise. As in Anger's histrionic screenplay in which Lucifer had risen, the theater of cruelty was on its way to becoming bona fide, apocalyptic violence.

In the summer of 1969, "the Process," as it came to be known, issued an edict in the *Fear* edition of its cult magazine. The Lamb of God and the Goat of Satan would become as one presence in the world. "Pure love descended from the pinnacle of heaven, united with pure hatred raised from the depths of hell." A month later the prophecy appeared to have been consummated.

The Manson murders in southern California were immediately perceived as something other than indiscrimate, "serial killings." Manson himself was portrayed eventually by both the press and the Los Angeles prosecutors as a berserk hippie who, like John Hinckley, Jr., and the Son of Sam killer, had gone on a rampage after hearing "voices" from the black cellar of the mind. But the personality of the killer and his oddball "theology" lent a decidedly different impression. The voices were well-honed themes of calculated destruction that had been whispering down through the ages in the occult underground. Manson, of course, was branded paranoid and schizophrenic. Yet his psychological imbalance could best be construed as the practical outworking of "process" thought, which throughout the sixties' "days of rage" had in one form or another attracted a classy congregation.

The American dream of democratic harmony was shattered with multiple assassinations. The ruins were aflame with riots in the black ghettoes and uncounted uprisings on college campuses. Nihilism was king. The chaos of the hippie movement with its cry of "make love, not war" and the chaos of the war in Vietnam itself, together with the social unrest that accompanied it, intermingled and fused like so many flushings into a larger cultural sewer. Love and hate were hardly distinguishable. In the feral brain of Charles Manson, they became one exploding nebula of cosmic insight.

Abused severely and eventually abandoned as a child, Manson was a hardened criminal who had spent more of his years behind bars than in a normal, social environment. Though uneducated, he was extremely street smart, and the result was that he plunged into the kind of career that befitted his warped genius—he became a con artist. During one of his brief stints between jail sentences, Manson studied pop psychology, hypnosis, magic, and the occult—in particular, Scientology. His familiarity with Scientology made him particularly susceptible years later to receiving de Grimston's gospel. His criminal connections, which were extensive because of his life as a jailbird, gave him the "business" clout and savvy to translate de Grimston's rhetorical ravings into occult *Aktion*.

Manson was an occult entrepreneur. Yet at the same time he was a tactician with tremendous personal skills and a baroque imagination. Of all members of the American counterculture over the last several generations, Manson was the great mastermind of aesthetic terrorism. Even the murder of Hollywood actress Sharon Tate and the LaBianca family was more an artistic "happening" than most people realize. As the prosecution argued during the trial of the Manson organization with a matter-of-fact edge of realism, it is doubtful that Manson thought his actions would precipitate a race war leading to the downfall of America, after which he and his followers would emerge as the supreme rulers. Instead, it is more likely that Manson was attempting to magically manipulate and control social events. The killings were not political assassinations so much as they were were ritual, or sacrificial slayings. In keeping with the symbolism of Crowley and the fantasies of the aesthetic terrorists, the slayings were intended as supernatural "triggers" for the apocalyptic upheavals that magicians since early in the century had been expecting.

A hippie and a reputed ex-con and Process member by the name of Blaine, according to Sanders, having met up with Manson in San Francisco, predicted that Charlie would be a "great man" in the near future because "he knows all about magic." Manson had stolen the name for his religious group from the original nomenclature of the Process. Manson simply called his cult "the Final Church," which suggests strongly that he was bent on executing de Grimston's revelations.

According to Sanders, Mary Anne de Grimston thought she was the manifest, universal power of the archwitch Hecate, decanting the powder of death into the cups of the Great Beast and the Scarlet Woman in Anger's *Inauguration*. Sanders goes on to explain that Mary Anne, who seems to have been the power behind her husband's throne, saw herself as the sculptress of something called "the Fear," which was what Manson sought to unleash in the summer of 1969. Brother Ely, a distinguished representative of the Process hierarchy, had an inspiration about promoting the Fear by recruiting biker gangs as the cult's own Nazi "brown shirts."

The bikers, however, were not sufficiently "spiritual" to carry out ritually correct mayhem and refused to cooperate in the plan. So Manson took over the command and designed a campaign with slogans and metaphors drawn from the Beatles' albums and the Book of Revelation. He called his project "helter skelter."

The idea of helter skelter was extremely good Process Church theology. It connoted, in effect, the unleashing of the cataclysmic evils of the end times in order to align the powers of Satan with the majesty of Christ. It was a transcendental balancing act. Manson had taken the name "helter skelter" from the Beatles' song and the concept from what he regarded as the "secret" meanings behind the cut "Revolution 9" on the *White Album*. "Revolution 9" was the apocalyptic substantiation of Revelation 9, the chapter in the Bible that tells of blowing the "fifth trumpet" and opening the "bottomless pit" from which fly scorpionlike creatures "with hair like women's hair," commissioned to torture a third of humankind.

Manson believed his "family," with their long hippie tresses, were in fact the appointed agents of wrath and mutilation. He even holed up his "family" at a remote location in Death Valley, where he thought was located the entrance to the bottomless pit. When "helter skelter" was finished, he would return with his legions of doom to their foul abode inside the bowels of the earth.

Perversely, helter skelter was, in Manson's thoughts, an expression of divine "love." Manson taught his disciples that love and the infliction of fear upon the population were identical. Until 1969, Manson had proseltyzed for the Haight religion of "love is all, love is groovy." In 1969 he was pronouncing the "opposite," which he said was not really a contrariety anyway. The distinction between hate and love was an illusion clutched by the unenlightened soul. Manson's crowd began to dress up like the Process in black capes and other forms of black attire in order to practice "getting the Fear."

The pages of the *Fear* issue of the Process publication were replete with images of holocaust. On the back was a flaming pink skull. Out of the skull's mouth issued a marching phalanx of Nazi storm troopers parading over masses of people burning up in a fire. At the lower right could be seen the evil visage of Hitler and a Buddhist monk in flames. The head of page 1 read, "Next issue: DEATH."

Death came not too long after midnight on August 8, 1969, at the lavish and highly protected home of actress Sharon Tate and her movie producer husband Roman Polanski on Cielo Drive in the Hollywood hills. Exactly what happened has been documented and reconstructed thousands of times over in police files, court depositions, and hardcover accounts of the Manson murders. The issue is not so much the chain of events as the real motives for the crime, which over the years have remained a gnarled skein of second-guessing, official puzzlement, and facile psychologizing. The presumption that Manson's trained killers—"creepy-crawlies" they christened themselves—were out to kill and terrorize all of southern California until Armageddon ensued just does not fit the facts or the commonly ignored "ritual" structure of their acts.

The Mansonites committed only two murders, which, though spectacular, were not all that random. It has been fairly well established that Manson knew his victims very well. He may even have had personal grudges against them. There is firm evidence that Manson himself was enmeshed in a vast, drug and pornography procurement racket that implicated many of the Hollywood stars, including Roman Polanski. Manson was known to have crashed parties—or in some cases was even invited to parties—that many of the celebrities in Sharon Tate's social network attended.

One hypothesis, which has been perhaps overstated, is that Sharon Tate was knocked off in vengeance for a drug deal that had gone sour. But Sharon herself seems to have been a relative innocent. When the Mansonites broke into the Polanski home, Sharon was pregnant and had nothing else on her mind besides becoming a mother. As the Manson maniacs repeatedly stabbed the other occupants of the house before finally killing Tate herself, the distraught Sharon pleaded, "Please, I'm going to have a baby. All I want to do is have my baby."

The birth of another "baby," however, had been responsible in part for Sharon's ascent in Hollywood. On June 15, 1968, Polanski's film *Rosemary's Baby* held its premiere. At the time the movie was called the "best advertisement for satanism ever made," and it grossed almost $20 million while playing to overflowing theaters and capturing an Academy Award nomination. *Rosemary's Baby* was about the birth of the "Devil's child" in mid-Manhattan in the mid-1960s. LaVey performed in the brief scene where Satan impregnates the woman who bears his son.

If one understands the mythology and eschatology of the Church of Satan, it takes very little guile to draw the inference that *Rosemary's Baby* was an allegory of the birth of the demonic eon, no matter what it was precisely termed. The heroine, played by Mia Farrow, is an ingenue housewife whose actor husband conspires behind her back to make her into the "bride of Satan." The deal is struck with a kindly old couple in the upstairs apartment, who turn out to be high priest and priestess of a powerful satanic coven. In the end, the couple discloses that the husband has been promised fame and success in his acting career in return for making the "Devil's bargain."

While there is no indication that Polanski, who was in Europe at the time of the murders, had "sacrificed" Sharon, the birth of Rosemary's baby and the death of Sharon Tate's baby has an odd parallelism. Sharon, it was rumored, had been initiated into the occult, perhaps even the

Church of the Process. At least she starred in a succession of horror films just prior to her death, such as *The Fearless Vampire Killers*. And on August 8, 1988, the leadership of a satanic organization in San Francisco calling itself the Abraxas Foundation on Evil held a celebration to commemorate the nineteenth anniversary of Sharon Tate's "sacrifice." The aesthetics of terror had become part of the liturgical calendar.

The rudimentary problem in analyzing "Satan's underground" in the current era has always been making plausible connections among the activities and misdeeds of particular groups, or covens, that might somehow lay bare a deeper layer of organization than the conventional wisdom would posit. The controversy over whether there are indeed systematic conspiracies of satanists nationally or worldwide is a tired one, however. For the argument pretends to revolve around whether criminal satanists work together in some lockstep, bureaucratic arrangement, like the FBI or the CIA, or whether they merely do what they do spontaneously without benefit of outside backing or communication.

The issue, however, is far more thorny. The aesthetics of terror has always been an ideological conspiracy to remake the world. And the power of media messages and symbols to activate the psyches of significant segments of the population brooks no dispute. It is true that Susan Atkins, one of Manson's followers, at one time worked as a dancer for Anton LaVey in his collusion with nightclub impresarios. It is known that Manson had a close association, not only with members of the Church of the Process, but with the remants of Crowley's organizational structure—the O.T.O. in southern California.

But the personal and institutional nexus is much less important than the collusive strength of the occult constructs themselves. The sense of apocalypse can be infectious, even among those who do not know each other. The thousands of fans of a rock group like Megadeath do not have to legally "conspire" among each other in order to share the same affection and anger. It is the "show" and the rallying words of their beloved celebrities that unite them and engender a uniform response.

Similarly, in the twentieth century, satanists began to "market" themselves to the masses. Manson was influenced. So was Pete Roland. All today's satanists do not need to be pen pals or have secret meetings or collect national dues in order to have a common set of passions and an impact. They just have to listen to the same music and read the same books. It requires only a certain modicum of literacy to become an aesthetic terrorist—and a satanist.

NOTES

1. Alberto Moravia, "The Terrorist Aesthetic: Of Artists, Stockbrokers, and Other Jacobins," *Harper's*, June 1987, p. 38.
2. Thomas McEvilley, "Art in the Dark," in Adam Parfrey, ed., *Apocalypse Culture* (New York: Amok Press, 1987), p. 88.

3. John Zerzan, "The Case Against Art," in Parfrey, *Apocalypse Culture*, p. 135.

4. Adam Parfrey, "Aesthetic Terrorism," in Parfrey, *Apocalypse Culture*, p. 115.

5. Parfrey, *Apocalypse Culture*, p. 117.

6. Quoted in Martin Esslin, *Antonin Artaud* (New York: Penguin Books, 1976), p. 124.

7. Antonin Artaud, *The Cenci*, trans. Simon Watson Taylor (New York: Grove Press, 1977), p. 7.

8. Antonin Artaud, *Selected Writings*, trans. Helen Weaver (New York: Farrar, Straus and Giroux, 1976), p. 244.

9. Ibid., p. 99.

10. Parfrey, *Apocalypse Culture*, p. 62.

11. Greil Marcus, *Lipstick Traces: A Secret History of the Twentieth Century* (Cambridge, MA: Harvard University Press, 1989).

12. Ibid., p. 443.

13. Quoted in P. Adams Sitney *Visionary Film*, (New York: Oxford University Press, 1974), p. 106.

14. Kenneth Anger, "Invocation of my Demon Brother," *Film Culture* (Spring 1970), p. 1.

CHAPTER 6.

The Age of Satan

The Satanists are marching, where the vague moon vapor creeps, while the night wind to their coming like a thunder's herald sweeps. They are clad in ancient grandeur, while the world unheeding sleeps . . . The truth about Satanism is far more frightening than anything people might *expect* to see."

——ANTON LAVEY *in a 1975 interview with writer Dick Russell*

Until quite recently, the truth about satanism was not something people really wanted to see.

The conventional wisdom was that, if there was such a thing as satanism at all, it was so well hidden and nefarious that no one could fathom its secrets *or* that it was all charade and harlequinade—a clever and financially lucrative spoof of every private anxiety and closet superstition of the American middle classes.

When LaVey started holding his "midnight magic seminars" on Friday evenings in 1960, and when on the evening of April 30, 1966— *Walpurgisnacht* in the occult calendar—he declared the arrival of the Age of Satan, it all seemed like good theater. With its chilling black interior, its art deco geegaws, and its lifelike, automated mannequins of tarts and bar floozies, LaVey's house at 6114 California Street in San Francisco served throughout the Vietnam era as a kind of discreet, haute-hip tourist attraction. LaVey performed both "satanic weddings" and "satanic funerals" to apprehend the interest of the press. He also kept a full-grown circus lion that scared the neighbors with its roar. With deliberate parody, LaVey called himself "the black pope."

A contemporary observer noted that in attendance at both the magic seminars and the rituals of the Church of Satan were physicians, lawyers, engineers, teachers, former members of the FBI, IBM executives, and even street cleaners. At one gathering of eight, half were either Ph.D.'s or Ph.D. candidates. The same writer noted that LaVey was never raided because he had a warm relationship with the San Francisco police. The highlight of the ceremonies were "cursing sessions" in which participants sought to destroy or harm by magic their real, or fancied, enemies.

Adolfo de Jesus Constanzo (left) with his bodyguard. This photograph was one of the items found when the Federales raided Constanzo's home in Mexico City. Photograph © Brad Doherty. Used with permission.

Five alleged members of a cult linked to the murders of fifteen people in Matamoros, Mexico, stand before cult paraphernalia at a news conference May 5, 1989. Alvaro de Leon (second from left) admitted to killing the cult's leader, Constanzo. Sara Maria Aldrete Villarreal (far right) was said to be one of the cult's spiritual leaders. Photograph © Reuters/Bettmann Newsphotos. Used with permission.

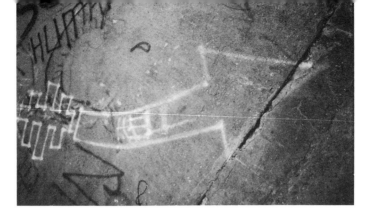

Satanic heavy metal symbolism at site of Denver, Colorado, skateboard rallies. The three-barred cross is used by the Abraxas Foundation, a satanist skinhead organization. Photograph by Carl A. Raschke.

Satanist graffiti on garage door in Denver, Colorado. The message reads: "And when you go home this weekend, be sure to tell your mother SATAN." Photograph by Carl A. Raschke.

Site of a satanic ritual discovered in an abandoned house in rural Indiana. Symbolism on the floor is employed in conjunction with "magic circle." Photograph by Bruce W. Yonker. Used with permission.

Scenes from a recent satanic ritual depicting a communion service using one of the participant's own blood (the man in the middle picture has cut himself on the chest). The design of the altar and the ceremony depicted exactly match Aleister Crowley's prescriptions. Photographs by Bruce W. Yonker. Used with permission.

A Satanic baptism, using a naked woman as an altar, performed in 1967 by Anton Szandor LaVey, founder of the Church of Satan. Child in center is LaVey's daughter Zeena, now a spokesperson for her father's religion. Photograph © Associated Press/Wide World Photos. Used with permission.

Aleister Crowley, twentieth-century religious showman and spiritual ancestor of contemporary satanism, shown in 1934 dressed in "magical" attire. Crowley called himself "The Beast 666." Photograph © Associated Press/Wide World Photos. Used with permission.

Convicted mass murderer Charles Manson, with Nazi swastika scratched on his forehead, walking to court in Los Angeles. Manson, whose notorious "family" murdered movie actress Sharon Tate in the summer of 1969, is a hero and cult figure to present day satanist skinheads. Photograph © Associated Press/Wide World Photos. Used with permission.

Serial killer Richard Ramirez, known as the "Night Stalker," displaying the satanic symbol of the five-pointed star, or pentagram, during a courtroom appearance in 1985. Ramirez was found guilty of murder. Photograph © Associated Press/Wide World Photos. Used with permission.

Dr. Michael A. Aquino, a colonel in U.S. Army intelligence, who has drawn Pentagon investigations for his leadership of an offshoot of the Church of Satan known as the Temple of Set. Photograph by Linda O. Blood. Used with permission.

Ritual child abuser Frank Fuster arrested in Florida. The Fuster case, though not well publicized, was similar to the McMartin preschool affair in which seven defendants were acquitted. Fuster was convicted by a jury in Miami. Photograph courtesy of the Miami Herald. *Used with permission.*

Raymond Buckey (second from right) and his mother, Peggy McMartin Buckey, in court in January 1986 at the start of their trial for felony child abuse and conspiracy charges in the McMartin Preschool case. Left is attorney Dean Gits, representing Mrs. Buckey, and second from left is Daniel Davis, representing Buckey. Photograph © Associated Press/Wide World Photos. Used with permission.

Raymond Buckey reads through papers in Superior Court in Los Angeles. Two and one half years from the start of the trial, jurors began deliberations on the longest criminal proceeding in U.S. history. Photograph © Associated Press/Wide World Photos. Used with permission.

Rock star Ozzy Osbourne holding an inverted cross. Photograph © Ralph P. Fitzgerald. Used with permission.

Gene Simmons, a member of the rock group KISS. Photograph © Lynn Goldsmith. Used with permission.

General Hershey, head of the federal draft system during the period of the Vietnam War, was evidently a frequent target of abuse.

He was born Howard Anton "Tony" LaVey on April 11, 1930, in Chicago, as his biographer says, to "a travelling liquor salesman." That may or may not be true. During Prohibition, nobody sold liquor in Chicago except the well-known rivals of Elliot Ness. His family moved to San Francisco in the early thirties, and stayed until 1947. By his early teens, LaVey had developed a strong interest in the occult and was fascinated by such roguish magicians as Rasputin, Cagliostro, and Crowley. He dropped out of high school in his junior year and joined the Clyde Beatty circus.

In the winter of 1947, LaVey was working for the Pike Amusement Park in Long Beach, California, where he became steeped in stage magic. He married his first wife, Carole, the daughter of a Wells Fargo Bank executive in 1950. The following year, chiefly to avoid the draft, he enrolled in San Francisco's City College, where he studied criminology. In 1952 he acquired a job as a police photographer, which according to his own account drilled him in the seamy affairs of life and made him completely cynical about the human conditon. He quit his job as police photographer and instead took up playing the organ at the Lost Weekend nightclub.

As early as the late 1960s, LaVey proclaimed that he had a "mission" and a "legacy" to fulfill. He said he envisioned a time—the fruition of the Age of Satan—when satanic emblems, rather than crosses, would rise from church roofs. LaVey added that he was going to make hatred and defiance of authority not only respectable but a socially powerful force.

In 1971, *Newsweek* magazine, however, dismissed LaVey as "a man unworthy of the devil's trust." He was a con artist, but he certainly posed no danger to the world. Although the same publication observed that a number of sickening crimes could be traced specifically to "deranged" individuals associated with LaVey's Church of Satan, the consensus remained that LaVey was a highly successful scalawag and buffoon.

The view seemed unshakable, in spite of the unsettling circumstances surrounding the untimely death of actress Jayne Mansfield.

May Mann, author of *Jayne Mansfield: A Biography*, claimed not to have had any previous communication with the dead until 1967. That was the year the buxom movie star was killed in a tragic automobile accident along with her lawyer and lover, Sam Brody, on a highway outside of New Orleans. In the preface, Mann says that Mansfield came back in her "spiritual" state, demanding that May complete the biography she was about to put down for good and tell the world everything that had gone on in her life, including her strange "affair" with the founder of the Church of Satan, Anton LaVey.

Mann indicated she had planned to dump the nearly complete book, chiefly because "the behind-the-scenes aspects of Mansfield's life were too awful." Mansfield, however, continually appeared to her in dreams, pleading that she reconsider her decision. "World famous psychics" hounded her, Mann said. Finally, Mansfield got through by the help of one of Mann's friends, Yvonne Avery, who claimed that she had been one of the world's foremost psychics as a child. "Tell all of the conversations we had the night before my death and everything I confided to you at all times during the years" was the urgent psychic message from one of Hollywood's shrewdest and most successful publicity seekers.

The daughter of a lawyer, Mansfield was born Vera Jane Palmer on April 19, 1933, in Bryn Mawr, Pennsylvania. Her father died when she was three, and most of Mansfield's early life was spent under the care of a very strict mother. After Mansfield's mother married Harry Peers, a traveling sales engineer, the family moved to Dallas. At fourteen, Mansfield was raped by one of the boys at school. She picked out a handsome older lad named Paul J. Mansfield, confided to him she was pregnant, and persuaded him to wed her in secret. Mansfield lied about her age to obtain the marriage license. Paul joined the army, and Mansfield went away to college with the agreement that after his two years of officer training, they would move to Hollywood to allow her to venture a career as a film star. Events proceeded as planned, except that Paul moved back to Texas from Hollywood after only a brief stay, and she remained with her three-year-old daughter, Jayne Marie. Paul had wanted an average, everyday, all-American girl for a wife, not a temptress of the silver screen.

Hollywood was a bitter struggle, but Mansfield managed to fetch a bit part in the film *The Female Jungle*. At twenty-two her full-bosomed figure immediately typecast her in the "sex goddess" roles, for which she eventually became infamous. Soon Warner Brothers hired her, and shortly thereafter she did some time on Broadway as well as in Las Vegas. Mansfield showed herself a prodigy at pulling publicity stunts, such as a fake kidnapping of herself. By now a divorce was in progress, and Mansfield had many impassioned suitors.But she fell for "Mr. Universe" Mickey Hargitay, who built her a house known as the "Pink Palace" with thirty bathrooms and a heart-shaped pool, all in the pastel color that was her trademark.

After having been assigned to Fox Studios, she married Hargitay in an "intimate little ceremony" that turned out to be the most stunning media event of the season. The marriage lasted through two more children until Mansfield divorced Mickey in Mexico to marry an Italian. The Italian was unable to secure his own divorce, however, and Mansfield at twenty-nine consoled herself by marrying another man of the same nationality named Matt Cimber, a twenty-eight-year-old director. Two more children followed, but Mansfield soon tired of Matt. Affairs ensued, including one with a twenty-year old Venezuelan. She never remarried, even though the obsessive Sam Brody, a boyfriend and an attorney in whose automobile she finally met her death, reportedly asked her over and over again. At her death, the divorce with Cimber was still not final.

According to virtually all the Hollywood gossip columnists, Jayne was preoccupied with sex, astrology, and religion. In an interview she once said that "in physical relationships, everything goes. The wildest form of love is beautiful. I don't see how you can make a floral arrangement out of it. It should be animalistic. It should be beautiful. It should be tender. It should be brutal, sadistic." Mansfield had been bewitched by the lethal mixture of occultism, vanguard sexuality, and the undercurrents of brutality and sophisticated squalor that had been the hidden regime of Hollywood for generations. In time, she tired of raw hedonism, and began to flirt with Catholicism. She was especially attracted to the incense, the golden altars, the solemnity of the Mass, and the august tonality of the cathedral settings. It was difficult for her emotionally, however, to remain the great American sex symbol and still practice Catholicism. In the end, she chose something similar, but at the same time quite divergent—*satanism.*

It was all in good fun perhaps. "It was all for laughs," said Mansfield of her meeting in 1966 with Anton LaVey and her subsequent initiation as a high priestess of the Church of Satan. LaVey escorted her through his home, which he told her was "the First Satanic Church of the Devil." He showed her some candles on the altar, which he said contained the power of death and would bring down a curse on anyone who touched them. Her boyfriend Brody, who tried to keep a close rein on Mansfield, was not at all gladdened with her fondness toward the Prince of Darkness. When he returned to the altar room, Brody became angry. In order to spite LaVey, Sam lighted the forbidden candles on the altar, which only the Devil himself supposedly had the authority to light. LaVey became furious and proclaimed that Satan himself had cursed Brody and that he would be killed within a year. LaVey was serious, but Brody laughed, thinking it all a gigantic jest.

LaVey called Mansfield into a back room and instructed her solemnly that "no one laughs at the Devil!" LaVey darkly prophesied that Brody would meet death in a car crash—not one, but a succession of them, and that anyone else in his company would also die. LaVey demanded that Jayne rid herself of Brody forthwith. Mansfield, however, could not easily take leave of a man who maintained control over the actress through blackmail, physical abuse, and dramatic and tearful gestures of repentance and requests for forgiveness, not to mention the purchase of expensive jewelry. Later it was discovered that Mansfield's own money had been used for the gifts. At the same time, Mansfield began to advertise and promote the Church of Satan in the same fashion a famous sports star does testimonials for children's charities. In one instance she shocked the American military brass on a tour with the G.I.'s in Vietnam by asking for a satanic religious service.

The series of predicted car crashes began, but Mansfield apparently felt she could outwit both Brody *and* LaVey. Brody made her drunk one night and snapped photographs of her naked with a man she nad never seen before. Mansfield alleged that Brody had slipped knockout drops in her drink and that she had been framed. Brody threatened to turn the photos over to the judge and release them to the press and the scandal magazines to prove Mansfield was an unfit mother for her children.

Jayne told biographer Mann that she trusted the "Devil's curse" to destroy Brody first, if only she could endure his ravages for a while longer. Parroting LaVey, Mansfied said with a mocking laugh, "You know something? Satan has been the best friend the church, I mean conventional religions, ever had for he's kept them in business all of these years!"

The San Francisco newspapers were abuzz with gossip that Mansfield had been anointed the new "high priestess" of the Church of Satan. Jayne denied it. A better public relations gimmick, however, could not have been invented.

Mansfield was less sure of what she was doing by early 1967. The car wrecks, regular thrashings by Brody, freak accidents (including the mauling of one of her children by a lion), pipes bursting at the Pink Palace, and the resulting bad publicity—all began to take a toll. Mansfield and her friends began to believe LaVey had put a curse on the Pink Palace, although she appeared to scoff at LaVey's claims that he had the true "power of Satan." Like a naughty schoolgirl confessing to her mother that she had only appeared to go along with the raunchy behavior of the bad crowd, she insisted to Mann that she went to LaVey's black castle only because "it seemed a fun thing to do."

In the same breath, she gave Mann still another version of what actually happened when the curse was pronounced. She said that her primary attraction to LaVey had been sexual and that like any flippant starlet she had been captivated by his eccentricities, including the 500-pound lion he kept as a pet and the black hearse he drove. She said LaVey had fallen in love with her as well and had discretely proposed marriage, which she considered "a laugh."

LaVey showed Brody and Mansfield some ointments he claimed could supernaturally heal, murder, or inflict other kinds of unspecified magical results. She denied she had worn amulets with the Devil's symbols as well as the charms LaVey had given her. Instead she had taken them secretly to her priest and asked him if Anton LaVey indeed had possessed evil powers. According to Mansfield, the priest confirmed her fears and warned her about staying too close to LaVey or the world of black magic. Afraid to anger LaVey, however, Mansfield agreed to pose for publicity pictures with him, including one shot in which she came across exactly like the diabolical counterpart to a Playboy Bunny.

Whether produced by magic or not, the disasters in her life continued. The end came swiftly. Early on the morning of June 28, 1967, Mansfield was killed in a car crash outside New Orleans. Her head had been severed from her body during the accident. Brody and the chauffeur had been killed as well, although three of Mansfield's children survived with injuries. Anton LaVey, the Devil incarnate, has a different recall of events. "Yes, there was Sam Brody," LaVey told journalist Dick Russell in 1975. "He worked overtime at being detestable, kept her doped and liquored up and had guys fooling around with her in the bedroom while he took pictures. If she ever left him, he promised to ruin her career and see that she lost custody of her kids. He was despicable. Utterly despicable!"

Mansfield was a "charter member" of LaVey's church. The scuttlebutt was that he and Mansfield were secret lovers, but LaVey was known to exaggerate his attachments to gorgeous women, in particular blonde movie queens. At one time he had made similar representations about an affair with Marilyn Monroe. Did LaVey put a curse on Brody because he had somehow committed a ritually inappropriate act, as Mann suggests, or because he saw Brody as the "despicable" other man, as a sexual and possibly even a magical rival. The power of the inverted pentagram may have been complicated by the passions of a deadly love triangle.

LaVey could barely suppress his most deeply-drawn and absolutely icy hatred for Brody even when talking to a reporter about him eight years later. Brody was slime, an absolute predator, LaVey mused. On one occasion, according to LaVey, Brody picked up twenty young, black toughs on a San Francisco street with the pretext that Jayne Mansfield had "invited" them all to a party at LaVey's mansion. Brody then brought them back to LaVey's place, where they wreaked havoc and minor vandalism. The Devil threatened to unleash his Ethiopian lion, phoned the police, and that was the beginning of the end for Sam Brody, as far as LaVey was concerned.

There is no question that LaVey was infatuated with Mansfield, as he had been at one time with Marilyn Monroe. The Devil prefers blondes, or so a new version of the cherished maxim might go. A question persists, however: if he placed such a howling curse upon Brody, why did he allow Mansfield to be killed in such a gruesome manner? LaVey said he could only warn her and that he could not hold her hand or accompany her twenty-four hours a day. When he received word of the debacle, LaVey was almost clinical in his description, if not saddened—the Devil cannot show emotion—by the precise outcome of this particular "working." "I was in my den, clipping a picture out of the newspaper of myself placing flowers on the grave of Marilyn Monroe. And when I turned the page over, I saw there'd been a picture of Mansfield on the other side and I . . . *I'd* cut straight across her neckline."

The use of the first person in the above citation appears to offer a peremptory insight into the strange and dexterously guarded psychology of the man who took the underground religion of satanism and recruited for it a sprawling, consumer clientele. While LaVey throughout his writings and interviews has repeatedly disclaimed that "supernatual" machinations and invocation of real spirits are involved, in the same breath he has arrogated to himself magical honors and titles and lent the plain impression that the Church of Satan held tight rein over the forces of hell. In Mansfield's case, the Devil—or LaVey, depending on your perspective—*did* do it magically!

In *The Satanic Bible*, LaVey had prescribed carefully how to kill an enemy by unseen intermediaries—all quite legal, but not necessarily morally justifiable. Was LaVey proud of his "working" in the case of Mansfield and Brody, or was it just one further example of a satanist's own painful, "tragic," bittersweet, and Lear-like meditation on the human condition?

Why did the beheading of Mansfield coincide magically with LaVey's memorial for Marilyn Monroe, another blonde bombshell who became the ethereal Venus-girl consecrated at the eternal shrine of American male lust, only to be "sacrificed" in a similar spooky and untimely death. The irony was that Matamoros mass murderer Constanzo, a proven criminal in the occult underworld, had also been obsessed with the person and destiny of the 1950s fairy princess.

About the time of his flirtations with Mansfield, LaVey was married to Diane, another young blonde who met him while she was an usher in a local movie theater. Diane had adored him and given her very heart and soul to him in the early, entrepreneurial phase of the Church of Satan. Diane seemed to have been jealous of Mansfield, too, but it is not evident she was aware of LaVey's fetishisms toward a pantheon of celluloid goddesses.

LaVey, who has given interviews to the press on the average of once a decade, told journalist Dick Russell what he *really* had in mind for the "legions of satanists." Contrary to the line cult apologists continue to push, as though they were comfortably kept guard dogs trained to spring to their haunches and bark at the approach of truth, LaVey let Russell know he did not intend to become simply a circus entertainer feeding off annuities and the memories of the Church of Satan.

It should also be noted that Russell probably could not have written what he did without LaVey's approval. "Anton Szandor LaVey has a master plan," wrote Russell, "and he doesn't think he will need force to achieve it. He expects it might come to him as naturally as the 25,000 followers who already carry his red card declaring themselves CITIZENS

OF THE INFERNAL EMPIRE. Before he dies, Anton LaVey believes that he and an elite force of Satanists will rule the world."

The final statement sounds very much like the typical, overly exercised "Christian" scare tactic that apologists for cults are constantly reminding us cannot by any stretch of reason have a basis in fact. Russell's interview with LaVey, however, did not appear in *Christianity Today*. It was published in *Argosy*—that literary bunker of the nonnonsense, macho mentality. LaVey, the "recluse" in 1975, was a far different character than the supposed vaudeville personality who had conspired to keep the cameras clicking all through the Vietnam era. That was also the same year in which a long-stewing crisis described by Michael Aquino, LaVey's most notorious trainee in demonic showmanship, allegedly overtook the Church of Satan.

According to Aquino, the crisis was precipiated by the crass commercialism and hucksterism of LaVey himself. LaVey started selling religious offices in the Church of Satan to anybody who would sign a check. The move horrified Aquino. He believed satanism should be kept chaste and "ethical" like the Holy See itself, even though the medieval church had always thought *simony*—after Simon Magus, the magician who offered to buy power from the apostles—was quite proper behavior for the evil liege of vice, corruption, and general scalawagery.

LaVey's decision to set up a service business for mail-order magi was very much in keeping with his original design both to compromise all and to lay bare the hypocrisy of all, perhaps even the hypocrisy of Aquino. In any event, that is how the Church of Satan became thousands, if not hundreds of thousands, strong despite the habitual bridling and sniffing of the cult apologists who at the drop of a glove will stick up their dukes and shout, "Paranoid!"

The controversy between LaVey and Aquino centered on how to build the "elite" of the future. Aquino wanted the bluest of blue-blooded, intelligent stock. LaVey looked toward a new satanic sanhedrin to oversee a society awash with luxury, instinctual freedom, and Babylonian excess. The so-called nine satanic statements devised by LaVey as the would-be catechism of the Church of Satan dwell upon this theme. According to the statements, Satan is the cipher for every kind of forbidden pleasure and vice—indulgence rather than abstinence, "vital existence" as opposed to pie-in-the-sky, wisdom instead of "hypocrisy," vengeance and not mercy, love for those "deserving" of love, as well as every conceivable form of physical gratification. The same "ethic" had been enunciated, of course, by rakes for hundred of years, and on the surface there seemed to be very little difference between LaVey's satanism and the scurrilous doings of the Hell Fire Club.

In short, LaVey all along has harbored his own weird version of the American dream, the kind that was nurtured in the girlie magazines and pornography shops of the forties and fifties. The postwar period was a golden age for LaVey, and Marilyn Monroe was its golden girl.

If Mansfield was the incarnation of his most devilish desire, Marilyn was the cue for his confession of a mortal past, including the possibility of human frailty. "I left [Marilyn] for someone else," LaVey told Russell ruefully, meaning his first wife. Throughout the fifties, he said, he pined over Marilyn. She even sent him her famous "Golden Dreams calendar," which he shyly locked up.

In LaVey's imagination, *l'affaire* Marilyn was in no way something gloomy and sinister. His accounts do not vary much from a successful, middle-aged executive reminiscing about his Tom Sawyer escapades while growing up in Small Town, USA. His relationship was ostensibly of short duration, but it was intense and exciting. He and Marilyn met when they both were down on their luck. They had to make love in the back seat of a car.

LaVey has frequently been called an incurable romantic. Not only does he furnish both his life and his soul—if there is anything left of it—with the cheap and kitschy icons of many bygone gilded ages. He is in love with the images of alluring and unattainable beauty, if not virtue. If Carmen, the dark gypsy in Bizet's Romantic opera, was the doom of even the most hardened soldier, Marilyn the blonde waif has been something of a psychic peril for LaVey.

LaVey divulged to Russell a rather striking and eerie incident from that period of his life that in the retelling sounds very much like a bunch of kids camping out at the graveyard on Halloween. According to LaVey, he and Marilyn would park the car and neck beside one of Frank Lloyd Wright's famous houses. Built for a wealthy shoe manufacturer during the 1920s on the outskirts of San Francisco, the house was meant to imitate Mayan architecture. The couple loved the place because it was storied to be one of those more-than-simply-haunted houses, similar to the mysterious and possessed hotel in Stephen King's *The Shining*.

An ancient Mayan curse had supposedly settled upon the house. The houseboy had gone berserk and murdered seven people within the precincts. The original owner was ruined financially in the midst of the Depression. The wife of the second owner committed suicide by leaping from one of the towers. Marilyn was enthralled with the site and with its legends, LaVey said. Was it an omen? A magical preview of peculiar things to come? Or, as we would say today in psychological jargon, a synchronicity?

For Russell, LaVey embroidered the tale about his sexual escapades with Marilyn in the dark during a visit with the writer to a comparable house in central Mexico at one of the world's most "magical" sites—in a town called Tepotzlan near the volcano Popocatepetl in the heart of Mayan country. LaVey and Russell took an excursion to Teptzlan to visit the home of a "writer" who is never named. The writer lived in "the kind of house Marilyn Monroe would have had," and the house compared remarkably with "the house where she died." Tepotzlan is where the cream of Mexico's witch community hangs out. The house is shaped like a trapezoid and therefore, according to LaVey, vibrates with awesome and primeval "energy" of the demonic.

LaVey drew a parallel between ancient Mexican—Mayan and Aztec—and German architecture, both of which reputedly convey a mood of brooding malevolence, even of apocalyptic peril. Mexican and German cultures have been nourished by "trapezoidal" shapes and angles, LaVey claimed. The feeling of the house at any given moment corresponded to the satanic vision of the future—oppressive, haunted, totally uncanny, not all too different from the life and death of Marilyn Monroe.

A rich physician bought Marilyn's own house after she was found mysteriously dead of an overdose of barbiturates, or so the coroner's report read. According to LaVey, the doctor's mother died in the house exactly one year after Marilyn's death. The doctor packed his bags and left. LaVey claimed he himself went to the house in 1973 on the eleventh anniversary of Marilyn's passing in order to "conduct an experiment." Melodramatically perhaps, LaVey would not reveal anything more to Russell, breaking off his narrative at that point with the teasing disclaimer that there were things he could not "speak about."

A footnote perhaps should be inserted here. A growing number of conspiracy buffs, investigative journalists, and private eyes are convinced Marilyn was murdered because of alleged liaisons with both John and Bobby Kennedy. The Kennedys' chronic womanizing is now out of the closet and on to the front pages of the scandal magazines. At least one documentary made in England has made a strong case based on some key, though admittedly circumstantial, evidence that the Kennedy brothers, in collusion with Peter Lawford, were sleeping with Marilyn on the sly. Marilyn's "little red diary," which supposedly contained secret matters of state as well as confessions of her love for the Kennedys, disappeared after her body was found.

A Los Angeles private investigator named Milo Speriglio, who has spent fifteen years looking into Marilyn's demise, claims Marilyn was privy to the abortive Bay of Pigs operation. Jack Clemmens, a retired Los Angeles policeman, argued Marilyn was murdered, because there was no glass or container by which she could have swallowed all the pills she was supposed to have downed. Reputed Mafia princess Judith Campbell, who reportedly slept with Jack Kennedy, was a friend of Marilyn's and apparently helped introduce the president to the movie queen. Did LaVey ever hear about the hanky-panky with the Kennedys? Is there any connection to Brody and Mansfield?

The connections would surely be "magical," even though LaVey seems to have been present in some way at all the great historical tragedies and explosions of the Vietnam decade. Moreoever, in his own devilish manner he appears to delight in the inferences. The contemporary partisans of punk rock apocalypse culture have drawn the same conclusion. Not only the death of Marilyn Monroe, but the death of Robert Kennedy was a grand act of "ritual sacrifice," the killing of the king and his blonde consort.[1]

It is entirely possible LaVey is kidding about himself and his importance for the world and that all this ethereal, wildly metaphysical, but "romantic" satanism is the concoction of an outsize ego. LaVey has over and over been called the "great showman," the midway barker who is so smart all he ever wants to do is turn a trick or pull off a con—and the bigger the con, the better. The problem is that too many observers, let alone "scholars" or "investigators," have made out LaVey for exactly what he is not—a caricature. Even if Romanticism and Marilyn Monroe alike are dead, the surviving romantics tend to take themselves all too seriously. Most people do not take LaVey seriously, but that does not go for LaVey himself.

At this writing, LaVey has been rumored in the occult underworld to have taken up a part-time residence in Colorado not far from the nerve center of the Strategic Air Command and the Consolidated Space Operations Center in Colorado Springs. Perchance the Devil who is "lord of this world," as the church fathers put it, wants to contemplate the trajectories of flight to other worlds. Perhaps he wants to use his black magic to keep us from going to other worlds or from disturbing his ageless reign.

In addition, LaVey spends a lot of time playing the organ. LaVey has claimed he first met Marilyn Monroe when he was playing the organ for a burlesque hall. She was the trained monkey; he was the organ-grinder. Whether LaVey really knew Marliyn Monroe at all, he kept alive the *myth* of his liaison with her as the most holy relic among the lyrical antiquities of the Church of Satan. Today he plays the organ in memory of Marilyn and, it has been reported, as a sort of dirge for Western civilization itself.

If the West collapses, it will deserve it, LaVey believes. The philosopher Nietzsche once wrote that if a world is teetering, the "artist" ought to give it a push. Since the sixties, LaVey has been following that advice. America and the West for him are the "Great Babylon," not a sinkhole of villainy and fornication, but a nest of phony national self-righteousness, hypocritical morality and religion, and of the sanctioned, but ineffectual "occultism" of science and technology.

LaVey spends hours playing "romantic" music on his great organ in order to "ease" the horror of the convulsions he feels taking place in the ether. Sometimes he messes up. LaVey has "confessed" to one interviewer that by getting angry one night as he pounded on the organ, he "caused" the Mexico City earthquake. It is not clear who was responsibile for the disaster in Soviet Armenia that upstaged Gorbachev's "peace in our time" speech to the United Nations. It may be that when LaVey looses his temper, it is because he is overwhelmed with the memory of Jayne, or Marilyn.

Aquino purports to know LaVey better than anybody currently living. "Sympathy for the devil" may mean that it is easier for one ghastly embodiment of the collective human mind's darkness to appreciate the other. In his history of the Church of Satan, Aquino professes skepticism about LaVey's account of both his fling and his veneration for Marilyn. He compares the career of LaVey to a 1971 horror movie titled *The Abominable Dr. Phibes*, which may or may not have been an allegory of the rise and fall of the man whom the media by the late 1960s had dubbed "the black pope."

Dr. Phibes is about a retired vaudeville actor whose wife is killed in a major automobile mishap. The doctor becomes a recluse and sets about to murder, by chilling and demonic devices, the false physicians who had allowed his wife to perish. Phibes has his wife's body embalmed and keeps it in his house. At the same time he whiles away hours on his gothically grotesque organ and entertains himself with a lifelike mannequin "big band" from the 1930s. His hideous powers are sufficient to create in Pygmalion fashion a beautiful young apparition named Vulnavia, who acts as his purely sexual "familiar." Marilyn, says Aquino, was LaVey's Vulnavia. Aquino also makes the bald statement that LaVey's version of what happened with Marilyn Monroe is "wholly fictitious." Evidently LaVey disclosed most of the details of his affair with Marilyn to a Robert Slatzer, a mutual friend. Aquino contends Slatzer also expressed doubts about the authenticity of the relationship, that Marilyn had never mentioned it to him and that no literary remains were taken from her belongings after her death. It would have been unusual for Marilyn to go around blabbing to her Hollywood friends about a relatively short amour years before when both she and the fellow were young and as yet unnoticed by the world. Before LaVey became famous, the matter probably would not have crossed her mind. After he did gain celebrity status as the Devil himself, the disclosure might have ruined her career. There are many middle-age businessmen who regale their fishing buddies about the time they dated, or even slept with, so-and-so back in high school when she was just a pom-pom girl who could barely pass plane geometry.

Aquino's willingness to dismiss LaVey's preoccupation with Marilyn, however, is less significant than what he does make of the Jayne Mansfield episode. That affair happened, Aquino admits, but the sensationalist media has made far too much out of the "curse." And besides, LaVey was never interested in her. Aquino says he even asked her mother, who could not confirm the affair, as proof positive of LaVey's lack of candor.

A second impartial source was LaVey's wife, Diane, who denied LaVey had ever telephoned Jayne. Did LaVey, who may have been pining over the recently departed Marilyn while straining to manifest a new Vulnavia, just walk into the kitchen and tell Diane that the Great Satan had a new flame? Probably not. Aquino becomes even more pedantic as he refutes LaVey's claim that Brody was the target of a well-aimed curse. LaVey told *Hustler* magazine in 1979 that Mansfield wanted Brody out of the way. (Remember, her attorney lover boy would routinely humiliate and thrash her.) LaVey also told *Hustler* that, to oblige her, Anton pronounced "the ultimate curse—the death rune." Now, says Aquino, "in point of fact there was .no 'death rune curse' in the ceremonial inventory of the Church of Satan." And he adds that "the Church of Satan's familiarity with rune-lore, in any case, was not extensive." Gee whiz! Could it possibly be that LaVey the "clown," LaVey the entrepreneur, LaVey the artful director of psychodrama could have concocted a "rune curse" for Jayne's benefit? Jayne was not exactly a paragon of purity, integrity, and unsullied innocence herself. And LaVey was far more likely to have conspired to engage in some closet sort of homicidal, supernatural skullduggery in order to put out of commission an archrival and to endear himself to Vulnavia—that is, Jayne Mansfield—than to make sure his "rune" ritual could be found in the authorized handbook of satanist maledictions. Aquino might have made sure he was keeping kosher; LaVey was, and has always been, a different story.

LaVey's saga of the triumph and tragedy of his beloved "golden girls," even if embroidered slightly in the telling for his followers, can be easily understood in terms of his theatrical mind-set—aesthetic terrorism gone "pop." The magical personality is a grandiose and narcissistic one. What happens on the world stage is but a manifesting—in fine, a "working"— of the desires, fantasies, and strivings of the lonely madman himself. To rudely paraphrase Descartes, "I think, therefore, it happens. Marilyn becomes metaphor for the sordid history of the twentieth century." Thus says the satanic subconscious: "My one symbol of honesty and childlike naivite has died an untimely death; my own romantic past is obliterated. Let chaos ensue. Usher in the age of fire, the epoch of Satan." LaVey once told the *National Enquirer* that satanists only advocate what most Americans practice. Satanism is not subversion. It is only a wry kind of psychoanalysis. But LaVey the unsung messiah figure should not be given short shrift as well. At one time he predicted that by 1985 all the world's religions would bow before the evangel of Satan. In the sixties he had identified 1984 as the year when more unspeakable things would occur than what was ever dreamed by Orwell. Both prophecies were off the mark.

But LaVey has been somewhat insightful about the pervasive nature of the corruption that he himself, Aquino's denials notwithstanding, has been trying to foment. "We are the new establishment," he has boasted. The spreading incidence of satanic murder cases may vindicate his words. Did LaVey create the "new establishment"? With his own furry and clawed hands did he perform confirmation ceremonies for tomorrow's streetside child molesters, cannibals, and heavy-metal mental perverts? A young man from Pete Roland's home town, who had been raised since a tender age as an acolyte in the local parish of the Church of Satan before turning to Christianity, said with a straight face, "LaVey knows all, sees all. You can't do anything in the religion without LaVey's authority."

It may not be all so simple. The Devil does not have to be perceptibly present to exercise dominion. The early Christian saints knew that was the case. The Devil has only to give permission for human beings to do what comes naturally to them. LaVey has declared over and over that satanism equals the return of what is most repressed, as the terrorist avant-garde has exulted as well. And what is more repressed than the taboos on killing and violence? The sexual taboos have been virtually removed by now. Bare breasts and exposed crotches are not at the cutting edge of the pornography industry any longer. Now it is "snuff" movies where women or children are actually murdered on camera. Could not the same logic be operating inside the cathedrals of religious, IRS-endorsed, Church of Satan–style devilry?

It does not take a universal conspiracy in the formal, political sense to postulate the real existence of all that nasty stuff clipped from the newspapers these days that is called satanism. Aquino probably has never carved a pentagram on the behind of a baby. Hitler, it is reported, hated the smell of blood, and as late as 1945 he was a vegetarian. Even Anton LaVey may never have broken the law, even though it would seem to be a contradiction of his own philosophical principles. But the issue is really moot. When the piano man starts playing, one never knows how many will go out the door dancing. In this case, the music seems to have wafted all the way out into the countryside.

In understanding the message of satanism and its impact on culture, one must not pay a great deal of attention to the self-conscious, high-minded hokum that one reads in the for-public-consumption writings of the movement's leading lights or cult apologists. The argument generally runs as follows:

- Satanism is an established religion with canons and rituals as well as an elitist philosophy that cannot appeal to everyone.
- The theory that there is a current epidemic of satanist crime is overblown. No evidence has been found of any satanic murder—a patent untruth—and if one were found, it would not be satanic at all, merely the work of sick and perverted people who happen to be aping the beliefs and doctrines of the Church of Satan.
- All the fuss about satanist corruption and criminality adds up to nothing more than a hysterical tremor, or a conscious plot, on the

part of Christians to stir up the passions of persecution against a misunderstood and abused religious sect.

Such a view, for example, permeates an earlier "definitive" book on the subject entitled *Satan Wants You: The Cult of Devil Worship in America* by Arthur Lyons. The purpose of the book, which came out right after the swell of reports about sensational crimes with satanist connections began to hit the media, is to disarm concern that there might be anything of significance afoot. No evidence has been found linking satanic religion to satanic crime, and when satanist symbols appear at crime scenes, it is the leavings of sheer charlatans and pretenders. Although Charles Manson professed satanist beliefs, he was not a satanist. The current satanic scare is but a revival of the venerable witchcraft myth. It is similar to the Jewish conspiracy myth. Nor have there ever been real satanists in past history. It is just good old-fashioned Christian psychological projection.

Books like Lyons's count as neither serious reporting nor scholarship. They are cleverly worded appeals to prejudice, particularly the high-brow know-nothingism that sees the world as its own kind of mythic, Manichean battle between enlightened libertinism and the moral fanaticism of Middle America. Lyons never presents the countless cases where "evidence has been found." And he tries to show that the "evils" ascribed to satanism are really those of "fundamentalist Christians"—another stereotype without specificity.

Such writings employ strategies of persuasion familiar to students of propaganda:

1. *Appeal to authority.* In this case, the authority is the "satanist expert" who has studied the cults first-hand and therefore knows so much he or she does not really have to produce documentation or conduct an argument.
2. *Inversion of the subject.* It is not the crooks who are at fault, but the police for persecuting them.
3. *Pseudo-distinction.* Satanists who are caught doing things that look bad are by definition not satanists at all (however, if Jimmy Swaggart does wrong, it is hypocritical behavior typical of all Christians).
4. *Thought-stopping clichés.* Satanism is the fearful construct of right-wing paranoids.
5. *Genetic fallacy.* Some crazy fundamentalists (not to mention some sober police, of course) carry on about satanist conspiracies; therefore, satanists cannot in any way be conspiring.

Lyons' book belongs to a genre of literature and scholarly outpourings these days known as *cult apology,* most of which are written from a "sociological" perspective. Cult apologists are usually social scientists or general authors who hang around offbeat religious groups for such a span of time that they tend to become one with the group mind. Many of them prefer to play "anthropologist" or become involved with the group in such a manner that they think they can begin to profoundly understand the group from the inside.

Among ethnologists this tendency is known as "going native." There are stories of famous anthropologists who went native and never returned to either civilization or sanity. A few cult apologists, usually the ones who study organizations like the Unification Church, actually receive material favors from the group they are supposedly studying "objectively," which does not exactly leave them with a disinterested cast of mind. Whether anybody actually greases their palms, however, is largely irrelevant. Most of the rewards cult apologists receive are "psychic," not financial. The cult adores them, puffs them up, makes them seem important.

Many cult apologists are academics who have only marginally made it in the traditional route to authority, status, and prestige. The fact that the world largely ignores them is offset by the friendship, comaraderie, and fawning that cult members show toward them. In gratitude they become unwitting public relations spokespeople. And, like all public relations flacks, they tend not to question what the cultists tell them. Many of them also start out as civil libertarians who assume that, because someone wants to stop what some religious person is doing, the motive must logically and infallibly be bigotry, pointy-headedness, or a lust to persecute. In the case of satanists, the bigotry argument is probably believed, if satanists consistently believe anything, only by Aquino.

Lyons, who all the way back in 1970 wrote about LaVey and satanism in a quite adulatory manner as a sort of spiritual wave of the future, pleads rather unconvincingly, for example, that virtually all the kinds of incidents detailed so far in this book are fantasies and fables. Like cattle mutilations and UFOs, they constitute the making of an "urban legend"—a popular story spread by word of mouth that is soon accepted as true. The bogus whisperings of urban legends are then, according to this model, amplified and allowed to run amok by an irresponsible and sensation-crazed mass media.

Stories about satanists are supposedly like reported trick-or-treat poisonings. They are nought but dark hauntings and things that go bump in the night, things that strike a primal chord in middle-class America's fantasy soul while mining the mother lode of human credulity. Antisatanism is a huge conspiracy of the malicious and the stupid, including hordes of people with Ph.D.'s and impressive professional certificates. The *National Enquirer* writes about satanist cases; therefore, none of the claims can be true. So do many sheriffs' magazines. There are spurious and unproven cases, of course, all of which Lyons cites. Conveniently, he never mentions any of the other ones. Many, many murder allegations are never proven and never solved, which does not mean according to the canons of empirical inference that no one ever commits murder.

One of the favorite gambits of the cult apologists is a rhetorical sleight of hand that, for want of a better descriptor, might be dubbed the *unsupported, categorical denial,* betoken in the phrase "no evidence has been found . . ." Lyons plays the "no evidence has been found" ditty with the skill of a concert master. The musical score for "no evidence" is composed in the style of "someone who knows." A person with some sort of seemingly authoritative credentials—preferably a cult apologist who knows how to sound as if he "knows"—will very quickly and tersely describe what procultists or anticultists are saying.

Usually, the summary is a caricature, intended to make the anticultists appear fanatical, half-cocked, ill-informed, or all of the above. Then the "expert" will add a concluding sentence, like a dashing and billowing "John Hancock" at the bottom of the Declaration of Independence, which states peremptorily, "But, of course, no evidence has been found . . ."

Lyons, for instance, cites the police investigation of the Finders cult in Washington, D.C., which had been accused of child abuse. There had been suspicion that the Finders had been dabbling in satanism, though neither the press nor the police took the presumption seriously, and Lyons notes correctly that "no evidence was found" to that end. He also observes that no bodies were found. The fraud in such a position is that, from the beginning, no one in law enforcement, or even cult investigation, really thought the Finders were into satanism. Lyons, of course, does not discuss any of the hundreds of other cases where genuine satanism does seem to have cropped up.

The impact of the "no evidence has been found," ploy is to shut off all further reflection on what is happening. Since no evidence has been "found," the case is now closed. The same effect is often achieved by defendants who in organized crime hearings, take the Fifth Amendment over and over. The aim is to impart the spurious impression that because the guilty party constantly protests his innocence, he *is* innocent.

Lyons's book was written prior to Matamoros, and hence the "no evidence has been found" stance seems to have been attenuated. But the most interesting argument of the cult apologists in their Herculean effort to assure the public that no evil is ever done by satanists, only by Christians, can be found in a recent article by Chas S. Clifton in *Gnosis* magazine. Clifton hypothesizes that the reason so many therapists, police, and "ritual abuse" victims are telling stories about satanism is because of an outsize manifestation of "astral plane reality"—or, in nonoccult terminology, the outpouring of archetypal consciousness fed by "centuries of imagination."

The theory is both weird and silly, and it reveals the extent to which fanatical denial plagues the American intelligentsia on this very topic. The aesthetic terrorists are suddenly discovering that somebody took them seriously—i.e., heard them cry, "Fire!"—and they are now denying any responsibility for the stampede. At the same time LaVey has been bad-mouthing all the "wanna-be" satanists who do not live up to his standards of amoral perfection when they commit amoral acts. He has been selling books by the millions counseling people not to take morality seriously. While he has denounced Christianity for taking offense at satanism, he has presided over, performed, and sold the franchise for a "religious" enterprise that is liturgically and rhetorically centered on establishing an adversary relationship to Christianity in *extremis*.

LaVey has defended satanism time and time again as nothing more than "psychodrama." Yet when LaVey's own description of the "choice of a human sacrifice" has been peddled to millions of people worldwide over two decades with virtually no discretion, it is difficult to take seriously the protestation that the Church of Satan should not be held accountable somehow for acts of perversity.

But we must return to one of our first disturbing questions. Does black magic mean death, mutilation, and sacrifice? In order to earn a black belt in satanism, so to speak, is it necessary to move beyond the unlimited satisfaction of strictly sexual drives to the appeasing of every possible tendency and lust, to materializing every "evil imagining of the heart," as the Bible says human beings were doing before the Deluge? If the logic of satanic involvement, as LaVey stresses repeatedly, comes down to the progressive casting off of all moral restraints—those remnants of a twilight "Christianity"—for the sake of heightened human "self-awareness," then what is next? Hitler was mainly monstrous, but it is possible to sustain the momentum of "evil" only so long by flashing pictures of a guy who is known to history primarily for saturation bombings of civilians and the mass extermination of Jews.

The Mayan house that LaVey visited in central Mexico yields a clue or two. The Mayans were not just storm-troopers. In occult lore they were the magical masters of the universe because they supposedly understood the hidden meanings of the motions of the stars. They also performed dread, horrible, but carefully orchestrated and "scientific" sacrifices of live human beings to the forces of the underworld, according to archaeological evidence. The evidence of human sacrifice was reported by scholars at a recent conference at Dumbarton Oaks sponsored by Harvard University. According to Arthur Demarest of Vanderbilt University, human sacrifice among the Mayans was a "fundamental element."

Nobody knows exactly what the Mayans were up to. Until the last ten years archaeologists have assumed that the terrible bloody oblations done dutifully at Mexico City by Indian priests to their sun god before the eyes of the Spanish conquerors were the sick invention of the Aztecs. The priest would lay the living victim on a stone altar spread-eagle, plunge an obsidian knife into his chest cavity, rapidly make an incision, and tear the still-beating heart out of the body. He would then eat the heart. The eating of the heart symbolized the reinvigorating of the powers of the world and the transfer of the "life force," bestowed originally by the sun, to the priest, who was really a magician. Eating the hearts of victims, many of whom were warriors captured in battle, would give the priest-magician sufficient occult energy to perform correctly and diligently the rituals necessary to keep the sun god himself from dying. Constanzo's cult used Aztec sacrificial practice both in Matamoros and in Mexico City to suit their own grotesque purposes. It is now known, however, that the Aztecs adapted the practice from the Mayans, who were previously thought to be a culture of benign and peaceful scholars governed by astrologer kings.

Why did the Mayans behave in the way today's satanists might truly envy? The Mayans watched the night skies. They developed what is perhaps the most precise system of time-reckoning the ancients, including the Egyptians and the Babylonians, could have contrived. They had a profound, if still a "metaphysical," comprehension of the passage of time. Unlike their Old World counterparts, they did not believe time is one enormous circle that winds back upon itself. Time is a series of what might be called "star waves" on which each god, like an invisible surfer, rides across the days, months, and years. When one wave has crested, an age is over, and another wave builds and breaks across the shore of human experience.

In differing versions of occultist lore, wave cresting is the eon of Horus, or in LaVey's parlance, the Age of Satan. Crowley's rule that the "bloody sacrifice" must be enacted in order to ensure the advent of the new age is a sort of "art deco" imitation of Mayan mysteries and mythology. Artaud, visionary of today's aesthetic terrorism and "theater of cruelty," was fascinated with ancient Mexico. In his 1936 speech to students entitled "What I Came to Mexico to Do," Artaud said bluntly, "I came . . . to look for a new idea of man." And he added, "We expect from Mexico a new concept of Revolution," what he in his jottings termed "a sensibility of the flayed." Mexico would provide the laboratory for the consciously political, anti-European, and anti-American "great idea of pagan pantheism."[2] This "Mexico mystique" also has had a profound impact on LaVey. It was in the blood of Constanzo.

Satanism is so "frightening," according to LaVey, because it is so "human"—as Nietzsche would say, "all-too-human." Satanism is not just atheism; it is the extreme version of a conscious choice to live in a world without God or without values or without obligation to others or without scruples. For hundreds of years Western intellectuals have sold their ancient patrimony to buy into the idea of a world with God. In Roman times it was called Epicureanism. Later it was known as hedonism, and in the eighteenth century it was "materialism." Last century it was best exemplified in the thought of Nietzsche, who wanted his own elite to create a universe in the wake of the death of the deity.

The difference between LaVey's satanism and these venerable life philosophies is that the latter were assumed to be too refined, or too toxic, to teach to the masses. The great unwashed would inevitably confuse free thinking with anarchy, the argument ran. Aquino represents the older free-thinker's point of view. So does LaVey, to a point. "Satan is only a symbol," he is fond of saying. But if you encourage somebody to "kill," and they go out and actually kill, not realizing that you used the verb in a "symbolic" or magical and not a literal sense, where does the responsibility lie?

When LaVey decided in the mid-seventies to sell his own brand of indulgences to the masses, he made satanism into a crude belief system, exactly what Aquino to this day denies it is. LeVey stripped it of intellectual pretense and made it exactly what it has become—an ideology of hate and an incitement to "revolutionary" violence. The Nazis were caught up in much the same web. But the brown shirts had more direct orders—kill Jews!

LaVey has no primal rage toward Jews, nor toward any particular ethnic group for that matter. He is too sophisticated and too "worldly" to be a racial mystic or a bigot. But he does hate the average American. He hates "ordinary people" and the celebration thereof. He hates democracy and equality. In an interview in 1986 with the *Washington Post Magazine*, LaVey gesticulated to writer Walt Harrington about what might be called the "conspiracy" of average Americans—many of whom probably go to church, read the Bible, vote for politicians who promise passage of antivice laws—in the same way that Hitler would have become apoplectic over the *Protocols of the Elders of Zion,* a forged document from earlier in the century purporting to be master blueprint of Jews to take over the world. Most people are useless and insignificant, LeVey fumed. They might just as well "never have lived at all."

Earlier, LaVey talked about another "average" American who demanded service at a fast-food restaurant." If someone put a gun to his head and blew him away, who would care?"[3] The satanists call them "zeroes." Harrington observed that satanists are fond of thinking that, other than themselves, "the world is full of idiots and fools and chumps."

Maybe that is why the Devil prefers blondes. Blondes are unusual. Marilyn Monroe was extremely unusual, both in her life and her death. Yet on the screen, and it seems also in her own private dreams, she was the near perfect mirror of very average, middle American fantasies of girl-next-door normality. That was her seductive power. It was even more so with Jayne Mansfield. By 1986, LaVey was protesting that he did not "kill" Jayne Mansfield. He told Harrington that her death and decapitation, despite the curse, was all a weird "coincidence." As the Devil has started to age, his children may have abandoned his stern authority and learned indeed to "go for it," even if that disqualifies them as "real" satanists.

Pete Roland, for one, never knew Anton LaVey. In a chemical stupor, he killed a close friend—a drug-dealing, small-change cultural castaway from a Missouri town. Roland, too, was part of the floating debris. But he did not, as far as we can tell, dream of blonde movie stars.

NOTES

1. James S. Downard and Michael A. Hoffman II, "King-Kill/330: Masonic Symbolism in the Assassination of John F. Kennedy," in Parfrey, *Apocalypse Culture*, p. 239.
2. Antonin Artaud, *Selected Writings*, p. 357ff.
3. Walt Harrington, "The Devil in Anton LaVey," *Washington Post Magazine*, February, 23, 1986, p. 7.

CHAPTER 7.

The Strange World of
Dr. Michael Aquino

Up is down, pleasure is pain, darkness is light, slavery is freedom,
madness is sanity . . .

——ANTON SZANDOR LaVEY

"In the last few months, in the USA, an ancient evil has surfaced." Thus
began the November 1985 edition of *Magical Link*, the newsletter of the
Berkeley O.T.O. The "ancient evil" was what the newsletter called "the
blood libel"—a legendary accusation of orthodox Christianity that Jews
abducted Christian babies and made sacrifices of them in horrid,
clandestine rites. According to the libel, frequently used by clerics and
monarchs in Catholic and Eastern European countries to incite pogroms
up through the nineteenth century, the Jews used the blood of Christian
children for their own nefarious magical undertakings.

Historically, the blood libel seems to have been a dodge by aristocrats
practicing satanism. And inside the Church itself, it was an attempt to pin
the blame for the occasional discovery of ritual child murders on a
despised minority. The most notorious of the blood libel documents was
the *Protocols of the Elders of Zion*, which appeared around the turn of the
century. The *Protocols* purported to be the testament of a secret nest of
very high-ranking, Jewish conspirators bent on world conquest.

Research by the religious historian Norman Cohn suggests that the
Protocols, in actuality, was a forgery sponsored by the Russian secret police
and authored by an inner core of Russian occultists known as "the-
osophists." Amusingly, the very occultists who in the past were largely
responsible for spreading the blood libel about Jews have begun to claim
that the Christians have been using it against them, when in fact most of
the charges of sanguinary doings against contemporary satanists have
come from secular police investigators, prosecutors, and the media.

A vocal fraternity of publically professed, "orthodox satanists" have
begun to counterpunch against all the media coverage of ritual abuse.
Addressing its readers with the Crowleyite flourish of "beloved
Thelemites," the anonymous writer declaims:

The news media have carried stories, and one major TV network has actually aired a documentary on the quaint subject of Satanist child murder. There are people who deliberately use the grief of parents as an unspeakable road to power.

Like a scene from *The Untouchables* where Capone denounces Eliot Ness for dishonesty and treachery, the normal perception of fair is made to seem foul, and the foul fair. It is the Christians who are out to besmirch and spread the blood libel against the upstanding, decent, "good people." The Christians are consolidating their regiments for the massive assault on satanist virtue!

Today the cry is out against Witches and Satanists. The pogrom is being mounted in the halls of the U.S. Congress; and you, dear reader, are the intended goat of public sacrifice! Because Witches in the present day are more often middle class and above average education, it may be possible to prevent the burning again . . .

The most prominent "victim" of the blood libel had been Aquino. *Newsweek* magazine had tabbed him "the second beast of Revelation" in the wake of charges filed against him and another Presidio employee by the San Francisco Police Department for alleged child molestations at a day-care center at the Presidio, where he was stationed. The allegations included the following:

- Children said they were taken by day to private homes, including two on army property, where they had been sexually molested.
- Other children talked about a "googoo" game in which they were urinated and defecated on by a "Mr. Gary."
- Pencils were used to doodle on the skin and genitals of the children and were also inserted in a child's anus.
- A gun was pointed at the head of another adult in front of the children.
- There were five confirmed cases among the children of chlamydia, a sexually transmitted illness.

Those particular charges were later dropped against Aquino and his associate. Parents of the children who were allegedly abused said it was because of strong pressure from the army on the federal investigators and the San Francisco police. Prosecutors blamed the well-known difficulties of prosecuting child abuse cases in the first place. Just before this book went to press, however, authoritative sources within the military, who requested anonymity, reported that another investigation of Aquino had been opened by civilian law enforcement in California.

A one-time Eagle Scout and former stockbroker, Aquino was born of an Italian Catholic father and a Protestant mother. He graduated from high school in Santa Barbara, California, in 1964, and was ranked tenth in his class. He then went to college and later joined the army. He received his master's degree in political science from the University of

California at Santa Barbara with a specialty in Western European political affairs. He also received his doctorate from here. Starting in 1981, he allegedly reported directly to the Joint Chiefs of Staff.

In October 1988, Oprah Winfrey invited Aquino to answer for himself before millions of television viewers. Aquino, who has a widow's peak and raised eyebrows that make him a dead ringer for the Prince of Darkness—he says he was born that way—has been incensed that satanists are receiving such a bad rap in the press and that their reputations are being skewered by born-again crusaders. His epiphany in the presence of Oprah was his initial pistol shot of righteous wrath. In response to the "scare tactics" of the fundamentalists, Aquino said he was prepared to put satanism "in a little context." Satanism is a "phenomenon in human culture" that reaches back for millenia. It is a "sense of awareness," an "element in the human soul" that distinguishes itself from nature.

At this point, Aquino's wife, Lilith—her name is the same as the great she-demon in Jewish lore—intruded into the discussion. With her jet-black hair, heavy eyebrows, and a midnight aura that would make Elvira envious, Mrs. Aquino, like her husband, seems terribly "witchy." She does not claim to have been born that way, however. Oprah inquired whether she and hubby are in the business of doing "evil." "No," said Lillith. "Evil is a very uniquely personal term. I think everyone has their own definition of evil."

The comment could just as easily have been made by Shirley MacLaine. Evil does not really exist; it is only those hyped-up, overzealous Christian folk with their red necks, receding foreheads, and squint eyes who have invented the term. Devilment is not at all the same thing as wickedness, Dr. Aquino goes on to explain. Christians, and indeed all "conventional religions," loathe satanists because they "fear this sense of being separate from the universe that satanists glorify and that satanists are interested in exploring." Because Christians, unlike satanists, are afraid to be "separate from the universe," they represent people like Aquino "as a devil, as something evil and vicious."

But what is satanism? Oprah begged. According to Aquino, "satanism is a recognition that humanity, unique among life forms, is something that can perceive itself as an actor against the rest of the material universe, that we can reach out and we can change it."

People in general, and Christians in particular, are terrified of acting "ethically and responsibly," according to Aquino. Satanists believe that there is a "quality in the human soul that makes it different from all other life forms," and that agency has been present from the beginning of evolution. It has been called by different names, but the ancient Egyptians called it "Set."

Aquino prefers to designate those who would tread in the Dark Master's footsteps as *Setians* rather than satanists. Set was the shadowy, outlaw god of ancient Egypt. In Egyptian mythology, he was the "evil" brother of Osiris, the good god of the Nile and of abundant crops. Set was born of, and ruled over, both the night and the dead season of the year. He was the god with "terrible" eminence, the emperor of rage and destruction.

Following the familiar, mythic pattern of the "jealous" brother that pops up so much in the ancient imagination—Cain and Abel, Jacob and Esau, to name a few—Set murdered Osiris, hacked him to pieces, stuffed his remains in a wooden chest, and sent it floating down the Nile toward the sea. In less graceful versions, Set lopped off Osiris' male member. The goddess Isis went out searching for what was left of Osiris, including his immortal manhood.

Aquino has drilled it into his followers that the name *Satan* is a corruption of *Set*. Scholars of antiquity do not necessarily agree with this etymology, but it has allowed for a certain pride of place among followers of the Temple of Set. The ancient meaning of the name, according to a principal authority, is "instigator of confusion, deserter, drunkard." He was, as the French scholar H. Te Velde has phrased it, "the personification of violence." Set was the great outlaw deity—the god of strangers, plunder, and barbarian invasion. While Aquino has gone to excessive lengths to make the principles *Setianism* sound wholesome and sanitary, the name itself belies such an interpretation.

Aquino has designated himself "high priest" of the Temple of Set, the successor organization to LaVey's Church of Satan. Aquino's story is that he stumbled on satanism by accident. In 1968, he was attending the premiere of the movie *Rosemary's Baby*, where he espied LaVey's entourage from the Church of Satan. The spectacle fascinated him, and he began to make inquiries. He decided that, contrary to public perceptions even today, LaVey was "serious and sincere in what he was doing." A few months later Aquino left for Vietnam, where he both served as an expert in psychological warfare and joined the Church of Satan.

The Church of Satan "was largely a social gesture of outrage against what was felt to be the hypocrisy of conventional society . . . whereby virtuous values were espoused and then disregarded in the way that society conducts its day-to-day activities," Aquino informed Winfrey.

Oprah asked if there were human and animal sacrifices at the temple, a question that made Aquino indignant. According to Aquino all the public brouhaha over bloody altars and ceremonial killings must be attributed to a system that "perverts" Satan. To explain "that kind of perverted behavior to anyone you would have to take people who had been brought up in a system where the term 'Satan' represented something perverted, which I would lay at the doorstep of the Christian value system, and say that what you have here are the Christians gone wrong." The "bad" satanists are really "Christians gone wrong"—fallen angels or corrupted saints, so to speak. The "good satanists" are the only people who should properly be called satanists, that is, people who worship themselves as entities separate from the universe, not people who dance naked around a fire and chant, "Hail, Satan."

Aquino says that satanists work "for the good of humankind." Satanism is a distinctive brand of human psychology. It is not unlike New Age metaphysics, insofar as every human being "looks within himself or herself" and "seeks . . . to explore this freedom of the will." Set, of course, should not be confused with the avuncular spirit who talked for years through psychic Jane Roberts and was the source of her many Seth books, including the original *Seth Speaks*. The other Set in recent years has been unveiling the most ancient truths through his preselected "channel," Michael Aquino.

In *The Book of Coming Forth By Night*, written in 1985, Aquino describes how he had a number of peculiar dreams and visions, which climaxed during the first week of June. It was Aquino's act of one-upmanship to the giving of Crowley's *Book of the Law*.

The Equinox has succumbed to my Solstice, and I, Set, am revealed in my Majesty . . . I am the ageless Intelligence of this Universe . . . and from my manifest semblance, which alone is not of Earth. *Known as the Hebrew Satan,* I chose to bring forth a Magus, according to the fashion of my Word. He was charged to form a Church of Satan, that I might easily touch the minds of men in this age they had cast for me.

The "word of Set" was that he gave his "Magus," that is, Aquino, a new "Diabolicon" containing the ancient wisdom. The end result was an ethereal coup d'etat in which LaVey was displaced and Aquino was to become "Magus V of the Aeon of Set." The Aeon of Set superseded LaVey's Age of Satan, which in turn had replaced Crowley's new eon of Horus.

Interestingly enough, the cosmic utterances of the Great Intelligence of the Universe have less to do with the indescribable essence of all things than they constitute a catty putdown of LaVey, Aquino's mentor and archrival in the satanist movement. When high goverment officials receive, or give, the boot from office they generally will write a book revealing insider secrets and telling how downright deceptive or dorky their immediate colleague was. Don Regan's tattling about Ronald and Nancy Reagan's dabbling in astrology is a well-known example. So far as the Temple of Set was concerned, however, the literary hatchet job had to come from the Primeval Presence himself.

The tension between Aquino and LaVey, however, is of importance only because it offers insight into the off-camera workings of the minds who made satanism a trend in today's America. Aquino was one of the leaders of the satanist "church" in the 1960s and 1970s. In fact, he was its scribe, historian, and philosopher. Aquino chafed at the power and publicity accumulated by LaVey. From Aquino's own writings one draws the distinct impression that all along he could not stand to be second or, even worse, third banana. LaVey was a Barnumesque promoter who, if he did not accept the master's adage that "there's a sucker born every minute," at minimum he held in cynical, low esteem the idealists and crusaders of the world. There is genuine debate over whether LaVey has ever wanted to be taken seriously. Aquino, however, always has.

Aquino has proclaimed the use of satanism to "do good"—the diametric reverse of LaVey's catechism of lust and surfeit. LaVey came from the rough-and-tumble streets of San Francisco. Aquino was born into the the bluest of blue-blood families. Aquino himself wrote of LaVey that he was only comfortable among "outlaws and outcasts" and that he was "ultimately uncomfortable in the company of the uncorrupt." Satanism, for Aquino, is not vice but the most laudable form of "human potential" or New Age philosophy. "Satan" has nothing to do with "evil." Satanists "have a very high set of personal ethics;" it is Christianity that villifies "the devil."

According to Aquino, "Satanism" is not at all a philosophy of degeneracy, as LaVey made it out to be. LaVey's "midnight magic seminars" were from the outset a circus sideshow—the ambience and method of operation that LaVey knew exactly how to manipulate. The lectures involved startling "demonstrations," including the purported eating of a dish of human flesh, which Aquino says was actually leg of mutton roasted with exotic herbs. The seminars drew a regular clientele, many of which stayed around to become the nucleus of the Church of Satan itself.

Yet LaVey carried his "theater of cruelty" a little too far, says Aquino. Not only the death of Jayne Mansfield, but a number of rowdy, public stunts contributed to the demise of whatever genuine magical prestige in the occult underworld LaVey might have enjoyed. For example, LaVey decided to advertise his organization by sponsoring a "topless witches sabbath" in San Francisco's North Beach. One of the dancers he signed up for the ballyhoo was a woman whose stage name was "Sharon King," whose real name was Susan Atkins of the Manson family.

The problem with the Church of Satan, Aquino has explained disdainfully, is that it was not a real church. Rather, it could best be described as "atheism with psychodrama." While LaVey was supposedly helping the disenfranchised middle class have its unchained fantasies and immoderate libidos through calculated ritual and pageantry, he was also beginning to sense, according to Aquino's account, a transpersonal reality shimmering in the lightless crypts of carnal passion. While Satan, for LaVey, was nothing more than an ape suit, Set was a true entity, a "dark god."

As it happened, Aquino grabbed the dim, incomprehensible sense of Set away from LaVey and ran with it. And, he contends, the Church of Satan was transformed, not necessarily with the acknowledgement of Anton LaVey, into the Temple of Set.

Aquino's "ethical" satanism, stressing the aspiring of the mortal grain of consciousness toward higher selfhood, would not sound so interesting had he not been for years a lieutenant colonel in the U.S. Army with a top security clearance. According to Aquino himself, the army had been apprised of his "religion" since the beginning of his military career in 1968. The army was probably not unduly concerned, because insofar as they looked upon Aquino as a satanist, his piety was recognized as one of many possible, legitimate options in the command's own handbook for chaplains.

Aquino himself, of course, was rumored to have been responsible for having the Church of Satan included in the handbook in the first place. The manual remarks dryly that "the Church does not proselytize but welcomes inquiries from honest potential Satanists who hear about the Church from the various books about it, the mass media or word-of-mouth." It goes on to say that "the Church of Satan stands as a gathering point for all those who believe in what the Christian church opposes," but that "the Church of Satan is not to be confused with 'Satanist' groups which have been found to engage in illegal acts."

It is not clear how long the army has known about Aquino's peculiar genus of satanism. But the San Francisco police have been exceptionally interested since about 1980. The interest crested in November 1987 when police raided a house where a three-year-old girl told police she had been molested by a sinister-looking man named "Mikey" who snapped pictures of her in the bathtub and sexually mistreated her in a room with black walls and a cross etched on the ceiling. The girl later spotted "Mikey" in the PX at the Presidio army base in San Francisco, where Aquino was stationed. The girl said she thought "Mikey" was Aquino. The girl also said she recognized Mrs. Aquino. Meanwhile, authorities had found evidence of ongoing child abuse at the Presidio day care center. A three-year-old boy had also been molested, and the cops turned up six cases of sexually transmitted infection in fifty-eight other charges at the center. A thirty-four-year-old civilian day-care worker at the Presidio facility, who was also a Southern Baptist minister was arrested. At first, the charges were dismissed. But subsequently, Hambright was indicted anew on twelve counts of sodomy, oral copulation, and lewd conduct. Hambright later died of AIDS.

Although charges were never formally filed against Aquino, the supreme magus of the Temple of Set was infuriated. "I never met the child in my life," he declared. "I am not a crazed pedophile." With the publicity surrounding the Presidio arrest, Aquino went on his own personal campaign to discredit the San Francisco police and to launch a campaign against the anti-cultists who had intrigued to embarrass him and besmirch the fine character of orthodox satanists, who are really nothing more than Boy Scouts in black robes. Sniveling that he had been the goat of callous victimization because of his *outré* religious beliefs, Aquino began to speak out. Within several months he was before the cameras chatting with Oprah.

A news reporter looking into the Presidio scandal just before it broke on the national wire asked the Pentagon about Aquino. The response was a stone wall of official silence. One public relations spokesperson even said Aquino was not in the army. After that fact could no longer be suppressed, there came a response that was distinctly Aquino's and in certain measure LaVey's—the principled appeal to conscience and the protection of religious liberty. "Aquino has an absolute constitutional right [to his beliefs] . . . unless there is illegal behavior associated with it," said an army spokesperson. The army then began an investigation of its own day-care centers and transferred Aquino from his position at that time with top-security clearance at the National Defense University in Washington, D.C. At the time of this writing he works at a personnel station outside of St. Louis and reportedly runs a computer bulletin board, called Weirdnet, for subscribing satanists. Weirdnet is not in any way sponsored by the army.

A police intelligence report on Aquino, numbered #81-776 and dated July 1, 1981, states the following: "[The Temple of Set] is a small group but nonetheless has several hundred members and operates on a national level. Aquino is the official head of the organization and rules the organization through a council of nine, who are in fact his chief lieutenants."

The two "lieutenants" mentioned in the police intelligence report are a woman named Willie Browning (at the time a captain in the U.S. Army Reserve in an intelligence unit out of Los Angeles) and a reserve army officer by the name of Dennis Mann. According to the report, Mann "too is involved in Intelligence activities." On December 29, 1982, Mann wrote a letter, which was forwarded to the U.S. Army Intelligence and Security Command at Fort George G. Meade, Maryland, requesting files pertaining to himself under the privacy act. San Francisco police had a telephone conversation with a "Lieutenant Colonel" Jones and a "Mr. Burkley" concerning the Temple of Set. At that time the army concluded that police concern about the temple "was not a criminal matter" and referred the issue to army intelligence, with which Aquino was employed. Another army memo dated November 18 and signed by Donald P. Press, Director of Counterintelligence, discloses that "a check of the files of the Federal Bureau of Investigation concerning the Temple of Set reflected no record of such an organization."

A final memo of December 9 to the commander of U.S. Army Forces in Fort McPherson, Georgia, states that "information mentioned in paragraph 2, basic letter, concerning Michael A. Aquino, was favorably adjudicated and Top Secret clearance granted 9 June 1981 by the U.S.

Army Central Personnel Security Clearance Facility. . . . Recommended the investigative file pertaining to Michael A. Aquino be reviewed at the U.S. Army Central Personnel Security Clearance Facility, Fort George G. Meade, Maryland 20755." It was signed by "John W. Richards, LTC, GS, Chief, Intelligence and Security."

Aquino denies that satanists harm people.

In the autumn of 1981, Aquino wrote and circulated within the Temple of Set a document known as "The Wewelsburg Working." A *working* in the magical lexicon is a set of ritual acts that allegedly influence future events. It is like a time-release capsule on the astral plane. Its aims and accomplishments, which are not made manifest until the *working* is complete, must be uttered in the strictest secrecy and with solemn dedication in order to realize the "will" of the magician. Aquino defines a *working* as any formal operation of black magic, which may last for a few hours or be a complicated ceremony "lasting a year or more."

Aquino carried out this particular *working* at the North Tower of the Wewelsburg castle in Westphalia Germany where Nazi SS leader Heinrich Himmler had supposedly outfitted a chamber to conduct black magic in order to "enhance" the outcome of World War II. The Wewelsburg castle itself—let alone the use of the place for satanic ceremonies among the Nazi leadership—seemed to have vanished from history. Aquino reviews how he tracked down the legends and found the place so as to rekindle for the world once again the flame of Hitlerian occultism. Hitler's magic would be the tonic that weaned satanism away from its predisposition toward self-indulgence, brutality, and bestiality. It would give him power over LaVey, and it would make the Temple of Set, as Aquino put it, into the "perfect initiatory medium." In short, Aquino endeavored to appropriate for himself the cosmic-magical powers of Heinrich Himmler's SS, which allegedly permeated the Wewelsburg castle. According to Aquino, Himmler had taken over the Wewelsburg and refurbished it for "black magical" doings. The chambers of the castle, still intact, he discovered were "nothing less than an SS laboratory for experiments in 'conscious evolution'." Its design was to amplify thinking.

The aim of LaVey's Church of Satan had been to advance such "evolution" by abolishing the repressive mechanisms of the subconscious. The exclusive focus on unbridling the instincts, however, contributed to the licentiousness and organizational anarchy that ultimately unraveled the Church of Satan. In the aftermath, Aquino boasts, it became necessary to set up a different, more traditionally "occult" body that would serve as a "perfect initiatory organization," one which was truly ethical in scope. Like Plato's academy, the Temple of Set would be devoted only to the achievement of intellectual and spiritual prowess.

Yet Aquino's Platonic, or perhaps we might say "hermetic," seminary was beset with problems and ultimately disbanded because of a "conspiracy" of senior devotees. The conspiracy was beaten back, but in consequence Aquino was driven to the very painful conclusion that his organization had suffered from the excesses of too many overly "evolved" intellects. Aquino, therefore, set about to carry through an unprecedented "magical working" at Wewelsburg to put the growth of the temple on a new trajectory. Wewelsburg served such an end mightily, because in occult lore it was the "middle point of the world."

At the Wewelsburg Aquino felt himself "energized" as never before. Absent was the Hollywood hype and vaudevillery of LaVey, the midway atmosphere that had drawn so many casual seekers and pleasure-loving rakes, yet seemed to bar true spiritual supplicants.

For Aquino, the visit to Wewelsburg was not much different than an American undergraduate's pilgrimage to the cathedral of Chartres or the Sistine Chapel in Rome. The castle, according to Aquino, is constructed according to very ancient "Gnostic" principles, such as the recurring use of the number twelve. In addition, the castle had twelve central SS offices, for each lieutenant general in the cadre.

At the center of the castle is the Marble Hall with the signs of the zodiac. A domed and airy room called the Hall of the Dead is situated beneath the North Tower. At the crown of the dome is a swastika. A central pit serves as a focus for the light of the stars, sun, and moon streaming from four window clefts. Aquino became ecstatic when, he says, he experienced the immense "energy" converging at the spot. It was more than a magical place; it was what occultists would term the most majestic of "power points." Aquino asked the curator to let him spend the day in the pit and launched, according to his own narrative, into the working that would save satanism and purify it of its gross elements, thereby rescuing it from the horrors of the "disproportionately evolved intellect."

Meanwhile, Aquino was able to manage a tart, historical reflection as perhaps his parting salute to the monuments of the Nazi mind and era. He noted that 1,235 inmates of the Niederhagen concentration camp had perished as part of the Wewelsburg renewal project. The camp did not signify the horrors of human depravity. It was but a reminder of "a certain unique quality in mankind" together with the "penalty which mankind pays for that quality." Mrs. Aquino told Oprah Winfrey "You don't see any endorsement of Nazism. We're talking about occult practices of the Third Reich. We're not talking about their political and their social behavior, their criminal behavior. And that's very explicit in our literature."

Nazism has sometimes been called a religion as much as a political movement. Its own ethic was racist and elitist—only the pure, Aryan genius that flowered in German culture should be allowed to survive in the world. The Nazis did their notorious concentration camp experiments, and until the horrid finale of the war continued to engage in the most outlandish forms of genetic engineering, because of their obsession with fabricating a "super race" of exceptionally intelligent beings.

In an important sense the Nazis as a political movement were *magicians,* and the Third Reich was their working. They aimed to conjure up the primal powers of the cosmos for the sole purpose of bringing forth by night a whole new order of human, and most likely "superhuman," existence.

The "initiatory polices" of the Temple of Set stress the elitism that was at the heart of the Nazi mind set. Only the exceptionally brilliant and creative need apply. Nazism could be construed as a higher species of magic. Could the mastery of the political in some still murky and enigmatic way be what Aquino's "erudite" satanism amounts to? In an extensive bibliography to be used for the edification and instruction of Temple of Set initiates, Aquino devotes an entire section to "Fascism, Totalitarianism, and Magic." In a paragraph of annotation to the section, Aquino talks about fascism and nazism as "a very powerful area of magic" of which the ramifications are largely "unrealized by the profane."

In January 1984, Aquino disseminated to his admirers a curious little essay entitled "Notes Toward Project Andromeda." Aquino starts off by quoting Adolf Hitler on architecture and music—"Is it not in these disciplines that we find recorded the paths of humanity's ascent? When I hear Wagner, it seems to me that I hear rhythms of a bygone world. I imagine to myself that one day science will discover, in the waves set in motion by the *Rheingold,* secret mutual relations connected with the order of the world."

Aquino wonders what Adolf Hitler would make of Paul Kantner and the Jefferson Starship. Aquino appears in a photograph amiably jawing with Kantner in front of a radio microphone. Kantner and Aquino appeared together on a talk show with a Catholic priest and an evangelical Christian minister from southern California to respond to accusations that satanic lyrics had been *backmasked*—that is, recorded in such a way as to sound audible if the vinyl platter were played backwards—on the Starship's albums. Grace Slick of the Starship—formerly the Jefferson Airplane—launched the sixties generation on the pursuit of infinite consciousness through a psychedelic blow-out of the mind in her song "White Rabbit," claims Aquino. Aquino explains how the Devil "talks" through Kantner's music.

Aquino cites Kantner's curious notion of a "computer assisted telepathic amplification technology"—ESP through rock 'n' roll. The electrical energy of the brain occurs as wave packets, each one with varying energy. The frequency range for most conscious or semi-conscious processes are between one and about twenty-three cycles per second. Brain waves, like all electrical phenomena, observe the laws of resonance. The fact of resonance can be observed when a pair of tuning forks are placed side by side, and one is struck. The resonant energy in the first fork causes the second fork to vibrate in a seemingly spontaneous and "ghostly" manner. The resonance effect often appears remarkable, if not miraculous, to the scientifically unlettered because a strong vibration in one system can be induced by a relatively minor stimulus in a different system.

Brain waves are also affected by sympathetic resonance between systems. A pulse of mechanical energy, such as a sound vibration, can cause resonance in the electrical portion of the brain in the same fashion that a rhythmically flashing light can bring about, or "entrain," the waves of the human brain. The theta-wave band at about three to seven cycles per second tends to be connected with parapsychological states or happenings, according to Aquino.

The "cash value" of such research for the satanist is the ultimate activation of latent potentiality locked within a select minority of human creatures evolving into a "super race," according to Aquino. The sounds of the band would be amplified, according to Aquino. And through computer-assisted technology it would produce rhythmic waves within the theta range—approximately three and a half to seven cycles per second—at decibels that would yield resonance in a concert hall. If all the concert goers "focused their wills on the same thing," and the energy of thought as affected by the concert was beamed into the ether, then a powerful "magical" working would take place.

The venture would even have a decidedly "humanitarian" outcome. The object lesson for satanists can be found in F. Paul Wilson's novel *The Keep*. *The Keep* is the saga of German soldiers during World War II who encounter a bizarre and antiquated cluster of ruins deep in the Carpathian Mountains. One by one the soldiers are murdered by a mysterious force of evil. Incarcerated in a subterranean honeycomb is a "Being of Darkness far elder and more powerful than anything guessed at in mankind's childish mythologies." Aquino compares the geometry of the Keep with the structure of the architecture in Wewelsburg castle. More strikingly, he says, the force within the Wewelsburg is now loosed upon the world as a consequence of his ritual.

Forces and workings have the ring of so much abracadabra, but the logic of occult thinking has its very pragmatic and even "scientific" application as well. Such an application Aquino terms *Lesser Black Magic*, or LBM for short. It takes little imagination to infer that there are unmistakable military uses of LBM. LBM otherwise encompasses propoganda, mind control, the discretionary unleashing of terrorists—all the conceivable instruments in the arsenal of a magician whose workings take totalitarian political form.

So far as the Temple of Set is concerned, LBM permits total manipulation of the psychology of a target population. Since Aquino all along has been in some branch of military intelligence and, despite constant publicity, has not received any public reprimands, demotions, or dismissal for his activities, it would be too far-fetched to read Aquino's writings as sheer nonsense. While the army itself may not countenance the practice of LBM, if you use the military's own, blander form of *techspeak* and refer instead to the type of activity termed *PSYOP*—for "psychological operations"—what Aquino has in mind becomes slightly more intelligible.

In this context an article titled "From PSYOP to MindWar: The Psychology of Victory," which was composed by Aquino and which he claims was sent to the prestigious Washington publication *Military Review*, becomes relevant. On the cover to the article, which was distributed among temple members, was the inscription "HEADQUARTERS, IMPERIAL STORMTROOPER FORCE/Office of the Chief of Staff/MindWar Center/Hub Four." Apparently Aquino, who rarely gives any hint of humor, was letting us in on a little word sketch of his ideal self—Darth Vader in the flesh!

Aquino cites a body of literature on the subject of electronic ESP called *psychotronics,* and he exults that the army already has in its possession an *operational* that charts the minds of both neutrals and enemies and aims to alter them according to American strategic interests. Psychotronics is itself a *technology* of black magic.

A novel called *Black Magic,* which cropped up on paperback book racks in the early 1980s, is all about a desperate, ultra secret struggle between U.S. and Soviet intelligence operatives in which the deployment of psychotronic weaponry is at stake. In the novel, the United States loses out to the Russians, who have been planning all along to press their strategic advantage in the development of such weaponry in a surprise attack against American missle installations. The canard that "the Russians are ahead of us" in psychotronic research and applications was loudly, if not widely, recited about the same time in occult circles and among a very few military representatives. Some short-lived and inconclusive psychotronic experiments were supposedly undertaken at the Stanford Research Institute in California in order to counter the presumed Russian threat.

An article published in *Omni* magazine called "Psi Soldiers in the Kremlin" gave weight to this suspicion. In the article, Larissa Vilenskaya, a Soviet defector who once worked at a "radioelectronics" institute in Moscow, tells from first-hand experience about carefully controlled and stringently guarded investigations into the possiblities of mind control using psychotronic devices. A gadget known as "Lida" apparently uses electromagnetic signals to change, remotely, what a person is feeling or thinking. A former Soviet KGB agent named Nikolai Khokhlov told *Omni* the Soviets were using electromagnetic beams to influence the world and to engulf the United States itself with extra low frequency waves in the range of two to twenty hertz, the kind that Aquino claims are the basis of the satanist's lesser black magic. As for the assertion that the Soviets have outgunned us in the undeclared psychic radiation war, Aquino assures us that we should not be alarmed.

According to Aquino's "MindWar" article, the United States lost in Vietnam because it was not skilled and aggressive enough in the execution of PSYOP. Aquino recommends that the army forget about useless "leaflet and loudspeaker" routines and concentrate instead on the strengthening of a "national will to victory." Such a tack entails changing the hearts and minds of civilian populations by remote technology—in other words, black *political* magic. Aquino baptizes this black political magic *MindWar*. MindWar must reach into the very subcortices of those who would be caught up in it. It must penetrate into their homes, their places of entertainment, their jobs. America's defeat in Vietnam took place not in the jungles but in the streets of its own cities, Aquino declares.

Aquino apparently taught, or learned from, LaVey about MindWars. *The Satanic Rituals* describes in detail the Nazi ceremony of the "electronic theater" involving an electrostatic generator and a low-frequency, resonant brain-wave transmitter in order to open a "window" to the fourth dimension. The symbolism and accouterments resemble Aquino's Wewelsburg working. In his introduction to *The Satanic Rituals*, LaVey lauds psychotronics as an "awesome" new tool of sorcery.

A MindWar blitzkrieg would envelop everyone; it would deploy not just psychotronics but world satellite telecommunications and electronic media. Aquino compares MindWar to the grasping of the mythical sword Excalibur of Arthurian legend. The hero who had the strength, will, and wisdom to draw it from the rock would seize command of armies and kingdoms. Excalibur, nonetheless, would be directed first and foremost at the people of the United States. Although PSYOP units, Aquino admits, cannot under present laws take aim at American citizens within their national boundaries, such constraints are misguided inasmuch as they are predicated on the belief that propoganda is "a lie." MindWar would not tell half-truths or even practice "deception." Like satanism itself, it must remain highly ethical. MindWar evinces a "whole truth" that cannot be considered brainwashing. Brainwashing seeks to disassemble the rational mind and foster a zombie-like compliance with the agenda of the brainwasher.

MindWar, like the "ideals" of satanism itself, is a strong elixir to be savored by the seasoned palette of the "evolved" intellectual. The meaning of MindWar is that the subject should *believe* it has made its decisions freely and without constraint. MindWar must not be detectable.

Is MindWar, therefore, just another expression for lesser black magic, which means the usually unconscious manipulation of people, perhaps even the *American people,* against their will, though in a very "ethical" sense of the word? According to Aquino, the use of LBM by one group against another is not necessarily invidious. Diplomacy often requires subterfuge and coercion of leadership "behind the scenes." A serious LBM covert operation would go undetected both by the people involved and at the international level.

From Aquino's viewpoint, psychotronics and MindWar espionage can naturally be seen as "scientific" extensions of the religion of Set. They are Setian metaphysics and morality made practical for the advantage and benefit of the human race en masse.

At the same time, it should be pointed out that Setian "human-itarianism" is not really some kind of overarching and all-compassing benevolence toward human beings, regardless of their talents or station in life. Setianism is a cool, gentrified—one might even add "yuppified"—style of Nazi elitism, although in all fairness to Aquino, his strange, romantic preoccupation with Hitler and the SS has been shorn of the latter's genocidal anti-Semitism and racist insanity. If Hitler had not built the crematoriums and ordered the extermination of Jews, Aquino suggests, he might have turned out to be a "good" satanist, after all. Setianism is what might be called a "human potential" therapy. It preaches self-advancement by cultivating one's transcendental, magical, and psychic powers. The secret resides, as it did for Crowley, in the act of "willing."

But what is "willing"? In the English language, will suggests an unconscious faculty rather than a sublime, superbly *conscious* agent or entity. *Will* is really a verb, not a noun. Nietzcheanism, and Crowleyism for that matter, metaphysically mixed apples and oranges. If willing is all that is, as Nietzsche and Crowley really said, what is the will that wills?

To solve this philosophical puzzle, Aquino invents the notion of *Xeper,* an Egyptian word that, he says, implies the emergence into time of the immortal and undefined essence of consciousness itself. Whereas LaVey stressed human finitude, Aquino accentuates immortality. Pronounced *khef-fer,* the word is the Egyptian hieroglyphic for the transformation of existence into eternity.

The Wewelsburg working allegedly "affirmed" the continuation of the personality as Xeper force. Psychotronics expands the grappling of the *Xeper* to achieve a state of ultimacy. The goal of Setianism, or authentic satanism, is to know all things and control all things, especially those of the spirit, without any God intervening or ordaining rules. The Prince of Darkness is so named because he has established his own universe without a more authoritative model from which to work.

For Aquino, satanists are in substance not all that different from Mormons, Christian Scientists, or perhaps somewhat eccentric Episcopalians. Not only does all this stuff about sacrificing babies, carving upside down crosses on the bellies of corpses, quaffing blood, and despoiling in the name of the evil lord of this world smack of totally unfounded hysteria, but the cops themselves are obviously crazy, too. Those wicked

Christians, who got thrown to the lions by the Romans, are now about to engage in a homicidal campaign against the honorable, high-principled, and Rotary Club satanists.

Is it actually so impertinent and hoaky to think satanism might be up to something other than, as Lyons tells us and Aquino insists, engaging in a little street mime? To raise suspicions about people who openly and deliberately go around flaunting the paradigmatic emblems of death, cruelty, and utter desolation in music, in literature, and in ceremonies—a little more than granting licenses for fraternity bashes, romps of randy sex, or playing hookie from Sunday Mass, as it turns out—is not entirely unreasonable.

Do satanists then mean the exact opposite of what they say? LaVey says they do. The only people who do that consistently are schizoids, pathological liars, and masters of the totalitarian PSYOP. The most outspoken satanists are definitely not schizos. So what is left? The Nazis discovered that the essence of propoganda was "the Big Lie." They realized that if you say something totally outlandish and unbelievable, and you say it loud enough, people will start to believe it.

It is not just Methodists from Moline, Illinois, who have called Satan the "father of lies." Jesus said Satan was a "liar and a murderer" from the beginning. A lot of Egyptians felt the same about Satan, or Set. So did the Persians and the Muslims.

Furthermore, does Aquino's fascination with the Nazis, if he is to be taken seriously, mean that you can have the heart of Hitlerism without six million dead Jews, or the twenty-two million people who died in World War II? Is Aquino's script for MindWar nothing more than a sort of sci-tech, updated "art-deco" version of the fantasy game "Dungeons and Dragons"? Is Aquino just another kook and an eccentric? After all, did Aquino not replace LaVey and become installed by the invisible masters of the universe themselves as the Magus of the latest, black aeon, as the spiritual Lord Goombah of the High Church of Satan, a.k.a. the Temple of Set?

The irony, of course, is that a painstaking investigation of historic occult practices in the twentieth century shows that much of Aquino's Setian doctrine was gleaned directly from Crowley and reworked with all the appropriate mumbo jumbo to give an added mystique to LaVey's pop, farcical cult. In Crowlean mythology, Set and his guardian angel "Aiwass" are one and the same. Thus, Aquino's alleged "revelation" from Set turns out to be a cheap imitation of Crowley's communication in Cairo. As the occultist Kenneth Grant observes, "Crowley established contact with the Great White Brotherhood," the alleged magical and invisible prefects of the planet, "when he identified himself with the Beast 666, and with Set or Shaitan [Satan]."[1]

The lore of Set is not some post-sixties disclosure from beyond but has remained an integral feature of O.T.O. tradition since its early days. The

Egyptian god Set was associated with the star Sirius B, and the "desert of Set" with the stellar expanse in that portion of the sky. Aquino used the supposed "word" of Set to exorcise the influence of LaVey, but the language and recondite symbolism went back to Crowley. The peculiar tale of Aquino and of his relationship to the Church of Satan raises a question that has not been posed adequately. To what degree is contemporary, "public" satanism merely a continuation and refinement of the beliefs and practices of the O.T.O., which prior to the Vietnam era were highly secretive?

Finally, what is the correlation between the O.T.O.'s "magical" influence and leadership and the siege of satanism throughout American culture? Has a beast conjured up in the fusty cellars of the occult underworld been let loose, either deliberately or accidentally? Are schoolboy satanism and the "orthodox" religious variant completely divorced from each other, or are we witnessing the revenge of the son against the father?

The controversy over day-care abuse at the Presidio was not isolated. In 1987 alone, the army received complaints of nine similar child-abuse incidents at their facilities. Earlier flaps had developed at the U.S. Military Academy in West Point, at Fort Dix in New Jersey, and at a day-care center in West Germany. Twenty-two families filed $66 million in personal injury claims against the army in connection with the Presidio case. Although charges against Aquino were dismissed, Gary Hambright who was arraigned in the case, pleaded innocent and suggested he might be taking the rap for others possibly involved in the alleged molestations. After long legal maneuvering and bickering between army and federal investigators and the San Francisco police, the case against Hambright was shelved as well.

After the charges were dropped against him, Aquino went on the stump to make accusations of a Christian plot against him. The culprit in Aquino's mind was an assistant chaplain at the Presidio who had allegedly trumped up the allegations. Aquino sought to have the chaplain court-marshalled. Aquino gave no consideration to the fact that Hambright himself was a Christian minister.

Aquino also wrote a four-page letter to the head of a children's advocacy group in southern California with the warning that Christian persecution of satanists was mounting nationwide. He compared his followers to the Jews of Nazi Germany, who remained too meek to stand up to their tormenters and those who accused them of "heinous crimes." For purpose of argument this time, the Nazis were the bad guys.

Meanwhile, the army rallied to the defense of Aquino on the grounds that Aquino had a constitutional right to be a satanist. Presidio spokesperson Bob Mahoney told the press that Aquino was a good soldier and "did his job." "That he has religious beliefs that are contrary to what most people consider to be the norm does not disqualify anybody from military service. The military swears to uphold and defend the Constitution of the United States. That includes freedom of religion." Aquino told Temple of Set members in a newsletter that "when our back was turned . . . we were indeed struck." He warned, "We are going to go after the source of this rot, NOW, and not rest until these twisted people [i.e., the Christians] have been exposed for what they actually are."

The army apparently had little interest in prosecuting the case from the outset. Even when multiple allegations of abuse were filed by parents, the army did not close down the installation for almost a year, even though centers under state jurisdiction are routinely shut down at even a hint of unseemly activity. During the height of the investigation, the Child Adolescent Sexual Abuse Referral Center (CASARC) at San Francisco General Hospital told the army to expect multiple victims. But the "army did not want to believe that," according to a CASARC employee, quoted in the newspaper. The army said flatly, "We have no reason to believe that other children have been victimized."

Sex abuse problems, if not ritual crime controversies, had been relatively common at the Presidio, however. John Gunnarson, the Presidio's top day-care official, had been the object of an investigation in 1982. Gunnarson had been accused by a female Presidio employee, Pearl Broadnax, of assaulting her. Those charges were dismissed for lack of evidence. According to a deputy sheriff in Santa Clara County who had been assigned to the investigation of the original complaint against Gunnarson, the matter had to do with Broadnax's charges that serious child abuse was routine at the center. An army captain wrote a letter to the commander of the Presidio reporting that three child-care center staff members had been threatened with loss of their jobs if "they speak out and tell the truth."

On April 19, 1988, the army held an open house for a new $2.3 million day care facility at the Presidio, while parents of the allegedly abused children held a press conference protesting that the feds had done a whitewash of the case.

The new day-care facility had to be built because on September 22, 1987, one of the old buildings in the Presidio complex, where the child abuse had putatively occurred, burned down. Coincidently, September 22 is the autumnal equinox, a high holy day for satanists. Three weeks later another fire wreaked $50,000 in damages to four classrooms at the center, including what had been Hambright's.

Satanism has also been reported in the past at the Presidio. About the time of the Gunnarson investigation, San Francisco police had received a report of a man dressed in black who took a little girl down to the creek in a nearby park. Screams could be heard. Police raided a gardener's shack and found a mannequin with a gun aimed at the door, a giant pentagram on the floor, and doll's heads all over the ceiling. The investigating officer told his superior that "we've got a cult at the Presidio," but he was ordered to let the matter rest.

Linda Goldston, a San Francisco Bay Area reporter, did an on-site inspection of the Presidio's military intelligence unit, and found graphic indications of ongoing satanic practice nearby. Within a concrete bunker in back of the intelligence building Goldston found the words *Prince of Darkness* painted boldly in red. The concrete batteries apparently had been converted to what Goldston described as "ritual chambers."

Next to *Prince of Darkness* she uncovered the inscription *Die* along with a list of names that had been crossed out with heavy black paint. Another wall was covered with *666,* and in the center of the floor appeared partly burned logs. On the wall facing the military intelligence barracks was an enormous pentagram, and in the rear were visible black and white candle drippings. In a building farther up the street was a large drawing of Satan, or perhaps Set, with red eyes and horns. The latter building was locked tight with no entrance granted to outsiders under any circumstances.

Gini Graham Scott, a Bay Area sociologist, wrote a book in 1983 titled *The Magicians* about the Temple of Set, to which she attached the pseudonym "Church of Hu." She termed temple members "Hutians." "The Hutians," she concluded, "represent a potentially growing threat to society" and add to a "growing climate of fear and hatred."[2]

The ancient Egyptians also seemed to doubt that Setians were decent and honorable people. They even had a ritual to "overthrow Seth and his gang," which was conducted daily in the Temple of Osiris, the dominant religion of the day, which antedated Christianity by millenia. As one scholar of antiquity notes, Set "stood for sterility, the desert, mindless force, and violence."[3]

A waxen red image would be made of "the miserable Seth" and bound with the tendons of a red ox. Then the devotee would tread on the image with the left foot, cast a spear into it, and cut it to pieces with his knife. The remains would then be thrown into the fire, so that nothing remained. In the meantime, the celebrant would chant: "Robber! Lord of lies, king of deceit, gangleader of criminals . . . braggart among the gods, who causes enmity and occasions murder . . . lord of looting, who rejoices at greed, master-thief who suscitates theft; the [one] who gives offense . . ."

NOTES

1. Kenneth Grant, *Outside the Circles of Time* (London: Frederick Muller, 1980), p. 270.
2. Gini Graham Scott, *The Magicians: A Study of the Use of Power in a Black Magic Group* (New York: Irvington Publishers, 1983), p. 199.
3. E. C. Krupp, *Echoes of the Ancient Skies: The Astronomy of Lost Civilizations* (New York: New American Library, 1983), p. 18.

Part III.

MISE EN SCENE

CHAPTER 8.

Heavy Metal Music and the New Theater of Cruelty

I've always wondered what human flesh tastes like.
—GENE SIMMONS, KISS

ITEM: In Reno, Nevada, twenty-year-old James Vance and his parents initiated a lawsuit against the heavy metal rock group Judas Priest. The suit alleged that subliminal messages on the rock group's album induced young Vance to enter into a suicide pact after listening to the group's "Stained Glass" album. Vance survived in a hospital on life support systems for more than three years. After filing the suit, Vance died.

ITEM: In Indio, California, John McCollum, nineteen, drank excessively the night of October 27, 1984, while listening to Ozzy Osborne's "Suicide Solution." During the binge he obtained a pistol and shot himself. His father sued. Osborne, however, denied there is any connection between his music and suicide.

ITEM: Ricardo "Richard" Ramirez, the so-called Night Stalker killer implicated in at least fourteen murders and twenty assaults, was apparently intrigued by the satanic themes of AC/DC's 1979 *Highway to Hell* album. The album contains the song "Night Prowler." Ramirez's father attested to his son's drug problem, which Richard acquired while living in El Paso, Texas. The father further indicated that his son's "satanism" may be an appendage to his son's confused and narcotic state of mind, to which the music contributed. Ramirez was convicted in 1989 of murder.

ITEM: In Townsend, Massachusetts, state police studied music videos to try to find clues in the murder of Priscilla Gustafson, thirty-three, and her two children. The accused murderer, seventeen-year-old Daniel J. LaPlante, said he had been watching music videos on MTV cable networks the day the killings happened. LaPlante told his interrogators that he was "really into videos," and police wondered if he had engaged in copycat behavior. The previous year LaPlante had been arrested and ordered to stand trial for the kidnapping and an alleged attack on a fourteen-year-old Townsend girl. LaPlante was convicted by a jury.

ITEM: In Jefferson Township, New Jersey, teenager Thomas Sullivan, Jr., stabbed to death his mother Betty Ann, thirty-seven, in the basement of the family's home. Afterwards, he set the living room couch on fire in an apparent effort to burn down the house and kill his father and younger brother. Then he fled and committed suicide by slitting his wrists while leaning against a neighbor's backyard shed. The entire week before the slaying, young Sullivan had been singing a rock song about blood and matricide.

Police divulged that Sullivan—a talented student, Boy Scout, and outstanding athlete—had been a member of an adolescent satanic group in the area. He was also a fan of metal music, the lyrics of which he recited constantly. Before the tragedy, Sullivan had confided to some friends that he had a vision of Satan, who instructed him to murder his family.

ITEM: In Fullerton, California, two teenage lovers, who friends said were "obsessed" with devil worship, savagely killed the girl's mother by stabbing her with a knife and pummeling her with a wrench. In exactly the same community, another youth offered a prayer to Satan, then shot his father to death. Police were convinced that heavy metal music was to blame. "Basically, the music teaches that you don't have to listen to your parents, and that you should live life the way you want and screw the world," said Darlyne Pettinichio of the Orange County probation department.

ITEM: In Denair, California, police and city officials were alarmed by vandalism and grave desecration, including strewing about the bones of a seventy-seven-year-old man. Later the walls of the high school itself were defaced with occult graffiti, including 666. The majority of the scribblings were the names and lyrics of heavy metal groups, including Venom, AC/DC, and Ozzy Osborne.

ITEM: A Tennessee psychiatrist informed a Senate committee that heavy metal music is "poison" for disturbed adolescents, not to mention substance abusers. It is also "like throwing gasoline on the fire of hatred and resentment that's already burning," said Dr. Paul King, clinical assistant professor of child and adolescent psychiatry at the University of Tennessee. According to King, more than 80 percent of his adolescent patients have listened to heavy metal for long stretches of time as a daily routine. They were familiar with all the words and wrote them in notebooks and on desks while class was going on.

ITEM: Police in Britain were stifled in their efforts to come up with suspects in the serial gang rapes of London women. Victims reported that one of the rapists had a telltale spider's web tattoo on his hand. Another sported a tattoo with the letters MAR. Both tattoos were insignia of the heavy metal group Marillion, which sings about rape and mayhem.

ITEM: Vandalism of more than $200,000 to the Holy Rosary Cemetary in Hopelawn, New Jersey, spurred an investigation in 1986 of a group of about twenty youths. "The 'common thread' among the people who have perpetrated acts of satanic vandalism in Middlesex County the past few months was use of drugs and the influence of heavy metal music," said county prosecutor Alan A. Rockoff.

Investigators made the connection when they stumbled upon a shack in a forested area with the inscription "Welcome to the metal church." The interior walls of the "church" were strewn with pentagrams and the names of heavy metal musicians, including Ozzy Osborne. On a nearby tree could be seen the number 666 in a mosaic of steel tacks. The cops found drugs and beer cans with pellet holes in them.

Police also unearthed a notebook with the following inscriptions: *heroine, white punks on dope, motorhead, killers, Harley Davidson, Charlie Manson, Helter Skelter, smoke dust, suicidal vengeance, sabotage.*

An intelligence report prepared by the Middlesex County prosecutor's office summarized the development of the case as well as the connection between heavy metal and mounting vandalism. In 1985, the D.A.'s office was advised of an incident in which a cemetery in South River, New Jersey, was attacked. Several youths, local "heavy metallers," were apprehended. In February of the following year, unknown assailants in nearby Perth Amboy spray-painted the word *Slayer* and inverted crosses onto a church. On April 8, the incident at the Holy Rosary Church occurred. Seven stones were desecrated using a magic marker. Graffiti included the words *Venom, Satanas Luciferi Excelsi*, and *Satan 28*.

On May 19, approximately seventy tombstones at a Jewish cemetery near Woodbridge were defaced. In this context the Nazi swastika appeared beside the familiar *Slayer*. In heavy metal circles, *Slayer* is an acronym for "Satan Laughs While You Eternally Rot." Four juveniles were taken into custody after making what the police called "terroristic threats involving Satanic overtones" against a high school teacher. The following is the text of an actual police interrogation:

Are you a follower of heavy metal music?
Yes.
What groups?
Slayer, Creator, Possessed, SOD, Sultic Frost, Metalica.
How do the words make you feel?
Like, violent. The music gives me a feeling of strength.
Do you believe in God?
No, not really.
What do you do at Hell Parties?
Take drugs, light fires, chant things to the devil.

"Hell parties" take place in desolate areas. Sometimes animals are sacrificed, and drugs are regularly ingested. LSD, or mescaline, is the "drug of choice" at hell parties. The genre of the music is called *thrash*, or *speed metal*. It is also known as *black metal* or *satanic rock*. The groups that make the sound have names like Testament, Exodus, Violence, the Forbidden, Death Angel, Megadeth, Anthrax, Suicidal Tendencies, Venom, Exciter, Warhead, Slayer, and, of course, Metallica. The trailblazer of this trend was Black Sabbath, who gained notoriety through its use of gothic melodies and satanic lyrics.

But is heavy metal really bad for people, especially adolescents? Parents have objected to both the notes and lyrics of rock since Elvis "the Pelvis" started gyrating and wiggling in sexually explicit contortions to the strains of "Heartbreak Hotel." And if no one can blame rock music directly for the 300 percent rise in adolescent suicides or the 7 percent increase in teenage pregnancies, it may surely be more than a negligible factor.

Lead singer Brian Bubenheimer of the group Nocticula would like to "make it" as a rock star. "I may be a hard-core, underground, death-morbid-thrash metal vocalist," he said, "but I'd never do harm to nobody." The larger world outside the music is full of hollow values, hypocrisy, and stupidity, and it is fraught with the possibility of the species' extinction as well as sundry global horrors—the stuff that LaVey says should make anybody want to become a satanist. The metaler knows that he might easily be annihilated in a nuclear holocaust. He might even have to get a job.

Adolescents aged thirteen to eighteen are the prime listening audience for heavy metal. Enthralled by noise levels that fluctuate at the threshold of pain—125 decibels or more—the kids run a risk of serious damage to their hearing, even if their psyches are not immediately at peril. It is doubtful whether the heavy metal "freaks" can even hear the lyrics, let alone decipher them, at live performances. Sociology professor Lorraine Prinsky, who surveyed 265 California teenagers about their musical tastes and habits, concluded that the majority of heavy metal listeners did not have the slightest notion of what their favorite songs were about."Teenager's understanding is different from an adult understanding of things".

As such, sexual innuendo, occult references, even basic metaphors go utterly uncomprehended by the younger listeners, she insisted. Part of that may be because a complete understanding of popular music lyrics requires a degree of sophistication in literary analysis that is lacking in most young people. When the song says "lick me" or "slip it in" and so on, however, as the majority of heavy metal album cuts do, it is difficult to accept that the kids have no idea what the subject matter entails.

Jane Norwood of the Parent's Music Resource Center (PMRC) has a less cheery perspective. PMRC was founded and spearheaded by Tipper Gore, the wife of Tennessee senator Albert Gore, Jr., who ran unsuccessfully for the Democratic presidential nomination in 1988. Gore made headlines in the mid-1980s for the public hearings she initiated on the content of rock albums. The hearings were roundly jeered by the music industry. Norwood told the press, "I'm very happy to hear that of the children they interviewed, the majority were more interested in songs of love. However, what the PMRC is concerned with is the seven percent listed in the study who do listen to songs that glorify sexual violence. Unfortunately, there is a subculture of kids who listen to this kind of music, and violence is occurring."

Prinsky remains unconvinced of the association "because if they don't understand the lyrics, how can it affect their behavior?"

If it is all just a Halloween costume party, or the high school misfits' senior prom, the question then seems to be, what should Johnny or Jenny wear? Black primarily, but one might also observe accents of blood-red and a hint or two of white—mainly to put to rest charges that heavy metal is the music of absolutely bad "bad guys." Black satin and tight-fitting leather pants would have a certain charm. And you can attach your studs and spikes to leather arm bands or belts. Cut the fingers out of your black gloves. If the spikes leave sufficient room, append handcuffs or chains to the belt.

Of course, these tokens of torture and violence could be strung about one's neck, too. Black net stockings look better on the arms. And one should not forget the single earring—another accessory in the shape of a cross, to show either your "medieval" insignia à la Conan the Barbarian or your subtle, snarling contempt for Christian society. Just a little more eyeliner and one is ready to go. Still, if all one does is "dress metal" but somehow fails to identify personally with all the violence, one could be labeled a "poser."

Symbols might include the names of the heavy metal groups: upside-down pentagrams; the word *ZOSO*, meaning the three-headed guard dog at the gates of hell; *NATAS*, or Satan spelled backwards; swastikas; the words *helter skelter*; and the drawing of a fist with extended index and little fingers—the "Satan sign."

Perhaps what we have here is not an avant-garde slice of entertainment but a new morbidity. Aquino, who thinks rock music through its vibratory effects will change the consciousness of American civilization, is voluble about the "fatal attraction" of prospective young satanists to heavy metal. In an article called "The Cloning of Nikki Sixx"—Nikki Sixx is part of Motley Crue—"edited" by Michael Aquino, he observes that in the 1980s, when all soothing illusions of Americans have been obliterated, "younger America" must respond "with passionate frustration" at having come so near to achieving material paradise yet having been denied it.

Heavy metal, which he compares with the torchlight processions in Nazi Germany, is "an explosion of fury," a righteous eruption of barbarous emotion. Heavy metal is art, says Aquino, albeit of the terroristic stamp. All the good causes these days have evaporated—the environment, AIDS, the homeless—except for evil.

According to Dr. Paul King, the University of Tennessee psychiatrist who testified about heavy metal music before a Senate committee, the 1980s have been earmarked by "a vacuum of aimless rebellion and personal impotency." Only heavy metal music remains to ignite the emotions. King's studies of adolescent patients admitted for drug and psychological problems give us a clue about what is at stake with heavy metal. Disturbed adolescents, regardless of whether they are on drugs, display a staggering incidence of violent behavior and sexual promiscuity. This debility goes hand in hand with their immature brain's capacity to control adequately the erotic and aggressive drives. The abuse of drugs renders the situation lethal. Music preference research points to a sizable sample of "disturbed" adolescents who wile away their hours engrossed in "disturbing" music.

The strains of violence, fury, hate, insurrection, primitive sex, and, as the kids call it, "head banging" in heavy metal music cements a neural bond with all stripes of alienated adolescence. The incitement of heavy metal, however, is markedly increased when an adolescent abuses drugs in his or her day-to-day activity. Such a diagnosis certainly was borne out in the case of Pete Roland. The music instantly becomes the most impressive furniture in the mental housing of chemically dependent youth.

Heavy metal is to heavy drug use as lotteries are to compulsive gamblers. It is hard to say whether one "causes" the other. The chemically dependent adolescent adopts a life-style of swagger, brutality, theft, and sexual excess—all of which is reinforced by the yowling and bellowing of the metal groups.

The inflammatory message of heavy metal music is, as might not be surprising, "religious"—in the sense that it proclaims a higher power overseeing the universe. The power, however, is not God or even fate. It is *violence*—often the most irrational and uncontrollable violence engineered by the Archfiend himself, whom unsophisticated minds have a hard time identifying as "psychodrama" or "symbol."

The power and violence of the satanic is something toward which youngsters bereft of hope, and with a stunted conscience, can easily gravitate. Children who find it difficult to identify a coherent value system, or who were raised with no values at all, still must identify with something. That was Pete Roland's profile. All children—and in a very large sense teenagers are yet *children*, whether they say so or not—give heed to the feeling of a Higher Power. Troubled and abused youngsters, through a sort of insidious imprinting of experience, believe the Higher Power must be evil. Heavy metal affirms this "theology" and institutionalizes it in the music.

Consider, for example, the number "Eat Me Alive" by Judas Priest. The song hymns the florid sorts of ecstasies that should ensue from forcing a participant to have oral sex at gunpoint. Venom's album cover of *Welcome to Hell* announces that the group is "possessed by all that is evil" and that death of "your God" is demanded.

Great White and Motley Crue offer more than casual acceptance of rape in their lyrics, and the album covers themselves are lurid. *Exiter* shows a woman trying to stave off an ice-pick murderer, while *Gravedigger* displays a cross driven into a skull.

In *Anthrax* we contemplate a metal fist destroying a person's face. Stage theatrics might include simulated intercourse, oral sex, anal penetration, necrophilia, sadomasochism, satanic sacrifice, sundry barbaric rites, physical abuse of women, and perhaps the imbibing of blood from a skull. One of the band members may "lighten" things up by exposing himself—or herself. Consequently, it is not uncommon for knifings, fights, plundering, and rape to occur amid the musical brawling during a metal concert.

Dr. Thomas Radecki, M.D., chair of the National Coalition on Television (NCTV), says that heavy metal music "is a rock subculture of intense violence" and that the preponderance of heavy metal is an adulation of "violence for violence's sake." Metallica has leaped past the million-seller mark with the release its album *Master of Puppets*. Slayer's latest *South of Heaven* has sold over half a million. It is enormous cash flow for record merchandisers and the companies who turn their products out. The music business has found out that "smut sells" in the same way that movie producers figured out long ago that sex and violence mingled with the monstrous could change a B-grade thriller into a box-office smash.

When NCTV monitored over 1300 rock music videos from MTV, WTBS's Night-tracks, and the USA network, it learned that 44 percent of all music videos were replete with sounds and images of rage, violence, and threats of violence. Ferocious rivalries between male and female propounded the message that sexual brutality is not only normal but highly gratifying.

Heavy metal is audio pornography at extreme decibels. When he was surgeon general, C. Everett Koop remarked that:

society has become much more concerned about the way pornography has begun to invade both our public and our private lives. At one time, the public's concern was focused almost exclusively upon book stores and movie theaters that specialized in pornography. But today's hucksters of pornography have invaded cable television, the world of popular music, telephone communications, and the whole new field of home video recorders.

While smut sells, however, it also spreads "disease," which sometimes flares into epidemics if not quarantined. Why should it be so arduous for

America's intelligentsia to countenance the proposition that heavy metal music influences alienated youth? If we already grant the premise that pornography might motivate a child molester, why not entertain the thought that lyrics that scream *kill, mutilate, maim, torture, obliterate* might actually spur someone with a deranged brain to perform precisely those acts?

It should not take a prodigious genius to figure out that a hundred thousand young men with violent or homicidal tendencies, after listening day after day and hour after hour to music with accompanying video that celebrates explicitly the sorts of deed that might have even discomfited the Marquis de Sade, might just *possibly* pose a social problem. Stir drug abuse into a foul brew, set aflame pubescent hormones with some great new variants on "Saturday night fever"—e.g., rape, incest, suicide, whippings, bondage, bisexuality, nihilism, black magic, vampirism, werewolves, cannibalism, disembowelment, assorted hideous tortures, necrophilia, hari kari, beheading, flaying, castration, concentration camps, assassination—and the effects will probably not be at all trivial.

One rock video seems to encourage parricide itself, as in the Sullivan episode. In a segment put out by Twisted Sister there is a scene where a father who objects to his son's music is peremptorily "executed" by the boy. The boy then turns into the lead singer of the band, exulting "I WANT TO ROCK!"

The controversy surrounding heavy metal cannot be dismissed merely as a case of overwrought, ax-wielding moral crusaders and know-nothings making excessive ado about what is actually harmless psychodrama. The see-no-evil attitude of so many among the American intelligentsia, raised for years on the insipid dogma that any moral outrage coming from the middle class must be a menace to civil liberties, has helped trivialize the question.

Heavy metal, they consistently tell themselves, is only *this* generation's style of protest, as were pomade and leather jackets in the James Dean years and strings of beads and copulating in the park during Vietnam. The devil's sign is to kids born in 1972 what the peace sign was to those whose birth certificates say 1950. And after all, the two hand gestures do look considerably alike. If the kids are simply "acting out," a problem of content arises: What, in fact, are they acting out?

The great twentieth-century playwright Bertolt Brecht wrote productions with such a political and realistic intent that the actors sometimes were supposed to march off the stage, down the aisle, and out into the street to kindle a demonstration. It was his more urbane version of the terrorist aesthetic, Artaud's theater of cruelty. Satanism was originally "art" in this sense, although not something necessarily spontaneous or "unplanned." The Church of Satan did a very precise job of strategizing and shepherding the era of the Evil One. The hippies unleashed the sexual urge itself with their love-ins and their naked-savage mode of undress. The Church of Satan took custody in loosing the dark drives of humanity. The rationale was already there in the rhetoric of the sixties. It was not just "do your own thing." It was also, as a memorable slogan on the side of a building in Berkeley in 1968 said, "F—— civilization." That sensibility may have been the stalking horse for heavy metal.

For a long stint, the more tenebrous and the sleazier sermons of the sixties, were confined to manifestoes of the California in-crowd and to the street philosophers of the day—Charlie Manson's confederacy. Then those sermons went public through the medium of rock in the seventies. Heavy metal music was invented in London. The "ideas" trickled from the pop culture of fascism that had been preserved since the 1930s. The styles and images were drawn from the regalia of the biker gangs that roamed the highways and transported drugs across America. The lyrics came from the psycho wards.

Although the music industry would like what they perceive to be a socially liberal and forever credulous America to imagine that disgust with heavy metal is some outback, fundamentalist fad, the fact remains that health professionals are starting to abhor the business themselves. If heavy metal is nothing but pornography, then the effervescence of such an attitude is quite understandable. According to a publication of the American Academy of Pediatrics (AAP), a lot of current rock music and rock videos represent a type of "new morbidity" tied in with "psycho-social factors that can threaten a child's world as tragically as polio did a generation before."

The AAP argues that long-term exposure to heavy metal can warp a child's worldview, which is really a kind of long-term, psychological disfigurement. The fault with heavy metal is that its social effect or influence has been amplified through the television component of rock video, particularly the kind that is run regularly on MTV. What the songs themselves say is scurrilous enough.

But those who scoff at parental concerns about heavy metal, including some behavioral researchers who staunchly maintain the kids do not pay any attention to what they are hearing, ignore the fact that the lyrics are not meant to be important by themselves. Rock composers have understood this principle since the salad years of Elvis and Little Richard, with the exception of the late sixties when pop music often did try to get across an identifiable "social message." Rock is characterized by its totalizing impact.

Rock in the music world dovetails with the cycle of what is called *modernism* in art, which began at the turn of the century with Picasso's cubist paintings that did not compare with anything the average gallery viewer would recognize. It is not what the painting is "about," the defenders of modern art have been saying all along. Bob Dylan himself, after making the switch about 1964 from social protest or "movement" songs to surrealistic serenades such as as "Highway 61" and "Rainy Day

Women," mouthed this view in a spoof of an interview with *Playboy* magazine. When asked what his songs were really "about," Dylan deadpanned: "Oh, some are about three minutes. Some are about five minutes."

Generally speaking, the meaning of rock is what it *is*, an artist would contend, or it is what it *does*. The words, or the content, do not really count. It all converges on the response of the listener. The trifling fifties lyrics "Don't step on my blue suede shoes" or "Peggie Sue, I love you" are hardly different from "your mercury mouth in the missionary times" of Dylan, according to this theory. Fortuitously and perhaps with grim irony, they also compare with Z. Z. Top's "She likes whips and chains, she likes cocaine."

The point is to get the listener to react, not ruminate. It is also to provoke an upsurge of the irrational so far as is possible. It is to make somebody mad, usually parents and school officials, which will then titillate the voyeuers or the rebellious among the young. It is *pornography* —nothing less, nothing more. And the history of pornography is the process of conditioning an audience to react favorably to more intense and obscene jolts.

Pornographic shock may have its genesis in the music of the Rolling Stones, who were the first to challenge directly the values of Christian civilization with their intonations of "painting it black" and "sympathy for the Devil." In the seventies, Vincent Furnier, the son of a Mormon preacher who adopted his stage name "Alice Cooper" from a legendary seventeenth-century witch, dressed up as Dracula in drag and began beheading dolls on stage. That was further shock.

In the eighties, the performers are trying to convince their audience that killing real babies might be the next, ineffable thrill. That is about as close as one can get to the audio version of snuff movies. It may be "ritualized," but after all so is satanism. Heavy metal belongs to a so-called avant-garde art form that has stayed veiled from the eyes of mass audiences, the style known as aesthetic terrorism.

In 1985, the *Wall Street Journal* reported that a fat sheaf of neuro-psychological research has shown remarkable, and complex, relationships between music listening and brain organization. Roger Shepard, a professor at Stanford University, believes that certain kinds of music "mesh effectively with the deep cognitive structures of the mind." Heavy metal seems to mesh with the limbic brain, the most primitive and potentially violent stratum of cerebral processing.

The typical American teenager "tunes into" some form of rock music on the average of five hours per day. That is almost the average number of hours spent in a school classroom. In fine, the messages of rock music are about equal in "influence" to that of teachers. What about the influence of "Satan"? Said a former drummer with a well-known metal band, "I find myself basically evil. I believe in Satan just as much as I believe in God. You can use either to get things done."

Adolescent satanism is the pedagogy of contempory rock's aesthetic terrorism. It does indeed get things done. The stupidity of the see-no-evil crowd, the self-styled civil libertarians who prate that the music has little or no impact on social developments, becomes blatant when one considers that the emblems of Satan and suggestions of so-called devil worship used in heavy metal performances are indeed, as the rockers themselves contend, stage props. The props have a purpose. They are designed to "evangelize," not so much for some sort of organized and structured church of Satan, but for a summoning of the steely determination of "young America" to take charge, as the brownshirts did in the dusky streets of Weimar Germany.

Heavy metal rock videos and heavy metal magazines are often nothing more than crude but ruthless commercials for what in Nazi speech was called the "triumph of the will." The aesthetics of heavy metal videos are often copied from Nazi propoganda films. And heavy metal is by and large propoganda.

Deena Weinstein, a tenured professor of sociology at DePaul University who has become the academic authority to which defenders of heavy metal turn these days, does not, however, view the matter as such. According to an article about her in the *Chronicle of Higher Education*, Weinstein's favorite band is Manowar, and her favorite songs by the group are "Master of Revenge" and "Violence and Bloodshed." Weinstein wears metal T-shirts to class and hangs out with the thrash groupies. In consequence, the *Chronicle* called her "an intellectual with an edge on many of her colleagues" and rhapsodized, "Never has heavy metal needed an articulate spokesman more."

Metal music—even though it keens on day and night about death, torture, suffering, vampirism, self-destruction, and bestiality—is entirely "life-affirming," according to Weinstein, and is a valuable "cultural form." The problem lies with cultural snobbery. "Can one argue that Chuck Berry is better or worse than Beethoven?" she asks. "Can one argue whether Mendelssohn is superior to Manowar?"

Like the cult apologists who sociologize about satanism as merely a symbolic manifestation of all the faults with "decadent Christians," Weinstein agrees with the metalers themselves that the music is merely providing an outlet for righteous rage against something or other. Heavy metal "demonstrates what's going on in the society, and, insofar as it changes, it registers the changes that are going on," she said. The same argument was made by a member of the band Slayer at a music industry conference in New York, which Weinstein moderated. As for the problem with heavy metal, he observed, "It's not us. It's at home. The problem starts at home."

The sentiment has been echoed by some other experts. The Reverend Don Kimball of Santa Rosa, another partisan of the "metal-is-healthy" contingent, argues that even though metal may become a belief system in its own right, it is a way by which parents can "hear the hurts" in their kids. Kimball says that overcoming bad relationships and lack of communication should be attempted, rather than shutting down the music.

Joseph Katarba, sociologist at the University of Houston, argues that rock has always been construed as "a threat to the moral fiber of America's youth, whether it's Elvis Presley or the Rolling Stones, or heavy metal." The family, however, is "the most likely place to look for the source of aberrant behavior. If you have to depend on Megadeth to see what's up in life, there's something else wrong there. In fact, heavy metal is probably a useful mechanism for the release of adolescent feelings."

The release of feelings may also have real social consequences. Not too long ago an album by the band Frankie Goes to Hollywood hit the stores. On the liner sleeve was the following wry observation: "Manipulation of children's minds in the field of religion or politics would touch off a parental storm and a rash of Congressional investigations. But in the world of commerce, children are fair game and legitimate prey."

The late Jimi Hendrix was just as blunt. "You can hypnotize people with music and when they get at their weakest point, you can preach into their subconscious minds what you want to say." Nikki Sixx adds, "The one thing I got from Hitler was the idea of the Nazi youth. I believe in the Motley youth. The youth of today are the leaders of tomorrow. They're young, they can be brainwashed."

One of the classic techniques of brainwashing is to alter the key symbol, or concept, by which people steer their loyalties and organize their experiences. In the lingo of Edward Schein, a pioneer in the psychology of brainwashing techniques, this ploy is known as "unfreezing." The Chinese Communists during the Korean War learned how to "unfreeze" the ideas and attitudes that made American prisoners of war fiercely patriotic and resistant to the mental tortures their captors inflicted.

The Chinese Communists were not so much interested in bullying and physically degrading American prisoners in the manner the Japanese did during World War II. They wanted the "souls" of the internees. They were interested in "reforming" the thought of the P.O.W.'s in such a way that they talked and behaved like Maoists, which would be the ultimate "proof" to the world of the perfection and certainty of Marxist-Leninist ideology. So in order to brainwash, they first had to strip bare, annihilate, or unfreeze the captive's basic system of beliefs. One of the ways you unfreeze a belief system is to convince the victim that everything he deemed good is now evil and everything he longed for is impossible. Slavery is freedom. Lies are truth.

The chief objective of the satanist message in reforming the thought of today's young people is not just to encourage rebellion against parents or to implant in them coy doubts about traditional morality, as rock used to do. The aim is to ingrain in the kids the "deeper" message that parents are the quintessence of apocalyptic evil.

The message would not have taken hold in earlier generations when parents exerted stronger authority. It is impossible to generate an utter falsehood out of its opposite. The Korean P.O.W.'s were made to believe America hated them and had abandoned them because they were not allowed to receive letters or have any contact with others of their compatriots. To create an idol there must first be a psychological vacuum. The absent, capricious, and sexually abusive father of Pete Roland became a blank slate upon which the "thought reform" processes that create the governing symbol of the evil, all-powerful father began to write. In rock video, the process can be done through the transformation of the images of the father himself.

Dee Snider has gleefully described the method of "unfreezing" involved in the particular video mentioned earlier. In the video there is a scene with a "strict" middle American father, who berates his son for too much loud rock music. The father twits the son for making a mess out of his life, but the boy is unmoved. Instead he is suddenly transmuted into a demonlike personality and asserts in "an exorcist-like voice" that all he wants is "to rock." The actors in the video, according to Snider, then "proceed to destroy Daddy" and to "smash him with doors, pull him by the hair." Daddy is destroyed, but he now is reborn as "the Devil," as one might expect. Daddy is Snider himself, the all-powerful rock icon who is an extension of the personality of the disturbed youth.

The real Daddy is unfrozen. Says Nikki Sixx, "The Devil is any authority that tells you what you can or can't do. It can be your boss, your teacher, or your parents!" The social order is unfrozen, and violence reigns. Violence is the sole solution.

Pete Roland was especially fond of a Metallica album titled *Kill 'em All*. A security guard at a concert by the Scorpions told the press that "it was wild. . . . There was vomit and blood everywhere. . . . This band drives the kids into an uncontrollable frenzy." Drugs go with heavy metal as wine flowed, of necessity, through the Dionysian frenzy. The drugs heighten the sensation. They give the courage to think, believe, and perhaps do all those horrible things the musicians are glorifying as part of the "psychodrama." Substance abuse is not only one other "perversion" or form of degeneracy that adds to the aesthetic terrorism. It is a necessary and sufficient condition thereof.

Drugs have always been the standard players in the tool kit of thought reform. Drugs not only intensify perceptions and incoming messages to the brain, they create a general receptivity for new messages. They help break down old habits of feeling and responding. They are a torch for unfreezing.

King's clinical research indicates that 59.1 percent of all patients admitted chiefly for drug abuse made heavy metal their "first choice of music," as opposed to only 39.3 percent for otherwise disturbed patients. Moreoever, 74.4 percent of all chemically dependent patients were involved in violence. About 50 percent indulged in stealing, and 71.9 percent were into violent sexual activity. All along the spectrum, the portion of the same group with average psychiatric disorders was considerably less, indicating that the connection between the drugs and appropriation of the lyrics of the music was quite lethal.

According to King, "the music preference study shows that a large number of disturbed youngsters listen to music with unconventional themes of violence, hate, rebellion, primitive sex, abuse of women, and glorification of Satan. When an adolescent's life-style includes drugs, this preference is even more likely."[1] If heavy metal were simply a reflection on social breakdown, as its apologists demand, this correlation would not show up in the statistics.

Heavy metal influences social behavior because it is a "religion," as King has written in an oft-quoted article in the *Journal of the Tennessee Medical Association*. In an age when traditional religion can barely, if at all, inculcate values and identity, heavy metal spans the breach. Religion is typically about a sense of reverence for supernatural power. In heavy metal the reverence is for the omnipotence of evil. Hence, the controlling symbol of that power would be Satan, at least as far as Western civilization is concerned.

In heavy metal "evil acts are glorified to new heights in concerts," writes King. It is not just the presentation but the constant glorification that can eventually lead to insane and overly violent acts.

That sentiment helps the concerned critic of heavy metal deflect the cliche-ridden and insipid rejoinder that violence is ever present in society anyhow. Such an answer follows the familiar logic of "everybody's doing it," which all kids use against their parents when they want to do something not necessarily for their own good. Unfortunately, too many opinion-makers use a sophisticated swatch of the same argument. Their argument runs as follows: We see violence on television. There is violence on the urban streets at 2 A.M. There is violence in the military weapons we fund and ship to foreign nations. There is violence in families. There is violence in the news media. Heavy metal is a parodying protest against the prevalence of violence in today's culture.

The argument would be ludicrous were it not obnoxious. Every petty criminal, every political tyrant, every mass murderer, every aggressor has used virtually the same argument to justify the motive for the magnitude of the violence committed.

Heavy metal does not mirror the violence so much as it artistically stylizes, aggrandizes, beautifies, weaves a spell of enchantment around what would otherwise be lesser and ordinary violent behavior. And so violence becomes more than letting off steam or even "getting even" with real and fictitious abuses. Heavy metal is a true aesthetics of violence. It is a metaphysics. It is the tactic of consecrating violent terror, of divinizing it. That is why it has become the foundation of the "religion" of satanism. Most people are not naturally sadists or torturers in giving vent to their violent impulses. Cruel and unusual violence—the stuff that is wound into the very tapestry of heavy metal "art"—cannot occur unless the imagination is stimulated and trained not only to perform it, but to enjoy it.

Dr. L. D. Tashjian, chair of the department of psychiatry at Mount Sinai Hospital in Philadelphia, has found significant effects of rock music on the formation of values and worldview among children. "We find seven- and eight-year-olds," he told a national magazine, "who listen to lyrics extolling sexual sadism, bondage, bestiality, and at this very impressionable age such messages can seriously warp their sexual orientation. The younger child or the potentially disturbed youth is liable to be profoundly and dangerously influenced."

It is also untrue that heavy metal is to this generation what "Love Me Tender" or "I Want to Hold Your Hand" was to the early baby boomers. Joe Stuessy, professor of music theory at the University of Texas in San Antonio, observes that "there is a new element in the music, a meanness of spirit—outright hatred—that was not present in the early days of rock."

Heavy metal does more than dissolve the inherent inhibitions against violence. It actively fosters, configures, anneals, reinforces, and purifies the most vicious and depraved tendencies within the human organism. That was the Nazi secret. Violence must become mythological in order to be political. The lead time is a little less than a generation. In that respect, heavy metal is a laboratory experiment that has a lot to do with an emergent politics. It is a psychological refinery for the manufacture of *real* monsters.

What about the propogation of satanism as a belief complex? Does the music make a difference, or is Satan simply a convenient, poetic trope for what otherwise would still be violent urges and behavior? "The devil never came to me, he spoke to me through the music," Pete Roland told his shrink.

It was the lyrics from Metallica that both inspired and drove Roland to bludgeon Steve Newberry. What about when they wail, "I killed your baby tonight," or "It's time to die"? What about the album title *To Live is to Die*? Does Metallica "preach" satanism to adolescents in such a manner that an evangel causes a conversion from sociality to homicidal sociopathy? Metallica is not at all apologetic. Says Metallica's James Hetfield, "Don't take it literally."

Many of the kids probably do not take it literally. They take it allegorically, or at least "morally," as the medieval churchmen would have said. The "moral" sense of the heavy metal texts, which slowly leave their impression on the whole of the rock industry, is that there is no morality; and therefore immorality, or no morality, is the stage-sanctioned norm. "Feels so good to be so bad!" goes the tagline of an album by Badlands.

The credenda of virtually all the metal groups is that raw sensuality with a violent pulse, dearth of conscience, and the big *A* of anarchy should be the new social imperative. In that respect, LaVey's "nine satanic statements" have become a twittering commonplace among the bands themselves. The sensibility is complete cynicism and also "passing the buck." *Metal* magazine itself called Metallica the "triumph of the garbage band." Garbage sells only because it smells, and that is the thrust. Lars Ulrich, another Metallican, has remarked that they simply offer "an honest interpretation of what's going on in front of us." Or, as the magazine puts it, "they've stripped away the high-gloss, 'bullshit factor' and stood firm, guitars set on kill. And the world seems to be listening."

It is easy to speculate about why the world is listening. The pornography of violence has oversold itself so that what was once postured as social critique rapidly congealed into an institutional form of nihilism. In an age where all barriers and taboos have broken down, the only remaining contrivance for shock is to proclaim the end of all civility. The message of Metallica's "Justice for All" is that there is no justice, except the justice of the jungle. The violence itself was packaged as a metaphysics, so that the young begin to believe that society is thoroughly corrupt, which it is not, and that all human beings are refuse, which they are not. But in the metal culture, the music and the reality are indistinguishable, just as in the magical world of satanist believers from Crowley to Constanzo, evil power is the ultimate datum of experience—it must be mastered, or it will master you. Thus, one metal freak who signs his letters "Magick" à la Crowley can sneer,

Why do these single-minded, shallow-life people tweak when they hear about the devil on a record? Hey, this is *reality*; this is part of *life*. Most of these bands are just stating what's going on in the world. It isn't going to go away once they stop singing about it.

It probably will not go away immediately, any more than the craving for cocaine will not abate the instant one stops using cocaine. The addiction of neurochemistry and the addiction of media-generated belief systems have a certain psychological isomorphism.

The classical criminal mind has been noted for a similar kinetics of reasoning: I am corrupt, therefore society is corrupt, therefore I will corrupt it even further because *corruption* is a moral term that has no meaning. Therefore, I will do whatever I like, which is violence and corruption; therefore, I am only reflecting what is going on in society; therefore, I am quite justified in corrupting society.

It is no accident that drugs, heavy metal, brutality, and wanton violence have all become the grisly ensigns that wave above the human desolation as we move toward the third decade of the Age of Satan.

The heavy metal bands make a fetish of their "honesty" in depicting how sordid all of life is. But there is one metal celebrity who considers himself even more honest than the others because he admits to practicing satanism. His name is King Diamond.

A Danish performer, Diamond paints his face with a red, white, and black "fright mask" that entails bat wings superimposed on the eyes and an inverted cross on the forehead. He says he has performed satanic rituals, but he asks that he not be "judged" for his religious beliefs. He insists he does not sacrifice cats or kill babies, but he does have "certain feelings" on which he is compelled to act through his music and on stage. "I don't see anything I do as being a sin. So I don't run around with a bad conscience for that."

Neither did the Hardy boys.

NOTES

1. Paul King, "Heavy Metal Music and Drug Abuse in Adolescents," *Post-Graduate Medicine*, April 1988, pp. 297–98.

CHAPTER 9.

Fantasy Role-Playing Games and the Devil's Bargain

Welcome to the land of imagination. You are about to begin a journey where magic and monsters are the order of the day, where good and evil, law and chaos, are forever at odds . . .
    ——Introduction to the game "Dungeons and Dragons"

Michael Aquino describes the 1928 novel *Seven Footprints to Satan* as a "satanic manifesto." In the book, the character who calls himself Satan exists for three aims—to collect unique and beautiful things, to manipulate lives and events for entertainment value, and for the gambler's love of the game.

"Satan" would have delighted in the University of Michigan in 1979 when child genius James Dallas Eggbert III disappeared into the eight-and-a-half-mile maze of heating tunnels beneath the campus. Criticism and pressure to get the best grades apparently contributed to Dallas's severe depressive state. All Dallas really cared about academically was computers. He did not know how to explain to his parents the trouble he had fitting in socially with older college age students. Nor did he know how to explain to his mother he was gay. He could not divulge to them anything about the drugs he took, or the obsession with the nighttime games of "Dungeons and Dragons" in the dark tunnels, where the "dragon's breath," or jets of hot steam, could scald a player without warning.

Dallas had originally planned to commit suicide with qualudes and had left a cryptic map as a clue to where his body could be found. The attempt failed, however, and Dallas crawled out for help to his friends in the gay community.

Detective William Dear's account of the solving of Dallas's disappearance uncovers more than just a troubled teenager's story. Apparently, hundreds of students, and even professors, played the dangerous game of "Dungeons and Dragons," sometimes even in costume, in the twilight tunnels where reality and fantasy flowed together.

Other colleges, such as Southern Methodist University and the California Institute of Technology, were also known for their tunnels where such escapades were commonplace. But the tunnels at MSU could be used for sinister purposes as well. Several unsolved rapes and robberies had transpired. Outside the campus in a nearby woods, the Tolkien Society met once a year for rituals celebrating the birth of Gandolf the Magician. Pentagrams were carved in the trees and Dear even witnessed a student group apparently trying to channel Gurdjieff.

Dear was not concerned in 1979 with the darker workings of satanism on a college campus. Few people were. "I suspected most of it was an excuse to get drunk or moderately high and was not to be taken too seriously," he writes. Evidence found on the tunnel walls included thirteen spray-painted names and other graffiti messages like "This Way to Middle Earth." Dear writes:

Later I learned that thirteen was the designated number for a witches coven, and that the MSU students who dabbled in witchcraft and black masses and such read books like *The Satanic Bible* passed around helix-shaped Egyptian bracelets, and engaged in a variety of bizarre rites that were sure to drive their parents wild.

Dallas was passed around the gay community from one house to another, almost like a chain letter. Drugs and sex were provided to keep him high or perhaps to keep him controllable. He became afraid by the third move, when he was told he could not leave. Sent by bus to New Orleans with vague promises of help and threats if he told anyone where he had been and who he had been with, the drugs wore off. Eventually, Dallas called home and was rescued by William Dear. No names were ever revealed in connection with his ordeal. Tragically, Dallas's problems were not to be resolved. On August 11, 1980, Dallas squeezed the trigger of a gun aimed at his temple and was silenced forever.

Child psychologists since Piaget have noted that the formation of conscience, or its dismantling, often depends on the imaginative materials their culture, or their parents, supply them. The Germans had a word that could mean both "education" and "formation," and it came from the same root as the word for "imagination"—*Bildung*. If the *Bildung* of heavy metal music has been to teach the throwing of nihilistic tantrums, the value content of the so-called fantasy role-playing game known as "Dungeons and Dragons," which detractors have charged with leading to the practice of satanism, may be suicide and despair.

ITEM: The Fresno, California, school board ruled against "devil worship and the study of the black arts on school time." A course called "Literature of the Supernatural" was withdrawn from three high schools in the wake of protests by some parents. School board member John Oomasian told a reporter that the council took the steps after one teacher allegedly conducted a "Luciferian mass" in the classroom itself to illustrate what the "supernatural" is all about.

The teacher described to the teenagers the ceremony of laying out a naked woman on a mattress and placing a cross athwart her breasts. The teacher contended the course was designed to "encourage reading and scholarship." The school board branded it thinly disguised pornography.

ITEM: In Fremont, California, three adolescents and an adult male were arrested and charged with the murder of fourteen-year-old Kellie Jean Poppleton. Officials disclosed that the girl had served as an informer to police about a junior high drug ring. Prior to her death the girl's assailants had sexually molested her. Two days before the slaying, Kellie had written for her teacher an essay about playing the fantasy game "Dungeons and Dragons" while smoking marijuana.

"I can really get into the game," Poppleton wrote. "I can almost see the Orcas coming after me and a spell being cast on me. It's so realistic. I begin to feel like a medieval warrior in a cold damp dungeon fighting for power, gold and glory. It might get a little carried away at times, but I finally come back to Earth."

ITEM: In Montpelier, Virginia, sixteen-year-old Irving "Bink" Pulling II crept into his parents' bedroom, snatched a revolver from the nightstand, sauntered outdoors, and fired a bullet through his chest. Pulling had the profile of a completely "normal" teenager, and his parents were not only stunned, they were incredulous. Young Pulling had been secretly embroiled in the game "Dungeons and Dragons" (D & D). A suicide note was found along with a morass of game literature and material. The youth had been introduced to D & D through a special school program for the "gifted and talented."

Another player in the "game" had recently laid a "curse" on Bink. The curse went something like this: "Your soul is mine, I choose the time. At my command, you will leave the land. A follower of evil, a killer of man." Within hours Bink was dead, the victim of, as the cult apologists might say, "an overactive imagination."

Bink's mother, Pat Pulling, today is an activist campaigning to force "fantasy role-playing games" such as D & D off the market. Her organization, Bothered About Dungeons and Dragons (BADD), has been quite successful in bringing serious questions about the psychological safety of the game to public and professional attention. Pulling also filed a $10 million lawsuit against two of the boy's teachers and the maker of the game, TSR Hobbies, Inc. of Lake Geneva, Wisconsin.

ITEM: A Florida couple, Pat and Mary Dempsey, told how their high school son Mike, who killed himself, was a "well-balanced boy with no mental problems" before experimenting with fantasy role-playing games. His preoccupation with the game, they submitted, led him to become unduly withdrawn and sullen. The boy lost interest in all his favorite pasttimes, such as chess and water-skiing, and became virtually impossible to discipline. "When asked to do a chore, he would walk by as if he was in another world," the parents said.

Gradually the boy's role-playing fantasies turned into obsessive realities. "He asked me to make a real medieval sword, and when I didn't, he made some deadly weapons" that were found after his death, according to his mother. He began to branch out into other occult oddities—voodoo, astrology, tarot—and believed that playing D & D would magically secure him good grades. Section 19 of the D & D masters guide has this terse commendation of "Suicide Mania:" "This form of insanity causes the afflicted character to have overwhelming urges to destroy himself or herself whenever means is presented."

ITEM: Larry Swartz, a seventeen-year-old Maryland youth, was convicted and sent to a psychological correctional institution for the murder of both his parents. Swartz insisted to the local newspaper that he was innocent, and even he could not understand why he was accused of such a heinous deed. Swartz said the only problem with jail was that he would not be allowed to do what he loves most, and what he used to do all the time—play D & D.

ITEM: "Dungeons and Dragons" was permanently banned from activity period at the Copley-Fairlawn Middle School in Akron, Ohio. One of the parents, John Sobolewski, with two children in school, had protested that the game encourages "arson, murder, torture, rape, and highway robbery."

But in Sacramento, California, the school board contemplated banning the playing of the game for entirely different reasons. Board member George Marsh noted that the Supreme Court bars religious activity from public facilities, and D & D is "religious." His reasoning: the game promotes the teaching of witchcraft, a recognized religion in America.

ITEM: In Oakland, California, Juan Kimbrough, fourteen, was shot by his fifteen-year-old brother as the climax to an intense session with D & D, according to homicide detective Jerry Harris. "It was really a tragic thing," Harris said. "They were playing a game that deals heavily with fantasy death and used the gun as a kind of prop." Harris pointed out that many D & D enthusiasts believe that "to die in combat while playing the game is nothing, because there are spells which can be cast to bring you back. Unfortunately, that's not the way it works in real life."

ITEM: A thirteen-year-old Ohio boy was found to have hanged himself in his own room. The kid was practicing "autoerotic hanging"— sexual stimulation received from hanging himself by one of the ropes of his sleeping bags. He was acting out a fantasy apparently from the game "Dungeons and Dragons." "Other family members stopped playing the game with him when he began to refer to it as though he were actually living the game," his sister confessed.

ITEM: In Arlington, Texas, a teenager who blasted himself in front of his drama class with a sawed-off .410 shotgun was known to have been a devotee of D & D. "We thought it was a fake," a classmate noted. We just couldn't figure out where he got all the stage blood. But then, it just kept on coming."

Apparently, fantasy role-playing can turn bizarre. Several months later Arlington detectives received five anonymous tips about a double homicide in a local park that may have had a relation to D & D. Stephanie Jennings, eighteen, was slain along with her fiance. Their throats were slashed. Stephanie was playing D & D at the time.

ITEM: Timothy Grice, twenty-one, of Lafayette, Colorado, also committed suicide by shotgun. A detective report made this dry comment: "D & D became a reality" for young Timothy. "He thought he was not constrained to this life, but could leave and return because of the game."

In the same locale, Daniel Ethan Erwin, sixteen, and Stephen Ray Erwin, twelve, were found to have carried out a mutual suicide pact as part of a fantasy associated with D & D. Lafayette police chief Larry Stallcup observed, "My understanding is that once you reach a certain point where you are the master, your only way out is death. That way no one can beat you."

ITEM: Danny Rameta of Traverse City, Michigan, and Lisa Dunn, his eighteen-year-old girlfriend, confessed they were prompted to go on a murder spree that killed four people in northwest Kansas because of the fantasy game "Dungeons and Dragons." "It's not just a board game," he told a press conference. "It's a lot deeper than a board game." Rameta said he had five friends who were locked up because of the game. One was named Jim Gainforth, convicted of killing a gas station attendant in Traverse City. Upon his capture, Rameta had produced a hand-written note containing some doggerel poetry that yet lay bare his passion for the "game."

In the poem Rameta wrote the "many shall die" in seeking "treasure." Rameta also said that the "challenge" of the game is to "kill off all the other characters." So he did.

Heavy metal, "Dungeons and Dragons," the Black Mass, the wearing of chains and spikes—call it "psychodrama," "letting off steam," experimenting with symbols. So is satanism, we are told. The salient point is that many parents, ministers, counselors, police officers, and mental health workers think there exists some kind of interlocking grid of relationships between pop culture and the siege of destructive behavior in America.

The satanists say it would be bumptious, fanatical, and paranoid to make such a deduction. Fantasy role-playing in such a medium, unfortunately, has become more than a board game for America's bright, brash, and beautiful. There are spin-offs and accessories to D & D, such as coloring books for young children with such titles as *Tunnels and Trolls* and *Hellpits of Nightfang*.

In D & D, players assume the identity of a given character—an elf, a thief, a fighter, a cleric, or a magician or "magic-user," a "halfling" or mixed-breed of human and subhuman, a dwarf. The game, however, has no game board; it is played through psychodramatic techniques that may engage an individual's time for hours or for days or even for years. The kids who are playing the game may construct their own private "society" to keep the game moving. It is purely an elaboration of their minds.

The purpose of the game is to persevere in an involuted maze of dangers. The reward of survival is "treasure," guarded by monsters, as is the case in both myths and fairy tales. In the meantime, the player seeks to triumph step by step over adversity through the acquisition of wealth and "magical" prowess. Players have their own weapons as well as native abilities, such as "wisdom" or "intelligence" or "charisma," decided by a toss of the dice. The "dungeon master," who sets up and guides the game, is responsible for tracing out an entire field of play—where is the treasure? what magic will be effective? and so on.

Critics of the game do not blame it for enriching a child's imagination. Even intricate fantasy lives are alright, they say, provided a line can be drawn somewhere between life and the imagination. The danger arises because the game is itself so elaborate, so compelling, and therefore so *seductive*. The more complex the game, the more time and energy must be devoted to learning and playing it. The more time and energy involved, the greater the "investment" that must be psychologically protected. Gary Gygax, inventor of the game, admits the game can "take over" somebody's personality.

"When you start playing out a fantasy, it can really eat up time and capture you totally," Gygax says. At the same time, "most people can handle it, but there probably are exceptions. You can get very emotionally involved." And because the same emotions stem from the fantasy of making your way and struggling through the world by stealth, subterfuge, and sorcery, the game is a natural analogue to the knotted mysteries of the occult.

D & D, of course, is not the only "fantasy" of this type perpetrated in the world today. If one does not adopt the hypothesis that D & D is a "witch's conspiracy" to pervert adolescents, which unfortunately many opponents of the game at times happen to fall into, then one can begin to see that the game has evolved almost ineluctably out of a gnawing hunger in today's culture for something that might be characterized as "occult fantasy." The snug relationship between occult fantasy and the actual practice of the occult is well established in history. Writers such as H. P. Lovecraft and Edgar Rice Burroughs, progenitor of the Tarzan and Jane tales, were practicing occultists.

L. Ron Hubbard, architect of the controversial religion known as Scientology, openly and consciously decided to convert his science fiction work into a working belief system upon which a "church" was set up. Science fiction, "science fantasy," pure fantasy, and the world of esoteric thought and activity have all been intimately connected historically.

The present fantasy role-playing craze seems to have its roots in the popularity of the J.R.R. Tolkien books about dragons, wizards, elves, and evil empires that took the publishing industry by storm in the 1960s. D & D characters, as well as certain "plots," have been imported in one way or another from Tolkien's fantasy emporium. Tolkien captured the imagination of sixties youth during the Vietnam and hippie days because he was essentially writing fairy tales for grown-ups. And the sixties generation was, in a quite profound manner of speaking, the generation that did not want to grow up. And still today it does not want to, as the popularity of New Age nonsensicalities and non sequiturs shows. Even today there are aging Tolkien fanatics who have learned to "speak" the language of his elves in preference, say, to studying Japanese or Spanish.

In addition to possessing exceptional intelligence, Bink Pulling, was a "sensitive" boy, his mother explained. Perhaps that is a euphemism for saying he was impressionable or suggestible. Suggestible children tend to take "ideas" and devour them, even act on them, without testing them. Bright children may fall for D & D because the ordinary world is too drab and boring for the ambitions of genius. Bink shot himself as a "move" in the game. His mother recalled that

he became something that he apparently could not deal with. He was more tormented than depressed. He felt very bad, evil. His personality totally merged with his character. He was having violent urges and he felt he could not control them. In a suicide note, he wrote he had been summoned to do evil and that he did not want to hurt anyone, so this was the only way.

A statement issued by the Lafayette, Colorado, police department following the death of Timothy Grice made an analogous observation: "After looking into the game of Dungeons and Dragons, it has become apparent that Dungeons and Dragons became as much a reality for [Grice] as anything else." Grice was completely certain that he had "psionic" or exceptional mental powers, the sort of fantasy that would appeal to a kid who was told he was not only special but "gifted and talented." Because he believed he would be reborn, Gryce took along his own "survival kit." The idea apparently came from his listening to a fantasy role-playing tape titled "The Last Unicorn."

Most psychologists concur that fantasy, like wheat germ or skim milk, is good for kids. But nutritionists also say that any good part of the diet is only "good" because it comes in its proper allotment or proportion. Until medical science discovered cholestrol, it was assumed that "overconsumption" of dairy products by children should not be a worry. Whole generations raised on those nutritional values fell victim to high blood pressure, obesity, and heart attacks later in life. The same holds for a diet of fantasy. Dr. Joyce Brothers, a psychologist who later in life became a well-known media personality, does endorsement for TSR Hobbies, Inc., the manufacturer of the D & D game.

D & D, according to Brothers, "provides an especially safe way for young people to meet their needs for excitement and adventure." In this age when everyone is concerned about "safe sex," we also find something called "safe fantasy." The game is so safe that if people are dying from it, that is their fault, according to the company's corporate relations department. If a kid blows himself or herself away or a guy like Danny Rameta starts knocking off his "enemies" one by one, it is unquestionably because they are demented.

"It's easy to blame other things rather than the underlying factor," a TSR spokesperson has said. "There have been two or three tragedies that were totally blown out of proportion."

The one salute-the-flag version of truth in which all psychiatrists concur is that the healthy personality, however defined, must know how to discriminate between fantasy and reality. One of the old tricks of brainwashing, perfected by military interrogators and even inquisitors centuries back, is to confound fantasy with reality. That way the victim will end up confessing to things he probably did not do. The first step in creating the confusion is to peddle the philosophical concept that there is no difference between the two—which is no different than Big Brother, or Anton LaVey for that matter, declaring that war is peace and freedom is slavery.

Here is how you learn to play "Dungeons and Dragons," according to the game's own players' manual. "Imagine: dragons are real. Werewolves are real. Monsters of all kinds live in caves and ancient ruins. And magic really works. Imagine: you are a strong hero, a famous but poor fighter. Day by day you explore the unknown, looking for monsters and treasures. The more you find, the more powerful and famous you become."

If one is really going to play "Dungeons and Dragons," it will be necessary to choose one's own "character," which, significantly, does not turn out at all to be like the funny little red plastic "man" in Clue or the silver top hat in Monopoly. The player and the character are one, not only in role, but in the deeper mind. The manual suggests that in selecting a character it is advisable to choose one that matches one's own abilities. For example, if one opts for a "fighter," one should be cognizant of the fact that "a fighter often isn't very smart." So "your character isn't as smart as you are."

On the other hand, it is expeditious to distinguish between real life and role-playing, the game counsels. Nevertheless, one learns very quickly that the game itself has a hidden hierarchy of values and that very discrete value choices must be made in order to come out a winner in the play. One can choose to become a fighter, but one will learn quickly that cunning is better than brawn, and magic is preferable to intellect. The fighter is no match for a poisonous snake, which can bring a player down and, in fact, is likely to do so. "Don't get killed! Live to fight another day!"

Heroes and heroines use magic to get their way. The beautiful heroine, who is strangely called a "cleric," "casts spells." That is, she uses sexual magic to get her way. The player can learn to be just as effective in magic as she is. In the game, clerics and magic-users rarely fight. They wave their wands and manipulate events with the sway of unseen forces. Fighters "get along" quite well with clerics. That is because if one is smart, one will choose magic over worldly exertion.

The following is a synopsis of the directions offered by the game maker to an introductory player. Because of the blurry line between reality and fantasy in the conduct of the game, it becomes somewhat difficult to ascertain whether D & D is not a rite of initiation as much as a safari through the land of imagination.

Against your better judgement, you choose the role of the fighter. The cleric—let us call her the "good witch" Glenda—and you stroll down the "passageway" together; the ghouls creep out of the darkness and *attack.* The magic cleric zaps them, invoking one of her vintage spells. Only clerics and magicians can do that, she says. If Glenda had not shown off her spells, the stupid fighter would be dead from the ghoul assault. The next job is to try a whack at the treasure behind one of the big, creaky, mysterious doors.

Treasure, after all, is what D & D is all about, unless it is about learning to be a magician. Unfortunately, the beautiful cleric's spells cannot open the door. She calls for a *thief* —an even more prestigious character in the roster of D & D characters. Thieves, by the way, are not "bad," says the cleric. One should not make moral judgments about them. Thieves "are adventurers too." The kinds of thieves that break into and desecrate churches might even be more commendable perhaps than "magic users."

At this point in the game there appears a fellow named Bargle who is known as a "bad," or black, magic-user. He is the don of the D & D underworld. He has the goblins in his employ. The fighter and the cleric hear Bargle conspiring with the goblins. Glenda says her spells are as devastating as Bargle's. Bargle wears a black robe and puts a spell in the path of the "adventurers," like nails in the road. The cleric charges and waves her magical mace at Bargle and his goblins, but the latter's black magic is apparently invincible. Finally, Bargle kills Glenda with a magic arrow he calls forth into existence by the strength of *his* spell. Glenda is gone, and the player is alone. Bargle laughs a most malicious laugh. As the player approaches Bargle, the black magic-user, however, his mien seems to change drastically. "Why, he doesn't look so bad . . . Bargle seems to be a pretty nice guy!" The game discloses black magic to be, in fact, good magic, just as Dr. Aquino tells us.

Bargle is suddenly transformed into a friendly psychotherapist or day-care director. "Feeling better?" he asks. "You were overcome with rage for a moment. Are you okay now?"

As for the dead cleric, Bargle "convinces" you that nothing can be done for her, anyway. Women are expendable, as many rock videos suggest. Magic-users are the ones who have been unfairly maligned over the years. It is only Christian morality that insists magic is unsavory and that women should be honored.

Yet you remain a moralist. You try to carry Glenda on your back back to town so she can at least have a Christian burial. Fool. The ghouls are after you, and the weight of her body loads you down. Still, you persevere. At last you return her body to the other clerics. The clerics hand you a vial of healing potion in return, should you run low on spells. As the sun sinks, you head for home, "thinking about your adventure and all you have learned." Through this sort of role-playing you learned about the "real world."

The other message of D & D, as the manual states, is that there are no winners, only survivors—quite a change from the old-fashioned knights-in-shining-armor tales of masculine bravado. You have to learn to work with magic; it is the only game in town, and as you swiftly discover, there is essentially no difference between black magic and white magic. "Good" and "evil" are whatever forces work for you, whatever gets you by. If you have to make a pact with the Devil, if you have to let go of your lady and divide the treasure with Bargle, you need not have compunctions.

The manual instructs us that in the first part of the game you played bad guys and good guys. Bargle, because he was a magic-user, appeared at first not to be so good. But the pedagogy of the game itself emphasizes that characters are neither bad nor good. They have what D & D calls "alignments," which sounds a little like astrology, as it is supposed to do. Glenda had an alignment called "lawful." Bargle was unlawful or "chaotic." He "had a different alignment than yours," which is not bad, just different. He was "selfish," but that does not make him bad.

You begin to recognize that magic-users are very special characters. They are really black magicians, but black magicians are not bad. "Magic-users start as the weakest characters, but can become the most powerful!" The "prime requisite" of a magic-user is intelligence. By using intelligence, you figure out that everything you have been taught as common sense is fluff and tomfoolery. Is taking a gun to your head, if a curse is cast, necessarily a "bad" thing? An immortal is indestructible after all.

Here are some of the things you, as a magician, might do. You can charm a person. "Bargle charmed you." You can "detect magic," meaning that whenever there is a magical spell cast, you will envison a glow. It is the D & D version of reading "auras," which you thought only psychics and other metaphysicians would attempt. You can magically shut any door or gate and keep them shut with your "wizard lock." You can levitate. You can employ the "phantasmal force," creating illusions of something you have previously seen.

The foregoing is a summary of what is known as "D & D Basic." Included in the basic modules are the game's own fables, histories, myths, and special legends, such as a lost city within a pyramid, the Hill of Horror, and the Keep on the Borderlands. There is an "expert" level in which the games become difficult and the fantasy world ever more beguiling. As the box that contains the game's basic set declares, "Dungeons and Dragons" is "specially designed to expand your Fun into a whole Fantasy Universe." In the early 1980s it was estimated that there were between 4 and 5 million regular players of "Dungeons and Dragons"in the United States. At last tally, the manufacturer grossed more than $30 million per year.

"Dungeons and Dragons" has been called a not-too-veiled entree into the occult. The accusation is only half correct; it is much more. D & D is really an elementary-level home study kit for "black magic." The expression "fantasy role-playing" is misleading. Most popular parlor games are, in an important sense, fantasy role-playing games.

For a brief time the player takes on a position, persona, a disguise, a set of behavioral traits that teach him or her something about how the world operates. "Monopoly" teaches old-style methods of real estate trading and asset appreciation. "Risk" is a primer in conventional military strategy. What distinguishes "Dungeons and Dragons" is its open-endedness. No board exists, and there are no real rules in force—only some vague limits and options for each character. The identity of the player and the character, even though they are formally separate, tend to merge.

The game itself is forbidding and labyrinthine. It is not a bare-handed joust with chance. But it is also far less a game of skill than one might guess. In a sense, each player is at the mercy of the "dungeon master," who arranges the terms of the game and in the covered illustration is pictured as a leering, almost malevolent figure. Half-demon, half-Mephistopheles, he is the one who already "knows" the tenor of life's darkest secrets, which the rest of us pursue like blindfolded, and often errant, idiots. The dungeon master can be "sadistic." Rarely is he benign, and the young players quickly internalize this "religious" view of affairs. They swiftly form a dependency on the wiles of magic to survive in a "demonic" world that they have allowed to be created for them by joining the game.

Some psychologists may cluck that the fantasy only recasts the complicated and sordid social world that young people confront daily. But such an excuse begs the entire question. Not only is such an excuse foolish, it is pernicious. Fantasy by definition is not a mirroring of the real world. It persists in critical tension with reality. Fantasy has long been considered "good" because it allows the dream-weaver to believe in the possibility of good, to climb insurmountable mountains, to reach out for the stars. In the days of Marvel Comics and Superman serials on television, fantasy was indistinguishable from heroism. Goodness triumphed. The same has always been true of fairy tales.

Furthermore, while fantasizing may be therapeutic in many cases, psychological studies have shown that strong doses of the fantasy may be harmful to some individuals. According to psychologists Sheryl Wilson and Theodore Barber, approximately 4 percent of the population comports with a profile they term *fantasy-prone personalities*. The fantasy-prone are not only highly hypnotizable, or suggestible, they also tend to experience their fantasies as *real*. They see imagined sights with both their eyes closed and opened. And they respond to their fantasies with emotions that in other people would be aroused by actual, sensory perceptions. The group is capable of experiencing "anything" in fantasy, and when embroiled in their fantasies, "they do not ask whether their experiences are real."

The fact that a significant, if not sizable, sector of the populace fails to distinguish fantasy from reality should give pause to the apologists who argue that fantasy is good for anybody. A smaller swatch of the population is severely allergic to particular chemicals, which requires regulation by federal agencies. If the content of the fantasies is threatening, suicide-inducing, or destructive in a variety of modes, the caveat against fantasy role-playing becomes even more pressing.

"Dungeons and Dragons" is not a libretto for the triumph of good. It is a knotted, tortured, and maddening script in which good and evil become progressively indistinguishable—and ambiguous. *Real* effort and *real* strength fail, as when the beautiful "cleric" dies an ignominious death in the dungeon. Since real deeds are now discredited, the very magical means that have been discarded by a society once brimming with self-confidence now acquire status once more.

Yet it is not just magic that the game commends. It is black magic as well. In black magic, the only law is chaos, the only "reasonable" option is self-will, craftiness, and the inflation of one's sense of importance. That is what D & D teaches. Nothing is what it seems; everything is the opposite of its appearance. Up is down, black is white, sanity is madness.

D & D does *not* actually let the child "create a world of their own," as one psychologist who should learn to speak in some idiom beside clichés was quoted in commending the game. Schizophrenics generate their own worlds, too. Because the game is so confusing, it makes the player feel like a victim. That perception constitutes the experience occultists for the most part desire. We are all victims, they plead, especially of God; so let us delight in victimizing each other even further. The world has cast a spell upon us. Let us cast spell upon spell back at it, even if those spells be blasphemies and curses. You will never overcome Bargle! His black magic is invincible, so learn to charm him as he charms you. He is your friend, after all. "You run at him, hoping for a chance to swing before he can complete the spell. But it's too late—a magical force touches your mind," says the game manual.

Once the "magical force" takes over, there is no telling how the reasoning processes of the child's occult fantasy will unfold. If the child thinks of black magic as "good magic," and of magic itself as the effective principle by which the traumas and anxieties of his or her young life are resolved, then there can be no distinction between initiative and aggression, between criminal or antisocial behavior and self-expression. The rule of magic says there are no boundaries. When someone puts limits in your way, they must not be heeded. You must defy them!

Such a scenario can be spied in the actual text of a "pact with the devil" made by a teenager and recovered by police. It is not clear what may have influenced the kid to make the pact, but it is certainly an illustration of a type of fantasy role-playing. The "contract" is even drafted in formal language and with a kind of lawyerlike precision that would be extremely comical if the ramifications were not downright appalling. The pact was obtained by Dr. Dale Griffis, a criminologist and former police captain from Ohio who has become the nation's leading spokesperson on problems of occult crime:

1. Lucifer you are bound to deliver to me immediately 100,000,000 American dollars in gold. The gold cannot be counterfeit, must not disappear in one's hand, and will not turn into any other object. It must be pure and the money has to be current money of America.

2. You will deliver to me every first and third Tuesday 2000 dollars in current money of the place that I'm at.

3. You will deliver to me the foregoing items to my hand and they will be of this world and not fake. This money and gold shall be mine to decide how to disperse it.

4. All the money and gold that I have shall be legal in all countries and states.

5. If I need a considerable sum of money at any given time you shall give to me from your hand to my hand, a treasure chest including the exact amount of cash in current money of the place and time which I am in.

6. You are bound to cause my body, soul, and my mind no injury during the time of the pact or any other that I desire. You shall guard me from any illness or fatal disease, or any other that I wish.

7. If I do obtain a disease or illness, you are bound to give me the exact remedies and cures. If I should die from this illness and/or disease, I shall be immediately released from your dominion and you'll reserect [sic] me to follow through again. Also if this should occur to any other that I wish, you shall do the same for them.

8. Our agreement shall begin on February the first 1988, and shall end on 9999 of the same day. During this time, I will age considerably and you are bound to make me young looking. Or when I turn 19, you shall maintain my looks for me and my bodily functions shall not deteriorate or age normally. My

bodily functions shall not be turned to normal functioning until 19 years before the end of this contract. In other words, I shall cease to age at 19 until 9980. I also will have the power to cause anyone else that I deem reasonable to live as long as they wish up to 9999. At which time they must destroy a human and repent.

9. During the time of the agreement if you shall not do as I ask or break any part of the contract, you forfeit my soul and I shall return to living a normal life, in Christianity. When my time finally runs out, you are to let me die, destroying what happened during the agreement, and letting me be judged as if I had never had this pact, and as if I had died when this began.

10. You are bound to make *anybody* do as I command or they perish in your name. You are to make me popular and loved by everyone, and let it be excepted my practice although I shall keep it a secret.

11. You are bound to transport me and any other to wherever I desire and you are to make me immediately fluent in any language and especially that of the country I am in. You are also to make any companion of mine to have the same power of language. When I am satisfied you are bound to transport me/us back to my/our homes, safely, without harm or pain or injury.

12. You are bound to protect me from any danger including bombs, firearms, guns, weapons, and any other sort of pain inflicted by man or you. Do not let my companions have the same power!

13. You are bound to assist me in any dealings with anyone of high ranking and you are to give me the power to ensnare them. You are to make me confident and know when you are helping me.

14. You are to transport me through time and any other. And when we are satisfied you are bound to take us back to our original time and space.

15. You are to preserve my and any others body in case of a holocaust.

16. You are to give me hypnotical powers and the ability to control any body to do anything I wish before you get your part.

17. You are bound to give forewarning of any plots against me and give me the secrets to overthrow them.

18. You are to take up any fights for me and send demonic assistance.

19. You are bound to give me understanding, intelligence, and any knowledge that I wish from you must be thorough and true. It cannot be false information or lies.

20. You are bound to make the justice turn to my favor.

21. You are bound to allow me to live an outward life like a Christian.

22. You are bound to teach me all remedies and cures for any disease or illness of today or yesterday.

23. You are bound to prevent anyone from knowing of our contract.

24. As often as I desire your presence, you are to appear to me in a loving form with no fowl [*sic*] smell.

25. You are to see that each and every person do my biding [*sic*].

26. You are to swear your allegiance and promise to do the foregoing and if you shall not, this contract is null and void.

27. In return for the foregoing, I will cause 13 men and women to commit suicide or I shall commit homicide.

The end—

The boy who authored the pact was fourteen and came from a broken home, which he tried to repair through magic. His fantasies became obsessive, and his school performance deteriorated drastically, while he entertained thoughts of suicide. Had he played D & D? Or was he reading too much fantasy material? Apparently he had even drawn an altar as in some crude Gothic romance with an inverted pentagram with candles burning at each point of the star. The pact starts off with a petition for money, the respectable kind of magic in today's world. It is the casting of a spell to obtain "treasure" whereby the game of life will somehow be "won."

But the treasure quest rapidly degenerates into a paranoid mania. What the boy really wants is to live forever, to attain magical power over death. In the folk tales, Satan usually grants the petitioner unrestricted wealth and enjoyment for *this*. In the end, however, he comes to collect. The falling due of the "note" is postponed in the boy's pact for 8000 years. In the meantime, such a dispensation must be jealously guarded from hordes of prospective "enemies." The achievement of a magic, immortal body requires vigilance and new powers.

It is not enough for one to enjoy endless vitality. One must have mastery over all the human race. And even Satan must bow—he must not demand anything in return. The stakes of such a game—psychologically speaking—are extraordinarily high. They may be too high for even the "inventor" of the game to play.

Not at all curiously, fantasy role-playing of this sort is what satanism and the occult have always been about. The novels, short stories, poems, and plays since the Middle Ages that deal with the subject of the so-called magician's bargain are not spun out of thin air. The request for immunity from death is at least as old as the legend of Faust.

Both the promise of magical immorality and fantasy role-playing, in fact, can be found within the secret domain of the Western world's most popular and broadly influential traditions of "esotericism"—Freemasonry. In a book entitled *Masonry and Its Symbols* and captioned *The Great Lessons of Masonry*, Harold Percival says flatly that the imagery of building the ancient temple, which has dominated the Masonic lodges over the centuries, is but a symbol of the construction of an immortal body. In the Masonic initiation process, the candidate is blindfolded, told things that he later learns are figurative or not literally true, asked to memorize mystical words and complex formulas.

The difference between the traditional forms of ritual initiation and today's occult role-playing lies, not in the means, but in the ends. The ultimate aim of ritual initiation is to achieve a stage of enlightenment, freedom, or philosophical knowledge. The role-playing is but an interim approach. It is an aid to training that at the conclusion can be discarded. The symbols of the imagination are revealed to the initiate, as in the ancient Greek allegories of Plato's cave, as but shadows of the real, brilliant light of the conscious mind's sun. Role-playing is undertaken to wean oneself from the power of fantasy, not confirm it.

The satanist, as can be detected in the fourteen-year-old boy's pact with the devil, is both an illusionist and a megalomaniac. He does not want to be changed. He resists all change, even death itself. He wants to command the world with his "powers." Today's adolescent fantasy role-playing games can be said to make "little satanists" for very good psychological, if not metaphysical, reasons. When you are taught to believe that the traps and pitfalls of an inherently evil world—signified as a dungeon—are so enormous, so abundant, and so bizarre that you can only survive by a magic without moral substance, you are likely to go off the deep end. You are even more likely to bow down and prostrate yourself before the Power that reputedly rules over the maddening mesh of wickedness. You are apt to identify with Bargle, or with Satan.

Psychological role-playing is meant, as in ritual initiation, to be a learning, not an addictive, experience. When young children play "house," for example, they are constructing simple mental models of the complex, family relations they will develop later in life. Usually children will "play at" something for a relatively short period of time, then move on to the genuine article.

The kind of role-playing that occurs with D & D, however, is not an attempt to learn or "model" anything. It is an increasingly desperate effort to achieve heightened fantasies of power. Complex fantasies of power by their own momentum give rise to paranoia. The more treasure the player gains, the greater the peril. Because there is no exit to the dungeon fashioned brick by brick in the mind, the "suicide solution" frequently seems the only cogent alternative.

If the solution is not suicide, it is rage and aggression in a desperate gambit to bring about a triumph of the will. The player of D & D finds himself or herself increasingly alone in a fantasy world of threats, feints, stratagems, and countermoves. There is no board to limit his or sense of where the game can, or should, be played. The game is one's fate. Like a Lear or any other tragic hero, it is not inconceivable that the only conceivable outcome is madness, or death.

The popularity of "Dungeons and Dragons" has led to the marketing of other fantasy role-playing games. A most curious and unsettling one, especially in light of the Matamoros murders, is called *The Aztec Circle of Destiny* by Bruce Scofield and Angela Cordova. The game is more an ancient Mexican version of the Ouija board or Tarot cards or the throwing of coins and yarrow sticks with the Chinese *I Ching*. But the implication is the actual inculcation of some version of the Aztec worldview, which of course necessitated human sacrifice. "The authors have sought to re-create a form of this Mesoamerican divinatory and astrological symbol system which, hopefully, will allow many more people to explore its possibilities," Scofield and Cordova write. "The symbols are primal and may evoke deep responses in some. The delineations, both for card divination and for astrology, are simply a first attempt to bring what was once lost back into practice."[1] If one comes up with the symbol "grass" for day twelve, one should consider "self-sacrifice," which may include "bleeding" or "cutting oneself," the manual says.

The manual does not openly counsel anything horrid or malignant. In most respects it is simply another New Age foray into long "forgotten" or "neglected" magical traditions, which dabblers today are invited to revive. But in the hands of a suburban American Constanzo or his ilk, the advertisement to "discover" the reality of Aztec magical practices could lead in directions that send disquieting flutters through the imagination. D & D could turn out to be relatively innocuous after all.

NOTES

1. Bruce Scofield and Angela Cordova, *The Aztec Circle of Destiny: Astrology and Divination from the Ancient Aztec World* (St. Paul, MN: Llewellyn Publications, 1988), p. 8.

CHAPTER 10.

Where Are the Children?

Hysterical parents? No, we're just mad as hell.
——One of the parents from the McMartin
day school in southern California

ITEM: An Indiana state trooper told reporters he had been investigating satanic cult operations in his locale since he arrested a child abuse suspect in March 1988, according to published accounts. Another individual associated with the case had already been sentenced to the state penitentiary for statutory rape and related crimes. The mother of the abused children had been apprehended in January for terroristic threats and endangerment of the welfare of her two sons, ages eight and fourteen. The boys testified they had been taken to satanic rituals entailing animal sacrifice. The boys said groups of twenty to thirty people, including children, participated in the rituals.

ITEM: Al Sarno, a psychiatrist in the Kansas City area, has said he has thirty-five clients who have been involved in satanic cults, either as victims or abusers. His clients have reportedly described rituals involving very brutal sexual abuse of children and the slashing of flesh, as well as urinating and defecating on victims. "Our minds are not prepared to deal with this kind of trauma," said Darrell Miller, a clinical social worker at a local mental health center. Miller added that three of his patients had reported witnessing human sacrifice.

ITEM: Kurt Jackson of the Beaumont, Texas, police department talked about satanic ritual abuse of children to a gathering of California psychologists. He said that crimes committed against children by "black satanic cults" are reaching epidemic proportions and that they encompass sexual abuse, child pornography, animal killings, human sacrifice, and forcing children to ingest drugs, blood, urine, feces, and human flesh. The same criminal activities involve donning robes in dark, candle-lit rooms, according to Jackson. Children become victims because "they make the worst possible witnesses in court, are easy to force into silence about the abuse, are trusting and easy to handle," he said.

On Tuesday, July 13, 1987, following three and one half years of legal skirmishes and pretrial hearings, the infamous McMartin case commenced in the superior court of Los Angeles. This was the child molestation case—discussed in chapter 3—involving alleged sexual and satanic abuse at the McMartin preschool in Manhattan Beach, California. The seven defendants were the former owners and operators of the preschool—Virginia McMartin, 78; Peggy Buckey, 58, the school's director who is also Virginia's daughter; granddaughter Peggy Ann Buckey, 29; grandson Raymond Buckey; and three instructors by the names of Babette Spitler, Mary Ann Jackson, and Betty Raidor. Later charges were dropped against five of the seven. Raymond and Peggy Buckey were left to stand trial.

The "McMartin Seven" were initially charged with twenty counts of felony child molestation. A count of conspiracy had been laid against the son. The defendants had pled not guilty to the charges. Their attorneys contended that the prosecution was guilty of what the satanists said their detractors always suffer from—paranoia and community hysteria. The primary evidence to be admitted in the first part of the trial was the testimony of thirteen young children, who were allegedly victimized at the school. The children told social workers and police investigators that they not only suffered from perverted sexual handling, they witnessed satanic practices, including people chanting in black robes and ritual sacrifice of babies.

The subject was lurid, and the credibility of many of the children appeared in doubt because the stories had changed slightly. The cry of witchhunt had been heard many times by those sympathetic to the defense. The children could be "confabulating," said some psychiatrists, meaning that certain events or incidents may have been fantastically embroidered by what they saw on television or suggestions may have been planted in their heads by well-meaning but irresponsible mental health professionals. Early interviews by the Children's Institute International (CII) may have been flawed, according to the district attorney's office in charge of the case.

At the nub of the McMartin case was testimony by the children themselves that they played a game called "Naked Movie Star" in which they were routinely photographed without clothes. The children's parents, as well as the prosecuting team, had suggested that child pornography was involved. *McMartin* was well on its way to becoming the national codeword for virulent and orchestrated child abuse. But what made the case even more chilling and sensational, though at the same time exceedingly tangled, was the contention that behind the systematic abuse were satanic practices and rituals. The allegations of satanic influences were abundant:

- A four-year-old at the preschool told his mother one day without any prompting, "I am the son of the devil." The child had been stretched out on the couch at times during the preceding days with glazed eyes and was constantly making two horns with his fingers.

- Several children said former teachers buried the bones of rabbits after mutilating them in front of the children. Another child claimed a pony had been hacked to death before their eyes.
- One boy said he had been forced to drink animal blood.
- A fourth-grade boy claimed he had been taken to the St. Cross Episcopal Church in Hermosa Beach where adults wearing dark robes and moaning with strange sounds sacrificed an animal on the altar. He also insisted that, he along with other children, were sexually abused in the storage room of Harry's Meat Market in Manhattan Beach.
- The children told prosecutors about an unidentified "devil house" where adults dressed in a Satan suit and a tiger costume.
- McMartin pupils identified as one of their tormentors a thirty-five-year-old handyman named Robert Winkler, arrested on separate child molestation charges. During a raid at the home of the man's girlfriend in Lomita, California, sheriff's deputies confiscated a black robe, a dark candle, and rabbit ears such as had been allegedly chopped off during a ritual at the preschool. Torrance, California, police officers had supposedly found "cult books" in Winkler's motel room, which at first they thought were not relevant to the crimes for which he was accused.
- A six-year-old girl said she had witnessed the killing of three babies. She also related that she had been tied up and compelled to watch the killing by gun of animals, kept in cages.

The insinuations of satanic practice at the preschool went hand in hand with declarations by the children that vile sexual acts had been perpetrated upon them. An eleven-year-old girl, whom the prosecution regarded as the lead witness because approximately a third of the child molestation counts involved her and her brother, told the court she had been forced into having intercourse, sodomy, and oral sex with one of the defendants. The child had spent many afternoons at the preschool and thus could have been expected to have longer exposure to the defendants. Her testimony was disturbingly explicit. She finished her recollections by saying the defendant held up a knife and a gun and threatened to kill her parents if she tattled.

From the start, the defense made a pitch that would become the trademark of child abuse perpetrators around the country. The children were "fantasizing," and the child therapists used the power of suggestion to influence the children. The defense showed a ninety-minute tape of the examination of a McMartin child coded "Jane Doe No. 10" by a therapist named Shawn Connerly. "From start to finish, Jane followed and Connerly led," wrote a local columnist. "The interviewer put the words in

Jane's mouth and the teacher-and-child dolls in her hands. Long after Jane had dropped out from apparent stress and fatigue, Connerly was still lecturing her about how 'all these bad people (the defendants) went to jail' because 'they're all sick, they're sick in the head.'"

One of the most damning testimonies was offered by George Freeman, forty-five, a career criminal with nine felonies on his record and an acquaintance of the defendant. When Freeman and one of the defendants had been in jail together, the defendant allegedly discussed openly having sodomized the two-year-old boy. It was the mother's complaint about Buckey that triggered the original McMartin investigation. Freeman said the defendant did not like having sex with women and that he had described an incestuous relationship with his sister. Freeman also said the defendant had shipped pornographic movies to Scandinavia through an agent in southern California and that once, on his way to South Dakota, he had buried a suitcase of sexually explicit, pornographic photos of himself and children.

The prosecution produced evidence that Buckey's mother and grandmother knew one of the defendant's might be a child molester. The evidence was a collection of diaries in the possession of Virginia McMartin suggesting that Peggy McMartin told her in the spring of 1983 that she had witnessed a youngster touch the defendant's genitals. Virginia McMartin denied having knowledge of this episode, just as she loudly protested at one point that she did not understand what the word *molestation* meant.

Early in the court proceedings, defense attorney Daniel Davis exhorted the jury to remember that "there are victims on both sides," predicting that the children would change their stories. He said that since there has been the women's movement, there will be in the future the children's movement. He also brought up the time-honored association with the McCarthy era. Once the scapegoats were witches; then they were Communists; today they are epitomized in the phrase *the molester*.

Davis called Freeman a pathological liar. Davis, however, infuriated trial judge William Pounders when he implied that Freeman had cut deals with prosecutors, who in turn had suppressed evidence about his role in a 1979 strangulation murder. The judge also rebuked Davis for questionable cross-examination tactics, ordering him to "sit down and shut up." The judge called his method of interrogation "totally improper and outrageous." Earlier Judge Aviva K. Bobb, presiding over the preliminary hearings that went on for most of 1985, reprimanded Davis and branded him "childish" for peeking at the prosecutors' notes. At one point a small boy, under fierce and unrelenting questioning from Davis, asked the judge, "Will you ask him to lower his voice please."

Davis also was accused of disrupting children's testimony by inserting dubious witnesses. He called in a local child abuse "expert" allegedly to cast suspicion on what the children had been stressing. A local newspaper reported that the expert had been ordered to halt examinations of child abuse victims in San Luis Obispo County because of complaints that he was actually victimizing children through abusive interrogations like that of Davis. Pounders observed that it seemed to him "no child could answer these questions" posed by the defense lawyers.

The assault on the credibility of the plaintiffs and the witnesses was one of the most massive campaigns ever staged in legal proceedings. The out-of-court sideshow, particularly with regard to the media, was also astounding. The most dramatic effort was to discredit, not only the mother who first complained and was subsequently found dead of an apparent suicide, but also McMartin's chief prosecutor, Lael Rubin.

Bill Brunetti, an investigator for the D.A.'s office, testified that Rubin had quietly maneuvered to put the mother in protective custody and under psychiatric care. His statement contradicted Rubin, who said she did not think the mother had mental problems until November 1985 toward the close of the preliminary hearing. Rubin labeled the representations outright "lies." Brunetti's views, however, were seconded by former McMartin prosecutor Glenn Stevens, who told the court that Rubin had confided to him that the woman was "weird or crazy."

Roger Gunson, cocounsel to Rubin, however, dismissed the idea that the chief prosecutor had been from the start wary of the mother, whose name was Judy Johnson. "Everyone who has described the mother prior to the preliminary hearing recalls her as lucid," he said. "By the end of 1985 she was a different person."

Judy Johnson was a Lutheran pastor's daughter. She lived not in a pink palace but in a pink cottage covered with roses. She believed in God and Jesus Christ, and she feared, though not in extremis, the power of Satan. None of those traits, however, were germane to her initial phone call to police. She suspected child abuse. Stevens had called her "bananas," "pathetic," and "freaking out."

The week before Christmas 1986, a liquor store named Super Sam's in Manhattan Beach made a routine delivery to Judy's house. Judy did not answer the door. The order was for a Pepsi six-pack and a flask of rum. When police and a neighbor found her body, she was sprawled naked and partly facedown. She had supposedly died of fatty metamorphosis of the liver, a physical complication of alcoholism. Initially the defense tried to put Judy on trial. Johnson must be insane, and so was the whole case. But Rubin countered, "It's a diversionary tactic, and the one thing that has angered me is that the real issue of what happened to those children and their families has been stuffed into the closet."

Born Judy Knutson in 1944 in Milwaukee, Wisconsin, Johnson's growing up was hard. Her adult life was even more difficult. Her father, the Reverend Myrus Knutson, called her "a gal of such courage." It took courage to challenge McMartin, of course, but her old man was referring to the manner in which she first dealt with the death of her mother and later with a divorce. When Judy's mother passed away, the girl "decided she was going to take care of her daddy and Steve," according to the father. Steve was Judy's brother.

In 1969, Judy was married, but the relationship began to deteriorate almost from the start. A trial separation was the immediate outcome. In 1978, she found out that her eight-year-old son, an only child, had an inoperable brain tumor. The doctors said the child had a relatively short time to live. Reenacting the moments of courage she exhibited earlier in life when her mother died, Judy threw herself totally into loving and caring for the child. Miraculously, the child lived. The ordeal drew Judy and her husband back together temporarily. Yet Judy now had little confidence in either the institution of marriage or the competency of medicine. She wanted to have her second son, born in 1980, at home instead of at the hospital. Her brother, who now lives in the state of Washington, claims he persuaded her to have the child delivered by a doctor. After the boy's birth, the parents were separated once more.

Judy put her second son, then two, in the McMartin preschool. According to Steve, who had been like "a second dad" and had a very close relationship with the toddler, the boy suddenly began to change in an inexplicable manner."I put the kid up on my lap to talk to him, and he just jettisoned off me, like I was a springboard," Knutson told a reporter. The child was also suddenly aggressive, hyperactive, and oddly vicious. One day for no apparent reason he began to punch Judy's brother in the genitals. The brother noticed bleeding around the child's anus, and Judy took the boy to a UCLA pediatrician.

The pediatrician's diagnosis was rectal trauma as the result of "forced entry," a signature of child molestation. On questioning the child, who was extremely bright and could almost read, the child said a man named "Ray" at the preschool had done things to him while a shower cap was put over his face to muffle the screams. Judy called the police. The police tried to interview the child, but he clammed up and would not speak to detectives. The police also noted that the child had been with his father during the time of the putative molestation.

The police were stumped. In order to solve the riddle, they polled the McMartin parents, who in turn made inquiries of their children. The cops tried to maintain confidentiality, but the outrage of parents quickly spread, and the media got wind. The many McMartin children were referred by the prosecution to therapists, where they were carefully examined for psychological and physical scars of abuse. During extensive, video-taped interviews, stories of animal killings, pornographic picture-taking, and satanic rituals dribbled out.

Meanwhile, the McMartin case was exploding into a national sensation. Yet amid the brouhaha, Judy was noticed to be doing something that she had not been known for—nipping at the bottle. Contrary to the suggestions of the prosecution, Judy had little contact with the McMartin parents. On one occasion, however, she walked into a parents' meeting completely soused. She vomited in the lady's room to the notice of many.

According to prosecutor Stevens, Judy was telling investigators ever more "fantastic" tales. The child had seen animals chopped up in a satanic orgy. The teachers supposedly said that if the child talked they would "come in the night and take him away." She also said her son had been raped again by a Los Angeles Unified School Board member and three models in a Nautilus Club advertisement. She also accused her own husband of molestation and filed for divorce.

A nurse at the UCLA medical center claimed Johnson had said the child had run away and was accosted in a park. Johnson said the following took place throughout the summer of 1983:

- A marine had chased Judy while she was driving down a road from Twentynine Palms.
- Threatening messages were left on her answering machine.
- Strangers were tapping on her door and running away.

In addition, Johnson hid behind the drawn drapes of her cottage, installing a metal rod to bar the door. Her oldest son began missing school routinely. On a mysterious "tip," social workers visited, but Johnson would not grant them entrance. The brother came down from Washington to find out what was going on. Johnson was holed up inside the house.

Knutson found the older boy playing in the garage. When he stopped to talk, his sister suddenly showed up with an unloaded shotgun and told him to get off the property. Convinced that his sister was "paranoid," Knutson called police and arranged to have her committed. For almost two weeks Johnson was held for psychiatric tests at the University of California Irvine medical center in Orange County. The county took the children away from her and gave them to the brother. Johnson followed, living in her old, Volkswagen van and trying to make contact with the children.

In September 1986, Johnson returned to Manhattan Beach. Three months later she was dead. Johnson's body was discovered by Manhattan Beach police officers at her home early in the morning of December 19, 1986. The cause of death was cited as internal hemorrhaging. The death occurred almost exactly at the time Judge Pounders had denied bail to Buckey in light of what he called "the repeated testimony of so many of the child victims" and the possibility Buckey might carry out reported threats against them.

There was some talk among McMartin parents that Johnson's death, like Marilyn Monroe's perhaps, had not been accidental. For one thing, she had not been hitting the bottle long enough to suffer the kind of fatality from which she supposedly succumbed, they said. And it was more than coincidental that she had died alone just before testifying. But those were just more "paranoid" rumors among hysterical parents, according to the defense and its supporters.

The defense contended that Johnson had always been an "unstable woman" and that she had fanned up hysteria within the parents group. Defense attorney Daniel Davis and his partner Dean Gits argued that the woman was a "social contagion" who spread "wild fantasies" in the minds of others. Moreover, the defense now staunchly maintained that since Johnson was dead, any trial was impossible. Pounders, however, ruled that a deceased witness does not "make or break" the case.

Meanwhile, a minor scandal was brewing over former prosecutor Glenn Stevens's apparent change of heart. Because of his outspoken putdown of chief prosecutor Lael Rubin and the remaining prosecution itself, Stevens drew the wrath of the parents' attorney Greg Mooney, who threatened a complaint to the state bar and slander litigation.

In addition, Stevens had been consulting with screenwriters who wanted to "expose" the McMartin parents, according to a newspaper account. It was learned that Stevens had asked certain writers not to go ahead with a story on the case because if convictions were obtained, it would make everybody, including himself, look bad. He also said some parents "want their kids to be molested because they can see dollar signs" from lawsuits and insurance money.

Virginia McMartin, the wizened matriarch of the clan, riled judges for calling their questions "dumb." At one point Pounders threatened to jail her for contempt. McMartin acknowledged on the witness stand that one of her own granddaughters thought her two children had been molested at the day-care center. "The family was upset that we had a traitor," Virginia McMartin said. She huffed that her granddaughter had been "brainwashed" by the therapists and staff members at CII. The granddaughter's children, aged seven and nine, were not witnesses in the case.

McMartin, through most of her testimony, gave the impression that the courts, the press, the child psychologists, and, the wicked parents were all engaged in a witch-hunt. During the preliminary hearing, she repeatedly broke into the examination with explosions of temper and fulminations at the judge. "I don't care what your orders are," she snapped at one point when an attendant sought to help remove her from the courtroom without her crutches. "Don't you dare touch me." In a different episode she screamed at the bailiff, "This awful court, these awful people, these awful lies."

Virginia McMartin described her own life to the court in glowing but poignantly tragic terms. The accusations against her had capped a series of misfortunes, interspersed by personal pluck and glory. Though born into an affluent family, Virginia McMartin's mother died at seventeen, and the daughter married young. Virginia's "happy" marriage lasted for twenty years, until McMartin's husband left for a younger woman. Left with little means of support, Virginia McMartin went to work as a secretary at a dancing school and went back to finish her college education. All the while the money was constantly running out, and she bounced around from one low-paying, part-time job to another.

Then in 1954 she obtained work at the child development center at Long Beach City College. Her work was so good she received a regular teaching position there. Through continuing education programs she came to know, and began to work closely with, highly respected and topflight personnel in early childhood education. She became interested and active in the Southern California Nursery School Association. "I served on their board of directors for several years." She also was befriended by an Elizabeth Woods, who created an annual scholarship.

After working at a school in Santa Monica and Long Beach, she came up with the idea of an institution of her own. She was teaching at a place known as Miss Dawn's School when she heard it was for sale. She said she did not have one cent of her own but "prayed about it daily" until her daughter Peggy came up with a chunk of the money. Miss Dawn extended a loan for the remainder of the amount. And in 1956 at the age of forty-nine she purchased what would become the McMartin school.

The McMartins would take the children routinely to the beach, Virginia McMartin told the court. And "for several years Glen took colored movies of the children in action and activities, and showed them at open house outdoors." The McMartin videos of children became a kind of trademark. Virginia McMartin, by her own account, attained a certain celebrity status. In 1964 she visited schools in New Zealand and Australia. "I was entertained by college presidents and school heads," she said. "In 1966, I visited schools in Denmark, Sweden, Norway and England. Again, I was royally treated and entertained."

In September 1966, a second McMartin school was opened at 931 Manhattan Beach Boulevard, with Peggy in charge. After a very short while the school was full. In 1966, McMartin was injured and had to use crutches, on which she hobbled routinely into the courtroom. "But, I have been determined to keep on anyway," she said. "I refused to bow down to pain and inactivity."

Virginia McMartin said she had a file card for every child that had ever attended her school—3,306 at the first school in twenty years and 2,024 at the second school in seventeen years. She bragged that twenty-five sets of twins had gone through the school, that she had received four citations for outstanding service, including the president's award from the Chamber of Commerce in 1968 and from the students at Mira Costa High in 1978 for the "Super Boaster award of merit."

Virginia McMartin sounded like a den mother and an exemplary citizen. Thus the horrible things said about her must have been because the therapists and the parents planted thoughts in the heads of the children. Parents, however, consistently refuted the charge that their children were coached by therapists at CII to dream up fantasies of satanism and abuse. "What's in it for us?" one of the parents asked. "Nothing, except to keep people off the street who would do these things."

One father said he and his wife had discussed with their daughter on at least six occasions the goings-on at the McMartin school. The daughter could not "remember" anything happening. But after one of the other children, a friend of his daughter, let the little girl know he had been able to "tell secrets" to the therapists, the daughter was also able to "recall" things that had happened.

Using anatomically correct dolls, the daughter showed how Raymond Buckey had molested her. The parent said he tried to comfort his daughter later with regard to having to talk about the alleged abuse incidents. He said that during her stay at the school the girl had awoken with fits of shaking during the night, that she had redness in the region of her vagina, and that she was dead set against taking a nap at the school. He said she grew "more defiant" toward her parents "and less warm and affectionate" toward her father and other male members of the family. The counseling at CII, however, had created a more "positive" relationship between the child and the family.

Dr. Roland Summit, assistant clinical professor of psychiatry and head physician at the UCLA Medical Center where Judy Johnson's child was first diagnosed, has been outraged at the propensity of the media and public officials to dismiss child abuse. He is also upset at the way in which abusers and their defenders routinely appeal to American's native fear of moral vigilantes, allowing an entire industry of abuse and exploitation aimed at America's young to flourish.

Summit has been a consultant to federal law enforcement agencies, customs, postal inspectors, and child protective services. He gave written testimony for the U.S. attorney general's commission on pornography in 1985. "I believe that as a people, as a nation and as a collection of child caring institutions we have maintained, like the three monkeys, a self-protective posture of see no evil, hear no evil, and speak no evil," Summit wrote. "Our need to deny is bolstered by the relentless irrelevance of protective institutions and the paralyzing, calculated confusion imposed by an unknown number of influential citizens whose private lives are devoted to the sexual subjugation of children."

According to Summit, it is more comfortable to believe in a happy childhood and a just society than to confront the tragic truth of child abuse. The fact of widespread child abuse, particularly in day-care centers, challenges the proud myth of the sixties generation, which said that institutionalizing the care of children was not only harmless, but productive to the goals of society. The tendency is to "despise young victims and defend the needs and motives of the aggressor," according to Summit.

The common libertarian argument that what is done in secret is acceptable, so long as it is not a menace to society, is frequently trundled out in its most banal, and therefore most lethal, format. Victim suppression is a fairly routine malfeasance. Legitimate crime victims may go to the police, "but sexual abuse of a child is not a legitimate crime." The same argument has been used for the problem of rape and rape victimization. Women who are raped are frequently accused of "asking for it."

Since so much child sexual abuse takes place within the family, the difficulties are compounded. Many sex crimes are never reported. In one survey, only 2 percent of assaults on female children were reported, if the offender was kinfolk. Only 6 percent of offenders who were not family members were reported.

The ambivalence of jurors and the stress of protracted adjudication upon their thought processes is also a major factor.

In an article entitled "Too Terrible to Hear: Barriers to Perception of Child Sexual Abuse," Summit wrote the following:

Sexual abuse of children, child pornography, with its companion vices of child prostitution and sexual molestation, is explained away, trivialized or simply denied whenever there is a risk of confrontation. While the greatest motivation for denial rests in each of us as adult individuals, our need to deny is bolstered by the relentless irrelevance of protective institutions and the paralyzing, calculated confusion imposed by an unknown number of influential citizens whose private lives are devoted to the sexual subjugation of children. . . . If there is an enthusiastic traffic in sex with children and if little kids are consumed for the sake of its production, how could such an empire stay in hiding?

According to Summit, the "empire" is safeguarded by what he terms "seven dimensions of denial" by society. These seven, in turn, "serve as protective camouflage" for the abusers.

The first problem is the denial that innocent children may be subjected to invisible horrors.

Recognition of child sexual abuse exploitation requires the ability to suspect trusted resources, to question one's own judgement and competence in selecting those resources, and to empathize with the terror and helplessness of a child who submits without questions or outcry.

Second is the phenomenon of "victim suppression." It is naturally presupposed that normal crime victims will complain. But child sexual abuse is not a normal crime. Often the child, especially a preschooler, does not understand he or she is being abused. It is only when the child informs parents that the truth comes out.

Third, the usual methods of intelligence and information gathering by law enforcement agencies break down in this arena. There are no "undercover agents" in families or day-care centers. The children are by and large the sole source of reporting, and only if one is fortunate or brave enough to tell a sympathetic adult on the outside what has happened will investigations proceed. Often, however, investigations are throttled because of the danger of treading on civil liberties and invading privacy.

Fourth, sex crimes apparently require criminal convictions in order to achieve "public validation." The demand in the rules of evidence for criminal proceedings that guilt be established "beyond reasonable doubt" makes it easy not just for defense attorneys but for the child abuse underground itself to cast doubt on the veracity of the accusers. Defense attorneys commonly use strategies, as happened in McMartin, of "aging the case" and "discrediting the victim." Once the preliminaries of a case, such as hearings, depositions, and pretrial motions, have been completed, the children as well as the public at large have laid the matter to rest in their own minds. The children themselves quickly learn that the glare of the stage lights and the "assault of endless adversarial examinations" is not a tour of civic duty, but an experience of horror, to be avoided at all costs.

Fifth,

anyone who participates in uncovering a suspected nest of exploitation may now be accused of coaching witnesses into false accusations. Defense attorneys and a few clinical expert witnesses are claiming that specialist interviews telegraph the interviewer bias to an impressionable child, who will respond with fantasies that are interpreted as real by the crime-seeking specialist.

In other words, any involvement by an adult is automatically singled out by the defense as having influenced the child, which is clinically implausible, but may sound good to a jury, especially if the claim is made with righteous bravado.

Sixth, "deliberate deception" sometimes occurs. The prevalence of pedophilia in contemporary society is not only documented but shocking. It is highly probable, according to Summit, that a judge or an attorney or a journalist may be up to their shoulders in the same moral morass as a defendant.

Seventh, conservatives in the child mental health professions do not often allow for the data that is coming into the system. The upshot is "conceptual chaos." "There is no reliable standard of proof and not even a scientific nomenclature for most of the phenomena associated with adult sexual interest in children."

Furthermore, the aversion to accepting the proposition that ritual crime may have been involved is also all too widespread. The cover-up has been going on for over a century. Child pornography, according to recent historical scholarship, flourished during the Victorian age. It is probably no coincidence that Crowleyite satanism and the exploitation of children were coupled to each other.

With its emphasis on respectability, legitimacy, and the honor of the family, Victorian society encouraged casual sexual intrigues and encounters. Prudishness in the daylight secretly spawned a broad psychological demand for night sexual adventure. Prostitutes who were tough, attractive, and competitive could prosper financially in such a setting. At the same time, the laws of the marketplace promoted a subculture of perversion and bestiality that was worse than what vice cops frequently uncover nowadays. An oversupply of the unforunate, particularly in Europe and America's teeming cities, outstripped the demand. Whoever was weak, diseased, pockmarked, or deformed could find themselves serving as clients for indulgence in the most squalid sexual aberrations at the price of a few coppers.

Child pornography flourished because of the medical risks attached to sex for hire. The younger the prey, the less likelihood a "gentleman" might contract disease. Pedophilia became quite the fashion during the 1880s. According to the chaplain of Clerkenwell Jail, grown prostitutes sought to augment their regular incomes by attempting to pass themselves off as young children.

Homosexual relations between consenting adults, despite the official nineteenth-century view of it as a Biblical abomination, was carried out quite extensively and in some quarters even openly. Ironically, the Victorian fears about male lust toward women provided a cover for homosexuality. Men were expected to keep intimate company with other men and to avoid close contacts with women, except for their mothers and wives. Homosexual liasons, particuarly among men, could easily mask as the kind of strong emotional friendships between men that were easily accepted and even celebrated. As a result, there were few male prostitutes during the period. If a man was gay, he might still even marry, and no one would be much wiser, inasmuch as failure to consummate a marriage was not entirely uncommon.

Child pornography, particularly the exploitation of little boys, blossomed because of a combination of the breakdown of urban families under the stresses of the factory system and the unspoken acceptance of male homosexuality, which did not have public outlets. Another element was the Victorian admiration for classical culture, which would have included the pedophilia of the Greeks, as the philosopher Plato extolled.

Oddly enough, sexual emancipation in the late twentieth century has engendered much the same tolerance for pedophilia and pornography as sexual repression did in the nineteenth century. The Victorians winked at child sexual abuse because it was an "outlet." Today we do not want to appear "uptight." The effect is identical. But, more significantly, the siren song of "freedom" and "liberation" that was the battle drum of the sixties cultural revolution has produced a pervasive ideology not only among today's baby boomers but among the intelligentia at large that offers the most hypocritical smokescreen for exploitation.

Child abuse is not seen as abuse at all in many of the pamphlets put out by pedophiles. Instead, they talk of "man-boy love" or "children's liberation" as if these were utopian achievements. The horror to traumatized and unconsenting children is never mentioned. The misty shibboleths of civil liberties is used to justify the most vicious forms of human degradation in much the same fashion as "state's rights" were exalted a generation or two ago by the most callous racists.

The impact of sixties values on the rise of child pornography can be seen in the statistics themselves. Ruth and Henry Kempe, the celebrated pioneers in the tagging and treatment of child sexual abuse, have stated that between the years 1967 and 1972—the cresting of the wave of new sexual mores—the tally of abuse cases reported to them increased *tenfold*. Neither the Constitution nor legal consensus, of course, has ever offered a whit of ballast for child pornography.

A landmark decision in 1982 by the Supreme Court held that twenty states with laws outlawing child pornography were not in any way infringing on basic rights. The interpretation of the law, however, may be less consequential than one might desire. It has been estimated that there are at present about 300,000 children shackled to the taskmasters of "kiddie porn." Most of the children are runaways or have never had families. Some are actually turned over to the traffickers by their parents. A twelve-year-old boy on the streets of a major city can earn about $1000 a day for doing "tricks."

As psychiatric social workers well know, children recruited into the kiddie porn syndicates are permanently scarred with feelings of worthlessness, rage, betrayal, and guilt. The syndicates themselves have also been changed into "concentration camps" for permanently abused children, many of whom are smuggled from south of the border. The children are passed around like after-dinner mints from wealthy pedophile to wealthy pedophile, then killed—that is, "snuffed"—or returned home.

A child from Mexico, according to one study by mental health professionals, "can be packaged, delivered, and sold deep within this country in a short time." Many foreign children are secreted into the United States and purchased by child molesters solely "for the purpose of killing," the study says. Foreign kids indeed are preferred, because an American youngster has a family and a school record. But if a child has been picked off the streets of Guadalajara or Acapulco, the tack is much simpler.

The traffic in snuff porn among children is increasing rapidly. The snuff phenomenon was first observed by police in the mid-1970s in connection with so-called trash bag murders in southern California.

Bodies of young men and boys with homosexual backgrounds were discovered in trash bags. Several were of Mexican heritage.

The traffic is also moving north to south. Author Robin Llyod testified before the U.S. House Select Committee on Education and Labor that an eleven-year-old fifth-grade boy from a small Texas community had been kidnapped by a procurer for a kiddie porn ring. When apprehended, the procurer told the cops that he had been offered $25,000 for every fair-skinned Anglo kid to be delivered to Mexico City. The FBI and the Texas Rangers have confirmed that the operation is still active. The Texas House Select Committee on Child Pornography disclosed in the late 1970s that investigators probing leads to organized crime in Houston, Dallas, and other major cities found that "slave" auctions for sixteen- and seventeen-year-old boys were routinely held in Mexico. Some of the boys were featured in brutal snuff or "slasher" movies.

Guy Strait, a hoodlum who has spent years in the kiddie porn business, reported to government investigators that recently the domestic Mafia franchise had been usurped by global syndicates. Kiddie porn itself may have become a financial subsidiary of worldwide drug shipping and laundering. And, like drugs, the enterprise of kiddie porn is experiencing galloping growth because of surges in "consumer" demand. It is all part of the mushrooming culture of decadence. Every culture, particularly a complex and affluent one, requires a peculiar religious "belief system" to hold it together and to offer a theory of salvation and damnation.

Satanism may be just what the doctor ordered.

The key ingredient in the confluence of satanism and crime—particularly in the southern portion of the United States—has been Caribbean blood magic. That ingredient was certainly in evidence in Matamoros. In Florida, it also figured in a day-care child abuse case that in many respects mimicked the McMartin affair.

Frank Fuster, a convicted child molester and murderer, and his wife, Iliana, were allowed by the state of Florida to operate the Country Walk Babysitting Service in the southwest Dade County residential development of Country Walk. Country Walk was a tranquil development with security guards, protective fences, bike paths, ambient wildlife, a community center, and spacious lots for the homes priced as high as $200,000. But as its inhabitants would soon discover, money does not necessarily buy safety for one's children. And in Florida, even a first-degree murder conviction is not, as it turns out, sufficient grounds for denying a petitioner a day-care license.

According to Florida physicians Joseph and Laurie Braga, experts in child psychology and early childhood education, national statistics predict one in four females, and one in six males, will be molested or raped by the age of eighteen. And these molested children become ideal candidates to become the abusers of tomorrow. As the main advocates for the prosecution in the Fuster case, the Bragas interviewed the children. The children's statements included descriptions of birds having been sacrificed, strange masks, and games. The statements were taped by videocamera. The children divulged intimate knowledge of aberrant sexual activity, including the rape of other children, drinking urine, and eating excrement. Nursery games like "Ring Around the Rosy" were perverted into rites involving hypnotic trances that built with intensity into explicit sexual activity.

The Fusters owned a $150,000 home. They also had flexible self-employment with a "mobile showroom" business delivering blinds and window treatments. In 1983, Fuster, then forty-eight, married Iliana, whom he represented as about twenty-one years of age. Later investigation determined that she was an illegal alien and was only seventeen. The Country Walk Babysitting Service began advertising services in 1983, although the facility was not properly zoned and the property association prohibited operating such a business in a residential area. Hundreds of parents availed themselves of the day-care center, and authorities suspected that, over time, up to twenty-five children were abused.

Police reports from 1980 onward showed that Fuster had been the purported victim of a robbery of over $3000 from his van and of aggravated battery, having been shot in the ear by an unidentified white male attacker. In addition, a man dressed as a law enforcement officer had once smashed the windows of his van. Fuster had also been convicted of homicide in New York and had served four years before receiving parole. He had been suspected of raping a girl he had picked up at a shopping center, and he was found guilty of lewd and lascivious assault on a nine-year-old female in 1982. In the latter instance he was paroled for two years. The charge expired in November 1984.

Why did the Country Walk children not let their parents know sooner what was happening to them? Perhaps even a two-year-old understands the warning, "If you tell, your mommy will die." The children knew Frank Fuster could make things die. They had watched him cut up birds. From the outset, Fuster asserted that the children were liars. If the videotapes the children had said were made of them could ever have been found, the prosecution would have possessed its "smoking gun." But Fuster removed the tapes before a warrant could be issued to search his residence.

Parents initially reacted with shock, guilt, and denial. Government officials in Florida reacted strongly to the widely publicized case by assembling task forces, drafting tougher legislation, and running on election platforms in 1984 denouncing child molestation. A wave of media attention brought to light at least fourteen other child abuse arrests. Forty illegal child-care facilities were shut down in a matter of weeks. An emergency session of the legislature was held in 1985, and some forty bills pertaining to child welfare were introduced.

After their arrest, the Fusters launched a variety of manuevers to win sympathy with the courts. A Spanish interpreter was hired during pretrial hearings, although prosecutors found that most of the letters written between the couple while in jail were in English. The defense could use two tactics, either a trial by diversion or simply "it didn't happen." But it proved difficult to explain to the jury how Frank Fuster's seven-year-old son Jaime came to be infected with gonorrhea of the throat or why Jamie's father had recently taken a photo of him seated on a toilet, the surrounding floor smeared thickly with excrement.

Fuster was born Francisco Fuster Escalona of Cuban parents. In 1969 he had been sentenced to ten years in jail on a manslaughter rap after a violent traffic dispute in which he shot another motorist through the heart. Throughout his term, however, Fuster was a model prisoner. His parole log indicated that he received no disciplinary reports. His cellblock officer described him as "a polite, cooperative individual who gets along well with others and is rated as being a good inmate." Fuster served out only three years of the sentence. In 1972 he was released from the Wallkill Correctional Facility. In the following ten years he attended real estate school, opened his own interior decorating business, and married for a second time. In 1981, Fuster was arrested for "lewd and lascivious conduct" with a nine-year-old girl. He had picked up one Hilda Gomez in a van and begun fondling her. The jury found him guilty.

It was something of a mystery how the Fusters were able to make the payments on the house in Country Walk. A month before the house purchase, Fuster set up a corporation called KDW Enterprises, Inc.—an "interior decorating business specializing in window treatments." Fuster actually installed blinds. There is little evidence Fuster made much money from the business. But he had little difficulty making a 10 percent down payment or meeting a monthly mortgage of $1161. Over a ten-year period, Fuster opened six bank accounts in Florida. Sometimes lump figures of $20,000 would be deposited. He explained that the sums were "unsecured loans" made by the good graces of "former clients."

The kiddie porn industry grosses $3 billion a year in the United States. The worldwide gross is twice that amount. Kiddie porn in which children are sexually abused before cameras, made to perform degrading acts, and sometimes even snuffed has become as common, and as popular, as eating out. If kiddie porn were merely an underground, secret, and unspoken diversion, it would be one thing. But the trend has even been given the dignity of an ideological movement, with advocates of what is fulsomely called children's liberation forming organizations, holding conventions, and staging press conferences to speak out against the "unfairness of an intolerant society" and to justify molestation as a "revolutionary act."

Frank Fuster saw himself as a "spiritual revolutionary"—of sorts. If he had known the term, he might even have called himself an aesthetic terrorist. For him, children were a kind of sacramental or sacrificial offering in the cult of power. Fuster read books on foreign policy, on guerilla strategy, on negotiation and treaty-making. He obviously had grandiose political designs, but child molestation was his unique, twentieth-century version of magic.

In addition, Fuster shared the currently fashionable, amorphous religious belief of the so-called New Age that every individual is God. Every night Frank read aloud to Jaime from a mysterious book called *I Am*—a magical text deriving from ancient occultism. Through "I Am affirmations," as they are called, one could become in Fuster's view a "divine man."

But the children did not see Fuster as a holy man. The disturbing behavior of the Country Walk children included nightmares of masks and monsters, excessive masturbation, French kissing, inserting of toys into rectums, fear of bathrooms, unusual toilet and bathing habits, and regression to infantile states. One little girl called the Fuster's residence where she had been raped "the house into which God could not see."

Senate bill 290, which passed in 1985, provided for a special interview room for the child victims to give evidence. A courtroom is too intimidating for a child. The law allowed children's sessions to be taped and admitted into evidence. The children, however, would not have to face their alleged victimizers.

The children's medical records showed that many had been treated with antibiotics for what was thought to be throat infections or strep throat. The tests turned up negative. The infections may have been throat gonorrhea. Iliana Fuster finally turned state's evidence against Frank after almost a year. She claimed that Frank had beaten her into submission and said Frank continually tried to insert a cross into her rectum, that he dosed her with drugs every night, that he tied her up, threatened her with a power drill, and forced her to have oral sex with and give drugs to the children.

The defense employed what appeared to be virtually the same tactics as in McMartin. The defense attorneys tried to prove that the children had been influenced to say what they did by the doctors Braga. Their technique of cross-examining the Bragas is familiar to attorneys who want to tear down the authority of expert witnesses. One engages in a lot of gobbledy-gook and verbal sleights of hand. Then one comes on strongly and says something like, "But you really don't think that, do you?" The inference the jury is supposed to draw is that because the defense attorney presumed such a fact in his rhetorical posturing, the fact must be suspect. But the effect is to intimidate. As in McMartin, the defense attorneys apparently sought to make the testimony so laborious and prolonged that the parents would withdraw complaints out of fear for the mental stablity of their children.

In addition, the defense brought in a person whom they dubbed a "child brainwashing expert," a Dr. Ralph Underwager who according to published accounts, toured the nation assailing "child abuse hysteria." Underwager held the thesis that child sexual abuse was nothing more than a hysterical fantasy spread by overzealous guardians of the social morality. Child sexual abuse rarely happens—that was Underwager's stance. Underwager also trotted out an impressive but convoluted Freudian argument about what he called the "seductive child" and "Oedipal fantasy." In other words, the parents were divesting themselves of their own emotional entanglements when they assisted in the "fabrication" of the molestation tales. It was Salem, Massachusetts—again and again. It was, of course, the proverbial witch-hunt.

Underwager was present at the founding in 1984 of an organization called VOCAL, for "Victims of Child Abuse Laws." VOCAL is supposedly a support group for "victims" of child abuse hysteria, including convicted child abusers. "VOCAL seeks to resist and change abuse of government power to foster witch hunts and violence to innocent people," one of its newsletters read. Underwager had never testified in Florida before. His "busy" schedule did not allow him to be deposed by the prosecution. He presented himself as a minister and as a psychologist and as an entrepreneur. Underwager had also had a crucial role in putting down allegations of child abuse in a famous case from Jordan, Minnesota.

Again, it just did not happen, Underwager had assured the public as he chimed in with the outrages of VOCAL. VOCAL sued the child-care therapists connected with those proceedings, asserting that their "manipulative" tactics had led the children to spin absurd yarns that were taken seriously by law enforcement personnel responsible for "false arrest."

There were sixteen actual charges against Fuster. He was accused of eight separate counts of sexual battery and seven lewd and lascivious assaults. The last count was a charge of aggravated assault compassing different acts committed on twenty-one children. The prosecution argued that Fuster on several occasions had threatened the children by wearing masks, making verbal threats, dancing naked, fondling sex organs, defecating and urinating in the presence of the children, by administering drugs, confining them against their will, and compelling them to eat excrement.

The defense laid out the litany of children's allegations as if by the force of nature they could *not* have occurred:

Now the government wants you to believe all the allegations these children eventually made about being abused. Now, these are children who also said that they ate heads, sipped ants through straws, saw doody monsters, broke a door into pieces, started playing sex games . . . rode on sharks and whales, had gone to college.

The children did not at all say it that way, but the collage was supposed to sound all too unbelievable. And the kids may have been mingling perceptions with hallucinations from certain pharmaceuticals Fuster was known to have readily available.

The Bragas told the court it was "expected and predictable" that the children would hide what was happening. Even adult survivors rarely tell, they said—which is true. Children invariably fear for their parents and for themselves. In general, they are afraid. Frequently overlooked in the debate over whether the children should be "believed" is that day-care providers *have* taken on the cast and the authority of "surrogate parents" for many preschoolers. In some cases, they command more respect than the parents themselves. This twist of events is both sad and shocking. It raises some fundamental issues about the long-term social effects of day care on a culture. But, quite simply, it also explains why the kids did not tell their parents. A four-year-old who is sexually molested by her father will usually not tell her mother. And in this context the children hesitated to tell their "other" parents.

In a wide range of clinical surveys, 70 to 90 percent of sexually abused children are molested by someone they already know. The closer they are to the molester, the less likely they are to talk. The majority of children at Country Walk, at McMartin, at the Minnesota facility—indeed, in most day-care homes—see their natural parents less hours per week than their "day parents." The earlier a child enters day-care, the more likely he or she is to develop a bond, either of fear or of trust, with the day-care provider. The child may even refuse to say things that would damage the day-care abuser. And the child is unlikely to go running to their nighttime parents, who the child knows put them in daycare, and complain about what is happening—unless the parent finds out, of course, and becomes upset. When the child does talk, it becomes, as California psychiatrist Lee Coleman stated on behalf of the defense, "obvious fantasizing."

When Fuster himself finally took the stand, the prosecution snared him in a net of revelations about what had been going on at Country Walk as well as in a birdlime of his own lies. The state laid exhibit number thirty-four before the court—thumb cuffs, a kind of torture implement, seized from among Fuster's belongings. Fuster identified it as a "ring" he had purchased for his son Jaime. Fuster had venereal disease. He had a "friend" who owned a pharmacy. He also took lots of pictures of children. The prosecutor trundled out a whole stack of them before the court.

The evidence was irrelevant, said Fuster, because he was innocent. He was a victim of a witch-hunt. The children had all been brainwashed. The real child abusers were the courts and the therapists, particularly the Bragas.

Fuster eventually was found guilty by the jury. He will be up for parole in the year 2150. The "witches" had been "persecuted" once again. The Fuster case was nominally about child abuse. But overall, however, it was scarcely different from McMartin.

Fuster was, by his own accounting, a religious man. The prosecution inquired of Fuster about the cross Iliana said he had attempted to shove up her private parts. During the police raid on Fuster's home, a detective had found the same cross concealed between the mattress and the bedsprings. Fuster said the cross, made of wood, symbolized "God as a human being on earth." If that "theological" statement could be squared with his recitation of the *I Am* affirmation, then Fuster was saying the cross signified his own self-deification—perhaps through magic.

In fact, Frank was Cuban and his religion was *santeria*. A *santeria* priest stated that the mysterious cross kept beneath the mattress was a talisman that "invoked" a spirit that would wreak evil on whoever slept in the bed. The dark ritual of the cross was known as "sleeping with the incubus."

The rituals witnessed by the children were never, for a number of reasons, introduced as evidence into the trial—the charges were "child abuse." But the *santeria* priest was able to describe them. The children had said they had watched the filming of such rituals and that they had taken part in them. The police never seized Fuster's infamous videotapes of such rituals, even though they were characterized on numerous occasions. The tapes must have had "power." While in prison, Fuster put a contract out on his former wife, Iliana, who he believed did him in by turning state's evidence. He did not offer his contract agent money, which he probably could have obtained easily. Instead he offered the tapes.

At the beginning of the McMartin trials, Los Angeles district attorney Robert Philibosian said publicly that the McMartin preschool was but a front for a child pornography ring. The grounds for this statement remain problematical to this day, and the accusations were never proven in the McMartin case, although suggestions of some kind of pornography activities continued to creep into the police reports and legal representations.

Yet *santeria*, or at least a satanist adaptation à la Constanzo for criminal use of what, from the standpoint of religious scholarship, remains an off-center, controversial but genuine folk cult of the Caribbean peasantry—may have had something to do with the McMartin case. It should be remembered that so-called orthodox satanists will pirate both ritual and psychic ingredients from recognized religions, or occult practices, all over the world in order to achieve their "black magical" goals. Anton LaVey in *The Satanic Rituals* says his religion is "a blend of Gnostic, Cabalistic, Hermetic, and Masonic elements, incorporating nomenclature and vibratory words of power from virtually every mythos."[1]

One interesting item about the McMartin episode that escaped notice by the press was a series of anonymous phone threats allegedly made to Jeanine Driscoll, mother of a McMartin victim, in 1985. The phone calls involved a series of what at first sounded like chanting in Spanish. Driscoll copied down the chant phonetically. A detective who understood cults identified the words right away. It was a *santeria* chant translated as "your time is up."

If the McMartin affair threw into relief a raddled web of alleged conspiracy, accusation, confusion, and denial, the Country Walk case revealed quite plausible connections between satanic abuse and the Latin American criminal underworld. This underworld included the child pornographers, and by extension perhaps, the drug traffickers who had propelled Constanzo with his satanism in his rise to power, although narcotics was never raised as a factor in the latter trial.

Narcotics also entered indirectly into another sensational, but not nationally publicized, case in Colorado, which involved alleged satanic child abuse. In that situation the cry of satanic abuse trumpeted for weeks by a leading Denver newspaper resulted in the removal from office of an anti-drug-crusading district attorney. When the case actually came to trial, the satanist elements of the case were dropped entirely, and one offender ended up with a conviction and a light sentence on minor charges. The same offender then repudiated his confession during the trial of the other defendant.

The incident also raised some rather disturbing questions about the role of the media and the use of the satanist issue in the manipulation of public opinion for overt political purposes.

It happened in Akron, Colorado—an expiring farm community on the plains east of Denver that progress and population trends had left to founder. In July 1985, a woman reported to Washington County Social Services that her daughter had come home with a new, sexually explicit vocabulary—including the words *cunt* and *testicles*. The little girl had been under the supervision of another "grandmotherly" woman, Hazel Riggs, sixty-seven, who ran a day-care center in Akron. In October, however, the Colorado Department of Social Services renewed Riggs's day-care license without much question.

In June 1987, the county social services agency began an investigation of the Riggs facility to look into charges of abuse allegedly occuring between August 1985 and April 1987. The sheriff's department was notified of the inquiry. In late August 1987, Riggs received an outline of the charges and closed the center. At the time, the charges revolved primarily around minor offenses.

In addition to concern about profanity, the complaints touched on an allegation that Riggs had been found napping with the children and that an unapproved relative had been found sleeping at her home. Satanism was not at all the issue.

The first report on the center by Bonnie Grover of the county social services hinted that sexual abuse may have occurred. In August, a number of children, all under four years old, who formerly had been under the oversight of Riggs, were taken to Grover and claimed they had been molested by one of Riggs's relatives. Grover and Washington County undersheriff Steve Vosberg recommended that the children should obtain counseling.

In May 1988, Vosberg got wind that the *Denver Post* was about to publish a major story on the case, and he searched the day-care center. When the *Post* article appeared, it gave an entirely new slant to the child abuse accusations. The *Post*, in a headline story, brandished evidence of ritual abuse of the children at the day-care center by hooded adults. "Satanism feared in eastern Colorado child-abuse case," the headline blared. "Rash of child-abuse cases arouse fears of Satanism in small town." The article, with the byline of Paul Hutchinson, also mentioned the sacrificial murder of a boy named "Bobby." The last name of "Bobby" was never divulged, and the corpse was never found.

Unlike the McMartin case, in which the satanism issue was forced into the public arena by trial attorneys and by parents conferring with each other after interviewing their own children, the Akron case was driven by the yellow journalism of the *Post*. The *Post*'s posture was quite understandable, since it had recently gone through several changes of ownership and was deeply in the red. The *Post* and the Scripps-Howard *Rocky Mountain News* were in an infamous and long-standing Colorado "newspaper war" to capture a shrinking market in a depressed local economy. This gave Denver's once prestigious paper an incentive to bend matters slightly. The *Post*, however, was probably not engaged in any malicious crusade, and it certainly did not invent any facts. It may have simply been led down the primrose path.

According to the initial *Post* article, "alarm" had "escalated" earlier in the year "after social workers and other officials consulted with Jim McCarthy, a self-described expert on satanism and a director of Bethesda PsychHealth Institute in Denver. According to one source, McCarthy said the Akron case had "definite satanic overtones." The paper added, "McCarthy, who claims to be a former occultist, confirmed his involvement in the case but refused further comment. McCarthy says he advises police nationwide in cases involving satanism." In this instance the presence of such expertise set off an enormous emotional charge.

A brochure for Bethesda PsychHealth claims that McCarthy "has been involved personally and professionally in the broad area of deviant social movements for 25 years, as a believing participant, a student and researcher, consultant and counselor, and a nationally recognized lec-

turer and trainer to education, religious, mental health and law enforcement agencies." On the cover of the brochure is the surly silhouette of a
teenager before a wall defaced by an inverted pentagram. The caption of
the brochure is "I sold my soul to the Devil. Now I know the price was too
high." Inside the brochure explains that the purpose of the institute "is to
address boldly the issues surrounding deviant social movements and to be
an educational and therapeutic resource to persons seeking assistance
with such issues."

After consulting with McCarthy, county and state social workers held a
meeting in Akron to provide information to social workers in nine other
northeastern Colorado counties about the incident. Plans were made to
develop training seminars for professionals in the area of ritual abuse.
"The children's stories were substantially similar enough" to make the
training necessary, noted K. C. Robbie, a field supervisor. In the
meantime, Irene Ibarra, director of the Colorado Department of Social
Services, had come to Akron and had asked the governor of Colorado,
Roy Romer, to conduct an outside investigation, presumably on the
premise that local law enforcement was not sufficiently zealous in
pursuing the matter of satanism. As it turned out, Romer and the
Colorado attorney general—both Democrats—did order such an investigation, the effect of which was to discredit Akron District Attorney
Doyle Johns and remove him from office in the upcoming general
election. Johns was a Republican.

The *Post* duly noted that Vosberg was "skeptical of any links to devil
worship." And he noted that "I'd like to know where (the children) are
getting these stories." Vosberg had not at all been playing the part of
jaded skeptic. Early in 1988 he had asked for assistance in his investigation from the Colorado Bureau of Investigation. The FBI also wondered
about where the children might be getting their stories. Agents interviewed children to identify victims with no results. The child relating the
story about "Bobby" first said the killing took place at a site near Merino,
Colorado. Then he changed his story and said it occurred near the town
of Atwood. The father of "Bobby," named "Joe," was supposedly of
Mexican descent, even though the supposed child victim was blonde and
blue-eyed. Neither the name nor the family of the child telling the stories
was ever made public.

Social workers reported a variety of afflictions among the children,
including depression and suicidal tendencies, nightmares, regressive
behavior, outbursts against other children, spells of fear and terror, and
general disgust. Throughout therapy the children described adults
brandishing knives, swords, power saws, and cattle prods. The children
also said they were smeared with their feces and forced to drink blood.
Again, like the McMartin pupils, they were allegedly threatened with
death if they revealed what had occurred. One mother said her daughter

had developed a "split" personality and essentialy "distrusted everyone" since attending the Riggs home.

A strong clue as to how the children may have begun "remembering" these things can be found in the differing summaries of the background to the case compiled by the *Post* and the local paper, the *Akron News-Reporter*. The local paper's version of events was quite different than that of the *Post*. For one thing, the *Post* series of articles, which contributed to the governor and attorney general assuming charge, gave the unmistakable impression that Johns and Vosberg were willfully sitting on their hands while satanists marauded around Akron.

The *News-Reporter*, on the other hand, disclosed that the sheriff's office had produced more than one thousand pages of reports from investigations but could not come up with enough evidence to file charges. The paper also observed that Johns had done "nearly everything possible to make a case" and had "two of the most experienced district attorneys in this state review the evidence." It also added acidly, "The conclusion of nearly everyone involved in the case is that not only is there no one to charge in the case, but that much of the story as reported in the 'Denver Post' probably never happened."

The *Post* story, however, may have been set up, if only inadvertently, by the actions of the state social services agency, which had already put its mark on Johns for political reasons. Because Riggs's home was licensed by the state and not by the county, Colorado social services had authority to enter the case, which they did in June 1987.

Mary Hetherington, a state investigator and child-care protection agent had been called into the case by Bonnie Grover of the county social services agency. Initially Hetherington interviewed three young children and made a referral for therapy. The therapists suggested child abuse, and Vosburg and Johns became involved. The state investigator, however, soon left the case in the hands of the sheriff's department. Johns then asked that Hetherington, the state investigator, immediately refer all of the children to Kempe Institute in Denver for therapy and assessment.

The Kempe Institute has been a pioneer and highly respected international authority in the examination of child abuse. Johns said, "We wanted early opinions from recognized experts as to whether we were dealing with child abuse." Hetherington, however, allowed the children to be interviewed only by certain psychologists, who Johns contended had "no experience in the field." Hetherington said that all her referrals to counseling went to M.D.- or Ph.D.-level individuals.

According to Johns, when he interviewed psychologists for the case at the bidding of Akron's victim compensation committee, he hired a particular Denver therapist on the belief that "she had experience working with the Kempe Institute." Apparently, the therapist had no connection with Kempe, but she did have ties with McCarthy's organization, as Hetherington herself told the *News-Reporter*. It was that therapist who apparently "made the connection from reports of children in November and December 1987 and in January 1988," and "she got Hetherington involved in a multi-party telephone conversation with a center for ritualistic abuse." Johns claimed that when he had instructed Hetherington "to send the three identified victims to the Kempe Institute for observation and to be interviewed," they wound up with that particular therapist instead.

The method of psychological evaluation used by the state was "questioned by the Kempe Institute," according to the *News-Reporter*. Most of the charges about satanism had come from one small boy, as opposed to many children in the McMartin affair. It was this reticence that reportedly prompted Johns to hold off filing charges. Johns was a hard-bitten, old-fashioned, rural representative of law enforcement with little experience regarding the complex issues surrounding child abuse cases. He believed in putting one's ducks in a row before stepping in. The strong community reputation of Riggs was also a deterrent in his mind. A retired rancher who had known Riggs for forty-three years said she "was a good, religious woman . . . not guilty of any criminal act of any kind." That opinion was not idiosyncratic for Akron.

However, McCarthy, state social services, and the state district attorney's office were convinced that satanic abuse lay beneath the fairly well-documented suspicions of child sexual abuse. In August, Romer ordered Colorado attorney general Duane Woodward to intervene in the case and to investigate Johns as well. Woodward was a Democrat who had bolted the Republican party a year before with a proclamation that his colleagues were not socially sensitive enough. Romer told the press that he had a "kind of instinct, an intuition, that whatever happened on the local level was not thorough."

At the same time, the Colorado District Attorney's Council, through its president, Denver D.A. Norm Early, wrote a letter to the *Post* stating that it was "particularly concerned about the seemingly unprecedented entry of the Attorney General into this singular local case pursuant to executive order."

In late October, just a few days before Johns faced reelection, Woodward issued arrest warrants against Riggs's grandsons. Woodward publicly accused Johns of impeding the investigation and said Johns's "priorities are not to do justice."

Romer told the press that "child abuse cannot be tolerated." He said that "we have to send a loud message to everyone that we're not going to tolerate it." Woodward also claimed in a story at the top of the front page of the *Post*, headlined "Johns tried to block case," that the Akron D.A. "called the chief judge in the 13th Judicial District and tried to convince him we were without authority to proceed." However, Chief Judge James

Leh said to the press that Johns called only "to question whether the case was being filed properly, not to prevent it."

The following Tuesday, Johns, who had served as the district attorney of Washington County for nineteen years, five more as deputy district attorney, and two as a municipal judge, was out of office, having lost in a landslide to his Democratic rival Jon Bailey. Johns was widely disliked by police and politicians in the Denver metropolitan area. In 1978 he ruffled feathers when he alleged that Denver law enforcement had failed to supply him with adequate information in his prosecution of a case against one of the city's district judges named John Brooks. Brooks had been arrested on charges of leaving the scene of an accident and driving under the influence of alcohol. The judge was eventually fined $158 on the reduced charge of driving while impaired, to which he pleaded guilty.

Finally, Johns had been active in the effort to interdict drug transporting and dealing in northeastern Colorado—a major hotspot. Some of his undercover operations against big-time cocaine dealers had been among the most aggressive and effective in the state, which was otherwise noted by many national experts, including the U.S. Justice Department, for comparatively weak enforcement. In a 1989 report, the Justice Department alleged that a number of drug barons were laundering money through massive resort holdings in the Colorado mountains.

At the time the Akron child abuse controversy surfaced in the press, a Sterling, Colorado, dealer was standing trial for a narcotics sale to Sterling police. The dealer was the reputed operator of a major drug ring of which fifteen had been recently shut down by a Morgan County team of police. In May 1985, twenty people from Brush were arrested for their participation in a Denver-based drug operation. In November 1986, two residents of nearby Brush were arrested in a drug sweep by Fort Morgan police and the Morgan County sheriff's office. And in the summer of 1988, a large spread of marijuana plants was confiscated by law enforcement agents at the Cattlemen's Inn in Brush. Also during the summer, Merrigwen Morrow, organizer for the Drug-Free Colorado program in Brush, told a local paper that in recent months there had been two drug-related shootings. Brush police chief Ken Baker said there was a "very strong" problem with drugs, especially marijuana.

Once the state attorney general took up the case, the issue of satanism was dropped. "They just didn't see it as pertinent to the case," a *Post* reporter who had worked on the story explained.

Riggs herself was never accused of sexual molestation, let alone satanic ritual abuse. She was indicted on two counts of accessory to the crime for obstructing efforts to investigate, locate, and charge her grandsons, who had been named as defendants in the actual child abuse. One grandson, Philip Schmidt, twenty-four, of Yuma, Colorado, was charged with three counts of sexual assault on a child, a count of sexual assault on a child using force, a count of criminal extortion for threatening the parents of one victim, and a count of incest. His brother, Michael, twenty-three, was named for three counts of sexual assault on a child. In October 1989—after the uproar precipitated by the *Post* had run its course—Philip and Michael signed statements admitting they had sexually abused children in the day-care home. Neither grandson had a previous criminal record of any serious nature.

Testimony in the trial of Michael Schmidt was kept away from the public because Judge Leh had put a gag order on the proceedings. Michael Schmidt was tried and convicted on one count of sexual molestation and has been sentenced to four years.

The same week that the alleged drug dealer's defense was presented, Johns was making a pitch to the Brush, Colorado, Rotary Club for his antinarcotics efforts. He was asked a question about the *Post*'s reporting of the Riggs affair. "Had it not been for the word 'witchcraft'," he quipped, "they probably wouldn't have done a story."

Unlike the cult apologists, Johns did not cry witch-hunt. But he did declare his intent to sue the *Post*, a threat which at this writing he has not carried through. It was the *Post* and the Colorado state social services, at the suggestion of McCarthy, who seem to have injected witches, or satanists, into the picture. The whole flap, which seems to have been well-engineered, had the effect of discrediting the notion that satanism could be a serious factor in day-care child abuse. If McCarthy was indeed a "former occultist," as the *Post* said, it may have been he who first entertained the suspicion of witches. On the other hand, McCarthy is quoted in the occult journal *Gnosis* as saying,

I've argued with the [Bethseda] staff that I don't believe these kids can be labelled 'self-styled Satanists.' That would imply that this is a religious act on their part and it's not, anymore than rape is a sexual act . . . Sacrificing animals may have the trappings of a religious act, but it has no transcendental end.[2]

Has the rash of child sexual abuse cases with attendant allegations of ritual crime added up to a contemporary witch-hunt? The charge has increasingly been trundled out not only in occult-related child abuse stories, it has also been aired with respect to the public uproar over satanism in general. The presumption of those who have been calling the matter a "witch-hunt" is that if children are telling stories about strange occurrences and about eerie figures dressed up in black robes, and if investigators are somehow listening to them, the whole slate of accusations must be concocted, just as they were in Salem, Massachusetts, during the Puritan era.

Witch-hunt has entered the stream of contemporary political rhetoric to denote hysterical, unfounded, and usually right-wing political campaigns of defamation, although in the Akron scandal the left-wing seemed to have been leading the charge. The McCarthy hearings during the 1950s—that is, Senator Joe McCarthy of Wisconsin—in which hundreds of government officials and public servants were accused of Communist ties, either past or present, are generally the point of reference for contemporary carryings-on about the danger of witch-hunts. Those who denounce witch-hunts are by and large insinuating that the whole notion of witches is a fabrication. The use of the term *witch-hunt* is, of course, ironic, since there are thousands of outspoken and self-proclaimed witches in America today.

In the 1950s, it was generally accepted that there were Communists—or at least Stalinist agents—infiltrating American government and social institutions. The FBI had arrested and obtained convictions for many of them. The popular television series *I Led Three Lives* was about an undercover G-man who brought to light the activities of Communists in America. The unspoken implication that to call something a witch-hunt automatically discredits the accusers often works to halt investigations, let alone honest reflection on the facts of the case. The word witch-hunt has become its own kind of thought-stopping cliché. It has also become an effective weapon in making investigators and prosecutors alike appear as fools.

Many ardent disbelievers, who hold that just about all claims of ritual abuse are due to witch-hunting, cite a series of so-called investigative articles by the *Commercial Appeal* in Memphis, Tennessee, in January 1988. The articles, which without doubt can be said to have a "point of view" on the matter, have had an unmistakable effect on national news reporting about satanic child abuse. For example, after an editor for the *Reader's Digest* had been embroiled for months with an inquiry into the subject, he suddenly pulled out and quashed the article because of the "findings" of the *Commercial Appeal*.

"It became a national witch-hunt. Literally." So ran the lead sentence of the *Commercial Appeal* series. The newspaper's "investigation" began with a brief notation of the McMartin case. Then:

In Manhattan Beach, one of the mothers made a handwritten statement that said her son had seen one of his teachers fly, and that three of his abusers had 'dressed up as witches'. The accusations mushroomed. Children in the two cities named hundreds of people—including one of the mothers—as child abusers. Before the criminal investigations in Jordan and Manhattan Beach were over, authorities would be unable to separate fact from fantasy. The guilt or innocence of the accused—and the extent to which children were abused—will never be known.

That is not exactly how matters shook out. There was a conclusion to the McMartin criminal case, although the civil suit is likely to throw all the undigested legal matter into the public arena once more. In the American system of justice, guilt or innocence is never suspended forever. The outcome of a jury trial, even if later it may be overturned by a higher court, is regarded as a definitive judgment of the accused. The results of the Fuster case somehow slipped past the critical scrutiny of the *Commerical Appeal*, although it used McMartin as a presumed litmus test of child abuse cases.

According to the *Commercial Appeal*, "a pattern emerged in Jordan and Manhattan Beach that later cases followed." For example:

> most cases evolved from a single incident involving one child, but investigators often triggered runaway inquiries that fed on publicity and parents' worst fears. Accusations were made against grandmothers, police officers, pastors, defense lawyers and even social services workers who investigated the complaints. Children's stories were the foundation of the cases—and they were almost completely uncorroborated by physical evidence or adult testimony. Allegations were spread from child to child and from city to city by the news media, parents, prosecutors, social service workers and consultants.

That was not true at all, as far as McMartin and Fuster were concerned. In the case of Akron, it was only two parties—a subscription-hungry urban newspaper and a governor who wanted a political rival gone.

If the *Post* helped devise a story in the sensationalist tradition of William Randolph Hearst, the *Appeal* series could be called an example of what in the sixties was branded "new journalism"—a montage of essay and advocacy masquerading as reporting. Some "new journalists" even went so far as to proclaim their actual disdain for the "facts." It was the political impact that counted.

The concrete political impact of the *Appeal*'s brand of new journalism is yet to be measured. But the techniques of distortion are quite familiar to scholars of rhetorical persuasion and propoganda. For instance, the bald assertion that "most cases evolved from a single incident involving one child" is a glittering generality that even the *Appeal* does not bother to substantiate. The authoritative tone of the newspaper purports to be sufficient evidence in itself. There is also the infamous "appeal to prejudice" in the phrase "accusations were made against grandmothers," as if elderly women, whoever and wherever they might be, are somehow incapable of commiting horrible crimes.

"Children's stories were the foundation of the cases—and they were almost completely uncorroborated by physical evidence or adult testimony." Here a version of the rhetorical trick "no evidence has been found" is subtly brought into play. It is simply the fallacy of the *argumentum ad hominem*, or "argument to the man." The character or reputation of a person making a statement is first faulted. Then the accusations against the person are taken as a refutation of the statement itself, even though it may have no bearing on the material evidence. The newspaper insinuates that because "children" are the source of information, the information itself cannot be trusted.

Children assuredly are given to fantasize, just as adults are prone to lie. The fact that some children fantasize, however, does not mean logically that any given youngster's testimony in court must be presumed fallacious. Just because certain adults, such as criminals or sociopaths, lie under oath does not mean all adults do the same. The symmetry between the two cases is obvious.

As juvenile psychiatrists have frequently observed, children do not as a rule deliberately make things up. Children describe through their own language and their own mind-sets what they see. The fact that adults did not corroborate what the children saw is irrelevant as well, since *child abuse* by adults is what remains at issue in the first place. Most women who are raped are not observed by other men or women. The only witness is the rapist. But such a statistical commonplace does not mean we refuse to believe rape victims.

"Allegations were spread from child to child and from city to city by news media. . . ." Exactly the same decrepit reasoning surfaces once more. Allegations about serial murders or terrorist bombings or money laundering are disseminated in the same way. The fact that news media report a story does not mean the story is a lie. Nor have behavioral scientists shown with any serious suggestion that allegations of criminal conduct are simply fabricated by the power of suggestion. People are just not that stupid.

In another article the *Appeal*, following basically the same text and wording of author Arthur Lyons, dismisses the satanist child cases for "bearing the traditional themes of urban legends—sex, religion, and horror." Just why these kinds of themes should be rejected at face value is extremely puzzling. An enormous portion of *actual* crimes are sex crimes. Most crimes by their very nature *are* horrible. And, as the Jim Bakker episode tells, criminal activity is *often* done under the cover of religion.

The category of "urban legends" was invented by sociologists not for the purpose of debunking those legends through the very use of the word, as the cult apologists do. It was devised to explain how stories, whether true or false, circulate in the streets and in the criminal underworld. The irony is that because human beings in the underground are forced to be very "street savvy" or worldly wise in order to survive, they tend to be far less credulous than suburban residents or urban professionals. Urban legends may be about sex and violence because sex and violence are the routine features of life in the underground.

The Akron case and the brazen editorial posturing of the *Commercial Appeal* under the pretense of reporting have confused the issue of the relationship between satanism and sexual abuse. As psychiatrist Roland Summit has stressed, there are powerful interests—the criminal interests—who want the public to remain confused. Whether babies are actually sacrificed by day-care providers in front of the eyes of kids is not nearly as relevant as the fact that drug-use or child pornography are strongly implicated.

The Family Violence Research Laboratory at the University of New Hampshire has issued a report showing that child pornography has been a key factor in 10 to 15 percent of 270 documented sex abuse cases in day-care centers. Remarkably, 40 percent of the sex offenders were females, which contradicts the conventional wisdom that women do not abuse children. Organizations such as VOCAL have been on-site in McMartin, and even Akron, to religiously denounce the witch-hunts and to demand immunity from prosecution and public hysteria. But, as child advocacy research shows, approximately 90 percent of sex abuse cases—whether satanic or not—are never prosecuted. The Denver chapter of the American Humane Association found that of 576 reported cases of child sexual abuse that came its way, only 8 percent could be considered false assertions. And even fewer false reports were made by children.

The fact of the matter is that satanism is creeping into the underworld of child pornography, drugs, and sexual abuse as an ideology that goes well with crime in the first place. Satanist "theater" may also be used by criminals, first to frighten and intimidate the children, then to devise stories that make the little witnesses lose their credibility—allowing the criminals to go free and to undermine the plausibility of the attack on child sexual abuse in the first place. The common cord that binds most of the controversy is that parents, who generally know their children, believe what they are being told or at least believe that some kind of serious trauma has happened and should not be dismissed by officials.

Some of the more far-out fantasies of young children that are the victims of ritual abuse, trotted into court by the defense to underscore how ridiculous the prosecution's case is, may simply be the result of slipping the kids LSD or similar hallucinogens, which can then be manipulated by the power of suggestion. Satanic cults are known by police all over the country to avail themselves of LSD in their ceremonies. A local television station in Denver filmed a sandstone cave west of the city next to a popular rock concert amphitheater. The cave was employed as a satanic ritual site for adolescents following concerts, where they would be given LSD and introduced into the experiential mysteries of the dark.

And as for the beheaded babies, it all may be a matter of aesthetic terrorism in a very clever sense of the word. Alice Cooper would ritually decapitate dolls onstage. And police in California raided a warehouse where cultists had reportedly been active. They found a whole cache of aborted fetuses.

NOTES

1. Anton Szandor LaVey, *The Satanic Rituals* (New York: Avon Books, 1972), p. 21.
2. Chas S. Clifton, "The Three Faces of Satan: A Close Look at the 'Satanism Scare,'" *Gnosis*, Summer 1989, p. 12.

Part IV.

APOCALYPSE NOW

CHAPTER 11.

The Metaphysics of Violence

The wolf is smarter than human fools could dream of.
———CHARLES MANSON

ITEM: In Huntington Beach, California, police concluded that neo-Nazi "skinheads" were the culprits behind a series of animal mutilations as well as a riot of graffiti that employed recognizable, satanic symbolism.

A similar incident was disclosed by law enforcement agents in the Great Basin region of the West, where two Utah skinheads—members of violent neo-Nazi gangs of youth—were indicted for the February 1988 slaying of a Las Vegas store clerk. The duo had been connected to a major, satanic cult in the community, which practiced routine rituals in an abandoned building. The Utah skinhead who murdered the store clerk thought he was engaged in an act of "worship," according to police. He believed through the act he would obtain the energy of his victim.

ITEM: In the suburbs of Washington, D.C., park police came across a mutilated deer beside a high school building, which was swathed in paint with inverted crosses and vicious racial epithets. A skinhead from Maryland, apprehended in another incident, was found to have burned a swastika into his chest with a coat hanger and had tatooed a pentagram as well as the familiar 666 on his shoulder. Police theorized the two incidents were connected.

ITEM: Tustin, California, citizens complained almost weekly about mutilations of their household cats, which police dismissed as insignificant. Inhabitants of the quiet Orange County municipality said they would walk out on their front steps to see the dismembered carcasses on their front lawns. Terrified residents resorted to keeping their cats and dogs inside each night.

Local police explained away the wave of terror as the work of "coyotes"—as some law enforcement agencies did with the cattle mutilations of the 1970s. Unfortunately, the nearest habitat for coyotes was in the mountains twenty miles away. Janet Hampson, whose cat had been murdered in the same, mysterious manner, argued that the "surgical precision" of the kills could not be attributed to animal predators, who generally slash, shred, and chew their victims. The blood was also carefully drained from the cadavers.

Some observers theorized the malefactors might be skinheads who have been active in Tustin recently. Fire-lit rituals were noticed at night in the large, cement storm drains and cisterns running through Tustin where the "coyotes" supposedly crouched. In the morning, skinhead scrawlings mixed with satanic sigils were visible on the tubular walls of the sewer system.

ITEM: In Kenton, Delaware, a white supremacist was sentenced to death for the murder of a local woman. A member of the Aryan Brotherhood, the man sported a satanic tattoo—the name "Abaddon," or the angel from the bottomless pit of hell in chapter 9 of the Book of Revelation.

ITEM: In Florida at a rally of the Ku Klux Klan, according to published accounts, Kevin Lindquist, fifteen, grabbed a microphone and hurled a racist polemic to the delight of his onlookers. Prior to taking the stage, Lindquist had identified himself by a pseudonym well known to students of satanism, but previously unheard at gatherings of the knights of the invisible empire. The pseudonym was "Aleister Crowley."

Since late 1988, satanism has undergone a metamorphosis, switching from private, cultic violence centering on the esoteric facets of "devil worship" to the blatant, street violence of neo-Nazi gangs, who combine such symbols as *666* with Hitler worship and anti-Semitic terrorism.

We go back to the summer of 1988. The gang graffiti is thick along the trash dumpsters and rust-brick facades along the alleys just east of Broadway and south of Colfax in Denver's Capitol Hill district like a lifetime of tattoos on a derelict seaman. The curious symbols and obscure but taunting messages that have usually been spray-painted in red and black are not, contrary to popular belief, simply the idle outbursts of disturbed adolescent imaginations. They are a language with a grammar and a structure all its own.

Gang specialists in California police departments began decoding the graffiti and listing it in training manuals over a decade ago. Some of the pictures are what might be described as gang "logos." They say, for example, in a subtle but menacing fashion, "I'm a Crip. I was here." Because of widely publicized street shoot-outs between rival black groups distributing crack and because of the movie *Colors*, an impression has grown that the gang problem is largely an affliction of the ghetto—the 1980s version of the Watts rioting that touched only those whites who happened to get in the way or ventured too close to the action.

This summer, however, the scene has suddenly shifted. An impending storm can be sensed from the graffiti. The latest statements on the buildings bear the combined signature of teenage satanism inspired by heavy metal music and the neo-Nazi style of virulent white racism that four years ago led to the assassination of Denver radio talk show host Alan Berg. One can spot the familiar devil's horns and the slogan *Christian death*, but there are also the initials *K.K.K.* and the moniker *Aryan Brothers* as well as the acronym *WAR*, which stands for "White Aryan Resistance." The acronym tells all.

Call him Gary. Gary is an aging and slightly balding veteran of the Hollywood rock music industry. Gary regards himself as an authority on the metal culture and, by extension, the pop ideology of nazism cum satanism that has sculptured the psyches of the new white gangs. The white gangs are commonly called "skinheads" after their shaved pates. They are a British import, an American adaptation of the bands of young thugs in paramilitary dress that first appeared in the back streets of London during the 1970s and became famous for their angry, sick music as well as their delight in terrorizing and beating up Pakistani immigrants. Their style of music has always been strongly political, according to Gary, and now it is developing into a kind of patriotic anthem for "oppressed whites" throughout the country.

The skinheads and other white gangs have been quietly rallying and fortifying themselves to confront the black cadres which, they believe, already rule the streets of America. They are talking of their own "revolutionary" Armageddon.

The whites have been organizing to regain control of the streets and will "clean up" the social rot spread by the "Zionist Occupation Government" that has given the Bloods and the Crips—black gangs known for urban drug trafficking and violent killings—free rein throughout America, Gary said. The rhetoric, of course, is altogether vicious, fulsome, and fanciful. But it is still a deeper symptom of both the dark, roiling passions that the gang problem represents and the almost religious fever that motivates the legions of self-professed warriors.

Social service professionals are fond of describing today's gangs in the familiar, textbook fashion as disturbed deviants who have achieved access to automatic weapons. Drugs are their currency of the realm. Ego and greed are the justification. Such a picture, however, is seriously flawed, primarily because of its lack of attention to gang ideology. The origins of the current gang menace can be found in the social violence and political turmoil of the late 1960s.

On the West Coast such revolutionary and terrorist groups as the Black Panthers, the Black Guerilla Family, and the Symbionese Liberation Army (which kidnapped newspaper heiress Patty Hearst) set up their own underground network within the prison system. They were countered by young Hispanic groups known as Venceremos and Nuestra Familia as well as Anglo organizations with such neo-Nazi names as the United White People's Party and the Aryan Brotherhood. The Aryan Brotherhood, according to testimony before the California state legislature, acquired close ties with the "family" of notorious serial killer Charles Manson.

The Aryan Brotherhood set the trend out of which emerged popular, adolescent satanism, noted for its fascination with Third Reich insignia and a cultivated criminal swagger. For example, the attribute used by the Aryan Brotherhood in California's Folsom Prison was the number 666 in a pyramid configuration. In the last several years the particular drawing has been observed on numerous walls and at cult ritual sites by law enforcement investigators.

In Denver, police have identified the dominant units as the White Aryan Youth and the White Aryan Resistance. A strange and extremely violent organization, which started in southern California, calls itself Psychic Youth and melds the more grisly iconography of satanism and nazism with a bizarre, racist revolutionary philosophy. One specialist has estimated that there are no more than two hundred to three hundred actual members of such hard-core groups, but their influence and messages have most likely spread much further.

In Douglas County south of Denver, the teenage Aryan gangs have begun to make their presence felt in the suburbs. They have been responsible for extensive vandalism in the quiet town of Castle Rock. In one instance, a skinhead squad broke into a church and destroyed its cross, replacing it with the upside-down emblem of satanism. Similar acts of desecration occurred the previous spring about twenty miles down the road near the town of Monument in northern El Paso County. At the time, police were perplexed regarding the culprits, but there are indications now that the Douglas County gangs may have been involved. It is all due, one local police officer confided, because of the "music."

Blaming it on the "music" may, from a criminological standpoint, be way too much of an oversimplification. But, like all clichés, an echo of truth can be detected.

One of the principal reasons the rock music culture functions as a powerful form of social influence is its ability to access the deep unconscious. The age-old psychological technique for attaining such access is what has come to be called hypnosis—a simple but not very well understood method of inducing trance and, hence, susceptibility to outside stimuli and suggestions. Hypnotic induction is frequently quite useful in political propoganda and the exaltation of the godlike stature of a charismatic leader, as Hitler's famous Nuremburg rallies in the early 1930s underscored. The words and thoughts emanating from the charismatic personality, which contain at the same time a very strong emotional charge, can be easily and lastingly imprinted on the mind of the crowd. The mechanism is what the psychologist G. H. Estabrooks has termed "social contagion," which he contends can be identified in a sweeping gamut of phenomena from the ritual drumming ceremonies of the primitive medicine men to Pentecostal religious services. In a different context, a number of psychological studies have shown that a hard, pulsating, repetitive rock beat can be as instrumental as a stage hypnotist or a charismatic leader in producing a trance state within an audience. The mob psychology and force of social contagion at rock concerts can temporarily induce what might be called religious frenzy and ecstasy, leading to a permanent effect on perceptions and values. A generation ago the rock scene with its trancelike ensemble of experiences was able to beget the mystical, utopian ideal of a "Woodstock nation." Today the heavy metal culture is causing mayhem and violence both on and off the stage. It is not only, as one critic of the rock industry has put it, a case of "superstars not realizing their own power of suggestion."[1] It is the all too obvious and virtually undeniable fact that rock music for masses of adolescent Americans, especially over the last twenty years, has become something much more than a source of entertainment. The music has acquired a mystique which has the cachet of transcendental truth for many. When the music poeticized primarily about peace and love, not too many people could object. When the music self-consciously seeks to revive the worst of Nazi fascism, it is an altogether different matter.

The constituency for this new, music-driven "metaphysics of violence" is a strange, multipersonality amalgam of former followers of Anton LaVey, neo-Nazis, and groupies attached in varying ways to the revived pop cult of Manson. Its publicity organ is a rock band and newsletter, designed for media consumption, dubbed Radio Werewolf.

The moniker *Radio Werewolf* comes from the radio broadcasts by German propoganda minister Goebbels at the end of World War II, encouraging the German nations to strike at the allies with all the ferocity of the ancient Teutonic warriors in service of the god Wotan. The "Werewolf Corps" was a last-ditch, terrorist lunge against the forces occupying a defeated Germany. The "Radio Werewolf Supreme Command" makes its own cynical statement after the fashion of the German propogandists and the aesthetic terrorists of the postwar era in its "indoctrination" manifesto:

Radio Werewolf is utilizing the powerful tool of "pop" culture, in which the impressionable youth of the world are so intertwined. Music, the lowest denominator of the media's cynical manipulation, must be used for more than the purveyance of mindless escapism. . . .

Employing the technique used in occultism of appealing to the primordial beginning of things—what scholars call the "prestige of origins"—the manifesto proclaims that it is more than music; it is the great, aboriginal force Aquino ballyhoos in his discussion of the motion picture *The Keep*. The ideas of Aquino are also strongly in evidence because of the linkage between psychotronics, music, and the alleged manifestation of the power of Satan.

"Throughout history," the manifesto begins, "man has been fascinated with the strange legend of an evil presence, an omnipotent, malevolent force that has manifested itself in many guises." In the prehistorical past, according to Radio Werewolf, these forces cowered in the darkness and were feared by all. "The ancient Egyptians worshipped this entity with secret, mysterious rites." The unmerciful forces of darkness, and their impersonations, have been idly brushed away as fantasy or fanatically suppressed in the name of true religion, the manifesto continues, but to no avail.

"Superstition? Irrational fears? Old wives' tales? Quite the contrary! These things are very real." Furthermore, "Radio Werewolf is that glorious force upon which all these legends, myths, and 'superstitions' are factually based. Radio Werewolf is but the current incarnation of this demonic manifestation." Finally, "employing time-tested subliminal techniques, Radio Werewolf has returned to rid this Earth once and for all of the sub-human parasites that have for too long hindered the spiritual evolution of the chosen."[2]

The Mansonite theology of "getting the Fear" becomes explicit in the Radio Werewolf literature. Fear is the secret of mystical illumination, it concludes, and only by becoming a friend of it can liberation take place. Horror is perhaps the most formidable "magical tool" in the soul's initiation. The werewolf is the ultimate symbol, or "archetype," of the beast that lurks in the subbasement of the minds of the chosen. Those who listen, and adore, the beast through the music will became one with the "lycanthropoic legions" bent on conquest.

Manson's fascination with wolfish metaphysics is well known. Manson regarded the wolf, or its desert cousin the coyote, as the embodiment of the "ultimate evil," which embraced both death and love simultaneously. Manson coined the word *coyotonoia*, or "coyote-mindedness," to convey the concept of both wickedness and stealth in the formation of the occult guerilla personality to triumph at the moment of "helter skelter."

The "werewolf" as the essential revelation of both absolute fear and absolute enlightenment for the current generation of *Illuminati* is given a rather arcane justification by Adam Parfrey in his essay "Latter-Day Lycanthropy." Christian morality, he says, resists the celebration of the werewolf, which betokens, in fact, the most pagan among "mystical states of ecstatic illumination." The medieval terror of the werewolf was derived largely from the peasant encounter with this sacred practice and pertains as well to the Viking wolf-warrior, or *berserker*, who, upon donning animal skins and achieving a mysterious kind of wolf-consciousness, became the most feral warrior Europe had ever confronted.

Crowley's cult of the beast, according to Parfrey, was founded in part upon the ideal of "lycanthropic transformation." And in subsequent O.T.O. rites, wolf-magic was used as a means of achieving "cosmic" and "unlimited" awareness. Crowley made more than a jape out of the familiar fact of the English language that *God* is *dog* spelled backwards. *God barks* was his aphorism, meaning that true transcendence can be realized through reversion to pure animal instinctuality. Satanism, therefore, signifies nothing more or less than the turning of the divine upside down, even in a very primitive, linguistic sense.

Lycanthropy, or "werewolfism," is also a key ingredient in Setianism, if we follow the analysis of such occultists as Grant and Michael Bertiaux. Sirius is the "dog star"; Set, its dark double. The secrets of Set coincide with the metamorphosis of human into wolf. The magician must become the wolf-beast in order to escape from the "circles of time" and the fate of a doomed planet. His "bloody sacrifice" is a magical means of ensuring this transformation.

If Radio Werewolf is the propoganda arm of the new pop underground of satanism cum nazism, the Abraxas Foundation on Evil is its death-worshiping think tank. The foundation, which at this writing lists an address on Jones Street in San Francisco, is the brainchild of Nikolas Schreck, confidant of Charles Manson and theoretician of apocalypse culture. One of his hallmarks is the motto "Long live death!"

Abraxas was a name referring to the ancient, dark godhead of the Gnostics, the figure whom the twentieth-century psychologist Carl Jung in his *Seven Sermons of the Dead*, written in the 1920s, magnified as "the god whom ye knew not, for mankind forgot it." Abraxas "begetteth truth and lying, good and evil, light and darkness, in the same word and in the same act. Wherefore is Abraxas terrible." Jung called Abraxas "true God," which has been repressed by Christianity. He is the pure psychic impulsion, the supreme reservoir of the instincts that surpasses all moral separation of good and evil.

Abraxas was also a major character in the popular novel *Demian* by Herman Hesse, who had undergone psychoanalysis with Jung. Demian is a shadowy figure, portraying the "wisdom" of the god Abraxas, who teaches the novel's hero, Sinclair, about the mysteries of good and evil. The overriding mystery is that good and evil are at bottom one. Demian instructs Sinclair, for example, in the Gnostic secret of Cain, the original fratricide in the biblical story. The "mark" of Cain, according to Demian has been misunderstood as a sign of murder and rebellion. In actuality, it is an arbitrary stigma consigned to those whom society has cast aside. Demian tells Sinclair that "people with courage and character always seem sinister to the rest." At the end of the novel, Sinclair troops over the carnage of World War II and discovers the meaning of the teachings of Abraxas "in the dark mirror."

Lycanthropy and the intuitive recognition of the wolf side of the personality is the central motif of *Steppenwolf*, another key novel by Hesse. The protagonist Harry Haller, an upstanding icon of the middle classes, comes to appreciate his lycanthropic nature by taking a tour through the "magic theater" of experience—a 1920s version of the psychedelic mind-tour. Harry has a mystic vision of the universal mind with all its joys and terrors, its sublimity and its morbidity, until he beholds the "wolf world" in all its horror, symbolized in the masses of corpses from the battlefield.

The credo of the Abraxas Foundation plays upon this type of thinking but with far more sinister, political overtones. Abraxas is the superior power of nature in which creation and destruction are "united and transcended," according to Schreck. The law of nature and the law of humanity are at loggerheads with each other. Human beings are disposed to call the natural instincts—the "law of the strong"—evil, giving rise to the "catastrophical situation which imperils this planet." The weak must be eliminated and the strong and fearless lionized.

Schreck, along with white supremacist Boyd Rice, helped engineer the "8–8–88" celebration in San Francisco, which took place at the Strand Theater on Market Street between Seventh and Eighth and not only memorialized the murder of Tate but also served, according to posters advertising the event, as a tribute to the infamous zodiac killer. The event was described by a city newspaper as a "satanic rally." Along with Schreck appeared LaVey's daughter Zeena and the Church of Satan's head himself. LaVey read from *The Satanic Bible*, while attendees in the front row chanted "Hail Sata-a-an." Clips from the extravaganza were shown on Gerald Rivera's special "Devil Worship: Exposing Satan's Underground," which aired in the fall of 1988. LaVey's appearance would seem to undercut Lyons's apology for LaVey that he has always kept the neo-Nazi right "at arm's length" from his own views.

The explanation for the ideological merger of satanism and neonazism can be gleaned from the essay by Donald Nugent "Satan is a Fascist," published in the April 1972 edition of the British publication *The Month* and analyzing the "unholy Trinity of Adolf Hitler, Charles Manson . . . and Anton LaVey." For both LaVey and the fascist, the "satanist and the superman are one," Nugent writes. He also points out that mysticism and humanism are the "two routes to satanism." Catharism mixed with the secular ideology of state control became Hitlerism. German mysticism mingled with LaVey's libertarian philosophy of *laisser-aller*, or "let anything pass," becomes the nine satanic statements.

Nugent also discusses Manson's fanatical racism; his sporting of Nazi swastikas, which he wears on his forehead to this day; and his own cryptic allusions to "supermen." He cites the congruity with LaVey's political objectives of a "benign police state" in which the weak are winnowed away. In the satanist mentality, according to Nugent,

the world is a hospital—and a mental hospital. The world is the lustful will to power, wanton destructive violence, man's inhumanity to man. The world is the Paradise that has been polluted. The world is the exploitative society, the place where nothing is holy and everything has its price. The world is a brothel.[3]

That has been LaVey's sentiment almost to the letter.

If the world is a brothel, then destruction and violence are the most justifiable course. All of one's corrupt surroundings must be unmasked, dismembered, and dispersed into nothingness. A mysterious Massachusetts group calling itself Blood Axis has taken up the call of the neo-Nazi satanist alliance. It uses the death's head and the slogan "Terminate" and messages such as "Kill Your Parents." The group has been involved in developing rock concert lyrics and stagings that openly glorify the cruelty of the Third Reich as well as the desecration of Christian and Jewish monuments. The burning of a creche in Cambridge, Massachusetts—although the group has not admitted to it—is an historical deed celebrated by Blood Axis.

But it has been in the recent cycles of the skinhead movement where the fusion of satanism as aesthetic terrorism and nazism as terror per se has been most pronounced. It was the San Francisco satanic mafia that made the skinheads political. Again, it has been through the music.

The musicologist behind the campaign of Radio Werewolf and the effort to create a "skinhead nation" has been San Francisco's Robert Heick, who set up shop in the Haight where the hippies used to hang out. It has been said that Heick "manufactures rage."

Heick also calls himself an apostle of LaVey's "new order," which is really neopaganism in the sense of the release of unbridled, manly, abysmally animal, and "white" impulses. In his room, Heick has a Ku Klux Klan poster with the British Union Jack draped across the window. He sings such memorable ditties as "nigger, get out of here" while demanding that the United States shut down all its borders to nonwhites.

Heick's music reflects the politics of white supremacy activist Tom Metzger, current head of the White Aryan Resistance. Metzger began his career as a member of the John Birch Society in the 1960s. Then he went on to work with the Klan in the seventies and finally with the White American Political Association in 1980. He has supported the line of the Aryan Nation radicals (the group that assassinated Jewish talk-show host Alan Berg in 1985 in Denver) about the United States as under the boot of the "Zionist Occupation Government," or ZOG for short. Metzger also envisions himself as a champion of the white, working class against the numberless predations of blacks, Asians, and Hispanics. Metzger has formed skinhead chapters out of his WAR machine in southern California. "Skinheads were born in violence," according to Metzger. "They're pissed off at the system. They're fighting every day. It takes somebody beaten down to stand up, and they have their place in the movement." Metzger exults, "Once we get the white people's minds right and we get rid of all these white traitors, the Jews will be a weekend operation, baby!"

According to police in California, the skinhead movement was responsible for a 121 percent increase in anti-Semitic vandalism in California alone. In one incident, skinheads accosted a black woman at a San Jose park and told her she would have to pay a "nigger toll." Otherwise, they would string her up on a tree. The incident was described as a heroic act by the Aryan Youth Movement, a subsidiary of WAR. "We support them all the way," one member of AYM professed. "Skinheads are our front-line warriors. They roam the streets and do what's necessary to protect the race."

Whereas the skinheads, formerly "punkers," had been mildly multi-racial or at least multireligious until the mid-1980s, the Abraxas influence changed things dramatically. The change started right in San Francisco. In the Haight, swastikas were carved on segments of sidewalk, and Buena Vista Park came to be known as Skinhead Hill. According to published accounts, Heick broke the window of an anarchist bookstore, and the cops began putting the pressure on skinheads by pulling them off the streets. The left-leaning political punkers—"peace punks," they were called disparagingly—were reviled as "Weimar liberals." In 1988, Heick led a sizable march of skinheads down Haight Street as part of "White Workers Day." Heick has recently proclaimed that he will be organizing the heavy metal freaks as part of his movement.

The more esoteric elements of the skinhead movement, putting as much emphasis on the satanism as on the nazism, have taken the name "Temple of Psychic Youth." The Psychic Youth logo—a crosshatch with one vertical bar and three horizontal ones that is sometimes overlain with a glaring skull—can be found increasingly among gang graffiti in urban settings. Psychic Youth has stylized the Manson cult, as well as the nine satanic statements. A Psychic Youth is "totally conscious" of his or her objects of desire, a manifesto reads, and "knows how to go about making that desire a reality." The manifesto also describes the means of channeling "sexual orgasm" into a powerful, magical force. Male Psychic Youth initiates, who describe themselves as "lone wolves," reportedly undergo ritual mutilation of the sexual organs and have shaven heads with monklike tails at the rear of the skull.

"Skinhead America," as the music hucksters call it, has been accountable for an increasing epidemic of random and brutal crime. In Florida, two skinheads bludgeoned a black man to death. In Portland, Oregon, a band calling itself East Side White Pride assaulted Ethiopian immigrants with baseball bats, leaving one dead. In Milwaukee, skinheads waded into a street dance with baseball bats and metal pipes and shot at black youths in a car. In Washington, D.C., three skinheads were arrested for a spree of "gay bashing" with baseball bats. In Atlanta, skinheads knocked a pair of women flat on the ground and shouted antilesbian obscenities. In Seattle, a sixteen-year-old girl was kidnapped and savagely tortured by five female skinheads.

The "metaphysics of violence" inherent in the Nazi/satanist complex is shifting swiftly, and radically, from aesthetic terrorism to a true fascist "metapolitics"—to invoke the language of Peter Vierick, historian of Nazi thought and ideology. Satanism has turned "revolutionary" in a manner that invokes the most terrible historical reminiscences.

There are seemingly simple, sociological explanations. The newsletter *Klanwatch* dryly observes that "both Skinhead gangs and satanic cults attract young people who are insecure, fiercely rebellious and resentful toward society." That, of course, has been the standard rationale for delinquency for more than a century. It is not some generic bugaboo of "frustration" or "alienation."

The current trend appears deeper and more baleful. The new scene has a litany of self-conscious bestiality and terrorism that even the public face of German nazism, bound by certain bourgeois scruples, would not acknowledge. A *USA Today* analysis seeks to dispense with self-serving clichés. It remarks that "we must first dispense with denial. In the face of increasingly visible Nazi skinhead organizing and its accompanying brutal violence, [one should] never dismiss the early signals—vandalism, slurs, Nazi sloganeering—as 'just kids,' 'juvenile pranks,' or any other such rationalizations."

The new cadres of Psychic Youth however, are extraordinarily upfront about their political agenda. An AYM pamphlet says, "Our goal is to create a network of white youth gangs and wolf packs across the nation . . . the Aryan Youth Movement salutes the wolf pack . . . for hunting down and causing the death of Negro Michael Griffith, and for physically beating with baseball bats Negros Cedric Sandiford and Timothy Grimes in the New York City area."

The siege of American culture runs the risk of turning into an onslaught, or as the name of one skinhead rock group suggests, a Coup de Gras. The message has always been LaVey's. As LaVey wrote in his conclusion to a lesser known book, *The Compleat Witch*, a sort of tongue-in-cheek, fashion-magazine guide for women to the clothing styles and life-styles of twentieth-century occultism, black magic is tantamount to the piety of the hunter. It is bound by the "rules of the chase." Although religious ideologies will rise and fall while "the Games will begin and end . . . man's basic nature will remain the same." It is only by means of self-understanding that the human being will be "able to embrace and cherish the demon within him. Then he can revel in his nature and feeling glad, move on to the Final Solution."[4]

NOTES

1. John G. Fuller, *Are the Kids All Right? The Rock Generation and its Hidden Death Wish* (New York: Times Books, 1981), p. 144.
2. Quoted in Parfrey, *Apocalypse Culture*, p. 18.
3. Donald Nugent, "Satan is a Fascist," *Month*, April 1972, p. 119
4. Anton Szandor LaVey, *The Compleat Witch or What to Do When Virtue Fails* (New York: Dodd, Mead, 1971), p. 266.

CHAPTER 12

Twilight of the Idols

And he said to them, "I saw Satan fall like lightning from heaven."
—LUKE 10:18

In a series of breezy, but perceptive essays, on late twentieth century culture, the Italian philosopher of language Umberto Eco compares the twentieth century, with its peculiar religious excesses, to the Middle Ages. The medieval period, like today, was an era of long-term transition, as opposed to adventure and construction, according to Eco. Therefore, he suggests, it is possible to imagine serious couplings between heroic romance, "the new satanism," and the popular mystique of King Arthur and Excalibur. Increasingly, science fiction with its vistas of the technological future intertwines with the neopagan and the medieval. The synthesis was first achieved with polished artistry in Lucas's *Star Wars* trilogy.

In the nineteenth century, the popular longing for the Middle Ages gave rise to the style of historical fiction found in Sir Walter Scott novels. It also revived for a spell the ideal of chivalry, expressed in the Victorian attitude of almost obsessive deference toward chaste women, while at the same time it conjured the incredibly seductive notion of the quest for the magical grail of power. The grail, as a symbol of the highest magical proficiency, and of eternity, may have been a driving wedge behind nazism itself.

As Trevor Ravenscroft claimed in his *Spear of Destiny*, Hitler may have been initiated during his youth into a form of black Tantrism, or sexual magic, similar to Crowley's, by the occultist Dietrich Eckart. Eckhart was the central figure in the influential circle of occultists known as the Thule Group, who had close ties with Crowley's organization. The Thule cult centered on the legend of the grail and the spear of Longinus, which supposedly rendered Christ his death wound on the cross. Even before Hitler's rise to power, the spear and grail had been mystical emblems of political sovereignty in Europe. The spear signified the eighth-century Frankish king Charlemagne's claims of a thousand-year "Holy Roman Empire." The grail represented the occult wisdom, or Gnostic vision of things, available to whoever destiny would allow to rule over the new

Reich. Ravenscroft, whose own occult leanings nonetheless have made him slightly suspect among academic experts, has argued that the struggle between totalitarian ideologies in the twentieth century has boiled down to a rivalry over who would rule in a reborn medieval empire.

Eco may be overstating the case when he says we have entered a "new Middle Ages" and something called "neo-medievalism" is the trend in images, politics, religion, and modes of communication. But he rightly observes that social fragmentation, the proliferation of ever smaller political units struggling for elusive power, and general insecurity is a norm now, as it was in those times. American hegemony is in decline at the same time as the worldwide empire of the Communist faith rapidly unravels.

"In these broad territories in the grip of insecurities, bands of outcasts roam, mystics, adventurers." In the Middle Ages there was a religious underground with striking affinity to today's counterculture. As it was true slightly less than a thousand years ago, "the borderline between the mystic and the thief is often minimal, and Manson is simply a monk who has gone too far, like his ancestors, into satanic rites."[1] The claim of a corporate ancestry of Catharism is far greater than a metaphor. It is the watershed of all modern systems of belief emphasizing the right of the human creature to revolt against the ultimate order of things, to sanctify the darkly instinctual in opposition to the hegemony of a universal morality or a supreme reality.

Eco describes several models, or views, of the medieval period. The one that pertains most directly to the contemporary moment, which the *engragees* of the last twenty years have, in the words of the Rolling Stones' song, "painted black," is what Eco dubs the "decadent" Middle Ages. Decadentism was nurtured throughout the nineteenth century and was at first "an invention of intellectuals." It then became the scaffolding for militant national restoration behind the snarling mask of nazism and fascism. But since the sixties, decadentism has joined itself with what Eco regards as the Middle Ages of occultism and "perennial philosophy"— "mixing up Rene Guenon and Conan the Barbarian, Avalon and the Kingdom of Prester John."[2]

The latter edges closer to what has commonly come to be known presently as New Age thinking, which is nothing more than a generic label for every conceivable kind of exotic religious enthusiasm and manner of magical dabbling. The Middle Ages had its own New Age, usually corresponding to the underground of anticlericals and the schools of heresy. Where magic, off-the-shelf metaphysics, and even the Gnostic traditions of occultism shade off into the violent and the criminal—as they frequently did even in the medieval epoch—we begin to descry the black chamber of psychic horrors and spiritual inversion we call the satanic. It is the act of desecration veiled as a cultural "redecoration," the swashing of black paint over the red door of avant-garde experiment and defiance. It is terrorism that has ripped off its civil disguise of aestheticism and become terror itself—straight and simple.

Up until the 1960s, the avant-garde had been in the business of shocking the powers that be with its eroticism, its mysticism, its sheer and mischievous nonsense. The "cultural revolution" of the sixties that took place in San Francisco's Haight Ashbury and at the Straight Theater, where "free love" was never freer and mind-exploding drugs were passed out like so many Tootsie Rolls, was largely street theater. It was, the social perfection of Artaud's dramatic theories. It was indeed, as LaVey has insisted, a kind of psychodrama enacting at the figurative, not the material, level an entire libretto of "discontents," as Freud would have it, concerning civilization. That all ended with Charles Manson.

Manson was not a satanist in the ordinary sense of the word. He was not an aesthetic terrorist. He was an Illuminist bent on changing the makeup of the world. The fact that "Mansonism" in recent years has become indistinguishable from neonazism, which in turn has absorbed LaVey's satanism, should come as no surprise. Manson was not in revolt against the bourgeois. Sharon Tate was not, contrary to the mythology that has evolved about her, cast in her Hollywood heyday as an archetype of Miss American Pie. She was the symbol of a beautiful innocence transfigured into darkness and despoilation—in LaVey's phrase, the "failure of virtue." She was created on the screen to give off airs of witchery as normality.

Her murder by the Manson "creepy-crawlies" was the ritual signature of the turning of America from aesthetic mockery of convention to its underlying secret, that is, the triumph of the predatory beast, of calculated savagery. Despite what the orthodoxy of American social liberalism continues to strut, satanism today is not—if it ever has been—a rejection of middle class values and a somewhat ingenuous expression of chronic adolescent "alienation."

Today's young satanists, as we see so vividly in the life of Pete Roland, are not shaking their fists against a repressive society. They grew up in an era when all the straw men of the old avant-garde had been torn asunder and hurled to the four winds. Roland had no object of rage, except the all-enveloping disorder and turmoil he experienced in every niche of his existence. The turbulence was everywhere—in his family, in his sense of values, in the music. He was the offspring of unrelieved personal terror and confusion, and he found symbolic flesh for that confusion and terror in Jim Hardy's minicult of Satan. He was the "younger brother" of an earlier generation of Charlie Mansons. He was the child of the children of the sixties.

The persistent notion among America's educated elite that satanism is not something substantive or significant, that it is essentially a bugbear of religious rubes, dies hard. Strangely, the *lack* of such a prejudice can be found in an unusual triad of the most incongruous of mentalities—

Christian evangelicals, secular cops, and religious satanists. It was the cops who first confronted the siege. It was the evangelicals who whispered, "I told you so." It was the religious satanists who first denied what was happening, then began to follow the lead of Nikolas Schreck and celebrate what was happening as a millenial new "humanism" of the wolf-man.

In all three instances we have a readiness to acknowledge what postwar American society with its mellow-yellow utopianism of the spirit, with its yearning for God's Kingdom without suffering or grace, has gazed at and blinked. That is, of course, the "fallen" character of human beings. On that score, LaVey has been more of a Presbyterian than most of today's Presbyterians. Let us lust, he has proclaimed. Traditional American liberalism has known only undifferentiated "feelings," not the ragings of the instincts.

In his essay "Gods of the Underworld," Eco has observed, perhaps far more insightfully than Americans themselves, that cultic terrorism has its sources in the ancient constitution of the human psyche. "Normal people try desperately to repress a reality that has been before their eyes for at least two thousand years," he opines. "Refusal to remember these things leads us then to see in terrorist phenomena the hand of the CIA or the Czechs. If only evil really did come always from across the border."[3]

Satanism *is* terrorism. It is the gestation of a permanent terrorist subculture in America that will bring the random violence and political intrigues of the Old World at last to the new. The new Mansonites bear some resemblance to Italy's Red Brigades. They are hardened, without a nagging division of conscience, apocalyptic in their view of matters, and determined.

In one sense, satanic terrorism has come from "across the border" because it was borne on the tide of the corruption of a people by drugs. Matamoros was not a fluke but a portent. Yet the siege itself has been possible because of a population waiting with open arms for the regiments of occupation. America has not truly known evil until today. Today it knows it, and the unnerving truth cannot be wished away.

Dr. Griffis's fourfold typology of satanists may be augmented somewhat to account for its own stated political and revolutionary strategies. Griffis himself has pointed out that the standard usage among certain "experts" of the term *satanic dabblers* is woefully misleading. One does not "dabble" in satanism any more than one "plays around" with heroin. The latter is forthwith addictive. The former creates certain and immediate bondage, as the Tarot card "the Devil" has wryly suggested for centuries. Americans have always sought to contain the threat of evil by means of therapeutic intervention. Therapeutic intervention requires that the subject be tamed, or at least rendered docile, before action is taken. Thus satanism must be reduced, like acne or anorexia, to a manageable adolescent disturbance. Such a posture hinges on the most incredible delusion that the symbol of the Devil does not at all mean what the symbol of the Devil has always meant for peoples, religions, and cultures. For a decade and a half the same myopia prevailed in an effort to "contain" the drug problem. But the problem continued to grow, like poisonous nightshade in the sheltered earthdamp, until it shifted suddenly within the ken of public awareness from a "social concern" to an international enemy with formidable financial clout and military might. The same is happening with satanism. Evil cannot be cajoled.

In order to do justice to what is at stake in the current siege of American culture, we must add to Griffis's categories the notion that satanism is also both *nihilism* and *terrorism* at once. The profile of the nihilist first appeared in the nineteenth century in Dostoyevski's novel *The Devils*. The nihilist is the saint with the yearning for God but with no faith in God. His faith is in politics. Dostoyevski's nihilists were literary versions of the fourteenth-century monster Giles de Rais. Originally the cohort in saintliness of Joan of Arc, de Rais turned his thirst for God upside down into unspeakable cruelty against humanity. A man with the passion for beatitude who gives up on God will become a satanist. There was something of this syndrome in Constanzo, although on the level of popular metaphysics. He became, in effect, something more than a religious huckster or a *narcotraficante*. He became a terrorist. In the last century he would have been called an Illuminist.

All through the seventies, satanism served as a counterreligion that used the marketing genius of LaVey to promote itself through the medium that America knew and loved best—sex, drugs, and rock 'n' roll. Then in the eighties something changed. Something changed drastically. What was called "hard rock" now became heavy metal. And it had a message. The Satan ensconced with the new lyrics became a power rather than merely a verbal cat-o'-nine-tails to flog the ethical sensibilities of the nation. The change was evident in the sound itself. It began with the punk scene. The messages became brawling and brutal. But even more significantly, the sound itself was stripped of all melodic tenor. The decibels and the beats per minute were precipitously increased. The effect was to swathe the brain in constant tonal simulations of fury and venomous anger. The end result is to erode the nervous system with noise, as drugs destroy the cerebrum.

Perhaps that is part of the conditioning process. Satanism may not really be a "religion" after all. Particularly in its musical incarnation, it is a means of propaganda and cultural warfare that is succeeding, as psychologist Edgar Schein would say, in "unfreezing" the prevailing belief systems and moral sensibilities. Satanists per se are not really serious, but the hucksters are. The members of the Matamoros cult were only part-time "believers." Most of the day they were engaged in rural guerilla warfare. Satanism had a purely pragmatic purpose. It enabled them to profit at the dope trade. Many of today's young satanists are not characterized, or motivated, so much by the will to do evil as they are by a metaphysics of exhaustion and hopelessness.

A culture of despair becomes ever easier pickings for the *narcotraficantes*, or the child pornographers or perhaps the professional terrorists themselves. Satanism has already yielded a climate of fear in middle-class quarters where fear had never flourished before. As in the concentration camps or in the torture chambers, pleasure becomes indistinguishable from pain, suffering from salvation. War is peace, and a truth is a lie. Interestingly, LaVey's paradox that freedom is slavery and darkness is light was also the motto of Big Brother in Orwell's *1984.*

Regardless of whether it actually happened, or whether the malefactors were satanists in black robes, stage magicians, or the therapists themselves, the tales told by the children at the McMartin preschool were not much different than the stories recounted by former prisoners-of-war. The common effect of child abuse, totalitarian forms of brainwashing, torture during imprisonment, and what has come to be called satanic ritualism is the obliteration of the normal personality and its replacement by a psychological automaton incapable of sympathy, feeling, or moral discrimination. A pervasive environment of bestiality and horror— Manson's "getting the Fear"—acts as a relentless acid to dissolve the self and refashion it according to the aims and strategies of the terror-craftsman. The old-style theater of horror known as melodrama performed the same function as the ancient Greek tragedies—it purged onlookers of both their emotions and anxieties.

To a large extent, even today's horror movies accomplish this objective. The new-style aesthetic terrorism seeks not to purge but to overwhelm. It succeeds not in relieving the viewer, or the *voyeur*, of his or her primal inhibitions but of confirming them as an indelible psychology of the thought-slave. The outcome of the siege, therefore, would be to bend society to the will of what the occultists themselves have called the "master of fear."

ITEM: In Alexandria, Virginia, two men were arrested by federal agents and held without bail on charges of conspiring to kidnap, molest, and kill a little boy for the making of a pornographic video. U.S. Attorney Henry Hudson said that Dean Lambey, thirty-four, of Richmond, Virginia, and Daniel Depew, twenty-eight, of Alexandria had plotted either to purchase or to abduct a child between the ages of eight and thirteen so that they could tape him while under torture for two weeks. According to Hudson, they had then planned to wash the body in acid to erase all signs of the torture and dump the remains in a marsh outside of Washington, D.C.

The two suspects had allegedly solicited their quarry on a computer bulletin board advertising itself as a resource "to assist people seeking contact with others interested in diverse sexual pursuits," according to police. One of the men had supposedly boasted he could buy a child for only $12,000, according to news reports. The enterprise was initially discovered by an undercover policeman, who turned the matter over to the FBI. Depew, a computer clerk, allegedly stored lurid descriptions of his sadomasochistic acts in a file called "vital info" on an office computer. Lambey reportedly told an undercover cop that "I think the pleasure of doin' it would be worth it."

News accounts of the incident failed to mention whether Lambey knew anything of the philosophy of "do what thou wilt" or whether he had read *The Satanic Bible* and its proposition that "the watchword of Satanism is INDULGENCE." The question, however, was largely irrelevant. Lambey, with or without "theological" justification, had acted on the same principles.

Lambey and Depew never carried through with their alleged scheme. The undercover cop followed them day after day to make sure they did not do what they allegedly said they were going to do. The cop did not consider their sick blustering late at night on-line to be just one more instance of "psychodrama."

That particular story had a happy ending. In the end, the power of evil, no matter how it might be sanitized or rationalized by its apologists, did not prevail.

Another God seemed to have been keeping watch on this occasion.

ITEM: In Salt Lake City, Utah, a group of sociologists of religion told the media that there is "not a shred of evidence" that satanism is a problem in America. David Bromley said at the annual meeting of the Society for the Scientific Study of Religion, held in late 1989, that "evidence disintegrates as close examination occurs" whenever satanism and crime are linked together. Bromley blamed concern about satanism on "collective histeria" generated by the media, Christian fundamentalists, and public overreaction to teenage antics.

James Richardson, another sociologist of religion from the University of Nevada at Reno, observed that the "satan scare" could be attributed primarily to the fundamentalist factor. Fear of satanists "fits neatly" with their "belief structure," he told the *Los Angeles Times*. It is but one of many ways, according to Richardson, of explaining "disturbing, anti-social behavior," the *Times* reported. J. Gordon Melton, director of the Institute for the Study of American Religion in Santa Barbara, California, added that "beyond several informal satanic groups and two or three serial killers . . . the reality of a satanist movement fades out quickly."

ITEM: "Devil worship is a folk myth," insists Shawn Carlson, author of a report issued by the Committee for the Scientific Examination of Religion. "Satanism and satanic crime are not a problem in this country—period. It's a complete farce, and it has caused egregious injury." Such "hysteria" is "spreading fear and mistrust of individuals and legitimate religious groups," Carlson was reported by a columnist for the *Dallas Morning News* to have stated. The same columnist also cited FBI agent Kenneth Lanning as saying that he had "not found evidence of a single true satanic killing in the United States."

ITEM: As Richard Ramirez, also known as "the Night Stalker" was sentenced in September 1989 to death in the gas chamber for butchering and raping more than a dozen people in southern California, he told the court: "Lucifer dwells within us all." Ramirez, who had flashed the devil's sign and shown the press a satanic pentagram on his hand during his 1985 arraignment, also warned that the forces he represented would wreak havoc in the world. At the sentencing Ramirez said, "You don't understand . . . and you are not expected to, you are not capable of it. I am beyond your experience. . . . Legions of the night, night breed. Repeat not the errors of the Night Stalker and show no mercy. I will be avenged."

ITEM: In September 1989 in Portland, Maine, a deaf teenage girl walked into a school to seek help. She had apparently been kidnapped several years earlier and moved around the United States, "possibly by satanists," FBI agent Paul Cavanagh informed the press. "From some of the drawings she was able to provide, it is believed that some of the people she was with since her abduction may have been tied to the occult," the FBI agent said. Cavanagh also said that psychologists and child-care specialists had gathered sufficient information "to believe she was abducted from California" in 1986, according to national wire service news accounts. The girl's story was later discounted.

ITEM: After the U.S. Army raided Panama and found Matamoros-style occult furniture in General Noriega's apartment, one member of the Committee for the Scientific Examination of Religion seemed to shift away from the orthodox view of "no evidence has been found." Gerald Larue, professor emeritus at the University of Southern California and a spokesperson for the committee, told Clifford May, international editor for the *Rocky Mountain News* and former foreign correspondent for the *New York Times*, that the connection between drugs and the occult was "common and easy to understand." The drug lords "appear to be using occult practices primarily as a form of social control within their underground empire," May wrote. According to the *Rocky Mountain News*, Larue apparently agreed. "Drugs induce an altered state of consciousness during which one may be more susceptible to occult rituals and influences," Larue told the Denver-based newspaper.

Even in the most adamant skeptics' minds, there seemed suddenly to be more than a few "shreds of evidence" that satanism was becoming a major national problem.

NOTES

1. Umberto Eco, *Travels in Hyper Reality: Essays*, trans. William Weaver (New York: Harcourt Brace Jovanovich, 1983), p. 80.
2. Ibid., p. 71.
3. Ibid., p. 96.

Sources

CHAPTER 1. THE HORROR

"Aldrete Claims She Was Tortured." *Brownsville Herald*, May 26, 1989.

"Alex Perez Tied the Knot for Aldrete." *Brownsville Herald*, April 20, 1989, p. 1A.

Angelo, Chris. "Sara Says Interpol Official Was in Cult." *Brownsville Herald*, May 14, 1989, p. 1A.

———. "Aldrete Said to Have Three Personalities." *Brownsville Herald*, May 11, 1989, p. 1A.

Baker, Lisa. "Another Hernandez Arrested." *Brownsville Herald*, April 18, 1989, p. 1A.

———. "Bizarre Tale Behind Deadly Cult Continues to Unravel." *Brownsville Herald*, April 16, 1989, p. 1A.

———. "Charges Added, Dropped for Dad of Cult Suspect." *Brownsville Herald*, May 26, 1989, p. 1D.

———. "Constanzo Dead; Aldrete Arrested by Mexico Police." *Brownsville Herald*, May 7, 1989, p. 1A.

———. "Court Papers Claim Torture of Cult Suspects." *Brownsville Herald*, July 2, 1989, p. 1A.

———. "Cult Drug Figure Charged." *Brownsville Herald*, April 26, 1989, p. 1A.

———. "Cult Drug Ring Had Police Ties." *Brownsville Herald*, April 13, 1989, p. 1A.

———. "DEA Doubts Constanzo Really Dead." *Brownsville Herald*, May 8, 1989, p. 1A.

———. "Defendant Linked to Matamoros Cult Files for Gag Order." *Brownsville Herald*, May 16, 1989, p. 1B.

———. "Drug Cult Linked to Chicago Syndicate." *Brownsville Herald*, July 16, 1989, p. 1A.

———. "Henry Cisneros Offers to Help Kilroy Search." *Brownsville Herald*, April 7, 1989, p. 1D.

———. "Hernandez Cops Plea in Marijuana Case." *Brownsville Herald*, July 20, 1989, p. 1A.

———. "Intensive Manhunt Launched." *Brownsville Herald*, April 16, 1989, p. 1A.

———. "Jaramillo 'Godson' Cops Plea, Walks Free." *Brownsville Herald*, July 23, 1989, p. 1A.

——. "Jamarillo Thought to be Linked with Chicago Mob Boss." *Brownsville Herald*, July 18, 1989, p. 1A.

——. "Jaramillo Associate is Linked to Covert Munitions Shipments." *Brownsville Herald*, July 30, 1989, p. 1A.

——. "Kilroy Among 12 Bodies Found at Killing Field." *Brownsville Herald*, April 12, 1989, p. 1A.

——. "Kilroy's Family Members Put Faith in God." *Brownsville Herald*, April 13, 1989.

——. "Lawyer Withdraws from Serafin Hernandez Case." *Brownsville Herald*, June 11, 1989.

——. "New Appeal Made in Kilroy Case." *Brownsville Herald*, April 10, 1989.

——. "Officers Told Not to Discuss Suspect Linked to Cult Case." *Brownsville Herald*, May 26, 1989, p. 1A.

——. "Search Continues for Missing Man." *Brownsville Herald*, March 17, 1989.

——. "Spring Break Marred by Violence." *Brownsville Herald*, March 19, 1989, p. 1A.

——. "Student Missing in Matamoros." *Brownsville Herald*, March 16, 1989, p. 1B.

——. "Valley Company Probed as Front for Drugs Ring." *Brownsville Herald*, July 17, 1989, p. 1A.

Belejack, Barbara. "Mexico City Neighbors Say Constanzo Kept Low Profile." *Dallas Morning News*, May 8, 1989, p. 5A.

Bendel, Mary-Ann. "Killings Aren't Satanic, They're Just Very Sick." *USA Today*, April 19, 1989, p. 7A.

"California Drug Raiders Discover Sacrificial Altar, Skulls and Animal Remains." *Brownsville Herald*, June 18, 1989.

Carney, Dan. "Ortiz Calls for Probe of Occult Worship." *Brownsville Herald*, April 13, 1989.

Cartwright, Gary. "The Work of the Devil." *Texas Monthly*, June, 1989, p. 78.

"Constanzo Cremated and Buried in Florida." *Brownsville Herald*, May 22, 1989.

"Constanzo, 'El Duby' Blamed for Los Sombreros Killings." *Brownsville Herald*, June 14, 1989, p. 1B.

"Constanzo's Body Returned to Miami." *Brownsville Herald*, May 21, 1989.

"Constanzo's Mom Appeals Theft Sentence." *Brownsville Herald*, May 24, 1989.

"Cult Chief Killed in Shootout." *Denver Post*, May 7, 1989, p. 1A.

"Cult Denied Bail." *Brownsville Herald*, May 16, 1989.

"Cult 'Godfather' Banned Use of Drugs by Gang." *Rocky Mountain News*, April 21, 1989, p. 163.

"Cult Moved to Second Prison, Constanzo's Body Unclaimed." *Brownsville Herald*, May 11, 1989, p. 1A.

"Cult Suspect's Relative Charged on 5 Counts." *Brownsville Herald*, May 31, 1989, p. 1B.

"Cult 'Temple' Goes Up in Flames." *Brownsville Herald*, April 24, 1989.

"Cultist Reportedly Ordered Own Death." *Dallas Morning News*, May 8, 1989, p. 1A.

"Cultist Trio Indicted in 15 Murders." *Dallas Morning News*, June 1, 1989.

Dailey, Rickey. "Texas Cults Centered in South of State." *Brownsville Herald*, April 14, 1989.

——. "Warner Bill Passes Committee." *Brownsville Herald*, May 5, 1989, p. 6A.

Davies, Nigel. *Human Sacrifice in History & Today*. New York: William Morrow, 1981.

"Death of Son Bonds Woman Artist to Cult Victim." *Brownsville Herald*, July 24, 1989.

Deutsch, Linda. "Echeverria In-law Held in Camarena Case." *Brownsville Herald*, August 15, 1989, p. 3A.

"Drug Cult May be Linked to $20 Million Houston Cocaine Bust." *Brownsville Herald*, April 19, 1989.

"Drug-running Cultist Ordered His Death." *Denver Post*, May 8, 1989, p. 6A.

"Ex-cop Guilty in DEA Agent's Murder." *Denver Post*, September 23, 1988.

"Extradition Said Unlikely." *Brownsville Herald*, May 9, 1989, p. 1A.

"Fear, Superstition Haunt Site of Cult Murders." *Denver Post*, April 30, 1989, p. 15A.

Flores, Veronica. "Former Satanic Priest Advises Local Parents." *Brownsville Herald*, April 28, 1989, p. 1B.

———. "Leader May Have Controlled Killers." *Brownsville Herald*, April 13, 1989.

———. "Miami Priest Says News Reports Skew View of Santeria." *Brownsville Herald*, April 16, 1989.

———. "Tamaulipas Want Suspects Extradited." *Brownsville Herald*, May 10, 1989, p. 1A.

"Friends Remember Kilroy With Love." *Brownsville Herald*, April 12, 1989, p. 1B.

Garza-Trejo, Hector F. "Under Mexican Legal System Cult Slayings Trial Likely to Take Year." *Brownsville Herald*, April 19, 1989.

Graving, Patrice. "Kilroys Want Military Aid in the War Against Drugs." *Brownsville Herald*, May 26, 1989.

"Gun and Drug Charges Sent to Grand Jury." *Brownsville Herald*, May 30, 1989, p. 1B.

Hancock, David. "Cult Member Says He Killed Constanzo." *Brownsville Herald*, May 8, 1989, p. 1A.

Hancock, Lee. "FW Devotee Defends Spirit Worship." *Dallas Morning News*, April 16, 1989, p. 13A.

Henneberger, Melinda, "Constanzo Used Charisma to Attract Followers." *Brownsville Herald*, May 15, 1989, p. 5A.

———. "Constanzo's Magic." *Dallas Morning News*, May 14, 1989, p. 1A.

Henneberger, Melinda, and David McLemore. "Fear Born of Rivalry Led to Ritual Killings." *Dallas Morning News*, April 23, 1989, p. 1A.

Hernandez, Basilio. "Big Change Noticed in Suspect." *Brownsville Herald*, April 14, 1989, p. 1A.

———. "Extradition Considered." *Brownsville Herald*, April 12, 1989, p. 1B.

———. "Missing Kilroy at Center of Probe," *Brownsville Herald*, April 16, 1989, p. 1A.

———. "Neighbors Saw Nothing Unusual." *Brownsville Herald*, April 13, 1989.

Herzfelder, Richard. "Mexican Police Raid Cult Residences." *Brownsville Herald*, April 16, 1989.

Hirsley, Michael. "Drug Thugs Seek Safety in Occult." *Chicago Tribune*, April 16, 1989, p. 5.

Hogg, Gary. *Cannibalism and Human Sacrifice*. New York: Citadel Press, 1966.

"How I Escaped a Bloody Sacrifice to the Devil." *Midnight Globe*, May 2, 1989, p. 39.

Hughes, Candace. "Aldrete Charged with Cult Murders." *Brownsville Herald*, June 11, 1989, p. 12A.

Husar, John. "Satanic Cults Growing in Preserves." *Chicago Tribune*, February 26, 1989, p. 16.

Kahn, Robert. "Aldrete Family Says Sara Was Kind and Loving Person." *Brownsville Herald*, April 18, 1989, p. 1A.

———. "Border Patrol Sector Chief Says Constanzo Was Being Probed As Suspect." *Brownsville Herald*, April 20, 1989.

———. "Constanzo Gay, Not a Drug User." *Brownsville Herald*, April 21, 1989, p. 1A.

———. "Cult Slayings Echo Killings in Agua Prieta." *Brownsville Herald*, April 13, 1989, p. 1B.

———. "Cult Victim Had Run-Ins with Both Police and Ring." *Brownsville Herald*, April 21, 1989 P 1B.

———. "Families Say Victims Were Not Into Drugs." *Brownsville Herald*, April 18, 1989, p. 1B.

———. "Police Jefe Believes Sara Aldrete Dead." *Brownsville Herald*, April 18, 1989, p. 1A.

———. "Santa Elena Murders are Result of More than Devil Worship." *Brownsville Herald*, April 16, 1989.

"Kilroy Family Was Extorted." *Brownsville Herald*, April 28, 1989.

"Kilroy's Friends Re-enact Night of Disappearance." *Brownsville Herald*, March 26, 1989, p. 1D.

Komarow, "Ex-Dictator Sought Help in Witchcraft." *Dallas Times-Herald*, December 23, 1989, p. A-1.

"Leader of Cult Ordered Own Death, Cohorts Say." *Rocky Mountain News*, May 8, 1989, p.2.

Levi, Isaac. "Aldrete Says Cult Members Live in Miami." *Brownsville Herald*, May 10, 1989, p. 1A.

"Local Law Enforcement Officers Recognized for Solving Cult Case." *Brownsville Herald*, May 28, 1989.

Longoria, Arturo N., and John Hamilton. "3 Ranches Raided, No Suspects Found." *Brownsville Herald*, April 18, 1989, p. 1B.

"Lucas Map Said to Show Border Cult Activities." *Brownsville Herald*, April 21, 1989, p. 8A.

Luque, Sulipsa. "Aldrete's Neighbors Express Disbelief." *Brownsville Herald*, May 8, 1989.

———. "Businesses Have Mixed Reaction to Killings." *Brownsville Herald*, April 16, 1989.

———. "Cult Suspect Attorney Seeks Protective Order." *Brownsville Herald*, May 24. 1989, p. 1B.

———. "Cult Suspects Given Hearing." *Brownsville Herald*, June 20, 1989, p. 3.

———. "Cult Suspects to Get Hearing." *Brownsville Herald*, June 16, 1989, p. 1B.

———. "Five Cult Suspects' Custody Status to be Decided Today." *Brownsville Herald*, April 21, 1989, p. 1B.

———. "Legal Confrontations in Cult Case Continue." *Brownsville Herald*, June 21, 1989, p. 1B.

———. "Matamoros Surprised and Saddened by Mass Killings." *Brownsville Herald*, April 12, 1989, p. 2A.

———. "Policeman is Arrested in Cult Case." *Brownsville Herald*, May 17, 1989, p. 1A.

———. "Ritual Killings Suspects Charged." *Brownsville Herald*, April 19, 1989, p. 1A.

Macias, Anna. "Alleged Witch Says She Was Tricked, Held by Cult." *Dallas Morning News*, May 9, 1989, p. 1A.

———. "Constanzo Dead, Sara Maintains She is Innocent." *Brownsville Herald*, May 9, 1989, p. 1A.

———. "Constanzo's Welcome: 'This is the House of the Devil.'" *Dallas Morning News*, May 14, 1989, p. 28A.

———. "Cult 'witch' Allegedly Ordered Leader's Death." *Dallas Morning News*, May 11, 1989, p. 22A.

Marcus, David L. "Lifestyle of the Rich, Infamous." *Dallas Morning News*, December 29, 1989, p. 1A.

McCullen, Kevin. "Cultists May Follow Drug Routes Into State." *Rocky Mountain News*, April 15, 1989, p.8.

McLemore, David, and Lee Hancock. "Cult Crimes Rising." *Dallas Morning News*, April 16, 1989, p. 1A.

———. "Procedure in Case Not Yet Clear." *Dallas Morning News*, May 8, 1989, p. 6A.

Medina, Dolissa. "Kilroy Campaign Seeking Effective Anti-Drug Policy." *Brownsville Herald*, July 3, 1989.

"Mexico Farm Yields a 13th Body." *USA Today*, April 14, 1989, p. 3A.

"Missing Student's Mother Prays for His Safe Return." *Brownsville Herald*, March 21, 1989.

"Missing Student's Parents Return Home." *Brownsville Herald*, April 3 1989.

Moore, Evan. "Satanism Probed in Florida Keys Killings." *Houston Chronicle*, September 24, 1989, p. 11A.

"More than 1000 Gather for Kilroy Funeral." *Dallas Morning News*, April 16, 1989, p. 15A.

Murphy, Joseph M. *Santeria: An African Religion in America.* Boston: Beacon Press, 1988.

"Official Linked to Cult." *Rocky Mountain News*, May 13, 1989, p. 50.

"People Pray for Slaying Victims, Cities." *Brownsville Herald*, April 17, 1989.

Pitkin, Thomas Monroe, and Francesco Cordasc. *The Black Hand: A Chapter in Ethnic Crime.* Totowa, NJ: Rowman and Littlefield, 1977.

"Police Continue Hunt for Student." *Brownsville Herald*, March 20,1989.

Ragan, Tom. "Botched Drug Deal, Cultist Linked." *Brownsville Herald*, April 14, 1989.

———. "Cultists Practiced Deviant Form of Palo Mayombe." *Brownsville Herald*, April 25, 1989, p. 1A.

———. "Family Has No Body Bag in Which to Bury Son, 14." *Brownsville Herald*, April 13, 1989, p. 1A.

———. "Matamoros Killings Spur Run on Cult Movie." *Brownsville Herald*, April 19, 1989, p. 1B.

———. "Suspect Says He Was Unaware Slaying Victim Was His Cousin." *Brownsville Herald*, April 17, 1989, p. 1A.

———. "The Search for Missing Relatives." *Brownsville Herald*, April 16, 1989, p. 1D.

Ragan, Tom, and Veronica Flores. "Slayings Are Called a Combination of Devil Worshipping Acts." *Brownsville Herald*, April 12, 1989.

"Ranch Booze May have Been Hallucinogen." *Brownsville Herald*, April 13, 1989.

Reaves, Gayle. "Lucas Says Cult Inspired Killings." *Fort Worth Star-Telegram*, April 22, 1984, p. 17.

Rendon, Ruth. "Kilroy to Bennett: Drug Policy Not Working." *Brownsville Herald*, July 19, 1989, p. 3A.

———. "Kilroy's Hometown in Shocked Mourning." *Brownsville Herald*, April 12, 1989.

Rivas, Maggie. "Cult Killing Suspect's Attorney Alleges Torture." *Brownsville Herald*, May 21, 1989.

———. "Matamoros Residents Relieved as Bloody Saga Comes to an End." *Dallas Morning News*, May 8, 1989, p. 6A.

Rowley, Storer H. "Mexico's President Invades Capital of Narcotics Traffic." *Chicago Tribune*, April 16, 1989, p. 5.

Ryan, Michael. "Manuel's Black Magic." *People,* January 22, 1990, p. 41.

Schutze, Jim. *Cauldron of Blood.* New York: Avon Books, 1989.

Shannon, Elaine. *Desperados.* New York: Viking, 1988.

Spense, Lewis. *The Magic and Mysteries of Mexico.* Philadelphia: David McKay, 1931.

"Suspected Leader of Drug Cult Grew Up in a Santeria Family." *Brownsville Herald*, April 13, 1989, p. 1A.

Swartz, Mike. "False Rumors Panic Many Valley Schools." *Brownsville Herald*, April 14, 1989, p. 1B.

Thatcher, Rebecca. "City Leaders Slam Geraldo's Cult Interviews." *Brownsville Herald*, April 20, 1989.

———. "Ritual Slaying Suspects Presumed Guilty by Judge." *Brownsville Herald*, April 23, 1989.

———. "Sara Aldrete Warned People Not to Touch Her Strange Pendants." *Brownsville Herald*, April 14, 1989, p. 1A.

———. "Teachers Say Matamoros Killings Should be Discussed." *Brownsville Herald*, April 13, 1989.

Thatcher, Rebecca, and Veronica Flores. "City Relieved at News." *Brownsville Herald*, May 8, 1989.

Trejo, Hector F. Garza. "Love, Faith and Forgiveness Urged by Mother of Slain Mark Kilroy." *Brownsville Herald*, April 14, 1989, p. 1A.

"2 Arrest Warrants Issued." *Brownsville Herald*, April 13, 1989.

Vaidhyanathan, Siva. "2 Bodies Found Near Matamoros." *Dallas Morning News*, April 17, 1989, p. 1A.

———. "4 Victims Were Double-Crossed Drug Dealers, Police Say." *Dallas Morning News*, April 16, 1989, p.14A.

Verrengia, Joseph B. "Gory Facet of Anasazi Surfaces." *Rocky Mountain News*, March 26, 1989, p. 20.

Vindell, Tony. "Cult Slaying Suspects Due to be Charged." *Brownsville Herald*, April 17, 1989, p. 1A.

———. "$15000 Reward Offered for Kilroy." *Brownsville Herald*, March 22, 1989, p. 1B.

———. "Grand Jurors in U.S. Indict Cult Suspects." *Brownsville Herald*, April 19, 1989, p. 1A.

———. "Grisly Site Surrounded by Tranquility." *Brownsville Herald*, April 12, 1989, p. 1A.

———. "Killing Ranch to be Excavated." *Brownsville Herald*, April 14, 1989.

———. "Kilroys Want to Take Son Home." *Brownsville Herald*, March 24, 1989.

———. "No Leads Yet in Kilroy Case." *Brownsville Herald*, March 21, 1989.

———. "Probe of Cult Drug Smuggling Continues in Mexico." *Brownsville Herald*, April 20, 1989, p. 1A.

———. "Suspects Tell of Kidnapping Mark Kilroy in Matamoros." *Brownsville Herald*, April 13, 1989, p. 1A.

———. "Suspects to be Tried by Napoleonic Code." *Brownsville Herald*, April 18, 1989, p. 1B.

———. "Three victims of Cult Killings Had Crime Ties." *Brownsville Herald*, April 16, 1989, p. 1A.

Wiest, Stephen. "Witches Pay Homage to Satan." *Milwaukee Journal*, November 1, 1975, p. 4.

Woodbury, Richard, "Cult of the Red-Haired Devil." *Time*, April 24, 1989, p. 30.

Yanez, Luisa. "Santeria to be Court Issue." *Brownsville Herald*, July 30, 1989, p.4A.

CHAPTER 2. MURDER ON MAIN STREET

Allsopp, Fred W. *Albert Pike: A Biography*. Little Rock, AR: Parke-Harper, 1928.

Bell, Leland V. *In Hitler's Shadow: The Anatomy of American Nazism*. Port Washington, NY: Kennikat Press, 1973.

Carl Junction Police Department. Advice of rights, Brent Dunham, December 8, 1987.

Carl Junction Police Department. Advice of Rights, Ronald Clements, December 8, 1987.

Carl Junction High School, Pupil records of Theron (Pete) Reed Roland, 1981–1987.

Chalmers, David Mark. *Hooded Americanism: The History of the Ku Klux Klan*. New York: Franklin Watts, 1981.

Daniel, A.E. Psychiatric evaluation, Theron Reed Roland II, January 17, 1988.

Dumenil, Lynn. *American Culture: 1880-1930*. Princeton: Princeton University Press, 1984.

Hardy, James. Letter to Theron Roland, February 18, 1988, postmark date.

———. Letter to Theron Roland, February 22, 1988, postmark date.

———. Letter to Theron Roland, March 7, 1988, postmark date.

———. Letter to Theron Roland, March 10, 1988, postmark date.

———. Letter to Theron Roland, March 12, 1988, postmark date.

———. Letter to Theron Roland, March 21, 1988, postmark date.

Hayes, Angela. Statement, December 11, 1988.

Hayes, Pat, and Ray Youngblood. Office of the Prosecuting Attorney, Interview with Brent Dunham.

———. Office of the Prosecuting Attorney. Interview with Jackie Slanger, May 23, 1988.

———. Office of the Prosecuting Attorney. Investigation reports, *State v. Theron Reed Roland II; State v. James Hardy; State v. Ron Clements*, December 8, 1987–April 6, 1988.

———. Office of the Prosecuting Attorney. Statement, Lance Michael Owens, December 14, 1987.

———. Hayes, Pat, Office of the Prosecuting Attorney, Statement, Theron Reed Roland II, December 8, 1987.

Heffland, Jack. Statement.

Higgins, Terry. Statement.

Imersol, Russ. Statement.

Jasper County Sheriff Dept. Evidence analysis report, case no. 87–1717, December 8, 1987.

Jones, Tamara. "Dead Pets to a Human Sacrifice." *Los Angeles Times*, October 18, 1988, p. 1.

———. "'Fun' Killers Now Paying Devil's Dues." *Los Angeles Times*, October 20, 1988, p. 1.

Lester, J. C., and D. L. Wilson. *Ku Klux Klan: Its Origin, Growth and Disbandment.* St. Clair Shores, MI: Scholarly Press, 1972.

Logan, William S. Diagnostic interview report on Ronald Charles Clements, January 26, 1988; March 12, 1988.

McDonald, Margaret E., M.D. Pathologist. Jasper County coroner's report, case number 91, December 8, 1987.

Meninger Clinic. Diagnostic interview report, psychiatric evaluation, Theron (Pete) Roland, January 25, 1988.

Missouri Police Department. Statement of rights, Pete Roland, December 8, 1987.

Parrill, Larry. Jasper County Sheriff Dept. Homicide report, December 8, 1987.

Pulling, Pat. List of articles found in Pete Roland's room, June 6, 1988.

Randolph, Mike, and Ray Youngblood. Interview with Ronald Charles Clements, December 7, 1987.

———. Interview with Ronald Charles Clements, December 8, 1987.

Randolph, Mike, and Jim Wiseman. Interview with Terra Smith, December 7, 1987.

Randolph, Mike. Officer, Jasper County Sheriff Dept. Offense report, case no. DR87–1717, December 7, 1987.

Roland, Theron Reed, II. School notebook and sketches, 1987.

———. Song lyrics written down, 1987.

State of Missouri, Dept. of Mental Health. Medical and psychiatric assessment, December 29, 1987.

State of Missouri v. James Hardy. Transcript of guilty plea, case no. CR188–1FX, April 29, 1988.

———. Warrant in felony case, no. CR487–1000F, December 8, 1987.

State of Missouri v. Ronald Charles Clements. Preliminary hearing transcript, case no. CR487–999F, December 30, 1987.

State of Missouri v. Theron Reed Roland II. Warrant in felony case, no. CR487–1001F, December 8, 1987.

Stowe, Douglas R. Statement, December 8, 1987.

Tourgee, Albion W. *The Invisible Empire: A Concise Review of the Epoch.* Ridgewood, NJ: Gregg Press, 1968.

Wiseman, Jim. Officer, Carl Junction Police Dept. Offense report, case no. 1987–371, December 8, 1987.

Wood, Brent. Statement, June 13, 1988.

Youngblood, Ray. Jasper County Sheriff Dept. Homicide of Steven Newberry, case#DR87–1717.

Youngblood, Ray, and Jim Wiseman. Interview with Jerry Dale Hoffman.

———. Interview with Jerry Dale Hoffman.

CHAPTER 3. BAD MOON RISING

Allen, Carole with Pat Metoyer. "Crimes of the Occult." *Police*, February 1987.

Anderle, Ruth Ann. "Spouse Guilty of First-Degree Murder." (Nederland, CO) *The Mountain Ear*, October 12, 1989, p. 5.

Andersen, Susan M., and Phillip G. Zim. "Resisting Mind Control." *USA Today*, November, 1980.

Bailey, Karen. "Lawyer: Warnings Unheeded in Slaying." *Rocky Mountain News*, February 18, 1986.

Barry, Robert J. "Satanism: The Law Enforcement Response." *National Sheriff*, February-March 1987.

Belko, Mark, and Henry W. Pierce. "Counselors See Rise in Teen Drug Cults." *Pittsburgh Post-Gazette*, December 13, 1988.

Berg, Melissa. "Fascination With Occult Spans Centuries." *Kansas City Times*, March 26, 1988, p. A19.

———. "Satanic Crime Increasing? Police, Therapists Alarmed." *Kansas City Times*, March 26, 1988, p. A1.

———. "Therapists Unlock, Heal Horrors of Satanic Abuse." *Kansas City Times*, March 26, 1988.

Boyer, Peter J. "Program on Satan Worship Spurs Controversy at NBC." *New York Times*, October 26, 1988, p. D1.

Brennan, Charlie. "Killer Blames Satan for Turn to Crime." *Rocky Mountain News*, Mar. 16, 1987.

———. "Police Battling Satan's Evil Shadow." *Rocky Mountain News*, March 15, 1987.

Cares, Clark H. "Evidence of Satanism Turning Up in American Forks Area, Police Chief Says." (Salt Lake City) *Deseret News*, May 8,1986.

Carroll, Peter. "Cult Crimes." *San Francisco Magazine*, August 1987, p.20.

Charlier, Tom. "Links to Abuse of Children Hard to Prove." *Commercial Appeal*, January 18, 1988.

Charlier, Tom, and Shirley Downing. "Facts, Fantasies Caught in Tangled Web." *Commercial Appeal*, January 17, 1988.

Clark, Jacob R. "On the Investigative Trail with Occult Cops." (New York) *Law Enforcement News*, November 15, 1988, p. 1.

———. "The Macabre Faces of Occult-Related Crime." (New York) *Law Enforcement News*, October 31, 1988, p. 1.

Como, John J. "Satanism Tales Make County Lawmen Uneasy." *Indiana Tribune-Democrat*, March 2, 1989, p. B1.

Cracraft, Jane. "Detectives Learn Manning Was Involved in Witchcraft." *Denver Post*, October 21, 1983.

Crutchfield, Catherine. "California Police Finding Evidence of Satanic Cults With Links to Crimes." *Crime Control Digest*, May 14, 1984.

Cult Awareness Network. "Teen Satanism Evident Across the Country." *CAN News*, January 1989.

Culver, Virginia. "Satanists' Mood Devilish on 'Dark Holiday.'" *Denver Post*, April 30, 1987.

"Drifter Anxious to Plead Guilty, His Sister Claims." (Colorado Springs) *Gazette Telegraph*, September 29, 1985.

"Drug Agents Arrest 3, Seize Satanic Material in Weld." *Rocky Mountain News*, August 27, 1985.

"Drug Dealers Try Black Magic as Police Repellant." *Tampa Tribune*, October 30, 1983.

Dunn, Darrell. "Police Learn to Identify Satanism." *Dallas Times Herald*, May 8, 1988.

Emery, Erin. "Stolen Gun Used in Five Grisly Deaths." (Colorado Springs) *Gazette Telegraph*, May 20, 1986.

"Father Says Satanism, Drugs Drove Son to Murder, Suicide." *Denver Post*, July 10, 1984.

Fiore, Faye. "In Search of Satan." (Torrance, CA) *Daily Breeze*, no. 90, 1985.

———. "Satanists Denounce Bizarre Behavior." (Torrance, CA) *Daily Breeze*, March 31, 1985.

Fleming, Jon. "Devil Worhip Tied to Bizarre Maine Murder." *Rocky Mountain News*, November 18, 1984.

Flood, Mary. "Devil Worship: What's Behind It?" *Houston Post*, September 15, 1985, p. 1A.

French, Ron. "It's an Evil World Out there." (Fort Wayne, IN) *News-Sentinel*, November, 1988.

Gilpin County (Colorado) court report, February 21, 1989.

Gosliner, Kathy. "Unlikely Group Gathers to Call on Satan For Help." *Rocky Mountain News*, July 22, 1973.

"Grand Jury Lacks Evidence for Charges in N.M. Slayings." *Rocky Mountain News*, November 29, 1986.

Griffis, D. W. *"Four Faces of Satan."* Tiffin, OH: D. W. G. Enterprises, 1989.

Hawthorne, Michael. "Governor Gets Satanic Crimes Bills." *Chicago Sun-Times*, June 26, 1989, p. 14.

Heckelthorn, Charles William. *The Secret Societies of All Ages and Countries.* New York: University Books, 1965.

"Ignacio Parents Reassured on Cults." *Rocky Mountain News*, July 15, 1989, p. 44.

"Jailed Teen Tied to Satan Cult Found Hanged." *Rocky Mountain News*, July 8, 1984.

Jimison, Susan. "Shrink Says Most Crazy People are Possessed by the Devil." *Weekly World News*, May 9, 1989.

Jones, Rebecca. "Abuse Experts Say McMartin Taught Lesson." *Rocky Mountain News*, January 19, 1990, p. 2.

Jones, Tamara. "Dead Pets to a Human Sacrifice." *Los Angeles Times*, October 19, 1988, p. 1.

Kult, Ann Heise. "Teen-agers' Satanism Interest Concerns Cedar Falls Officials." (Iowa) *Waterloo Courier*, April 27, 1986.

Lanning, Kenneth V. *"Satanic, Occult, Ritualistic Crime: A Law Enforcement Perspective."* Quantico, VA: FBI Academy, 1989.

LaVey, Anton Szandor. *The Satanic Bible.* New York: Avon Books, 1970.

Lenihan, Robert. "Cults Prevail Throughout Monroe, Official Says." (Stoudsburg, PA) *Pocono Record,* July 27, 1989, p. A1.

———. "Satanic Evidence Seized by Police." (Stroudsburg, PA) *Pocono Record,* July 28, 1989, p. A1.

———. "3 Charged in Satanic Cult Kidnapping." (Stroudsburg, PA) *Pocono Record,* July 26, 1989, p. A1.

Lilly, Jeff. "Evil in the Land." *Moody,* March 1989.

"Man Charged in Decapitation Murder." *Tampa Tribune,* March 3, 1985.

Marty, Martin E. "Who Corners the Market on Morality?" *Context,* August 15, 1986.

Miniclier, Kit. "Denver Man Found Dead; Teens Held." *Denver Post,* July 29, 1989, p. 1-A.

Morch, Al. "Is Brainwashing Possible?" *Santa Clara Magazine,* Summer, 1988.

Multimedia Entertainment. "Donahue Transcript #02136." 1984.

Mundy, John Hine. *The Repression of Catharism at Toulousse.* Toronto: Pontifical Institute of Mediaeval Studies, 1985.

Murphy, Pat. "Suspect Decribes Indiana Devil Worship." (Fort Wayne, IN) *News Sentinel,* January 13, 1984.

Nafsinger, Janie. "Crowd Jams to Hear the Evils of Rock." (Klamath Falls, OR) *Herald and News,* February 11, 1988.

Naysmith, Bette. "Letter to Mayor Richad M. Daley." Chicago: May 19, 1989.

"Night Stalker' Victim Clings to Life." *Rocky Mountain News,* August 27, 1985, p. 24.

Norris, Joel, *Serial Killers: The Growing Menace,* New York: Doubleday, 1988.

Parker, Eric. "Firestone Pair Jailed in 1982 Murder." (Colorado) *Longmont Times-Call.* March 22, 1989, P. 1.

Pollack, Susan R. "Devil Cult 'Explored' in Slayings." *Detroit News,* June 20, 1983.

"Preschool Operator Files Lawsuit." *Rocky Mountain News,* January 20, 1990, p. 42.

Raschke, Carl. "Satanism is a Symptom of Society's Moral Rot." *Gazette Telegraph,* June 3, 1988.

"Ramirez Pleads Innocent." (Colorado Springs) *Gazette Telegraph,* October 25, 1985.

Rice, Daniel. "Satanism Reports Concern Local Officials." *Charleston Daily Mail,* May 5, 1988.

Richman, Alan. "Haunted by Dark Suspicions, an Indiana Lawman Digs into a Mystery of Empty Graves." *People,* March 14, 1988.

Robey, Renate. "Defendant Not Smart Enough to Plan Murder, Lawyer Says." *The Denver Post,* October 20, 1989, p. 1B.

Ryckman, Lisa Levitt. "Satanic Teen Crimes Jolt Parents to Reality." (Vancouver, WA) *Columbian,* February 14, 1988.

"School Bomber Unstoppable, Friend Says." *Rocky Mountain News,* May 20, 1986.

Scruggs, Kathy. "Teen Fascination with the Occult Linked to Crimes Across Georgia." *Atlanta Constitution,* February 8, 1988, p. A1.

"Second Blaze Guts Boulder Fraternity Home." (Colorado Springs) *Gazette Telegraph,* November 11, 1985.

Shaw, Kent M. "Falling Prey to Satanism?" *Burlington Free Press*, January 17, 1988, p. 1A.

Simborski, Rosannie. "Parents, Teacher Urge Action Against Satanism." *Fort Collins Coloradoan*, March 20, 1988.

Singer, Margaret Thaler. "Coming Out of the Cults." *Psychology Today*, January, 1979.

Skertic, Mark. "Some Criminals Drawn to Satanism." *Fort Wayne Journal-Gazette*, May 6, 1988.

Spiritual Counterfeits Project. "Satanism & Neo-Paganism." Professional Seminar, March 6–7, 1986.

"Stalker: Slow Pace of Trial Tests Courts." *Los Angeles Times*, July 17, 1988, p. 1.

Stewart, Richard. "Officers Training to Beat the Devil." *Dallas Morning News*, May 28, 1989.

Stowers, Carlton. "Satanic Curses." *D Magazine*, June 1989.

Swickard, Joe. "Policewoman, Companion Face Trial in Satanic Sex Rituals Case." *Detroit Free Press*, June 21, 1983.

Szechenyi, Chris. "Deadly Rites: Satanism in the Suburbs." (Illinois) *Sunday Herald*, February 16, 1986, p. 1-1.

"Teen Gets 50 Years in Satanic Slaying." *Florida Times-Union*, May 26, 1989, p. B–6.

"Teen-age Loners Drawn to Satanism." (Stroudsburg, PA) *Pocono Record*, July 27, 1989, p. A1.

Tunnicliff, Robin. "Friends Deny Boys Belong to Cult." (Stroudsburg, PA) *Pocono Record*, August 1, 1989, p. 15.

———. "Man Denies Involvement in Satanic Activities." (Stroudsburg, PA) *Pocono Record*, July 30, 1989.

"Two Acquitted in Child Abuse." *Rocky Mountain News,* January 19, 1990, p. 2.

"2 Devil-Worshippers Found Slain in Castle Home." *Ft. Lauderdale News and Sun-Sentinel*, December 19, 1982.

"2 Teen-agers Held in Satanic Killing." *Rocky Mountain News*, July 8, 1984.

"12 Jurors Suspended in Time." *The Denver Post*, January 19, 1990, p. 16A.

Westin, Av, executive producer. "The Devil Worshippers." Transcript for *20/20*, ABC News, May 16, 1985.

Whitmire, John. "Satanic Youths Unnerve El Paso." *Houston Post*, February 23, 1986, p. 1D.

"Young Suspect in Cult Murder Kills Himself." *Tampa Tribune*, July 8, 1984.

CHAPTER 4. THE OCCULT UNDERWORLD

Arnold, Benjamin. *German Knighthood* 1050–1300. Oxford: Clarendon Press, 1985.

Brooks, Geraldine. "This Iraqi Sect Has a Devilish Time Explaining Itself." *Wall Street Journal*, June 2, 1989, p. 1.

Chancellor, E. Beresford. *The Hell Fire Club*. Volume 4, *The Lives of the Rakes*. London: Philip Allan, 1925.

Crowley, Aleister. *The Diary of a Drug Fiend*. York Beach, ME: Samuel Weiser, 1987.

———. *The Works of Aleister Crowley*, London: Foyers, 1905.

Danilewicz, M. L. "'The King of the New Israel': Thaddeus Grabianka (1740–1807)." *In Oxford Slavonic Papers.* Vol. I, 1968, p. 49.

Daraul, Arkon. *A History of Secret Societies.* New York: Citadel Press, 1961.

Drury, Nevill. *The Occult Experience: Magic in the New Age.* New York: Avery Publishing Group, 1989.

Emmanuel, Pierre. *Baudelaire: The Paradox of Redemptive Satanism.* Birmingham, AL: University of Alabama Press, 1970.

Goodrick-Clarke, Nicholas. *The Occult Roots of Nazism: The Ariosophists of Austria and Germany,* 1890–1935. Wellingborough, Northamptonshire, England: Aquarian Press, 1985.

Grant, Kenneth. *Outside The Circles of Time.* London: Frederick Mullen, 1980.

Grinspoon, Lester and James B. Bakalar. *Cocaine: A Drug and Its Social Evolution.* New Hyde Park, NY: Basic Books, 1976.

Heckethorn, Charles William. *The Secret Societies of All Ages and Countries.* New Hyde Park, NY: University Books, 1965.

Howe, Ellic. *The Magicians of the Golden Dawn.* York Beach, ME: Samuel Weiser, 1972.

Huysmans, J. K. *La Bas* (Down There). Dover ed. New York: Dover Publications, 1972.

King, Francis. *The Magical World of Aleister Crowley.* 1st American ed. New York: Coward, McCann & Geoghegan, 1978.

LaVey, Anton Szandor. *The Satanic Bible,* New York: Avon Books, 1970.

———. *The Satanic Rituals: Companion to The Satanic Bible,* New York: Avon Books, 1972.

Lambert, Malcolm. *Medieval Heresy: Popular Movements from Bogomil to Hus.* New York: Holmes & Meier Publishers, 1976.

Leary, Timothy. *Flashbacks: An Autobiography.* Los Angeles: J. P. Tarcher, 1983.

Levi, Eliphas. *Transcendental Magic.* Chicago: de Laurence Company, 1910.

Mannix, Daniel P. *The Hell Fire Club.* New York: Ballantine Books, 1959.

McCormick, Donald. *The Hell-Fire Club: The Story of the Amorous Knights of Wycombe.* London: Jarrolds Publishers, 1958.

Michaels, Jason. *The Devil is Alive and Well and Living in America Today.* New York: Award Books, 1973.

Monaco, James. *The New Wave: Truffaut, Godard, Chabrol, Rohmer, Rivette.* New York: Oxford University Press, 1976.

Moore, R.I, *The Origins of European Descent,* New York: Basil Blackwell, 1985.

Partner, Peter. *The Murdered Magicians: The Templars and Their Myth.* New York: Oxford University Press, 1982.

Percival, Harold Waldwin. *Masonry and its Symbols.* 4th ed. Dallas: Word Foundation, 1979.

Peters, Edward. *Heresy and Authority in Medieval Europe.* Philadelphia: University of Pennsylvania Press, 1980.

Regardie, Israel. *The Eye in the Triangle: An Interpretation of Aleister Crowley.* Las Vegas, NV: Falcon Press, 1989.

———. *What You Should Know About the Golden Dawn.* 3rd ed. Phoenix, AZ: Falcon Press, 1985.

Rhodes, Henry T. F. *The Satanic Mass.* Rev. ed. London: Arrow Books, 1973.

Roberts, J. M. *The Mythology of the Secret Societies.* New York: Charles Scribner's Sons, 1972.

Rose, Elliot. *A Razor for a Goat.* Toronto: University of Toronto Press, 1962.

Russell, Jeffrey B. *A History of Witchcraft: Sorcerers, Heretics, and Pagans.* London: Thames and Hudson, 1980.

Sanders, Ed. *The Family: The Story of Charles Manson's Dune Buggy Attack Battalion.* New York: E. P. Dutton, 1971.

Symonds, John, and Kenneth Grant. *The Confessions of Aleister Crowley: An Autohagiography.* New York: Hill and Wang, 1969.

Webb, James. *The Occult Establishment.* La Salle, IL: Library Press Book, 1976.

Wilson, Colin. *Aleister Crowley: The Nature of the Beast.* Wellingborough, Northamptonshire, England: Aquarian Press, 1987.

Zacharias, Gerhard. *The Satanic Cult.* London: George Allen & Unwin, 1980.

CHAPTER 5. THE AESTHETICS OF TERROR

Abrahams, Edward. *The Lyrical Left.* Charlottesville: University Press of Virginia, 1986.

Artaud, Antonin. *Selected Writings.* (trans. Helen Weaver) New York: Farrar, Straus, and Giroux, 1976.

————. *The Cenci.* (trans. Simon Watson Taylor) 1st Evergreen ed. New York: Grove Press, 1970.

Atkins, Susan, with Bob Slosser. *Child of Satan, Child of God.* Plainfield, NJ: Logos International, 1977.

Bainbridge, William Sims. *Satan's Power: A Deviant Psychotherapy Cult.* Berkeley: University of California Press, 1978.

Bermel, Albert. *Artaud's Theatre of Cruelty.* New York: Taplinger Publishing, 1977.

Boyers, Robert. *After the Avant-Garde.* University Park, PA: Pennsylvania State University Press, 1988.

Brown, Marilyn R. *Gypsies and Other Bohemians.* Ann Arbor, MI: UMI Research Press, 1985.

"California Evil." *Esquire*, March, 1970, p. 99.

Cate, Phillip Dennis, ed. *The Graphic Arts and French Society, 1871–1914.* New Brunswick, NJ: Rutgers University Press, 1988.

Crane, Diana. *The Transformation of the Avant-Garde.* Chicago: University of Chicago Press, 1987.

Esslin, Martin. *Antonin Artaud.* New York: Penguin Books, 1977.

Ferguson, Andrew. "Mad About Mapplethorpe." *National Review.* August 4, 1989, p. 20.

Fox, Howard N. *Avant-Garde in the Eighties.* Los Angeles: Los Angeles County Museum of Art, 1987.

Grant, Kenneth. *Outside the Circles of Time.* London: Frederick Muller, 1980.

Greenberg, Allan Carl. *Artists and Revolution: Dada and the Bauhaus, 1917–1925.* Ann Arbor, MI: UMI Research Press, 1979.

Hatfield, Julie. "Anything-but-basic Black." *Boston Globe*, July 19, 1989, p. 75.

Hayman, Ronald. *Artaud and After.* Oxford: Oxford University Press, 1977.

Innes, Christopher. *Holy Theatre: Ritual and the Avant Garde.* New York: Cambridge University Press, 1981.

Knapp, Bettina L. *Antonin Artaud: Man of Vision.* Chicago: Swallow Press, 1980.

Lacayo, Richard. "Leatherboy and Angel in One." *Time*, August 22, 1988, p. 74.

Leavens, Ileana B. *From "291" to Zurich: The Birth of Dada*. Ann Arbor, MI: UMI Research Press, 1983.

Lyons, Arthur. *The Second Coming: Satanism in America*. New York: Dodd, Mead, 1970.

Mano, D. Keith. "Detente with Satan." *National Review*, May 24, 1974, p. 595.

Marcus, Greil. *Lipstick Traces: A Secret History of the Twentieth Century*. Cambridge, MA: Harvard University Press, 1989.

Monaco, James. *The New Wave: Truffaut, Godard, Chabrol, Rohmer, Rivette*. New York: Oxford University Press, 1976.

Moravia, Alberto. "The Terrorist Aesthetic Of Artists, Stockbrokers, and Other Jacobins." *Harper's*, June 1987.

Parfrey, Adam, ed. *Apocalypse Culture*. New York: Amok Press, 1987.

"The Pleasure of the Chase." *Newsweek*, January 30, 1989, p. 82.

Poggioli, Renato. *The Theory of the Avant-Garde*. Cambridge, MA: Harvard University Press, 1968.

Quinlan, David. *Wicked Women of the Screen*. New York: St. Martin's Press, 1987.

Sanders, Ed. *The Family: The Story of Charles Manson's Dune Buggy Attack Battallion*. New York: E. P. Dutton, 1971.

Shattuck, Roger. *The Banquet Years*. Rev. ed. New York: Vintage Books, 1968.

Sikorski, Radek. "The Last Battle?" *National Review*, August 4, 1989, p. 19.

Sitney, P. Adams. *Visionary Film*. New York: Oxford University Press, 1974.

Sontag, Susan, ed. *Antonin Artaud: Selected Writings*. New York: Farrar, Straus and Giroux, 1976.

Terry, Maury. *The Ultimate Evil*. New York: Doubleday, 1987.

Timms, Edward, and Peter Collier. *Visions and Blueprints*. New York: Manchester University Press, 1988.

Webb, James. *The Occult Establishment*. La Salle, IL: Open Court Publishing, 1976.

Weiley, Susan. "Prince of Darkness, Angel of Light." *Artnews*, December 1988, p. 106.

Wellwarth, George. *The Theater of Protest and Paradox*. Rev. ed. New York: New York University Press, 1971.

"When the Worlds of Art and Politics Collide." *New York Times*, July 9, 1989, p. H1.

Zaehner, R. C. "The Wickedness of Evil: On Manson, Murder & Mysticism." *Encounter*, April, 1974, p.50.

CHAPTER 6. THE AGE OF SATAN

Alexander, S. "The Ping is the Thing." *Life*, February 17, 1967, p. 31.

Aquino, Micahel A. *The Church of Satan*. San Francisco: Temple of Set, 1983.

Atkins, Susan, with Bob Slosser. *Child of Satan, Child of God*. Plainfield, NJ: Logos International, 1977.

Clifton, Chas S. "The Three Faces of Satan." *Gnosis*, Summer 1979, p. 8.

Demarest, Arthur. "Overview: Mesoamerican Human Sacrifice." *Human Sacrifice in Mesoamerica*. Harvard Dumbarton Oaks Conference, pp. 31–33. Cited in Patrick Tierney, *The Highest Altar: The Story of Human Sacrifice*, New York: Viking, 1989, p. 12.

Ebon, Martin, ed. *The Satan Trap: Dangers of the Occult*. New York: Doubleday, 1976.

"Evil, Anyone?" *Newsweek*, August 16, 1971, p. 56.

LaVey, Anton Szandor. *The Compleat Witch or What to Do When Virtue Fails.* New York: Dodd, Mead, 1971.

———. *The Satanic Bible.* New York: Avon Books, 1970.

———. *The Satanic Rituals.* New York: Avon Books, 1972.

Lanning, Kenneth V. *Satanic, Occult, Ritualistic Crime: A Law Enforcement Perspective.* Quantico, VA: FBI Academy, 1989.

Lyons, Arthur. *Satan Wants You: The Cult of Devil Worship in America.* New York: Mysterious Press, 1988.

———. *The Second Coming: Satanism in America.* New York: Dodd, Mead, 1970.

Mann, May. *Jayne Mansfield: A Biography.* New York: Drake Publishers, 1973.

Michaels, Jason. *The Devil is Alive and Well and Living in America Today.* New York: Award Books, 1973.

Nomolos, Rev. Yaj. *The Magic Circle: Its Successful Organization and Leadership.* Toluca Lake, CA: International Imports, 1987.

Parfrey, Adam, ed. *Apocalypse Culture.* New York: Amok Press, 1987.

Russell, Dick. "The Satanist Who Wants to Rule the World." *Argosy*, June 1975, p. 41.

"Satanism: Rosemary's Babies." *Newsweek*, July 19, 1971, p. 22.

Spence, Lewis. *The Magic and Mysteries of Mexico.* Philadelphia: David McKay, 1931.

St. Clair, David. *The Psychic World of California.* New York: Doubleday, 1972.

CHAPTER 7. THE STRANGE WORLD OF DR. MICHAEL AQUINO

Aquino, Michael A. *The Book of Coming Forth by Night.* San Francisco: Temple of Set, 1985.

———. ed. *The Crystal Tablet of Set.* San Francisco: Temple of Set, 1983.

Cohn, Norman Rufus Colin. *Warrant for Genocide: The Myth of the Jewish World-Conspiracy.* Chico, CA: Scholars Press, 1981.

Goldston, Linda. "Army of the Night." *San Jose Mercury News*, July 24, 1988, p. 15.

———. "Satanist Accused of Molesting Girl." *San Jose Mercury News*, November 8, 1987, p. 1A.

———. "Sources Say Army is Probing Abuse Case." *San Jose Mercury News*, December 23, 1988, p. 1A.

Grant, Kenneth. *Outside the Circles of Time.* London: Frederick Muller, 1980.

Heidrick, Bill. "The Blood Libel." *The Magical Link*, November 1985, p. 1.

Krupp, E. C. *Echoes of the Ancient Skies: The Astronomy of Lost Civilizations.* New York: New American Library, 1983.

Merritt, A. *Seven Footprints to Satan.* New York: Boni and Liveright, 1928.

Scott, Gini Graham. *The Magicians: A Study in the Use of Power in a Black Magic Group.* New York: Irvington Publishers, 1983.

Temple of Set. "By-Laws." San Francisco: Temple of Set, July 30, 1982.

———. "General Information and Admissions Policies." San Francisco: Temple of Set, 1984.

———. "General Information and Admissions Policies, Revised." San Francisco: Temple of Set, N.d.

———. "Temple of Set Brochure Sent to Inquirers." San Francisco: Temple of Set, 1978.

Vallely, Colonel Paul E., with Major Michael A. Aquino. "From PSYOP to MindWar: The Psychology of Victory." 1983. Unpublished manuscript.

Velde, H. Te. *Seth, God of Confusion*. Leiden, Netherlands: E. J. Brill, 1977.

CHAPTER 8. HEAVY METAL MUSIC

Allen-Baley, Carole, and David W. Balsiger. "Heavy Metal: A Weighty Police Problem." Costa Mesa, CA: Writeway Literary Associates, 1986.

Aquino, Michael A. "The Cloning of Nikki Sixx." *Runes,* Temple of Set, January 21, 1986, p. 1.

"The Audience Was a Motley Crew." *Columbus Dispatch*, October 28, 1987.

"Backwards Were Satan Lyrics on Records Put." *Press-Enterprise*, April 28, 1982, p. A-1.

Bangs, Lester, edited by Greil Marcus. *Psychotic Reactions and Carburetor Dung*. New York: Alfred A. Knopf, 1987.

Belko, Mark, and Henry W. Pierce. "Counselors See Rise in Teen Drug Cults." *Pittsburgh Post-Gazette*, December 13, 1988.

Belko, Mark, and Michael A. Fuoco. "Officers Seek Crime Link to Satanic Cults." *Pittsburgh Post-Gazette*, December 14, 1988.

Berg, Melissa. "Satanists Classified by Police." *Kansas City Times*, March 26, 1988, p. A19.

Billiter, Bill. "Satanic Messages Played Back for Assembly Panel." *Los Angeles Times*, April 28, 1982, p. 3.

Britt, Bruce. "Thrash Shouts With Gloom." (Colorado Springs) *Gazette Telegraph*, December 13, 1988, p. F1.

Brodie, Ian. "Suicide Blamed on Song." *London Daily News*, January 16, 1986.

Burkhart, Joan. "Expert Sees Link Between Music, Troubled Teens." *Las Vegas Review-Journal*, March 16, 1988, p. 1D.

"California Probes Rock Music 'Devil.'" *Chicago Tribune*, April 29, 1982.

"Callers: Rock 'n' Roll Albums Need Rating System." *Orlando Sentinel*, September 24, 1985.

Carroll, Peter. "Cult Crimes." *San Francisco Magazine*, August 1987, p. 20.

Chambers, Iain. *Urban Rhythms: Pop Music and Popular Culture*. New York: St. Martin's Press, 1985.

Chung, Connie. "Transcript on 'Satan's Children.'" Washington, DC: WRC-TV, August 19, 1986.

Curtis, Jim. *Rock Eras: Interpretations of Music & Society, 1954–1984*. Bowling Green, OH: Bowlilng Green State University Popular, 1987.

Davis, Sheila. "Beating the Drums for Lyric Literacy." *Billboard*, July 26, 1986, p. 9.

DeCurtis, Anthony. "Study Refutes PMRC Claims, Says Kids Don't Listen to Lyrics." *Rolling Stone*, August 14, 1986, p. 11.

Dougherty, Steve, and Alexander Connock. "Metallica, Unapologetic Avatars of Transuranic Metal, Find Success. . . ." *People*, p. 73.

Eddy, Steve. "Crimes Rooted in Devil Worship Rising in County." *Orange County Register*, September 28, 1986, p. B1.

Flood, Mary. "Devil Worship: What's Behind It?" *Houston Post*, September 15, 1985, p. 1–A.

Fricke, David. "Heavy-Metal Justice." *Rolling Stone*, January 12, 1989, p. 46.

Gitter, Mike. "Metallica: Truth, Justice, and Some Mighty Brutal Riffs." *Metal*, September 1989, p. 27.

Goleman, Daniel. "Depression Tied to Excesses." *New York Times*, September 9, 1986.

Greene, Elizabeth. "Deena Weinstein, Sociology Professor and Heavy-Metal-Music Fiend." *Chronicle of Higher Education*, June 14, 1989, p. A3.

Griffis, Dale W. *A Law Enforcement Primer on Cults.* Tiffin OH: D. W. G. Enterprises, 1985.

———. Pamphlet and materials provided by Dale Griffis.

Hagigh, Jaleh. "Police Link Satan Site, Heavy Metal Rock Music." (Maryland) *Montgomery Journal*, January 9, 1986, p. 40.

Harrington, Richard. "What'd I Say." *Washington Post*, June 28, 1986, p. D7.

"Heavy Metal: Selling Satan or Songs?" (Bloomsburg, PA) *Press-Enterprise*, April 12, 1987, p. C-1.

Hiltbrand, David. "King Diamond: Could the Devil be Behind This?." *Philadelphia Inquirer*, August 25, 1987, p. 4-E.

Hornblower, Margot. "Youth's Deaths Tied to Satanic Rite." *Washington Post*, July 9, 1984, p. A1.

Jones, Tamara. "Experts Debate Influence of Violent Music on Youths." *Los Angeles Times*, October 19, 1988.

King, Paul. "Heavy Metal Music and Drug Abuse in Adolescents." *Post-Graduate Medicine*, April 1988, p. 295.

———. "Heavy Metal: A New Religion." *Journal of the Tennessee Medical Association*, December 1985, p. 754.

Kroon, Louis. "A Report on the Effects of Rock Music on Our Youth." Read to the President's Council, October 6, 1986.

Lamp, Rob. "The World of 'Dark Rock.'" *The New American*, February 17, 1986, p. 6.

Lebowitz, Lawrence J. "Ozzy Osborne Can be Saved." *Enterprise*, June 2, 1984, p. 1.

Li, Annette. "Sex, Drugs and Rock 'n' Roll." (Pacific, MO) *Tri-County Journal*, December 11, 1985.

"Man Who Sued Rock Group After Suicide Try Dies." (Colorado Springs) *Gazette Telegraph*, December 1, 1988.

Mann, Peggy. "How Shock Rock Harms Our Kids." *Reader's Digest*, July 1988, p. 101.

Menninger Clinic. "Diagnostic Interview Report." March 10, 1988.

Michioku, Sandra. "Rock Musician Claims 'Satanism in Records' Charge a Hoax." *Denver Post*, May 4, 1982.

Middlesex County Prosecutor's Office Intelligence Unit. "Intelligence Report: Relationship Between Heavy Metal Music and Religious Desecration." 1986.

Myers, Jim. "Heavy-Metal Bands Rock Generations." *USA Today*, August 18, 1986, p. 1D.

"Occult Alluring to Youth." *Calgary Herald*, March 7, 1987, p. E-1.

O'Keefe, Joe. "Psychiatrist Blasts Drugs, Heavy Metal." *Gulfport Sun Herald*, August 13, 1986.

Orman, John. *The Politics of Rock Music.* Chicago: Nelson-Hall, 1984.

Parents' Music Resource Center. "Lyric Sheets: Lyrics with Satanic References." Arlington, VA: Parents' Music Resource Center, information sent 1989.

———. "The Influence of Media on Adolescents." Arlington, VA: Parents' Music Resource Center, information sent 1989.

———. *Record* (newsletter) Summer 1989.

Parfrey, Adam, *Apocalypse Culture.* New York: Amok Press, 1987.

Pattison, Robert. *The Triumph of Vulgarity.* New York: Oxford University Press, 1987.

Perrin, Marlene. "Rock 'n' Roll Sermon Nets Listeners, Doubters." *Iowa City Press-Citizen*, March 15, 1985.

"Police Examine Music Videos in Mass. Deaths." (Manchester, NH) *Union Leader*, December 8, 1987.

Roberts, Alec. "Transcript on 'Devil Worship and Crime.'" New York: WPIX-TV, February 27, 1987.

Roland, Pete. "Song Lyrics that Pete Roland Has Listened to and Copied the Lyrics in His Own Handwriting." Arlington, VA: Parents' Music Resource Center, November 24, 1987.

Ryckman, Lisa Levitt. "Satan's Kids: A Look at the Dark Side of Teen Rebellion." *Las Vegas Review-Journal*, March 16, 1988, p. 1D.

———. "Satanism Leading Teens to Crime, Violence." (Pennsylvania) *Greensburg Tribune-Review*, February 14, 1988, p. B3.

Santangelo, Mike, and Ruth Landa. "Satan Scout Left Hints." *New York Daily News*, January 12, 1988, p. 2.

"Satan Worship, Rock Records Will be Subject of Hearing." (Palmdale, CA) *Antelope Valley Press*, April 25, 1982, p. 1.

Scruggs, Kathy. "Teen Fascination with the Occult Linked to Crimes Across Georgia." *Atlanta Constitution*, February 8, 1988, p. A1.

Sharp, Deborah. "Heavy-Metal Music Tarnishes Minds, Psychiatrist Says." *Fort Meyers News-Press*, May 19, 1986, p. 1B.

Shaw, Kent M. "Falling Prey to Satanism." *Burlington Free Press*, January 17, 1988, p. 1A.

Sims, Lydel. "Sdrocer dna natas." *Rocky Mountain News*, May 13, 1982.

Stipp, David. "What Happens When Music Meets the Brain." *Wall Street Journal*, August 30, 1985, p. 13.

Street, John. *Rebel Rock.* Oxford: Basil Blackwell, 1986.

Stuessy, Joe. *The Heavy Metal User's Manual.* University of Texas at San Antonio, September, 1985.

Szechenyi, Chris. "Deadly Rites: Satanism in the Suburbs." (Berwyn, IL) *Sunday Herald*, February 16, 1986, p. 1-1.

Torriero, E. A. "Evil Acts Put Fear of God in Town." *San Jose Mercury News*, September 5, 1986, p. 1A.

Turner, Patricia C. "Youths Seized as Cemetery Vandals; Lawman Sees 'Heavy Metal' Influence." *New Jersey Star Ledger*, June 1986.

U. S. Congress. Senate. "Proceedings and Debates of the 99th Congress, 1st Session, Amendment 702." *Congressional Record*, September 26, 1985. p. S.12171.

"What Entertainers Are Doing to Your Kids." *U. S. News*, October 28, 1985, p. 46.

Whitmire, John. "Satanic Youths Unnerve El Paso." *Houston Post*, February 23, 1986, p. 1D.

CHAPTER 9. FANTASY ROLE-PLAYING GAMES

Armacost, Elise. "Dark Spirits." *County Wide News* (Westminster, MD), November 5, 1986, p. 1.
"Classmates Stunned by Youth's Suicide in Front of His Drama Class." *Tampa Tribune-Times*, January 20, 1985.
Cottman, Effie. "Teen D & D Player Charged in Parents' Murder." *Maryland Gazette*, March 10, 1984.
Dager, A. J. "Freeway Killer." *Los Angeles Harold Examiner*, October 23, 1983.
Dear, William. *The Dungeon Master: The Disappearance of James Dallas Egbert III.* Boston: Houghton Mifflin, 1984.
"Deaths of Two Brothers May be Linked to Game." *Tampa Tribune-Times*, November 4, 1984, p. 10-A.
Evanosky, Barbara. "Sister Unaware Her Brother Engaged in Bizarre Fetish." (Ohio) *Lake County News-Herald*, April 30, 1983.
"Fantasy Game Ruled Honor Student's Life—and Death." *Weekly World News*, September 20, 1983, p. 8.
Gygax, Gary, and Dave Arneson. *Dungeons & Dragons Dungeon Masters Rulebook.* Lake Geneva, Wisconsin: TSR Hobbies, 1983.
———. *Dungeons & Dragons Players Manual.* Lake Geneva, WI: TSR Hobbies, 1983.
"Magic: A Deadly Solution." *Denver Magazine*, February 1985, p. 23.
"Occult Alluring to Youth." *Calgary Herald*, March 7, 1987, p. E-1.
"1 Killed, 3 Hurt in Shooting at Kansas School." *Tampa Tribune*, January 22, 1985.
Parents' Music Resource Center. "The Influence of Media on Adolescents." Arlington, VA: Parents' Music Resource Center, information sent 1989.
Percival, Harold Waldwin. *Masonry and Its Symbols.* Dallas, TX: Word Foundation, 1952.
Price, Joyce. "Police Investigate Death-Game Link." (Montevideo, MN) *News American*, April 28, 1985, p. 1B.
Schwarz, Ted. "Diary of a Phoenix Boy's Death." *Phoenix Magazine*, December 1985, p. 97.
Scofield, Bruce, and Angela Cordova. *The Aztec Circle of Destiny: Astrology and Divination from the Ancient Aztec World* (fantasy board game and manual). St. Paul, MN: Llewellyn Publications, 1988.
Sherwood, John. "The Real World of Dungeons & Dragons." *Washington Times*, March 19, 1984.
"Slaying of Girl Linked to School Drug Ring." *Baltimore Sun*, December 23, 1983.
"Teen's Suicide Tied to a Fantasy Game." *Manhattan Mercury*, February 10, 1985.
Toth, John. "Teen Enticed Into Sex, Say Prosecutors." *Houston Chronicle*, May 8, 1985, p.19.
Visser, Nancy. "Police are Told Game, Murders May Have Links." *Arlington Daily News* (Texas), May 16, 1985, p. 1A.
Wilson, Sheryl C., and Theodore X. Barber. "The Fantasy-Prone Personality." *PSI Research*, September 1982, p. 94.

CHAPTER 10. WHERE ARE THE CHILDREN?

"Akron Lawmen Investigate Satanic Child Abuse." (Sterling, CO) *Journal-Advocate*, May 23, 1988, p. 1.

Ashby, Charles. "Devil Worship Possible in Logan County." (Sterling, CO) *Journal-Advocate*, May 23, 1988, p. 1.

———. "Devil Worship, Abuse Probe Expands." (Sterling, CO) *Journal-Advocate*, May 27, 1988, p. 1.

Bass, Ellen, and Laura Davis. *The Courage to Heal: A Guide for Women Survivors of Child Sexual Abuse.* New York: Harper & Row, 1988.

Berg, Melissa. "Therapists Unlock Horrors of Cult Abuse." *Kansas City Times*, March 26, 1988, p. A19.

Burgess, A., ed. *Child Pornography and Sex Rings.* Lexington, MA: Lexington Books, 1984.

Campagna, Daniel S., and Donald L. Poffenberger. *The Sexual Trafficking in Children.* Dover, MA: Auburn House Publishing, 1988.

Carlson, Peter. "Divided by Multiple Charges of Child Abuse, a Minnesota Town Seethes. . . ." *People*, October 22, 1984, p. 35.

Charlier, Tom. "As Children Point, Critics Sound Off." *Memphis Commercial Appeal*, January 1988.

———. "Methods of Inquiry Pressure Children." *Memphis Commercial Appeal*, January 1988.

———. "Parents Sought Relief—in Court or in a Cause." *Memphis Commercial Appeal*, January 1988. p. A18.

———. "Prosecutors Honing Edge in Duel of Reforms, Rights." *Memphis Commercial Appeal*, January 1988.

———. "'Satan Factor' Complicates Trials." *Memphis Commercial Appeal*, January 1988, p. A9.

———. "Skeptics Find Legend, Not Satan, At the Core." *Memphis Commercial Appeal*, January 1988, p. A7.

———. "System Promotes Charges, Say Critics." *Memphis Commercial Appeal*, January 1988, p. A12.

Charlier, Tom, and Shirley Downing. "Facts, Fantasies Caught in Tangled Web." *Memphis Commercial Appeal*, January 1988, p. A1.

Clifton, Chas S. "The Three Faces of Satan: A Close Look at the 'Satanism Scare.'" *Gnosis*, Summer 1989, p. 12.

Como, John J. "Indiana Child-Abuse Case Linked to Satanism, Trooper Says." *Indiana Tribune-Democrat*, March 3, 1989.

Corcoran, Katherine. "Akron Child-Sex Charges Filed." *Denver Post*, October 28, 1988, p. 1.

———. "Convicted Akron Child Molester Receives Minimum Sentence." *Denver Post*, August 30, 1989, p. 1A.

Corcoran, Katherine, and Bill Briggs. "Woodard: Johns Tried to Block Case." *Denver Post*, October 29, 1988, p. 1.

Coulborn, Kathleen. *An Interdisciplinary Manual for Diagnosis, Case Management and Treatment.* New York: Columbia University Press, 1988.

Crewdson, John. *By Silence Betrayed: Sexual Abuse of Children in America.* Boston: Little, Brown, 1988.

———. "Satanism Haunts Tales of Child Sex Abuse." *Chicago Tribune,* July 29, 1985, p. 1.

"D.A. Johns Says Lack of Evidence in Daycare Case Backed by Experts." (Brush, CO), *Brush Morgan County News-Tribune,* August 24, 1988, p. 1.

"DA Declines Grand Jury, Attracts Public's Criticism." (Sterling, CO) *Journal-Advocate,* June 27, 1988, p. 1.

"DA Lists Reasons Why No Charges Filed in Riggs Case." (Colorado) *Akron News-Reporter,* July 28, 1988, p. 1.

"Day-care Sexual Abuse Case Jeoparized by 'Post' Articles." (Colorado) *Akron News-Reporter,* May 26, 1988, p. 1.

Downing, Shirley. "Ballard Case: Detours Along Road to Truth." *Memphis Commercial Appeal,* January 1988, p. A21.

———. "Children's Stories Here Have Ring of Familiarity." *Memphis Commercial Appeal,* January 1988.

———. "Families, Town Divided by Wave of Accusations." *Memphis Commercial Appeal,* January 1988.

———. "Former Suspects Find Their Place on List of Victims." *Memphis Commercial Appeal,* January 1988.

———. "Pioneer Case at McMartin Called Hoax." *Memphis Commercial Appeal,* January 1988, p. A4.

———. "Tales of Cult Abuse Spiral; Officials Seek Foundation." *Memphis Commercial Appeal,* January 1988.

———. "These are Days of Trial for Ballard." *Memphis Commercial Appeal,* January 1988.

Eberlie, Paul and Shirley. *The Politics of Child Abuse.* Secaucus, NJ: Lyle Stuart, 1986.

Ensslin, John C. "Day-Care Sex Scandal Saddens Akron." *Rocky Mountain News,* October 29, 1988, p. 12.

Ensslin, John C., and John Sanko. "Woodard Accuses DA of Bid to Block Sex-abuse Charges." *Rocky Mountain News,* October 29, 1988, p. 12.

Fuller, John G. *Are the Kids All Right: The Rock Generation and Its Hidden Death Wish.* New York: Time Books, 1981.

Goldston, Linda. "Army of the Night." *San Jose Mercury News,* July 24, 1988, p. 14.

———. "Considering the Victim First." *San Jose Mercury News,* May 21, 1987, p. 1A.

———. "Many Abuse Cases Fail to Get Resolved Because Few Are Trained to Investigate," San Jose Mercury News, May 18, 1987, p.13A.

———. "Sending the Abused Back Home." *San Jose Mercury News,* May 18, 1987, p. 1A.

———. "The Littlest Victims: Too Easy to Assault, Too Tiny to Resist, Too Young to Be Heard." *San Jose Mercury News,* May 17, 1987, p. 1A.

———. "The Riddle of Treating Abusers." *San Jose Mercury News,* May 20, 1987, p. 1A.

———. "Unlocking a Childhood of Abuse." *San Jose Mercury News,* May 19, 1987, p. 1A.

———. "When the Molester is a Child." *San Jose Mercury News,* May 17, 1987, p. 22A.

Gomez, David. "Youth Going to the Devil." *Rocky Mountain News*, November 1, 1988, p. 20.

Gould, Catherine. "Satanic Ritual Abuse: Child Victims, Adult Survivors, System Response." *California Psychologist*, May-June 1987, p. 9.

——. "Signs and Symptoms of Ritualistic Abuse in Children." Encino, CA: 1988.

——. "Symptoms Characterizing Satanic Ritual Abuse Not Usually Seen in Sexual Abuse Cases." Brentwood, CA: May 23, 1986.

Hollingsworth, Jan. *Unspeakable Acts.* Chicago: Contemporary Books, 1986.

Hutchinson, Paul. "Satanism Feared in Eastern Colorado Child-Abuse Case." *Denver Post*, May 22, 1988, p. 1A.

James, Jennifer, and Jane Meyerding. "Early Sexual Experience as a Factor in Prostitution." *Archives of Sexual Behavior.* January 1977, p. 31.

"Johns: Abuse Case Was Groundless." (Sterling, CO) *Journal-Advocate* , May 31, 1989, p. 1.

Kempe, Ruth S., and C. Henry. *The Common Secret.* New York: W. H. Freeman, 1984.

Kluft, Richard P., ed. *Childhood Antecedents of Multiple Personality.* Washington, DC: American Psychiatric Press, 1985.

Kohn, Alfie. "Shattered Innocence." *Psychology Today*, February 1987, p. 54.

LaVey, Anton Szandor. *The Satanic Rituals.* New York: Avon Books, 1972.

Makin, Kirk. "Satanic Child Abuse Cited by Aid Group." (Toronto) *Globe and Mail*, December 22, 1987, p. A12.

Maney, Ann, and Susan Wells, eds. *Professional Responsibilities in Protecting Children.* New York: Praeger, 1988.

Nathan, Debbie. "The Making of a Modern Witch Trial." *Village Voice*, September 29, 1987, p. 19.

"No Charges Planned in Akron Abuse Case." (Sterling, CO) *Journal-Advocate* , July 28, 1988, p. 1.

"Origins Similar, Endings Different in Sex Abuse Cases." *Memphis Commercial Appeal*, January 1988.

"Patterns Emerge Across Nation." *Memphis Commercial Appeal*, January 1988, p. A7.

Reinhold, Robert. "California Shaken Over Informer." *New York Times*, February 17, 1989, p. 1.

Richards, Gary. "A First in Preventing Abuse." *San Jose Mercury News*, May 21, 1987, p. 16A.

——. "Abuse Victims Turning to Civil Courts." *San Jose Mercury News*, May 18, 1987, p. 12A.

——. "Disquieting Time for Model Therapy Program." *San Jose Mercury News*, May 18, 1987, p. 13A.

——. "Fingerprinting is no Answer: Most Abusers Have No Record." *San Jose Mercury News*, May 21, 1987, p. 17A.

——. "They Claim to Be Falsely Accused, and They're VOCAL." *San Jose Mercury News*, May 17, 1987, p. 22A.

——. "'You Have to Take the Top Off,' Missy Screamed; 'That's the Game.'" *San Jose Mercury News*, May 19, 1987, p. 8A.

Roelofsma, Derk Kinnane. "Battling Satanism a Haunting Task." *Insight*, January 11, 1988, p. 48.

Rohsenow, Damaris J., Richard Corbett, and Donald Devine. "Molested as Children: A Hidden Contribution to Substance Abuse?" *Journal of Substance Abuse Treatment*, 1988, p. 13.

Rush, Florence. *The Best Kept Secret: Sexual Abuse of Children*. Englewood Cliffs, NJ: Prentice-Hall, 1980.

"Sex, the Devil, and Day Care." *Village Voice*, September 29, 1987, p. 23.

"Shades of Salem." *Memphis Commercial Appeal*, January 1988.

Silbert, Mimi H., and Ayala M. Pines. "Sexual Child Abuse as an Antecedent to Prostitution." *Child Abuse and Neglect*, May 1981, p. 407.

"Some Telltale Signs of Child Sex Abuse." *San Jose Mercury News*, May 19, 1987, p. 9A.

Spencer, Judith. *Suffer the Child*. New York: Pocket Books, 1989.

Summit, Roland C. "The Child Sexual Abuse Accommodation Syndrome." *Child Abuse and Neglect*, July 1983, p. 177.

———. "Too Terrible to Hear." Paper written in support of testimony before the U.S. Attorney General's Commission on Pornography, Miami, November 20, 1985.

Summit, Roland, and JoAnn Kryso. "Sexual Abuse of Children: A Clinical Spectrum." *American Journal Orthopsychiatry*, April 1978, p. 237.

"The Protection of Children is the First Job of Social Services." (Colorado) *Akron News-Reporter*, August 11, 1988, p. 1.

"Things That Go Bump in Victoria." *Maclean's*, October 27, 1980, p. 30.

"Underworld Tales of Terror Echoed Through the Land." *Memphis Commercial Appeal*, January 1988.

"Washington County People are the Biggest Victims in Child Abuse Story." (Colorado) *Akron News-Reporter*, June 2, 1988, p. 1.

Winfrey, Oprah. "Satanism." Transcript of the Oprah Winfrey Show. Chicago: WLS-TV, September 30, 1986.

"Woodard Takes Reins in Akron Abuse Case." (Sterling, CO) *Journal-Advocate*, August 2, 1988, p. 1.

Wooden, Kenneth. "How Sex Offenders Lure Our Children." *Reader's Digest*, June 1988, p. 149.

Wyatt, Gail Elizabeth, and Gloria Johnson Powell, eds. *Lasting Effects of Child Sexual Abuse*. Beverly Hills, CA: Sage Publications, 1988.

CHAPTER 11. THE METAPHYSICS OF VIOLENCE

Came, Barry. "A Growing Menace: Violent Skinheads are Raising Urban Fears." *Maclean's*, January 23, 1989, p. 43.

Coplon, Jeff. "Skinhead Nation." *Rolling Stone*, December 1, 1988, p. 54.

Fuller, John G. *Are the Kids All Right? The Rock Generation and its Hidden Death Wish*. New York: Times Books, 1981.

Hackett, George. "Skinheads on the Rampage." *Newsweek*, September 7, 1987, p. 22.

Killip, Chris. "Skinheads of Newcastle." *Society*, July-August 1987, p. 84.

LaVey, Anton Szandor. *The Compleat Witch or What to Do When Virtue Fails*. New York: Dodd, Mead, 1971.

Leo, John. "A Chilling Wave of Racism." *Time*, January 25, 1988, p. 57.

Martin, Jane Meredith. "Anarchist Conference a Radical Departure." *San Francisco Globe,* July 22, 1989.
Nugent, Donald. "Satan Is a Fascist." *The Month,* April 1972.
Parfrey, Adam. *Apocalypse Culture.* New York: Amok Press, 1987.
Reinhold, Robert. "Dozens of Cats Killed, Fears Spread in Suburb." *New York Times,* August 13, 1989, p. 12.
Sears, Eva. "Skinheads: A New Generation of Hate-Mongers." *USA Today,* May, 1989, p. 24.
Southern Poverty Law Center. "Skinhead/Satanists Mix Racism, Ritual Crime." (Montgomery, AL) *Klanwatch Intelligence Report,* August 1988, p. 4.

CHAPTER 12. TWILIGHT OF THE IDOLS

Blow, Steve. "Could It Be . . . Satan? Not Likely." *The Dallas Morning News,* November 12, 1989.
Dart, John. "Satanism Called Insignificant in U.S." *The Los Angeles Times,* September 25, 1989.
Eco, Umberto, *Travels in Hyper Reality.* (trans, William Weaver) New York: Harcourt Brace Jovanovich, 1983.
"FBI Seeks Identity of Deaf Teen Girl Whom Satanists May Have Abducted." *The Denver Post,* September 20, 1989.
May, Clifford D. "Occult May Be Ultimate Power Trip for Absolute Rulers Like Noriega." *Rocky Mountain News,* January 14, 1990.
Ravenscroft, Trevor. *The Spear of Destiny.* (First American paperback ed.) York Beach, ME: Samuel Weiser, 1982.
"Serial Killer Sentenced to the Gas Chamber." *Rocky Mountain News,* September 21, 1989.
Womack, Anita. "Two Accused of Plotting to Molest, Kill Boy for Pornographic Videotape." *Brownsville Herald,* August 31, 1989, p. 1.

Index